ALL GLORY TO ŚRĪ GURU AND GAURĀṄGA

ŚRĪMAD BHĀGAVATAM

of

KṚṢṆA-DVAIPĀYANA VYĀSA

येऽन्येऽरविन्दाक्ष विमुक्तमानिन-
स्त्वय्यस्तभावादविशुद्धबुद्धयः ।
आरुह्य कृच्छ्रेण परं पदं ततः
पतन्त्यधोऽनादृतयुष्मदङ्घ्रयः ॥

ye 'nye 'ravindākṣa vimukta-māninas
tvayy asta-bhāvād aviśuddha-buddhayaḥ
āruhya kṛcchreṇa paraṁ padaṁ tataḥ
patanty adho 'nādṛta-yuṣmad-aṅghrayaḥ

(p. 172)

BOOKS by
His Divine Grace
A. C. Bhaktivedanta Swami Prabhupāda

Bhagavad-gītā As It Is
Śrīmad-Bhāgavatam, Cantos 1–10 (50 Vols.)
Śrī Caitanya-caritāmṛta (17 Vols.)
Teachings of Lord Caitanya
The Nectar of Devotion
The Nectar of Instruction
Śrī Īśopaniṣad
Easy Journey to Other Planets
Kṛṣṇa Consciousness: The Topmost Yoga System
Kṛṣṇa, the Supreme Personality of Godhead (3 Vols.)
Perfect Questions, Perfect Answers
Dialectical Spiritualism—A Vedic View of Western Philosophy
Teachings of Lord Kapila, the Son of Devahūti
Transcendental Teachings of Prahlad Mahārāja
Kṛṣṇa, the Reservoir of Pleasure
Life Comes from Life
The Perfection of Yoga
Beyond Birth and Death
On the Way to Kṛṣṇa
Geetār-gan (Bengali)
Rāja-vidyā: The King of Knowledge
Elevation to Kṛṣṇa Consciousness
Kṛṣṇa Consciousness: The Matchless Gift
Back to Godhead Magazine (Founder)

A complete catalog is available upon request

Bhaktivedanta Book Trust
3764 Watseka Avenue
Los Angeles, California 90034

ŚRĪMAD BHĀGAVATAM

Tenth Canto
"The Summum Bonum"

(Part One—Chapters 1–5)

*With the Original Sanskrit Text,
Its Roman Transliteration, Synonyms,
Translation and Elaborate Purports*

by

His Divine Grace
A.C. Bhaktivedanta Swami Prabhupāda
Founder-*Ācārya* of the International Society for Krishna Consciousness

THE BHAKTIVEDANTA BOOK TRUST
New York · Los Angeles · London · Bombay

Readers interested in the subject matter of this book are invited by the International Society for Krishna Consciousness to correspond with its Secretary.

International Society for Krishna Consciousness
3764 Watseka Avenue
Los Angeles, California 90034

First Printing, 1977: 20,000 copies

Library of Congress Cataloging in Publication Data (Revised)

Puranas. Bhāgavatapurāna.
Śrīmad-Bhāgavatam.

Includes bibliographical references and indexes.
CONTENTS: Canto 1. Creation. 3 v.—Canto 2. The cosmic manifestation. 2 v.—Canto 3. The status quo. 4 v.—Canto 4. The creation of the Fourth Order. 4 v.—Canto 5. The creative impetus. 2 v.
1. Chaitanya, 1486-1534. I. Bhaktivedanta Swami, A. C., 1896- II. Title.
BL1135.P7A22 1972 73-169353
ISBN 0-912776-97-8

Table of Contents

CHAPTER THREE
The Birth of Lord Kṛṣṇa

CHAPTER FOUR
The Atrocities of King Kaṁsa   275

CHAPTER FIVE
The Meeting of Nanda Mahārāja and Vasudeva   319

Preface

We must know the present need of human society. And what is that need? Human society is no longer bounded by geographical limits to particular countries or communities. Human society is broader than in the Middle Ages, and the world tendency is toward one state or one human society. The ideals of spiritual communism, according to *Śrīmad-Bhāgavatam*, are based more or less on the oneness of the entire human society, nay, of the entire energy of living beings. The need is felt by great thinkers to make this a successful ideology. *Śrīmad-Bhāgavatam* will fill this need in human society. It begins, therefore, with the aphorism of Vedānta philosophy *janmādy asya yataḥ* to establish the ideal of a common cause.

Human society, at the present moment, is not in the darkness of oblivion. It has made rapid progress in the field of material comforts, education and economic development throughout the entire world. But there is a pinprick somewhere in the social body at large, and therefore there are large-scale quarrels, even over less important issues. There is need of a clue as to how humanity can become one in peace, friendship and prosperity with a common cause. *Śrīmad-Bhāgavatam* will fill this need, for it is a cultural presentation for the re-spiritualization of the entire human society.

Śrīmad-Bhāgavatam should be introduced also in the schools and colleges, for it is recommended by the great student-devotee Prahlāda Mahārāja in order to change the demoniac face of society.

kaumāra ācaret prājño
dharmān bhāgavatān iha
durlabhaṁ mānuṣaṁ janma
tad apy adhruvam arthadam
(*Bhāg.* 7.6.1)

Disparity in human society is due to lack of principles in a godless civilization. There is God, or the Almighty One, from whom everything emanates, by whom everything is maintained and in whom everything is merged to rest. Material science has tried to find the ultimate source of creation very insufficiently, but it is a fact that there is one ultimate source of everything that be. This ultimate source is explained rationally and authoritatively in the beautiful *Bhāgavatam* or *Śrīmad-Bhāgavatam.*

Śrīmad-Bhāgavatam is the transcendental science not only for knowing the ultimate source of everything but also for knowing our relation with Him and our duty towards perfection of the human society on the basis of this perfect knowledge. It is powerful reading matter in the Sanskrit language, and it is now rendered into English elaborately so that simply by a careful reading one will know God perfectly well, so much so that the reader will be sufficiently educated to defend himself from the onslaught of atheists. Over and above this, the reader will be able to convert others to accepting God as a concrete principle.

Śrīmad-Bhāgavatam begins with the definition of the ultimate source. It is a bona fide commentary on the *Vedānta-sūtra* by the same author, Śrīla Vyāsadeva, and gradually it develops into nine cantos up to the highest state of God realization. The only qualification one needs to study this great book of transcendental knowledge is to proceed step by step cautiously and not jump forward haphazardly like with an ordinary book. It should be gone through chapter by chapter, one after another. The reading matter is so arranged with its original Sanskrit text, its English transliteration, synonyms, translation and purports so that one is sure to become a God-realized soul at the end of finishing the first nine cantos.

The Tenth Canto is distinct from the first nine cantos because it deals directly with the transcendental activities of the Personality of Godhead Śrī Kṛṣṇa. One will be unable to capture the effects of the Tenth Canto without going through the first nine cantos. The book is complete in twelve cantos, each independent, but it is good for all to read them in small installments one after another.

I must admit my frailties in presenting *Śrīmad-Bhāgavatam,* but still I am hopeful of its good reception by the thinkers and leaders of society on the strength of the following statement of *Śrīmad-Bhāgavatam* (1.5.11):

tad-vāg-visargo janatāgha-viplavo
yasmin prati-ślokam abaddhavaty api

nāmāny anantasya yaśo 'ṅkitāni yac
chṛṇvanti gāyanti gṛṇanti sādhavaḥ

"On the other hand, that literature which is full with descriptions of the transcendental glories of the name, fame, form and pastimes of the unlimited Supreme Lord is a transcendental creation meant to bring about a revolution in the impious life of a misdirected civilization. Such transcendental literatures, even though irregularly composed, are heard, sung and accepted by purified men who are thoroughly honest."

Oṁ tat sat

A. C. Bhaktivedanta Swami

Introduction

"This *Bhāgavata Purāṇa* is as brilliant as the sun, and it has arisen just after the departure of Lord Kṛṣṇa to His own abode, accompanied by religion, knowledge, etc. Persons who have lost their vision due to the dense darkness of ignorance in the age of Kali shall get light from this *Purāṇa*." (*Śrīmad-Bhāgavatam* 1.3.43)

The timeless wisdom of India is expressed in the *Vedas*, ancient Sanskrit texts that touch upon all fields of human knowledge. Originally preserved through oral tradition, the *Vedas* were first put into writing five thousand years ago by Śrīla Vyāsadeva, the "literary incarnation of God." After compiling the *Vedas*, Vyāsadeva set forth their essence in the aphorisms known as *Vedānta-sūtras*. *Śrīmad-Bhāgavatam* is Vyāsadeva's commentary on his own *Vedānta-sūtras*. It was written in the maturity of his spiritual life under the direction of Nārada Muni, his spiritual master. Referred to as "the ripened fruit of the tree of Vedic literature," *Śrīmad-Bhāgavatam* is the most complete and authoritative exposition of Vedic knowledge.

After compiling the *Bhāgavatam*, Vyāsa impressed the synopsis of it upon his son, the sage Śukadeva Gosvāmī. Śukadeva Gosvāmī subsequently recited the entire *Bhāgavatam* to Mahārāja Parīkṣit in an assembly of learned saints on the bank of the Ganges at Hastināpura (now Delhi). Mahārāja Parīkṣit was the emperor of the world and was a great *rājarṣi* (saintly king). Having received a warning that he would die within a week, he renounced his entire kingdom and retired to the bank of the Ganges to fast until death and receive spiritual enlightenment. The *Bhāgavatam* begins with Emperor Parīkṣit's sober inquiry to Śukadeva Gosvāmī: "You are the spiritual master of great saints and devotees. I am therefore begging you to show the way of perfection for all persons, and especially for one who is about to die. Please let me know what a man should hear, chant, remember and worship, and also what he should not do. Please explain all this to me."

Śukadeva Gosvāmī's answer to this question, and numerous other questions posed by Mahārāja Parīkṣit, concerning everything from the nature of the self to the origin of the universe, held the assembled sages in rapt attention continuously for the seven days leading to the King's death. The sage Sūta Gosvāmī, who was present on the bank of the Ganges when Śukadeva Gosvāmī first recited *Śrīmad-Bhāgavatam*, later repeated the *Bhāgavatam* before a gathering of sages in the forest of Naimiṣāraṇya. Those sages, concerned about the spiritual welfare of the people in general, had gathered to perform a long, continuous chain of sacrifices to counteract the degrading influence of the incipient age of Kali. In response to the sages' request that he speak the essence of Vedic wisdom, Sūta Gosvāmī repeated from memory the entire eighteen thousand verses of *Śrīmad-Bhāgavatam*, as spoken by Śukadeva Gosvāmī to Mahārāja Parīkṣit.

The reader of *Śrīmad-Bhāgavatam* hears Sūta Gosvāmī relate the questions of Mahārāja Parīkṣit and the answers of Śukadeva Gosvāmī. Also, Sūta Gosvāmī sometimes responds directly to questions put by Śaunaka Ṛṣi, the spokesman for the sages gathered at Naimiṣāraṇya. One therefore simultaneously hears two dialogues: one between Mahārāja Parīkṣit and Śukadeva Gosvāmī on the bank of the Ganges, and another at Naimiṣāraṇya between Sūta Gosvāmī and the sages at Naimiṣāraṇya Forest, headed by Śaunaka Ṛṣi. Furthermore, while instructing King Parīkṣit, Śukadeva Gosvāmī often relates historical episodes and gives accounts of lengthy philosophical discussions between such great souls as the saint Maitreya and his disciple Vidura. With this understanding of the history of the *Bhāgavatam*, the reader will easily be able to follow its intermingling of dialogues and events from various sources. Since philosophical wisdom, not chronological order, is most important in the text, one need only be attentive to the subject matter of *Śrīmad-Bhāgavatam* to appreciate fully its profound message.

The translator of this edition compares the *Bhāgavatam* to sugar candy—wherever you taste it, you will find it equally sweet and relishable. Therefore, to taste the sweetness of the *Bhāgavatam*, one may begin by reading any of its volumes. After such an introductory taste, however, the serious reader is best advised to go back to Volume One of the First Canto and then proceed through the *Bhāgavatam*, volume after volume, in its natural order.

This edition of the *Bhāgavatam* is the first complete English translation of this important text with an elaborate commentary, and it is the first widely available to the English-speaking public. It is the product of the scholarly and devotional effort of His Divine Grace A. C. Bhaktivedanta Swami Prabhupāda, the world's most distinguished teacher of Indian religious and philosophical thought. His consummate Sanskrit scholarship and intimate familiarity with Vedic culture and thought as well as the modern way of life combine to reveal to the West a magnificent exposition of this important classic.

Readers will find this work of value for many reasons. For those interested in the classical roots of Indian civilization, it serves as a vast reservoir of detailed information on virtually every one of its aspects. For students of comparative philosophy and religion, the *Bhāgavatam* offers a penetrating view into the meaning of India's profound spiritual heritage. To sociologists and anthropologists, the *Bhāgavatam* reveals the practical workings of a peaceful and scientifically organized Vedic culture, whose institutions were integrated on the basis of a highly developed spiritual world view. Students of literature will discover the *Bhāgavatam* to be a masterpiece of majestic poetry. For students of psychology, the text provides important perspectives on the nature of consciousness, human behavior and the philosophical study of identity. Finally, to those seeking spiritual insight, the *Bhāgavatam* offers simple and practical guidance for attainment of the highest self-knowledge and realization of the Absolute Truth. The entire multivolume text, presented by the Bhaktivedanta Book Trust, promises to occupy a significant place in the intellectual, cultural and spiritual life of modern man for a long time to come.

—The Publishers

His Divine Grace
A. C. Bhaktivedanta Swami Prabhupāda
Founder-Ācārya of the International Society for Krishna Consciousness

PLATE ONE

Lord Brahmā, Lord Śiva and all the other demigods, having heard of the distress of mother earth, went to the shore of the ocean of milk. There they worshiped the Supreme Personality of Godhead Kṣīrodakaśāyī Viṣṇu, who lies on the ocean of milk, by reciting the Vedic *mantras* known as the *Puruṣa-sūkta.* While sitting in trance, Lord Brahmā heard the words of Lord Viṣṇu vibrating in the sky. Thus he told the demigods: "O demigods, hear from me the order of the Supreme Person, and execute it attentively without delay. The Supreme Personality of Godhead, Śrī Kṛṣṇa, who has full potency, will personally appear as the son of Vasudeva. For as long as the Lord moves on earth to diminish its burden by His own potency in the form of time, all of you demigods should appear through plenary portions as sons and grandsons in the family of the Yadus, and your wives should also appear in that dynasty. The foremost manifestation of Kṛṣṇa is Saṅkarṣaṇa, the origin of all incarnations within this material world. Before Lord Kṛṣṇa appears, this original Saṅkarṣaṇa will appear as Baladeva, just to please Kṛṣṇa in His transcendental pastimes." (*pp. 42–50*)

PLATE TWO

As the newly married Vasudeva and Devakī were ready to start for home, conchshells, bugles, drums and kettledrums all vibrated in concert for their auspicious departure. But while Kaṁsa, controlling the reins of the horses, was driving the chariot along the way, an unembodied voice addressed him, "You foolish rascal, the eighth child of the woman you are carrying will kill you!" Immediately the envious and sinful Kaṁsa caught hold of Devakī's hair with his left hand and took up his sword with his right hand to sever her head from her body. Fortunately, however, the great soul Vasudeva, who was to be the father of Kṛṣṇa, was able to pacify him. (*pp. 58–61*)

PLATE THREE

Devakī kept within herself the Supreme Personality of Godhead, the cause of all causes, the foundation of the entire cosmos, but because she was under arrest in the house of Kaṁsa, she appeared like the flames of a fire covered by the walls of a pot, or like a person who has knowledge but cannot distribute it to the world for the benefit of human society. Because Lord Kṛṣṇa was within her womb, Devakī illuminated the entire atmosphere in the place where she was confined. At this time Lord Brahmā and Lord Śiva, accompanied by great sages like Nārada, Devala and Vyāsa, and by other demigods like Indra, Candra and Varuṇa, invisibly approached the room of Devakī. There they all joined in offering their respectful obeisances and prayers to please the Supreme Personality of Godhead, who can bestow blessings upon everyone. (*pp. 143–154*)

PLATE FOUR

The Supreme Personality of Godhead, Viṣṇu, who is situated in the core of everyone's heart, appeared from the heart of Devakī in the dense darkness of night, like the full moon rising on the eastern horizon. The newborn child had very wonderful lotuslike eyes and bore in His four hands the four weapons conchshell, disc, club and lotus. On His chest was the mark of Śrīvatsa and on His neck the brilliant Kaustubha gem. Vasudeva could understand that this child was the Supreme Personality of Godhead, Nārāyaṇa. Having concluded this without a doubt, he became fearless. Bowing down with folded hands, he offered prayers to the child, who illuminated His birthplace by His natural influence. Next, Vasudeva's wife Devakī offered her prayers. The Lord, being very pleased by the prayers of His parents, responded, "O My dear mother and father, I appeared twice before as your son because I found no one else as highly elevated as you in simplicity and other good qualities. Both of you constantly think of Me as your son, but you always know that I am the Supreme Personality of Godhead. By thus thinking of Me constantly with love and affection, you will achieve the highest perfection: returning home, back to Godhead." After thus instructing His father and mother, the Supreme Personality of Godhead, Kṛṣṇa, transformed Himself into His original form as a small human child. (*pp. 208–265*)

PLATE FIVE

By the influence of Lord Kṛṣṇa's internal potency, Yogamāyā, all the doorkeepers of Kaṁsa's prison house fell fast asleep, their senses unable to work, and the other inhabitants of the house also fell deeply asleep. When the sun rises, the darkness automatically disappears; similarly, when Vasudeva, carrying the child Kṛṣṇa, appeared before the closed doors, they opened automatically, although they had been strongly pinned with iron and locked with iron chains. Since the clouds in the sky were mildly thundering and showering, Ananta-nāga, an expansion of the Supreme Personality of Godhead, followed Vasudeva, beginning from the door, with hoods expanded to protect Vasudeva and the transcendental child. Because of constant rain sent by the demigod Indra, the River Yamunā was filled with deep water, foaming about with fiercely whirling waves. But as the great Indian Ocean had formerly given way to Lord Rāmacandra by allowing Him to construct a bridge, the River Yamunā gave way to Vasudeva and allowed him to cross. (*pp. 269–270*)

PLATE SIX

When Kaṁsa heard that Devakī's eighth child had been born, he approached Devakī, grasped the newborn child by the legs, and tried to dash her against the surface of a stone. But the child, Yogamāyā-devī, the younger sister of Lord Viṣṇu, slipped upward from Kaṁsa's hands and appeared in the sky as the goddess Durgā, with eight arms, completely equipped with weapons. While celestial beings like Apsarās, Kinnaras, Uragas, Siddhas, Cāraṇas and Gandharvas worshiped her with all kinds of presentations, she spoke as follows: "O Kaṁsa, you fool, what will be the use of killing me? The Supreme Personality of Godhead, who has been your enemy from the very beginning and who will certainly kill you, has already taken His birth somewhere else. Therefore, do not unnecessarily kill other children." (*pp. 284–286*)

PLATE SEVEN

Nanda Mahārāja was naturally very magnanimous, and when Lord Śrī Kṛṣṇa appeared as his son, he was overwhelmed by jubilation. Therefore, after properly bathing and purifying himself and dressing himself properly, he invited *brāhmaṇas* who knew how to recite Vedic *mantras*. After having these qualified *brāhmaṇas* recite auspicious Vedic hymns, he arranged to have the Vedic birth ceremony celebrated for his newborn child according to the rules and regulations, and he also arranged for the worship of the demigods and forefathers. The experts in reciting old histories like the *Purāṇas*, the experts in reciting histories of royal families, and general reciters all chanted, while singers sang and many kinds of musical instruments, like *bherīs* and *dundubhis*, played in accompaniment. All the cowherd men, dressed very opulently with valuable ornaments, coats and turbans, approached the newborn Kṛṣṇa with various presentations in their hands. The beautiful *gopī* wives of the cowherd men were very pleased to hear that mother Yaśodā had given birth to a son, and after decorating themselves very nicely with proper dresses, ornaments, black ointment for the eyes, and so on, they hurried to Nanda Mahārāja's house. Offering blessings to the newborn child, the wives and daughters of the cowherd men said, "May You become the King of Vraja and long maintain all its inhabitants." They then sprinkled a mixture of tumeric powder, oil and water upon the birthless Supreme Lord Kṛṣṇa and offered their prayers. (*pp. 320–330*)

In Mathurā, India, this temple marks *Kṛṣṇa-janmasthāna*, the site of Lord Kṛṣṇa's appearance in this world.

SUMMARY OF THE TENTH CANTO

A short description of each chapter of this Tenth Canto is as follows. The First Chapter, which has sixty-nine verses, describes Mahārāja Parīkṣit's eagerness to learn about the incarnation of Lord Kṛṣṇa, and it also tells how Kaṁsa killed the six sons of Devakī because of his fear of being killed by her eighth child. The Second Chapter contains forty-two verses, describing the entrance of the Supreme Personality of Godhead, Kṛṣṇa, into the womb of Devakī to fulfill His mission of killing Kaṁsa. When Lord Kṛṣṇa was within Devakī's womb, all the demigods, headed by Brahmā, offered prayers to the Lord. The Third Chapter contains fifty-three verses. This chapter describes the appearance of Lord Kṛṣṇa as He is. The Lord's father and mother, understanding the Lord's appearance, offered prayers. Fearing Kaṁsa, the Lord's father brought the child from Mathurā to Gokula Vṛndāvana. The Fourth Chapter contains forty-six verses, which tell of a prophecy by the goddess Caṇḍikā. After consulting demoniac friends, Kaṁsa began killing all the children born at that time, since he thought this would be to his benefit.

The Fifth Chapter contains thirty-two verses, describing how Nanda Mahārāja performed the birth ceremony of Kṛṣṇa and then went to Mathurā, where he met Vasudeva. The Sixth Chapter contains forty-four verses. In this chapter, Nanda Mahārāja, following the advice of his friend Vasudeva, returns to Gokula and on the way sees the dead body of the Pūtanā demoness and is astonished at her having been killed by Kṛṣṇa. The Seventh Chapter, which contains thirty-seven verses, describes Mahārāja Parīkṣit's enthusiasm to hear about the boyhood pastimes of Lord Kṛṣṇa, who killed Śakaṭāsura and Tṛṇāvartāsura and showed within His mouth the entire cosmic manifestation. In the Eighth Chapter there are fifty-two verses, which describe Gargamuni's performing the name-giving ceremony of Kṛṣṇa and Balarāma and how Kṛṣṇa and Balarāma performed playful childish activities, crawling on the ground, trying to walk with Their small legs, and stealing butter and breaking the pots. This chapter also describes the vision of the universal form.

The Ninth Chapter, which has twenty-three verses, describes how Kṛṣṇa disturbed His mother while she was churning butter. Because she left Kṛṣṇa to see to the stove, where the milk was boiling, and did not allow Him to suck her breast, Kṛṣṇa was very angry and broke a pot of yogurt. To chastise her naughty child, mother Yaśodā wanted to bind Him with rope, but every time she tried she failed because of a shortage of rope when the time came to knot it. In the Tenth Chapter there are forty-three verses. This chapter describes how Kṛṣṇa, as Dāmodara, caused the twin Yamalārjuna trees to fall and how the two demigods within the trees were delivered by the mercy of Kṛṣṇa. In the Eleventh Chapter there are fifty-nine verses. This chapter describes how Nanda Mahārāja released Kṛṣṇa from the ropes, how Kṛṣṇa showed His mercy to a fruit seller while exchanging grains for fruit, and how Nanda Mahārāja and others decided to leave Gokula for Vṛndāvana, where Kṛṣṇa killed Vatsāsura and Bakāsura.

Chapter Twelve contains forty-four verses, describing Kṛṣṇa's pastimes with the cowherd boys in the forest and the killing of the demon named Aghāsura. Chapter Thirteen contains sixty-four verses, describing how Brahmā stole Kṛṣṇa's calves and His friends, the cowherd boys. Kṛṣṇa expanded His pastimes for one year, representing Himself as the calves and boys in forms exactly like their own. In this way He bewildered Brahmā, who at last surrendered when his illusion was over. The Fourteenth Chapter contains sixty-one verses. In this chapter, Brahmā offers prayers to Kṛṣṇa after fully understanding Him to be the Supreme Personality of Godhead. The Fifteenth Chapter contains fifty-two verses. This chapter describes how Kṛṣṇa entered Tālavana Forest with Balārama, how Balārama killed Dhenukāsura, and how Kṛṣṇa protected the cowherd boys and cows from the poisonous effects of Kāliya.

The Sixteenth Chapter contains sixty-seven verses. This chapter describes the chastisement of Kāliya by Kṛṣṇa, and it also describes the prayers offered by Kāliya's wives. In the Seventeenth Chapter there are twenty-five verses. This chapter describes why Kāliya entered the River Yamunā after leaving his home, Nāgālaya, one of the *dvīpas*, which according to some corresponds to the Fiji Islands. This chapter also describes how Garuḍa was cursed by Saubhari Ṛṣi, how the cowherd boys, Kṛṣṇa's friends, were enlivened when Kṛṣṇa emerged from the Yamunā, and how Kṛṣṇa stopped the forest fire and saved the sleeping inhabitants of Vraja.

The Eighteenth Chapter contains thirty-two verses, giving a description of Kṛṣṇa and Balarāma, Their picnics within the forest, the climate of Vṛndāvana in the summer and the spring, and Lord Balarāma's killing of Pralambāsura. Chapter Nineteen contains sixteen verses, describing Kṛṣṇa's entering the forest known as Muñjāraṇya, saving the cowherd boys and cows from the forest fire, and bringing them to Bhāṇḍīravana. Chapter Twenty contains forty-nine verses. This chapter describes the enjoyment of Balarāma and Kṛṣṇa in the forest with the cowherd boys during the rainy season, and it gives various instructions through analogies concerning the rainy season and autumn.

Chapter Twenty-one contains twenty verses, describing how Kṛṣṇa entered the forest of Vṛndāvana in the autumn, playing His flute, and how He attracted the *gopīs*, who were singing His glories. The Twenty-second Chapter contains thirty-eight verses, describing how the *gopīs* prayed to the goddess Kātyāyanī to obtain Kṛṣṇa as their husband and how Kṛṣṇa later stole the garments of the *gopīs* while the *gopīs* were bathing in the Yamunā. The Twenty-third Chapter contains fifty-two verses, describing how the cowherd boys, being very hungry, followed Kṛṣṇa's directions by begging some food for Him and themselves from *brāhmaṇas* engaged in performing *yajñas*. The *brāhmaṇas* refused to give food to Kṛṣṇa and Balarāma, although the boys begged for it, but the wives of the *brāhmaṇas* agreed, and therefore Kṛṣṇa bestowed His mercy upon them.

The Twenty-fourth Chapter contains thirty-eight verses, describing how Kṛṣṇa defied King Indra, despite Indra's position of prestige, by stopping the *indra-yajña* and instead worshiping Govardhana. The Twenty-fifth Chapter contains thirty-three verses. As described in this chapter, because the *indra-yajña* was stopped, King Indra was very angry, and to kill the inhabitants of Vṛndāvana, Vraja, he flooded the entire area with rain. Kṛṣṇa, however, accepted King Indra's challenge by lifting Govardhana Hill as an umbrella to protect Vṛndāvana and all the cows. The Twenty-sixth Chapter contains twenty-five verses, describing how Nanda Mahārāja, seeing the extraordinary activities of Kṛṣṇa, was struck with wonder and how he thus narrated for all the cowherd men the whole story of Kṛṣṇa's opulence, as foretold by Gargamuni. Chapter Twenty-seven, which contains twenty-eight verses, describes how King Indra, upon seeing Kṛṣṇa's unlimited power, worshiped Lord Kṛṣṇa, who was fully washed with milk supplied by the *surabhi* and who thus became known as Govinda. The Twenty-eighth Chapter contains seventeen verses. In this chapter Kṛṣṇa saves His father, Nanda Mahārāja, from the custody of Varuṇa and shows the cowherd men how Vaikuṇṭhaloka is situated.

The Twenty-ninth Chapter contains forty-eight verses, describing how Kṛṣṇa talked to the *gopīs* before performing the *rāsa-līlā* and how, after the beginning of the *rāsa-līlā*, Kṛṣṇa disappeared from the scene. Chapter Thirty contains forty-four verses, describing how the *gopīs*, being separated from Kṛṣṇa, went mad and began to wander in the forest in search of Him. The *gopīs* met Śrīmatī Rādhārāṇī, the daughter of King Vṛṣabhānu, and they all wandered on the bank of the Yamunā searching for Kṛṣṇa. Chapter Thirty-one contains nineteen verses, describing how the bereaved *gopīs* waited in great anxiety to meet Kṛṣṇa. Chapter Thirty-two contains twenty-two verses. In this chapter, Kṛṣṇa appears among the *gopīs*, who are fully satisfied in ecstatic love for Him. Chapter Thirty-three contains thirty-nine verses. In this chapter Kṛṣṇa appears in multiforms in the midst of the *gopīs*, with whom He dances in the *rāsa* dance. Then they all bathe in the River Yamunā. Also in this chapter, Śukadeva mitigates the doubts of Parīkṣit concerning the performance of the *rāsa-līlā*.

Chapter Thirty-four contains thirty-two verses. This chapter describes how Nanda Mahārāja, Kṛṣṇa's father, was swallowed by a big python, who had been a demigod named Vidyādhara but was cursed by Aṅgirā Ṛṣi. Kṛṣṇa rescued His father and saved this demigod simultaneously. Chapter Thirty-five contains twenty-six verses. This chapter describes how Kṛṣṇa went to the pasturing grounds with the cows and how the *gopīs* sang in separation from Him.

Chapter Thirty-six contains forty verses. This chapter describes Kṛṣṇa's killing of Ariṣṭāsura. It also describes Nārada's disclosure to Kaṁsa that both Rāma and Kṛṣṇa were sons of Vasudeva. Because of this disclosure, Kaṁsa arranged to kill both Rāma and Kṛṣṇa. He sent his assistant Keśī to Vṛndāvana, and later he sent Akrūra to bring Rāma and Kṛṣṇa to Mathurā. Chapter Thirty-seven contains thirty-three verses. In this chapter Kṛṣṇa kills the Keśī demon, Nārada worships Kṛṣṇa by narrating His future activities, and Kṛṣṇa kills the demon named Vyomāsura. Chapter Thirty-eight contains forty-three verses. This chapter describes how Akrūra went to Vṛndāvana and how he was received by Rāma-Kṛṣṇa and Nanda Mahārāja. Chapter Thirty-nine contains fifty-seven verses. This chapter describes how Rāma and Kṛṣṇa, having been invited by Kaṁsa, started for Mathurā. While They were ready on the chariot, the *gopīs* began to cry, and Kṛṣṇa sent His messenger to pacify them. Thus He was able to travel toward Mathurā. On the way, Akrūra was shown the entire Viṣṇuloka within the water of the Yamunā.

Chapter Forty contains thirty verses, in which the prayers of Akrūra are described. Chapter Forty-one, which contains fifty-two verses, describes the entrance of Rāma and Kṛṣṇa into the city of Mathurā, where the ladies were very jubilant to see these two brothers. Kṛṣṇa killed a washerman, glorified Sudāmā and gave Sudāmā His benediction. Chapter Forty-two, which contains thirty-eight verses, describes how Kṛṣṇa delivered Kubjā and how He broke Kaṁsa's gigantic bow and killed its caretakers. Thus Kaṁsa and Kṛṣṇa met. Chapter Forty-three contains forty verses. Outside the sporting arena of Kaṁsa, Kṛṣṇa killed an elephant named Kuvalayāpīḍa. Then He entered the arena and spoke with Cāṇūra. Chapter Forty-four, which contains fifty-one verses, describes how Kṛṣṇa and Balarāma killed the wrestlers named Cāṇūra and Muṣṭika and thereafter killed Kaṁsa and his eight brothers. Kṛṣṇa, however, pacified Kaṁsa's wives and His own father and mother, Vasudeva and Devakī.

Chapter Forty-five contains fifty verses. This chapter describes how Kṛṣṇa pacified His father and mother and celebrated the enthronement of His grandfather Ugrasena. After promising the inhabitants of Vṛndāvana that He would return very soon, Kṛṣṇa underwent ritualistic ceremonies as a *kṣatriya.* He took the vow of *brahmacarya* and lived in the *guru-kula,* where He studied regularly. By killing the demon named Pañcajana, He received a conchshell named Pāñcajanya. Kṛṣṇa rescued the son of His *guru* from the custody of Yamarāja and returned them. After thus offering *guru-dakṣiṇā* to repay His teacher, Lord Kṛṣṇa returned to Mathurā-purī. Chapter Forty-six contains forty-nine verses. As described in this chapter, Kṛṣṇa sent Uddhava to Vṛndāvana to pacify His father and mother, Nanda Mahārāja and Yaśodā. Chapter Forty-seven contains sixty-nine verses, describing how Uddhava, following Kṛṣṇa's order, went to pacify the *gopīs* and then returned to Mathurā. Thus Uddhava appreciated the ecstatic love felt for Kṛṣṇa by the inhabitants of Vṛndāvana.

Chapter Forty-eight contains thirty-six verses. This chapter describes how Kṛṣṇa fulfilled the desire of Kubjā by going to her house and enjoying her. Kṛṣṇa then went to the home of Akrūra. Satisfied by Akrūra's prayers, Kṛṣṇa praised him very much and sent him to Hastināpura to gather information about the Pāṇḍavas. Chapter Forty-nine contains thirty-one verses. As described in this chapter, Akrūra, following Kṛṣṇa's orders, went to Hastināpura, where he met Vidura and Kuntī and heard from them about Dhṛtarāṣṭra's mistreatment of the Pāṇḍavas. Informed of the Pāṇḍavas' faith in Kṛṣṇa, Akrūra advised Dhṛtarāṣṭra, and after understanding Dhṛtarāṣṭra's mind, he returned to Mathurā, where he described everything about the situation in Hastināpura.

Chapter Fifty contains fifty-seven verses. In this chapter, Jarāsandha, having heard that his son-in-law Kaṁsa was killed, attacked Mathurā to kill Rāma and Kṛṣṇa but was defeated seventeen times. When Jarāsandha was about to attack for the eighteenth time, Kālayavana, having been advised by Nārada, also attacked Mathurā. Thus the Yādava dynasty entered a fort in the midst of the water and lived there by mystic power. After giving full protection to the Yādava dynasty and conferring with Lord Baladeva, Lord Kṛṣṇa emerged from Dvārakā. Chapter Fifty-one, which contains sixty-three verses, describes how Mucukunda killed Kālayavana simply by glancing upon him.

Chapter Fifty-two contains forty-four verses. In this chapter, Mucukunda offers prayers to Kṛṣṇa, and then Kṛṣṇa kills all the soldiers of Kālayavana and returns to Dvārakā with their booty. When Jarāsandha attacked Mathurā again, Rāma and Kṛṣṇa, as if afraid of him, fled to the top of a mountain, to which Jarāsandha then set fire. Unseen by Jarāsandha, Kṛṣṇa and Balarāma jumped from the mountain and entered Dvārakā, which was surrounded by the sea. Jarāsandha, thinking that Kṛṣṇa and Balarāma had been killed, returned with his soldiers to his own country, and Kṛṣṇa continued to live in Dvārakā. Rukmiṇī, the daughter of Vidarbha, was very much attracted to Kṛṣṇa, and she sent Kṛṣṇa a letter through a *brāhmaṇa*. Chapter Fifty-three contains fifty-seven verses. Following Rukmiṇī's request, Kṛṣṇa went to the city of Vidarbha and kidnapped her in the presence of such enemies as Jarāsandha. Chapter Fifty-four contains sixty verses. As described in this chapter, Kṛṣṇa defeated all the opposing princes and disfigured Rukmiṇī's brother Rukmī. Then Kṛṣṇa returned with Rukmiṇī to Dvārakā, where they were united in a regular marriage. Rukmī, however, remained in a place known as Bhojakaṭa, being angry at his brother-in-law, Kṛṣṇa. Chapter Fifty-five, containing forty verses, describes the birth of Pradyumna, how Pradyumna was kidnapped by Śambarāsura, and how Pradyumna later killed Śambarāsura and returned to Dvārakā with his wife, Ratidevī.

Chapter Fifty-six contains forty-five verses. As described in this chapter, King Satrājit, by the mercy of the sun-god, received a jewel called Syamantaka. Later, when this jewel was stolen, Satrājit unnecessarily became doubtful of Kṛṣṇa, but Kṛṣṇa, to vindicate His position, retrieved the jewel, along with the daughter of Jāmbavān. Kṛṣṇa later married Satrājit's daughter and received a full dowry. As described in Chapter Fifty-seven, which contains forty-two verses, both Balarāma and Kṛṣṇa went to Hastināpura, having heard about the fire in the shellac house of the Pāṇḍavas. After Satrājit was killed by Śatadhanvā at the instigation of Akrūra and Kṛtavarmā, Balarāma and Kṛṣṇa returned to Dvārakā. Śatadhanvā left the Syamantaka jewel with Akrūra and fled to the forest. Thus although Kṛṣṇa killed Śatadhanvā, He was unable to retrieve the jewel. Finally the jewel was discovered and awarded to Akrūra. Chapter Fifty-eight contains fifty-eight verses. After the Pāṇḍavas finished living incognito in the forest, Kṛṣṇa went to Indraprastha to see them. He then married five wives, headed by Kālindī. After Kṛṣṇa and Arjuna set fire to the Khāṇḍava Forest, Arjuna received the Gāṇḍīva bow. The demon Maya Dānava constructed an assembly house for the Pāṇḍavas, and Duryodhana was very much aggrieved.

Chapter Fifty-nine contains forty-five verses. In this chapter, Kṛṣṇa, at the request of Indra, kills the demon Narakāsura, the son of the earth personified, along with the demon's associates, headed by Mura. The earth personified offers prayers to Kṛṣṇa and returns to Him all the paraphernalia that Narakāsura has stolen. Kṛṣṇa then bestows fearlessness upon the son of Narakāsura and marries the sixteen thousand princesses whom the demon kidnapped. Also in this chapter, Kṛṣṇa takes away the *pārijāta* plant from the heavenly planets, and the foolishness of Indra and others is described.

Chapter Sixty contains fifty-nine verses. In this chapter, Kṛṣṇa makes Rukmiṇī angry with His joking words. Kṛṣṇa pacifies Rukmiṇī, and there is a lover's quarrel between them. Chapter Sixty-one contains forty verses. This chapter contains a description of the sons and grandsons of Kṛṣṇa. At the time of Aniruddha's marriage, Balarāma kills Rukmī and breaks the teeth of the King of Kaliṅga.

Chapter Sixty-two contains thirty-three verses. This chapter begins the discourse concerning the abduction of Ūṣā, the daughter of Bāṇāsura, and the amorous pastimes between Ūṣā and Aniruddha. It also describes a fight between Aniruddha and Bāṇāsura and how Bāṇāsura seized Aniruddha with a snake-noose. Chapter Sixty-three, which contains fifty-three verses, describes how the strength of Lord Śiva was defeated in a battle between Bāṇāsura and the Yādavas. The Raudra-jvara, having been defeated by the Vaiṣṇava-jvara, offered prayers to Kṛṣṇa. Kṛṣṇa severed all but four of Bāṇa's one thousand arms and thus showed him mercy. Kṛṣṇa then returned to Dvārakā with Ūṣā and Aniruddha.

Chapter Sixty-four contains forty-four verses. In this chapter, Kṛṣṇa liberates King Nṛga, the son of Ikṣvāku, from a curse and instructs all kings by explaining the fault in misappropriating the property of a *brāhmaṇa*. In connection with the deliverance of King Nṛga, there are instructions for the Yādavas, who were puffed up with pride due to wealth, opulence, enjoyment and so on.

Chapter Sixty-five contains thirty-four verses. As described in this chapter, Lord Baladeva, desiring to see His friends and relatives, went to Gokula. In the months of Caitra and Vaiśākha, in the groves by the Yamunā, Lord Balarāma performed the *rāsa-rasotsava* and *yamunā-karṣaṇa līlās* in the association of His *gopīs.*

As described in Chapter Sixty-six, which contains forty-three verses, Kṛṣṇa went to Kāśī and then killed Pauṇḍraka, as well as his friend the King of Kāśī, Sudakṣiṇa and others. Chapter Sixty-seven, which contains twenty-eight verses, describes how Lord Baladeva, while enjoying with many young girls on Raivataka Mountain, vanquished the extremely mischievous ape Dvivida, who was the brother of Mainda and a friend of Narakāsura's.

Chapter Sixty-eight has fifty-four verses. As described in this chapter, when Sāmba, the son of Jāmbavatī, kidnapped Lakṣmaṇā, the daughter of Duryodhana, he was captured in a fight with the Kauravas. In order to free him and establish peace, Lord Baladeva went to Hastināpura as a well-wisher. The Kauravas, however, were uncooperative, and upon seeing their arrogance, Lord Baladeva began pulling their city of

Hastināpura with His plow. The Kauravas, headed by Duryodhana, offered prayers to Lord Baladeva, who then returned to Dvārakā with Sāmba and Lakṣmaṇā.

Chapter Sixty-nine contains forty-five verses. As described in this chapter, Kṛṣṇa exhibited His householder life with His sixteen thousand wives. Even the great sage Nārada was astonished at how Kṛṣṇa, having expanded Himself into sixteen thousand forms, was conducting His householder life. Thus Nārada offered prayers to Lord Kṛṣṇa, and Kṛṣṇa was very much pleased with him.

Chapter Seventy, which contains forty-seven verses, describes how Kṛṣṇa exhibited His daily ritualistic ceremonies and how He released the kings arrested by Jarāsandha. While Lord Kṛṣṇa was receiving a messenger sent by these kings, Nārada came to see Kṛṣṇa and told Him news of the Pāṇḍavas. Nārada informed Kṛṣṇa that the Pāṇḍavas desired to perform a *rājasūya* sacrifice, and Kṛṣṇa agreed to attend it, but He first asked for Uddhava's decision about whether to give preference to killing King Jarāsandha or performing the *rājasūya-yajña.* Chapter Seventy-one contains forty-five verses, describing the happiness of the Pāṇḍavas when Kṛṣṇa went to Indraprastha. By the inconceivable desire of Kṛṣṇa, Jarāsandha would be killed, and the *rājasūya-yajña* would be performed by Mahārāja Yudhiṣṭhira.

Chapter Seventy-two contains forty-six verses. By agreeing to perform the *rājasūya-yajña,* Kṛṣṇa gave Mahārāja Yudhiṣṭhira great pleasure. This chapter also describes the killing of Jarāsandha, the enthroning of his son, and the release of the kings whom Jarāsandha had arrested. Chapter Seventy-three contains thirty-five verses. After Lord Kṛṣṇa released the kings and restored their royal power, He was worshiped by Sahadeva, the son of Jarāsandha, and then He returned to Indraprastha with Bhīma and Arjuna. Chapter Seventy-four contains fifty-four verses. Mahārāja Yudhiṣṭhira offered prayers to Kṛṣṇa and offered Him the first worship in the *rājasūya-yajña.* To honor the Lord in this way is the foremost duty of every man, but this was intolerable to Śiśupāla, the King of Cedi. Śiśupāla began to blaspheme Kṛṣṇa, who thus severed the King's head from his body and awarded him the salvation called *sārūpya-mukti.* After the conclusion of the *rājasūya* sacrifice, Kṛṣṇa returned to Dvārakā with His queens. Chapter Seventy-five contains forty verses. As described in this chapter, Mahārāja Yudhiṣṭhira, after the *rājasūya-yajña*, performed the final ritualistic bathing ceremonies. Duryodhana was bewildered in the palace constructed by Maya Dānava, and thus he felt insulted.

Chapter Seventy-six contains thirty-three verses, describing how Śālva, one of the kings Kṛṣṇa defeated when He kidnapped Rukmiṇī, decided to rid the entire world of the Yādavas. To defeat the Yādavas, Śālva worshiped Lord Śiva, who rewarded him with an aerial car named Saubha. When Śālva fought with the Vṛṣṇis, Pradyumna smashed the car designed by Maya Dānava, but he was attacked by Śālva's brother, whose name was Dyumān. Beaten unconscious by Dyumān's club, Pradyumna was carried some distance away from the warfield by his charioteer, but later he lamented having been removed from the battlefield. Chapter Seventy-seven contains thirty-seven verses. In this chapter, Pradyumna recovers from his injuries and begins fighting with Śālva. When Kṛṣṇa returned to Dvārakā from Indraprastha, He immediately went to the battlefield where Śālva and Pradyumna were fighting. There He killed Śālva, although Śālva was powerfully equipped with illusory weapons.

Chapter Seventy-eight contains forty verses. As described in this chapter, a friend of Śālva's named Dantavakra and Dantavakra's brother Vidūratha were killed by Śrī Kṛṣṇa. Instead of taking part in the fighting between the Kauravas and the Pāṇḍavas, Baladeva, who had been staying at Dvārakā-purī, went touring holy places. Because of the misbehavior of Romaharṣaṇa, Baladeva killed him at Naimiṣāraṇya and appointed his son Ugraśravā, Sūta Gosvāmī, the speaker of *Śrīmad-Bhāgavatam*, to continue the discourses on the *Purāṇas*. Chapter Seventy-nine contains thirty-four verses. This chapter describes how the *brāhmaṇas* of Naimiṣāraṇya advised Baladeva to atone for the death of Romaharṣaṇa. After killing a demon named Balvala, Baladeva traveled and bathed in holy places until He at last came to the Battlefield of Kurukṣetra, where Bhīma and Duryodhana were fighting. Then He returned to Dvārakā and went again to Naimiṣāraṇya, where He instructed the *ṛṣis*. Then He left with His wife Revatī.

Chapter Eighty, which contains forty-five verses, describes how Sudāmā Vipra, a friend of Kṛṣṇa's, approached Kṛṣṇa for money and was worshiped by Kṛṣṇa, who reminisced with him about their boyhood at the *guru-kula*. Chapter Eighty-one contains forty-one verses. This chapter describes the friendly talks between Kṛṣṇa and His friend

Sudāmā. Kṛṣṇa very gladly accepted a gift of flat rice from Sudāmā Vipra. When Sudāmā Vipra returned home, he saw that everything there was wonderfully opulent, and he praised the friendship of the Supreme Personality of Godhead. With the gifts of the Lord, he enjoyed material opulence, and later he was promoted back home, back to Godhead.

Chapter Eighty-two contains forty-eight verses. This chapter describes how the Yādavas went to Kurukṣetra because of a solar eclipse and how other kings spoke to them of Kṛṣṇa. At this meeting, Kṛṣṇa satisfied Nanda Mahārāja and the residents of Vṛndāvana, who had also come there. Chapter Eighty-three contains forty-three verses, describing how the women assembed at Kurukṣetra engaged in topics of Śrī Kṛṣṇa and how Draupadī asked all Kṛṣṇa's queens about how they had married Him. Chapter Eighty-four contains seventy-one verses. As described in this chapter, when great sages went to see Kṛṣṇa at Kurukṣetra, Kṛṣṇa took this opportunity to praise them. Because Vasudeva desired to perform a great sacrifice on this occasion, the sages advised him regarding worship of Kṛṣṇa, the Supreme Personality of Godhead. After the *yajña* was performed, all who were present dispersed to their respective abodes. Chapter Eighty-five contains fifty-nine verses. At the request of His father and mother, Kṛṣṇa, by His mercy, returned their dead sons, all of whom were liberated. Chapter Eighty-six contains fifty-nine verses. This chapter describes how Arjuna kidnapped Subhadrā with a great fight. It also describes how Kṛṣṇa went to Mithilā to favor His devotee Bahulāśva and stay at the house of Śrutadeva and advise them about spiritual advancement.

Chapter Eighty-seven contains fifty verses, describing the prayers offered to Nārāyaṇa by the *Vedas*. Chapter Eighty-eight contains forty verses. This chapter describes how Vaiṣṇavas become transcendental by worshiping Lord Viṣṇu and then return home, back to Godhead. By worship of demigods, one may get material power, but this chapter describes how an ordinary living being in the material world can be favored by Lord Śrī Kṛṣṇa, and it establishes Lord Viṣṇu's supremacy above Lord Brahmā and Lord Śiva. Chapter Eighty-nine contains sixty-five verses, disclosing who is the best among the material deities. Although Viṣṇu is among the three deities—Brahmā, Viṣṇu and Maheśvara—He is transcendental and supreme. In this chapter we also find a description of how Kṛṣṇa and Arjuna went to Mahākāla-pura to deliver the son of a Dvārakā *brāhmaṇa* and how Arjuna was astonished. Chapter Ninety contains fifty verses. This chapter summarizes Kṛṣṇa's *līlās* and presents the logic of *madhureṇa samāpayet,* establishing that everything ends well in transcendental bliss.

CHAPTER ONE

The Advent of Lord Kṛṣṇa: Introduction

The summary of the First Chapter is as follows. This chapter describes how Kaṁsa, frightened by hearing an omen about his being killed by the eighth son of Devakī, killed Devakī's sons one after another.

When Śukadeva Gosvāmī finished describing the dynasty of Yadu, as well as the dynasties of the moon-god and sun-god, Mahārāja Parīkṣit requested him to describe Lord Kṛṣṇa, who appeared with Baladeva in the Yadu dynasty, and how Kṛṣṇa performed His activities within this world. Kṛṣṇa is transcendental, the King said, and therefore to understand His activities is the occupation of liberated persons. Hearing of *kṛṣṇa-līlā* is the boat by which to achieve the ultimate goal of life. Except for an animal killer or one who is following a policy of suicide, every intelligent person must strive to understand Kṛṣṇa and His activities.

Kṛṣṇa was the only worshipable Deity for the Pāṇḍavas. When Mahārāja Parīkṣit was in the womb of his mother, Uttarā, Kṛṣṇa saved him from the attack of the *brahma-śastra.* Now Mahārāja Parīkṣit asked Śukadeva Gosvāmī how His Lordship Baladeva, the son of Rohiṇī, could have appeared in the womb of Devakī. Why did Kṛṣṇa transfer Himself from Mathurā to Vṛndāvana, King Parīkṣit asked, and how did He live there with His family members? What did Kṛṣṇa do in Mathurā and Vṛndāvana, and why did He kill His maternal uncle Kaṁsa? For how many years did Kṛṣṇa reside in Dvārakā, and how many queens did He have? Mahārāja Parīkṣit asked Śukadeva Gosvamī all these questions. He also requested Śukadeva Gosvāmī to describe other activities of Kṛṣṇa about which he could not inquire.

When Śukadeva Gosvāmī began to speak about Kṛṣṇa consciousness, Mahārāja Parīkṣit forgot the fatigue brought about by his fasting. Enthusiastic to describe Kṛṣṇa, Śukadeva Gosvāmī said, "Like the waters of the Ganges, descriptions of the activities of Kṛṣṇa can purify the entire universe. The speaker, the inquirer and the audience all become purified."

Once when the entire world was overburdened by the increasing military power of demons in the form of kings, mother earth assumed the shape of a cow and approached Lord Brahmā for relief. Sympathetic to mother earth's lamentation, Brahmā, accompanied by Lord Śiva and other demigods, took the cow-shaped mother earth to the shore of the milk ocean, where he offered prayers to please Lord Viṣṇu, who lay there on an island in transcendental ecstasy. Brahmā thereafter understood the advice of Mahā-Viṣṇu, who informed him that He would appear on the surface of the earth to mitigate the burden created by the demons. The demigods, along with their wives, should appear there as associates of Lord Kṛṣṇa in the family of Yadu to increase the sons and grandsons in that dynasty. By the will of Lord Kṛṣṇa, Anantadeva would appear first, as Balarāma, and Kṛṣṇa's potency, *yogamāyā*, would also appear. Brahmā informed mother earth about all this, and then he returned to his own abode.

After marrying Devakī, Vasudeva was returning home with her on a chariot driven by Kaṁsa, her brother, when an ominous voice addressed Kaṁsa, warning him that Devakī's eighth son would kill him. Upon hearing this omen, Kaṁsa was immediately ready to kill Devakī, but Vasudeva diplomatically began to instruct him. Vasudeva stressed that it would not be good for Kaṁsa to kill his younger sister, especially at the time of her marriage. Anyone who possesses a material body must die, Vasudeva advised him. Every living entity lives in a body for some time and then transmigrates to another body, but one is unfortunately misled into accepting the body as the soul. If a person under this mistaken conception wants to kill another body, he is condemned as hellish.

Because Kaṁsa was not satisfied by Vasudeva's instructions, Vasudeva devised a plan. He offered to bring Kaṁsa all of Devakī's children so that Kaṁsa could kill them. Why then should Kaṁsa kill Devakī now? Kaṁsa was satisfied by this proposal. In due course of time, when Devakī gave birth to a child, Vasudeva brought the newborn baby to Kaṁsa, who, upon seeing Vasudeva's magnanimity, was struck with wonder. When Vasudeva gave Kaṁsa the child, Kaṁsa, showing some intelligence, said that since he was to be killed by the eighth child, why should he kill the first? Although Vasudeva did not trust him, Kaṁsa requested Vasudeva to take the child back. Later, however, after Nārada approached Kaṁsa and disclosed to him that the demigods were appearing in the Yadu and

Vṛṣṇi dynasties and conspiring to kill him, Kaṁsa decided to kill all the children born in these families, and he also decided that any child born from the womb of Devakī must be killed. Thus he arrested and imprisoned both Devakī and Vasudeva and killed six of their sons, one after another. Nārada had also informed Kaṁsa that in his previous birth Kaṁsa was Kālanemi, a demon killed by Viṣṇu. Consequently, Kaṁsa became a great enemy to all the descendants of the *yadu-vaṁśa*, the Yadu dynasty. He even arrested and imprisoned his own father, Ugrasena, for Kaṁsa wanted to enjoy the kingdom alone.

Kṛṣṇa has threefold pastimes—the Vraja-līlā, Māthura-līlā and Dvārakā-līlā. As already mentioned, in the Tenth Canto of *Śrīmad-Bhāgavatam* there are ninety chapters, which describe all these *līlās*. The first four chapters describe Brahmā's prayers for the relief of the earth's burden, and they also describe the appearance of the Supreme Personality of Godhead. Chapters Five through Thirty-nine recount Kṛṣṇa's pastimes in Vṛndāvana. The Fortieth Chapter describes how Kṛṣṇa enjoyed in the water of the Yamunā and how Akrūra offered prayers. Chapters Forty-one through Fifty-one, eleven chapters, tell of Kṛṣṇa's pastimes in Māthura, and Chapters Fifty-two through Ninety, thirty-nine chapters, relate Kṛṣṇa's pastimes in Dvārakā.

Chapters Twenty-nine through Thirty-three describe Kṛṣṇa's dancing with the *gopīs*, known as the *rāsa-līlā*. Therefore these five chapters are known as *rāsa-pañcādhyāya*. The Forty-seventh Chapter of the Tenth Canto is a description known as the *bhramara-gītā*.

TEXT 1

श्रीराजोवाच
कथितो वंशविस्तारो भवता सोमसूर्ययोः ।
राज्ञां चोभयवंश्यानां चरितं परमाद्भुतम् ॥ १ ॥

śrī-rājovāca
kathito vaṁśa-vistāro
bhavatā soma-sūryayoḥ
rājñāṁ cobhaya-vaṁśyānāṁ
caritaṁ paramādbhutam

śrī-rājā uvāca—King Parīkṣit said; *kathitaḥ*—has already been described; *vaṁśa-vistāraḥ*—a broad description of the dynasties; *bhavatā*—by Your Lordship; *soma-sūryayoḥ*—of the moon-god and the sun-god; *rājñām*—of the kings; *ca*—and; *ubhaya*—both; *vaṁśyānām*—of the members of the dynasties; *caritam*—the character; *parama*—exalted; *adbhutam*—and wonderful.

TRANSLATION

King Parīkṣit said: My dear lord, you have elaborately described the dynasties of both the moon-god and the sun-god, with the exalted and wonderful character of their kings.

PURPORT

At the end of the Ninth Canto, Twenty-fourth Chapter, Śukadeva Gosvāmī summarized the activities of Kṛṣṇa. He spoke of how Kṛṣṇa had personally appeared to reduce the burden on the earth, how He had manifested His pastimes as a householder, and how, soon after His birth, He had transferred Himself to His Vrajabhūmi-līlā. Parīkṣit Mahārāja, being naturally a devotee of Kṛṣṇa, wanted to hear more about Lord Kṛṣṇa. Therefore, to encourage Śukadeva Gosvāmī to continue speaking about Kṛṣṇa and give further details, he thanked Śukadeva Gosvāmī for having described the activities of Kṛṣṇa in brief. Śukadeva Gosvāmī had said:

jāto gataḥ pitṛ-gṛhād vrajam edhitārtho
hatvā ripūn suta-śatāni kṛtorudāraḥ
utpādya teṣu puruṣaḥ kratubhiḥ samīje
ātmānam ātma-nigamaṁ prathayañ janeṣu

"The Supreme Personality of Godhead, Śrī Kṛṣṇa, known as *līlā-puruṣottama*, appeared as the son of Vasudeva but immediately left His father's home and went to Vṛndāvana to expand His loving relationships with His confidential devotees. In Vṛndāvana the Lord killed many demons, and afterward He returned to Dvārakā, where according to Vedic principles He married many wives who were the best of women, begot through them hundreds of sons, and performed sacrifices for

His own worship to establish the principles of householder life." (*Bhāg.* 9.24.66)

The Yadu dynasty belonged to the family descending from Soma, the moon-god. Although the planetary systems are so arranged that the sun comes first, before the moon, Parīkṣit Mahārāja gave more respect to the dynasty of the moon-god, the *soma-vaṁśa,* because in the Yādava dynasty, descending from the moon, Kṛṣṇa had appeared. There are two different *kṣatriya* families of the royal order, one descending from the king of the moon planet and the other descending from the king of the sun. Whenever the Supreme Personality of Godhead appears, He generally appears in a *kṣatriya* family because He comes to establish religious principles and the life of righteousness. According to the Vedic system, the *kṣatriya* family is the protector of the human race. When the Supreme Personality of Godhead appeared as Lord Rāmacandra, He appeared in the *sūrya-vaṁśa,* the family descending from the sun-god, and when He appeared as Lord Kṛṣṇa, He did so in the Yadu dynasty, or *yadu-vaṁśa,* whose descent was from the moon-god. In the Ninth Canto, Twenty-fourth Chapter, of *Śrīmad-Bhāgavatam,* there is a long list of the kings of the *yadu-vaṁśa.* All the kings in both the *soma-vaṁśa* and *sūrya-vaṁśa* were great and powerful, and Mahārāja Parīkṣit praised them very highly (*rājñāṁ cobhaya-vaṁśyānāṁ caritaṁ paramād-bhutam*). Nonetheless, he wanted to hear more about the *soma-vaṁśa* because that was the dynasty in which Kṛṣṇa had appeared.

The supreme abode of the Personality of Godhead, Kṛṣṇa, is described in *Brahma-saṁhitā* as the abode of *cintāmaṇi: cintāmaṇi-prakara-sadmasu kalpavṛkṣa-lakṣāvṛteṣu surabhīr abhipālayantam.* The Vṛndāvana-dhāma on this earth is a replica of that same abode. As stated in *Bhagavad-gītā* (8.20), in the spiritual sky there is another, eternal nature, transcendental to manifested and unmanifested matter. The manifested world can be seen in the form of many stars and planets such as the sun and moon, but beyond this is the unmanifested, which is imperceptible to those who are embodied. And beyond this unmanifested matter is the spiritual kingdom, which is described in *Bhagavad-gītā* as supreme and eternal. That kingdom is never annihilated. Although material nature is subject to repeated creation and annihilation, that spiritual nature remains as it is eternally. In the Tenth Canto of *Śrīmad-Bhāgavatam,* that spiritual nature, the spiritual world, is described as

Vṛndāvana, Goloka Vṛndāvana or Vraja-dhāma. The elaborate description of the above-mentioned *śloka* from the Ninth Canto—*jāto gataḥ pitṛ-gṛhād*—will be found here, in the Tenth Canto.

TEXT 2

यदोश्च धर्मशीलस्य नितरां मुनिसत्तम ।
तत्रांशेनावतीर्णस्य विष्णोर्वीर्याणि शंस नः ॥ २ ॥

yadoś ca dharma-śīlasya
nitarāṁ muni-sattama
tatrāṁśenāvatīrṇasya
viṣṇor vīryāṇi śaṁsa naḥ

yadoḥ—of Yadu or the Yadu dynasty; *ca*—also; *dharma-śīlasya*—who were strictly attached to religious principles; *nitarām*—highly qualified; *muni-sattama*—O best of all *munis*, king of the *munis* (Śukadeva Gosvāmī); *tatra*—in that dynasty; *aṁśena*—with His plenary expansion Baladeva; *avatīrṇasya*—who appeared as an incarnation; *viṣṇoḥ*—of Lord Viṣṇu; *vīryāṇi*—the glorious activities; *śaṁsa*—kindly describe; *naḥ*—unto us.

TRANSLATION

O best of munis, you have also described the descendants of Yadu, who were very pious and strictly adherent to religious principles. Now, if you will, kindly describe the wonderful, glorious activities of Lord Viṣṇu, or Kṛṣṇa, who appeared in that Yadu dynasty with Baladeva, His plenary expansion.

PURPORT

The *Brahma-saṁhitā* (5.1) explains that Kṛṣṇa is the origin of the *viṣṇu-tattva.*

īśvaraḥ paramaḥ kṛṣṇaḥ
sac-cid-ānanda-vigrahaḥ
anādir ādir govindaḥ
sarva-kāraṇa-kāraṇam

"Kṛṣṇa, who is known as Govinda, is the supreme controller. He has an eternal, blissful, spiritual body. He is the origin of all. He has no other origin, for He is the prime cause of all causes."

yasyaika-niśvasita-kālam athāvalambya
jīvanti loma-vilajā jagad-aṇḍa-nāthāḥ
viṣṇur mahān sa iha yasya kalā-viśeṣo
govindam ādi-puruṣaṁ tam ahaṁ bhajāmi

"The Brahmās, the heads of the innumerable universes, live only for the duration of one breath of Mahā-Viṣṇu. I worship Govinda, the original Lord, of whom Mahā-Viṣṇu is but a portion of a plenary portion." (Bs. 5.48)

Govinda, Kṛṣṇa, is the original Personality of Godhead. *Kṛṣṇas tu bhagavān svayam.* Even Lord Mahā-Viṣṇu, who by His breathing creates many millions upon millions of universes, is Lord Kṛṣṇa's *kalā-viśeṣa,* or plenary portion of a plenary portion. Mahā-Viṣṇu is a plenary expansion of Saṅkarṣaṇa, who is a plenary expansion of Nārāyaṇa. Nārāyaṇa is a plenary expansion of the *catur-vyūha,* and the *catur-vyūha* are plenary expansions of Baladeva, the first manifestation of Kṛṣṇa. Therefore when Kṛṣṇa appeared with Baladeva, all the *viṣṇu-tattvas* appeared with Him.

Mahārāja Parīkṣit requested Śukadeva Gosvāmī to describe Kṛṣṇa and His glorious activities. Another meaning may be derived from this verse as follows. Although Śukadeva Gosvāmī was the greatest *muni,* he could describe Kṛṣṇa only partially (*aṁśena*), for no one can describe Kṛṣṇa fully. It is said that Anantadeva has thousands of heads, but although He tries to describe Kṛṣṇa with thousands of tongues, His descriptions are still incomplete.

TEXT 3

अवतीर्य यदोर्वंशे भगवान् भूतभावनः ।
कृतवान् यानि विश्वात्मा तानि नो वद विस्तरात् ॥ ३ ॥

avatīrya yador vaṁśe
bhagavān bhūta-bhāvanaḥ

kṛtavān yāni viśvātmā
tāni no vada vistarāt

avatīrya—after descending; *yadoḥ vaṁśe*—in the dynasty of Yadu; *bhagavān*—the Supreme Personality of Godhead; *bhūta-bhāvanaḥ*—who is the cause of the cosmic manifestation; *kṛtavān*—executed; *yāni*—whatever (activities); *viśva-ātmā*—the Supersoul of the entire universe; *tāni*—all of those (activities); *naḥ*—unto us; *vada*—kindly say; *vistarāt*—elaborately.

TRANSLATION

The Supersoul, the Supreme Personality of Godhead, Śrī Kṛṣṇa, the cause of the cosmic manifestation, appeared in the dynasty of Yadu. Please tell me elaborately about His glorious activities and character, from the beginning to the end of His life.

PURPORT

In this verse the words *kṛtavān yāni* indicate that all the different activities Kṛṣṇa performed while present on earth are beneficial to human society. If religionists, philosophers and people in general simply hear the activities of Kṛṣṇa, they will be liberated. We have described several times that there are two kinds of *kṛṣṇa-kathā*, represented by *Bhagavad-gītā*, spoken personally by Kṛṣṇa about Himself, and *Śrīmad-Bhāgavatam*, spoken by Śukadeva Gosvāmī about the glories of Kṛṣṇa. Anyone who becomes even slightly interested in *kṛṣṇa-kathā* is liberated. *Kīrtanād eva kṛṣṇasya mukta-saṅgaḥ paraṁ vrajet* (*Bhāg*. 12.3.51). Simply by chanting or repeating *kṛṣṇa-kathā*, one is liberated from the contamination of Kali-yuga. Caitanya Mahāprabhu therefore advised, *yāre dekha, tāre kaha 'kṛṣṇa'-upadeśa* (Cc. *Madhya* 7.128). This is the mission of Kṛṣṇa consciousness: to hear about Kṛṣṇa and thus be liberated from material bondage.

TEXT 4

निवृत्ततर्षैरुपगीयमानाद्
भवौषधाच्छ्रोत्रमनोऽभिरामात् ।

क उत्तमश्लोकगुणानुवादात्
पुमान् विरज्येत विना पशुघ्नात् ॥ ४ ॥

nivṛtta-tarṣair upagīyamānād
bhavauṣadhāc chrotra-mano-'bhirāmāt
ka uttamaśloka-guṇānuvādāt
pumān virajyeta vinā paśughnāt

nivṛtta—released from; *tarṣaiḥ*—lust or material activities; *upagīyamānāt*—which is described or sung; *bhava-auṣadhāt*—which is the right medicine for the material disease; *śrotra*—the process of aural reception; *manaḥ*—the subject matter of thought for the mind; *abhirāmāt*—from the pleasing vibrations from such glorification; *kaḥ*—who; *uttamaśloka*—of the Supreme Personality of Godhead; *guṇa-anuvādāt*—from describing such activities; *pumān*—a person; *virajyeta*—can keep himself aloof; *vinā*—except; *paśu-ghnāt*—either a butcher or one who is killing his own personal existence.

TRANSLATION

Glorification of the Supreme Personality of Godhead is performed in the paramparā system; that is, it is conveyed from spiritual master to disciple. Such glorification is relished by those no longer interested in the false, temporary glorification of this cosmic manifestation. Descriptions of the Lord are the right medicine for the conditioned soul undergoing repeated birth and death. Therefore, who will cease hearing such glorification of the Lord except a butcher or one who is killing his own self?

PURPORT

In India it is the practice among the general populace to hear about Kṛṣṇa, either from *Bhagavad-gītā* or from *Śrīmad-Bhāgavatam*, in order to gain relief from the disease of repeated birth and death. Although India is now fallen, when there is a message that someone will speak about *Bhagavad-gītā* or *Śrīmad-Bhāgavatam*, thousands of people still gather to hear. This verse indicates, however, that such recitation of *Bhagavad-gītā* and *Śrīmad-Bhāgavatam* must be done by persons completely freed from material desires (*nivṛtta-tarṣaiḥ*). Everyone within this material world, beginning from Brahmā down to the insignificant ant, is full of material desires for sense enjoyment, and everyone is busy in sense gratification, but when thus engaged one cannot fully understand the value of *kṛṣṇa-kathā*, either in the form of *Bhagavad-gītā* or in *Śrīmad-Bhāgavatam.*

If we hear the glories of the Supreme Personality of Godhead from liberated persons, this hearing will certainly free us from the bondage of material activities, but hearing *Śrīmad-Bhāgavatam* spoken by a professional reciter cannot actually help us achieve liberation. *Kṛṣṇa-kathā* is very simple. In *Bhagavad-gītā* it is said that Kṛṣṇa is the Supreme Personality of Godhead. As He Himself explains, *mattaḥ parataraṁ nānyat kiñcid asti dhanañjaya:* "O Arjuna, there is no truth superior to Me." (Bg. 7.7) Simply by understanding this fact—that Kṛṣṇa is the Supreme Personality of Godhead—one can become a liberated person. But, especially in this age, because people are interested in hearing *Bhagavad-gītā* from unscrupulous persons who depart from the simple presentation of *Bhagavad-gītā* and distort it for their personal satisfaction, they fail to derive the real benefit. There are big scholars, politicians, philosophers and scientists who speak on *Bhagavad-gītā* in their own polluted way, and people in general hear from them, being uninterested in hearing the glories of the Supreme Personality of Godhead from a devotee. A devotee is one who has no other motive for reciting *Bhagavad-gītā* and *Śrīmad-Bhāgavatam* than to serve the Lord. Śrī Caitanya Mahāprabhu has therefore advised us to hear the glories of the Lord from a realized person (*bhāgavata paro diya bhāgavata sthane*). Unless one is personally a realized soul in the science of Kṛṣṇa consciousness, a neophyte should not approach him to hear about the Lord, for this is strictly forbidden by Śrīla Sanātana Gosvāmī, who quotes from the *Padma Purāṇa:*

avaiṣṇava-mukhodgīrṇaṁ
pūtaṁ hari-kathāmṛtam
śravaṇaṁ naiva kartavyaṁ
sarpocchiṣṭaṁ yathā payaḥ

One should avoid hearing from a person not situated in Vaiṣṇava behavior. A Vaiṣṇava is *nivṛtta-tṛṣṇa;* that is, he has no material purpose, for his only purpose is to preach Kṛṣṇa consciousness. So-called scholars, philosophers and politicians exploit the importance of *Bhagavad-gītā* by distorting its meaning for their own purposes. Therefore this verse warns that *kṛṣṇa-kathā* should be recited by a person who is *nivṛtta-tṛṣṇa*. Śukadeva Gosvāmī epitomizes the proper reciter for *Śrīmad-Bhāgavatam*, and Parīkṣit Mahārāja, who purposefully left his kingdom and family prior to meeting death, epitomizes the person fit to hear it. A qualified reciter of *Śrīmad-Bhāgavatam* gives the right medicine (*bhavauṣadhi*) for the conditioned souls. The Kṛṣṇa consciousness movement is therefore trying to train qualified preachers to recite *Śrīmad-Bhāgavatam* and *Bhagavad-gītā* throughout the entire world, so that people in general in all parts of the world may take advantage of this movement and thus be relieved of the threefold miseries of material existence.

The instructions of *Bhagavad-gītā* and the descriptions of *Śrīmad-Bhāgavatam* are so pleasing that almost anyone suffering from the threefold miseries of material existence will desire to hear the glories of the Lord from these books and thus benefit on the path of liberation. Two classes of men, however, will never be interested in hearing the message of *Bhagavad-gītā* and *Śrīmad-Bhāgavatam*—those who are determined to commit suicide and those determined to kill cows and other animals for the satisfaction of their own tongues. Although such persons may make a show of hearing *Śrīmad-Bhāgavatam* at a *Bhāgavata-saptāha*, this is but another creation of the *karmīs*, who cannot derive any benefit from such a performance. The word *paśu-ghnāt* is important in this connection. *Paśu-ghna* means "butcher." Persons fond of performing ritualistic ceremonies for elevation to the higher planetary systems must offer sacrifices (*yajñas*) by killing animals. Lord Buddhadeva therefore rejected the authority of the *Vedas* because his mission was to stop animal sacrifices, which are recommended in Vedic ritualistic ceremonies.

nindasi yajña-vidher ahaha śruti-jātaṁ
sa-daya-hṛdaya darśita-paśu-ghātaṁ
keśava dhṛta-buddha-śarīra jaya jagadīśa hare
(*Gītā-govinda*)

Even though animal sacrifices are sanctioned in Vedic ceremonies, men who kill animals for such ceremonies are considered butchers. Butchers cannot be interested in Kṛṣṇa consciousness, for they are already materially allured. Their only interest lies in developing comforts for the temporary body.

bhogaiśvarya-prasaktānāṁ
tayāpahṛta-cetasām
vyavasāyātmikā buddhiḥ
samādhau na vidhīyate

"In the minds of those who are too attached to sense enjoyment and material opulence, and who are bewildered by such things, the resolute determination of devotional service to the Supreme Lord does not take place." (Bg. 2.44) Śrīla Narottama dāsa Ṭhākura says:

manuṣya-janama pāiyā, rādhā-kṛṣṇa nā bhajiyā,
jāniyā śuniyā viṣa khāinu

Anyone who is not Kṛṣṇa conscious and who therefore does not engage in the service of the Lord is also *paśu-ghna,* for he is willingly drinking poison. Such a person cannot be interested in *kṛṣṇa-kathā* because he still has a desire for material sense gratification; he is not *nivṛtta-tṛṣṇa.* As it is said, *traivargikās te puruṣā vimukhā hari-medhasaḥ.* Those interested in *trivarga*—that is, in *dharma, artha* and *kāma*—are religious for the sake of achieving a material position with which to gain better facilities for sense gratification. Such persons are killing themselves by willingly keeping themselves in the cycle of birth and death. They cannot be interested in Kṛṣṇa consciousness.

For *kṛṣṇa-kathā,* topics about Kṛṣṇa consciousness, there must be a speaker and a hearer, both of whom can be interested in Kṛṣṇa consciousness if they are no longer interested in material topics. One can actually see how this attitude automatically develops in persons who are Kṛṣṇa conscious. Although the devotees of the Kṛṣṇa consciousness movement are quite young men, they no longer read materialistic newspapers, magazines and so on, for they are no longer interested in such topics (*nivṛtta-tarṣaiḥ*). They completely give up the bodily understanding of life. For topics concerning Uttamaśloka, the Supreme Personality of Godhead, the spiritual master speaks, and the disciple hears with attention. Unless both of them are free from material desires, they cannot be interested in topics of Kṛṣṇa consciousness. The spiritual master and disciple do not need to understand anything more than Kṛṣṇa because simply by understanding Kṛṣṇa and talking about Kṛṣṇa, one becomes a perfectly learned person (*yasmin vijñāte sarvam evaṁ vijñātaṁ bhavati*). The Lord sits within everyone's heart, and by the grace of the Lord the devotee receives instructions directly from the Lord Himself, who says in *Bhagavad-gītā* (15.15):

sarvasya cāhaṁ hṛdi sanniviṣṭo
mattaḥ smṛtir jñānam apohanaṁ ca
vedaiś ca sarvair aham eva vedyo
vedānta-kṛd veda-vid eva cāham

"I am seated in everyone's heart, and from Me come remembrance, knowledge and forgetfulness. By all the *Vedas*, I am to be known; indeed, I am the compiler of *Vedānta*, and I am the knower of the *Vedas*." Kṛṣṇa consciousness is so exalted that one who is perfectly situated in Kṛṣṇa consciousness, under the direction of the spiritual master, is fully satisfied by reading *kṛṣṇa-kathā* as found in *Śrīmad-Bhāgavatam*, *Bhagavad-gītā* and similar Vedic literatures. Since merely talking about Kṛṣṇa is so pleasing, we can simply imagine how pleasing it is to render service to Kṛṣṇa.

When discourses on *kṛṣṇa-kathā* take place between a liberated spiritual master and his disciple, others also sometimes take advantage of hearing these topics and also benefit. These topics are the medicine to stop the repetition of birth and death. The cycle of repeated birth and death, by which one takes on different bodies again and again, is called *bhava* or *bhava-roga*. If anyone, willingly or unwillingly, hears *kṛṣṇa-kathā*, his *bhava-roga*, the disease of birth and death, will certainly stop. Therefore *kṛṣṇa-kathā* is called *bhavauṣadha*, the remedy to stop the repetition of birth and death. *Karmīs*, or persons attached to material sense enjoyment, generally cannot give up their material desires, but *kṛṣṇa-kathā* is such a potent medicine that if one is induced to hear *kṛṣṇa-kīrtana*, he will certainly be freed from this disease. A practical example is Dhruva Mahārāja, who at the end of his *tapasya* was fully satisfied. When the Lord wanted to give Dhruva a benediction, Dhruva refused it. *Svāmin kṛtārtho 'smi varaṁ na yāce.* "My dear Lord," he said, "I am fully satisfied. I do not ask for any benediction for material sense gratification." We actually see that even young boys and girls in the Kṛṣṇa consciousness movement have given up their long practice of bad habits like illicit sex, meat-eating, intoxication and gambling. Because Kṛṣṇa consciousness is so potent that it gives them full satisfaction, they are no longer interested in material sense gratification.

TEXTS 5–7

पितामहा मे समरेऽमरञ्जयै-
र्देवव्रताद्यातिरथैस्तिमिङ्गिलैः ।
दुरत्ययं कौरवसैन्यसागरं
कृत्वातरन् वत्सपदं स्म यत्प्लवाः ॥ ५ ॥
द्रौण्यस्त्रविप्लुष्टमिदं मदङ्गं
सन्तानबीजं कुरुपाण्डवानाम् ।
जुगोप कुक्षिं गत आत्तचक्रो
मातुश्च मे यः शरणं गतायाः ॥ ६ ॥
वीर्याणि तस्याखिलदेहभाजा-
मन्तर्बहिः पूरुषकालरूपैः ।
प्रयच्छतो मृत्युमुतामृतं च
मायामनुष्यस्य वदस्व विद्वन् ॥ ७ ॥

pitāmahā me samare 'marañjayair
devavratādyātirathais timiṅgilaiḥ
duratyayaṁ kaurava-sainya-sāgaraṁ
kṛtvātaran vatsa-padaṁ sma yat-plavāḥ

drauṇy-astra-vipluṣṭam idaṁ mad-aṅgaṁ
santāna-bījaṁ kuru-pāṇḍavānām
jugopa kukṣiṁ gata ātta-cakro
mātuś ca me yaḥ śaraṇaṁ gatāyāḥ

vīryāṇi tasyākhila-deha-bhājām
antar bahiḥ pūruṣa-kāla-rūpaiḥ
prayacchato mṛtyum utāmṛtaṁ ca
māyā-manuṣyasya vadasva vidvan

pitāmahāḥ—my grandfathers, the five Pāṇḍavas (Yudhiṣṭhira, Bhīma, Arjuna, Nakula and Sahadeva); *me*—my; *samare*—on the Battlefield of Kurukṣetra; *amaram-jayaiḥ*—with fighters who could gain victory over the demigods on the battlefield; *devavrata-ādya*—Bhīṣmadeva and others; *atirathaiḥ*—great commanders in chief; *timiṅgilaiḥ*—resembling great *timiṅgila* fish, which can easily eat large sharks; *duratyayam*—very difficult to cross; *kaurava-sainya-sāgaram*—the ocean of the assembled soldiers of the Kauravas; *kṛtvā*—considering such an ocean; *ataran*—crossed it; *vatsa-padam*—exactly as one steps over a small hoofprint of a calf; *sma*—in the past; *yat-plavāḥ*—the shelter of the boat of Kṛṣṇa's lotus feet; *drauṇi*—of Aśvatthāmā; *astra*—by the *brahmāstra; vipluṣṭam*—being attacked and burned; *idam*—this; *mat-aṅgam*—my body; *santāna-bījam*—the only seed left, the last descendant of the family; *kuru-pāṇḍavānām*—of the Kurus and the Pāṇḍavas (because no one but me lived after the Battle of Kurukṣetra); *jugopa*—gave protection; *kukṣim*—within the womb; *gataḥ*—being placed; *ātta-cakraḥ*—taking in hand the disc; *mātuḥ*—of my mother; *ca*—also; *me*—my; *yaḥ*—the Lord who; *śaraṇam*—the shelter; *gatāyāḥ*—who had taken; *vīryāṇi*—the glorification of the transcendental characteristics; *tasya*—of Him (the Supreme Personality of Godhead); *akhila-deha-bhājām*—of all the materially embodied living entities; *antaḥ bahiḥ*—inside and outside; *pūruṣa*—of the Supreme Person; *kāla-rūpaiḥ*—in the forms of eternal time; *prayacchataḥ*—who is the giver; *mṛtyum*—of death; *uta*—it is so said; *amṛtam ca*—and eternal life; *māyā-manuṣyasya*—of the Lord, who appeared as an ordinary human being by His own potency; *vadasva*—kindly describe; *vidvan*—O learned speaker (Śukadeva Gosvāmī).

TRANSLATION

Taking the boat of Kṛṣṇa's lotus feet, my grandfather Arjuna and others crossed the ocean of the Battlefield of Kurukṣetra, in which such commanders as Bhīṣmadeva resembed great fish that

could very easily have swallowed them. By the mercy of Lord Kṛṣṇa, my grandfathers crossed this ocean, which was very difficult to cross, as easily as one steps over the hoofprint of a calf. Because my mother surrendered unto Lord Kṛṣṇa's lotus feet, the Lord, Sudarśana-cakra in hand, entered her womb and saved my body, the body of the last remaining descendant of the Kurus and the Pāṇḍavas, which was almost destroyed by the fiery weapon of Aśvatthāmā. Lord Śrī Kṛṣṇa, appearing within and outside of all materially embodied living beings by His own potency in the forms of eternal time—that is, as Paramātmā and as virāṭ-rūpa—gave liberation to everyone, either as cruel death or as life. Kindly enlighten me by describing His transcendental characteristics.

PURPORT

As stated in *Śrīmad-Bhāgavatam* (10.14.58):

samāśritā ye pada-pallava-plavaṁ
mahat-padaṁ puṇya-yaśo murāreḥ
bhavāmbudhir vatsa-padaṁ paraṁ padaṁ
padaṁ padaṁ yad vipadāṁ na teṣām

"For one who has accepted the boat of the lotus feet of the Lord, who is the shelter of the cosmic manifestation and is famous as Murāri, or the enemy of the Mura demon, the ocean of the material world is like the water contained in a calf's hoofprint. His goal is *paraṁ padam,* or Vaikuṇṭha, the place where there are no material miseries, not the place where there is danger at every step."

One who seeks shelter at the lotus feet of Lord Kṛṣṇa is immediately protected by the Lord. As the Lord promises in *Bhagavad-gītā* (18.66), *ahaṁ tvāṁ sarva-pāpebhyo mokṣayiṣyāmi mā śucaḥ:* "I shall deliver you from all sinful reactions. Do not fear." By taking shelter of Lord Kṛṣṇa, one comes under the safest protection. Thus when the Pāṇḍavas took shelter at the lotus feet of Kṛṣṇa, all of them were on the safe side of the Battlefield of Kurukṣetra. Parīkṣit Mahārāja, therefore, felt obliged to think of Kṛṣṇa in the last days of his life. This is the ideal result of Kṛṣṇa consciousness: *ante nārāyaṇa-smṛtiḥ.* If at the time of death one can remember Kṛṣṇa, one's life is successful. Parīkṣit Mahārāja, therefore, because of his many obligations to Kṛṣṇa, intelligently decided to think of Kṛṣṇa constantly during the last days of his life. Kṛṣṇa had saved the Pāṇḍavas, Mahārāja Parīkṣit's grandfathers, on the Battlefield of Kurukṣetra, and Kṛṣṇa had saved Mahārāja Parīkṣit himself when he was attacked by the *brahmāstra* of Aśvatthāmā. Kṛṣṇa acted as the friend and worshipable Deity of the Pāṇḍava family. Moreover, apart from Lord Kṛṣṇa's personal contact with the Pāṇḍavas, Kṛṣṇa is the Supersoul of all living entities, and He gives everyone liberation, even if one is not a pure devotee. Kaṁsa, for example, was not at all a devotee, yet Kṛṣṇa, after killing him, gave him salvation. Kṛṣṇa consciousness is beneficial to everyone, whether one is a pure devotee or a nondevotee. This is the glory of Kṛṣṇa consciousness. Considering this, who will not take shelter at the lotus feet of Kṛṣṇa. Kṛṣṇa is described in this verse as *māyā-manuṣya* because He descends exactly like a human being. He is not obliged to come here, like *karmīs*, or ordinary living beings; rather, He appears by His own internal energy (*sambhavāmy ātma-māyayā*) just to show favor to the fallen conditioned souls. Kṛṣṇa is always situated in His original position as *sac-cid-ānanda-vigraha*, and anyone who renders service to Him is also situated in his original, spiritual identity (*svarūpeṇa vyavasthitiḥ*). This is the highest perfection of human life.

TEXT 8

रोहिण्यास्तनयः प्रोक्तो रामः सङ्कर्षणस्त्वया ।
देवक्या गर्भसम्बन्धः कुतो देहान्तरं विना ॥ ८ ॥

rohiṇyās tanayaḥ prokto
rāmaḥ saṅkarṣaṇas tvayā
devakyā garbha-sambandhaḥ
kuto dehāntaraṁ vinā

rohiṇyāḥ—of Rohiṇīdevī, the mother of Baladeva; *tanayaḥ*—the son; *proktaḥ*—is well known; *rāmaḥ*—Balarāma; *saṅkarṣaṇaḥ*—Balarāma is none other than Saṅkarṣaṇa, the first Deity in the quadruple group (Saṅkarṣaṇa, Aniruddha, Pradyumna and Vāsudeva); *tvayā*—by you (it is so said); *devakyāḥ*—of Devakī, the mother of Kṛṣṇa;

garbha-sambandhaḥ—connected with the womb; *kutaḥ*—how; *deha-antaram*—transferring bodies; *vinā*—without.

TRANSLATION

My dear Śukadeva Gosvāmī, you have already explained that Saṅkarṣaṇa, who belongs to the second quadruple, appeared as the son of Rohiṇī named Balarāma. If Balarāma was not transferred from one body to another, how is it possible that He was first in the womb of Devakī and then in the womb of Rohiṇī? Kindly explain this to me.

PURPORT

Here is a question particularly directed at understanding Balarāma, who is Saṅkarṣaṇa Himself. Balarāma is well known as the son of Rohiṇī, yet it is also known that He was the son of Devakī. Parīkṣit Mahārāja wanted to understand the mystery of Balarāma's being the son of both Devakī and Rohiṇī.

TEXT 9

कस्मान्मुकुन्दो भगवान् पितुर्गेहाद् व्रजं गतः ।
क्व वासं ज्ञातिभिः सार्धं कृतवान् सात्वतांपतिः ॥ ९ ॥

kasmān mukundo bhagavān
pitur gehād vrajaṁ gataḥ
kva vāsaṁ jñātibhiḥ sārdhaṁ
kṛtavān sātvatāṁ patiḥ

kasmāt—why; *mukundaḥ*—Kṛṣṇa, who can award liberation to everyone; *bhagavān*—the Supreme Personality of Godhead; *pituḥ*—of His father (Vasudeva); *gehāt*—from the house; *vrajam*—to Vraja-dhāma, Vrajabhūmi; *gataḥ*—went; *kva*—where; *vāsam*—placed Himself to live; *jñātibhiḥ*—His relatives; *sārdham*—with; *kṛtavān*—did so; *sātvatām patiḥ*—the master of all Vaiṣṇava devotees.

TRANSLATION

Why did Kṛṣṇa, the Supreme Personality of Godhead, leave the house of His father, Vasudeva, and transfer Himself to the house

of Nanda in Vṛndāvana? Where did the Lord, the master of the Yadu dynasty, live with His relatives in Vṛndāvana?

PURPORT

These are inquiries about the itinerary of Kṛṣṇa. Just after His birth in the house of Vasudeva in Mathurā, Kṛṣṇa transferred Himself to Gokula, on the other side of the Yamunā, and after some days He moved with His father, mother and other relatives to Nanda-grāma, Vṛndāvana. Mahārāja Parīkṣit was very much eager to hear about Kṛṣṇa's activities in Vṛndāvana. This entire canto of *Śrīmad-Bhāgavatam* is full of activities performed in Vṛndāvana and Dvārakā. The first forty chapters describe Kṛṣṇa's Vṛndāvana affairs, and the next fifty describe Kṛṣṇa's activities in Dvārakā. Mahārāja Parīkṣit, to fulfill his desire to hear about Kṛṣṇa, requested Śukadeva Gosvāmī to describe these activities in full detail.

TEXT 10

व्रजे वसन् किमकरोन्मधुपुर्यां च केशवः ।
भ्रातरं चावधीत् कंसं मातुरद्धातदर्हणम् ॥१०॥

vraje vasan kim akaron
madhupuryāṁ ca keśavaḥ
bhrātaraṁ cāvadhīt kaṁsaṁ
mātur addhātad-arhaṇam

vraje—at Vṛndāvana; *vasan*—while residing; *kim akarot*—what did He do; *madhupuryām*—in Mathurā; *ca*—and; *keśavaḥ*—Kṛṣṇa, the killer of Keśī; *bhrātaram*—the brother; *ca*—and; *avadhīt*—killed; *kaṁsam*—Kaṁsa; *mātuḥ*—of His mother; *addhā*—directly; *a-tat-arhaṇam*—which was not at all sanctioned by the *śāstras.*

TRANSLATION

Lord Kṛṣṇa lived both in Vṛndāvana and in Mathurā. What did He do there? Why did He kill Kaṁsa, His mother's brother? Such killing is not at all sanctioned in the śāstras.

PURPORT

One's maternal uncle, the brother of one's mother, is on the level of one's father. When a maternal uncle has no son, his nephew legally inherits his property. Therefore, why did Kṛṣṇa directly kill Kaṁsa, the brother of His mother? Mahārāja Parīkṣit was very much inquisitive about the facts in this regard.

TEXT 11

देहं मानुषमाश्रित्य कति वर्षाणि वृष्णिभिः ।
यदुपुर्यां सहावात्सीत् पत्न्यः कत्यभवन् प्रभोः ॥११॥

deham mānuṣam āśritya
kati varṣāṇi vṛṣṇibhiḥ
yadu-puryāṁ sahāvātsīt
patnyaḥ katy abhavan prabhoḥ

deham—body; *mānuṣam*—exactly like a man; *āśritya*—accepting; *kati varṣāṇi*—how many years; *vṛṣṇibhiḥ*—in the company of the Vṛṣṇis, those who were born in the Vṛṣṇi family; *yadu-puryām*—in Dvārakā, in the residential quarters of the Yadus; *saha*—with; *avātsīt*—the Lord lived; *patnyaḥ*—wives; *kati*—how many; *abhavan*—were there; *prabhoḥ*—of the Lord.

TRANSLATION

Kṛṣṇa, the Supreme Personality of Godhead, has no material body, yet He appears as a human being. For how many years did He live with the descendants of Vṛṣṇi? How many wives did He marry, and for how many years did He live in Dvārakā?

PURPORT

In many places the Supreme Personality of Godhead is described as *sac-cid-ānanda-vigraha*, possessing a spiritual, blissful body. His bodily feature is *narākṛti*, that is, exactly like that of a human being. Here the same idea is repeated in the words *mānuṣam āśritya*, which indicate that He accepts a body exactly like that of a man. Everywhere it is confirmed that Kṛṣṇa is never *nirākāra*, or formless. He has His form, exactly like that of a human being. There is no doubt about this.

TEXT 12

एतदन्यच्च सर्वं मे मुने कृष्णविचेष्टितम् ।
वक्तुमर्हसि सर्वज्ञ श्रद्दधानाय विस्तृतम् ॥१२॥

etad anyac ca sarvaṁ me
mune kṛṣṇa-viceṣṭitam
vaktum arhasi sarvajña
śraddadhānāya vistṛtam

etat—all these details; *anyat ca*—and others also; *sarvam*—everything; *me*—unto me; *mune*—O great sage; *kṛṣṇa-viceṣṭitam*—the activities of Lord Kṛṣṇa; *vaktum*—to describe; *arhasi*—you are able; *sarva-jña*—because you know everything; *śraddadhānāya*—because I am not envious but have all faith in Him; *vistṛtam*—in full detail.

TRANSLATION

O great sage, who know everything about Kṛṣṇa, please describe in detail all the activities of which I have inquired and also those of which I have not, for I have full faith and am very eager to hear of them.

TEXT 13

नैषातिदुःसहा क्षुन्मां त्यक्तोदमपि बाधते ।
पिबन्तं त्वन्मुखाम्भोजच्युतं हरिकथामृतम् ॥१३॥

naiṣātiduḥsahā kṣun māṁ
tyaktodam api bādhate
pibantaṁ tvan-mukhāmbhoja-
cyutaṁ hari-kathāmṛtam

na—not; *eṣā*—all this; *ati-duḥsahā*—extremely difficult to bear; *kṣut*—hunger; *mām*—unto me; *tyakta-udam*—even after giving up drinking water; *api*—also; *bādhate*—does not hinder; *pibantam*—while drinking; *tvat-mukha-ambhoja-cyutam*—emanating from your lotus mouth; *hari-kathā-amṛtam*—the nectar of topics concerning Kṛṣṇa.

TRANSLATION

Because of my vow on the verge of death, I have given up even drinking water, yet because I am drinking the nectar of topics about Kṛṣṇa, which is flowing from the lotus mouth of Your Lordship, my hunger and thirst, which are extremely difficult to bear, cannot hinder me.

PURPORT

To prepare to meet death in seven days, Mahārāja Parīkṣit gave up all food and drink. As a human being, he was certainly both hungry and thirsty, and therefore Śukadeva Gosvāmī might have wanted to stop narrating the transcendental topics of Kṛṣṇa; but despite his fast, Mahārāja Parīkṣit was not at all fatigued. "The hunger and thirst from my fast do not disturb me," he said. "Once when I felt very thirsty, I went to the *āśrama* of Śamīka Muni to drink water, but the *muni* did not supply it. I therefore wrapped a dead snake over his shoulder, and that is why I was cursed by the *brāhmaṇa* boy. Now, however, I am quite fit. I am not at all disturbed by my hunger and thirst." This indicates that although on the material platform there are disturbances from hunger and thirst, on the spiritual platform there is no such thing as fatigue.

The entire world is suffering because of spiritual thirst. Every living being is Brahman, or spirit soul, and needs spiritual food to satisfy his hunger and thirst. Unfortunately, however, the world is completely unaware of the nectar of *kṛṣṇa-kathā.* The Kṛṣṇa consciousness movement is therefore a boon to philosophers, religionists and people in general. There is certainly a charming attraction in Kṛṣṇa and *kṛṣṇa-kathā.* Therefore the Absolute Truth is called Kṛṣṇa, the most attractive.

The word *amṛta* is also an important reference to the moon, and the word *ambuja* means "lotus." The pleasing moonshine and pleasing fragrance of the lotus combined to bring pleasure to everyone hearing *kṛṣṇa-kathā* from the mouth of Śukadeva Gosvāmī. As it is said:

matir na kṛṣṇeirataḥ svato vā
mitho 'bhipadyeta gṛha-vratānām

adānta-gobhir viśatāṁ tamisraṁ
punaḥ punaś carvita-carvaṇānām

"Because of their uncontrolled senses, persons too addicted to materialistic life make progress toward hellish conditions and repeatedly chew that which has already been chewed. Their inclinations toward Kṛṣṇa are never aroused, either by the instructions of others, by their own efforts, or by a combination of both." (*Bhāg.* 7.5.30) At the present moment, all of human society is engaged in the business of chewing the chewed (*punaḥ punaś carvita-carvaṇānām*). People are prepared to undergo *mṛtyu-saṁsāra-vartmani*, taking birth in one form, dying, accepting another form and dying again. To stop this repetition of birth and death, *kṛṣṇa-kathā*, or Kṛṣṇa consciousness, is absolutely necessary. But unless one hears *kṛṣṇa-kathā* from a realized soul like Śukadeva Gosvāmī, one cannot relish the nectar of *kṛṣṇa-kathā*, which puts an end to all material fatigue, and enjoy the blissful life of transcendental existence. In relation to the Kṛṣṇa consciousness movement, we actually see that those who have tasted the nectar of *kṛṣṇa-kathā* lose all material desires, whereas those who cannot understand Kṛṣṇa or *kṛṣṇa-kathā* regard the Kṛṣṇa conscious life as "brainwashing" and "mind control." While the devotees enjoy spiritual bliss, the nondevotees are surprised that the devotees have forgotten material hankerings.

TEXT 14

सूत उवाच
एवं निशम्य भृगुनन्दन साधुवादं
वैयासकिः स भगवानथ विष्णुरातम् ।
प्रत्यर्च्य कृष्णचरितं कलिकल्मषघ्नं
व्याहर्तुमारभत भागवतप्रधानः ॥१४॥

sūta uvāca
evaṁ niśamya bhṛgu-nandana sādhu-vādaṁ
vaiyāsakiḥ sa bhagavān atha viṣṇu-rātam
pratyarcya kṛṣṇa-caritaṁ kali-kalmaṣa-ghnaṁ
vyāhartum ārabhata bhāgavata-pradhānaḥ

sūtaḥ uvāca—Sūta Gosvāmī said; *evam*—thus; *niśamya*—hearing; *bhṛgu-nandana*—O son of the Bhṛgu dynasty, Śaunaka; *sādhu-vādam*—pious questions; *vaiyāsakiḥ*—Śukadeva Gosvāmī, the son of Vyāsadeva; *saḥ*—he; *bhagavān*—the most powerful; *atha*—thus; *viṣṇu-rātam*—unto Parīkṣit Mahārāja, who was always protected by Viṣṇu; *pratyarcya*—offering him respectful obeisances; *kṛṣṇa-caritam*—topics of Lord Kṛṣṇa; *kali-kalmaṣa-ghnam*—which diminish the troubles of this age of Kali; *vyāhartum*—to describe; *ārabhata*—began; *bhāgavata-pradhānaḥ*—Śukadeva Gosvāmī, the chief among the pure devotees.

TRANSLATION

Sūta Gosvāmī said: O son of Bhṛgu [Śaunaka Ṛṣi], after Śukadeva Gosvāmī, the most respectable devotee, the son of Vyāsadeva, heard the pious questions of Mahārāja Parīkṣit, he thanked the King with great respect. Then he began to discourse on topics concerning Kṛṣṇa, which are the remedy for all sufferings in this age of Kali.

PURPORT

In this verse the words *kṛṣṇa-caritaṁ kali-kalmaṣa-ghnam* indicate that the activities of Lord Kṛṣṇa are certainly the greatest panacea for all miseries, especially in this age of Kali. It is said that in Kali-yuga people have only short lives, and they have no culture of spiritual consciousness. If anyone is at all interested in spiritual culture, he is misled by many bogus *svāmīs* and *yogīs* who do not refer to *kṛṣṇa-kathā*. Therefore most people are unfortunate and disturbed by many calamities. Śrīla Vyāsadeva prepared *Śrīmad-Bhāgavatam* at the request of Nārada Muni in order to give relief to the suffering people of this age (*kali-kalmaṣa-ghnam*). The Kṛṣṇa consciousness movement is seriously engaged in enlightening people through the pleasing topics of *Śrīmad-Bhāgavatam*. All over the world, the message of *Śrīmad-Bhāgavatam* and *Bhagavad-gītā* is being accepted in all spheres of life, especially in advanced, educated circles.

Śrīla Śukadeva Gosvāmī is described in this verse as *bhāgavata-pradhānaḥ*, whereas Mahārāja Parīkṣit is described as *viṣṇu-rātam*. Both words bear the same meaning; that is, Mahārāja Parīkṣit was a great devotee of Kṛṣṇa, and Śukadeva Gosvāmī was also a great saintly person and a great devotee of Kṛṣṇa. Combined together to present *kṛṣṇa-kathā*, they give great relief to suffering humanity.

anarthopaśamaṁ sākṣād
bhakti-yogam adhokṣaje
lokasyājānato vidvāṁś
cakre sātvata-saṁhitām

"The material miseries of the living entity, which are superfluous to him, can be directly mitigated by the linking process of devotional service. But the mass of people do not know this, and therefore the learned Vyāsadeva compiled this Vedic literature, *Śrīmad-Bhāgavatam*, which is in relation to the Supreme Truth." (*Bhāg*. 1.7.6) People in general are unaware that the message of *Śrīmad-Bhāgavatam* can give all of human society relief from the pangs of Kali-yuga (*kali-kalmaṣa-ghnam*).

TEXT 15

श्रीशुक उवाच
सम्यग्व्यवसिता बुद्धिस्तव राजर्षिसत्तम ।
वासुदेवकथायां ते यज्जाता नैष्ठिकी रतिः ॥१५॥

śrī-śuka uvāca
samyag vyavasitā buddhis
tava rājarṣi-sattama
vāsudeva-kathāyāṁ te
yaj jātā naiṣṭhikī ratiḥ

śrī-śukaḥ uvāca—Śrī Śukadeva Gosvāmī said; *samyak*—completely; *vyavasitā*—fixed; *buddhiḥ*—intelligence; *tava*—of Your Majesty; *rāja-ṛṣi-sattama*—O best of *rājarṣis*, saintly kings; *vāsudeva-kathāyām*—in hearing about the topics of Vāsudeva, Kṛṣṇa; *te*—your; *yat*—because; *jātā*—developed; *naiṣṭhikī*—without cessation; *ratiḥ*—attraction or ecstatic devotional service.

TRANSLATION

Śrīla Śukadeva Gosvāmī said: O Your Majesty, best of all saintly kings, because you are greatly attracted to topics of Vāsudeva, it is certain that your intelligence is firmly fixed in spiritual understanding, which is the only true goal for humanity. Because that attraction is unceasing, it is certainly sublime.

PURPORT

Kṛṣṇa-kathā is compulsory for the *rājarṣi,* or executive head of government. This is also mentioned in *Bhagavad-gītā* (*imaṁ rājarṣayo viduḥ*). Unfortunately, however, in this age the governmental power is gradually being captured by third-class and fourth-class men who have no spiritual understanding, and society is therefore very quickly becoming degraded. *Kṛṣṇa-kathā* must be understood by the executive heads of government, for otherwise how will people be happy and gain relief from the pangs of materialistic life? One who has fixed his mind in Kṛṣṇa consciousness should be understood to have very sharp intelligence in regard to the value of life. Mahārāja Parīkṣit was *rājarṣi-sattama,* the best of all saintly kings, and Śukadeva Gosvāmī was *muni-sattama,* the best of *munis.* Both of them were elevated because of their common interest in *kṛṣṇa-kathā.* The exalted position of the speaker and the audience will be explained very nicely in the next verse. *Kṛṣṇa-kathā* is so enlivening that Mahārāja Parīkṣit forgot everything material, even his personal comfort in relation to food and drink. This is an example of how the Kṛṣṇa consciousness movement should spread all over the world to bring both the speaker and the audience to the transcendental platform and back home, back to Godhead.

TEXT 16

वासुदेवकथाप्रश्नः पुरुषांस्त्रीन् पुनाति हि ।
वक्तारं प्रच्छकं श्रोतॄंस्तत्पादसलिलं यथा ॥१६॥

vāsudeva-kathā-praśnaḥ
puruṣāṁs trīn punāti hi
vaktāraṁ pracchakaṁ śrotṝṁs
tat-pāda-salilaṁ yathā

vāsudeva-kathā-praśnaḥ—questions about the pastimes and characteristics of Vāsudeva, Kṛṣṇa; *puruṣān*—persons; *trīn*—three; *punāti*—purify; *hi*—indeed; *vaktāram*—the speaker, such as Śukadeva Gosvāmī; *pracchakam*—and an inquisitive hearer like Mahārāja Parīkṣit; *śrotṝn*—and, between them, the listeners hearing about the topics; *tat-pāda-salilam yathā*—exactly as the entire world is purified by the Ganges water emanating from the toe of Lord Viṣṇu.

TRANSLATION

The Ganges, emanating from the toe of Lord Viṣṇu, purifies the three worlds, the upper, middle and lower planetary systems. Similarly, when one asks questions about the pastimes and characteristics of Lord Vāsudeva, Kṛṣṇa, three varieties of men are purified: the speaker or preacher, he who inquires, and the people in general who listen.

PURPORT

It is said, *tasmād guruṁ prapadyeta jijñāsuḥ śreya uttamam* (*Bhāg.* 11.3.21). Those interested in understanding transcendental subject matters as the goal of life must approach the bona fide spiritual master. *Tasmād guruṁ prapadyeta.* One must surrender to such a *guru,* who can give right information about Kṛṣṇa. Herein, Mahārāja Parīkṣit has surrendered to the right personality, Śukadeva Gosvāmī, for enlightenment in *vāsudeva-kathā.* Vāsudeva is the original Personality of Godhead, who has unlimited spiritual activities. *Śrīmad-Bhāgavatam* is a record of such activities, and *Bhagavad-gītā* is the record of Vāsudeva speaking personally. Therefore, since the Kṛṣṇa consciousness movement is full of *vāsudeva-kathā,* anyone who hears, anyone who joins the movement and anyone who preaches will be purified.

TEXT 17

भूमिर्दृप्तनृपव्याजदैत्यानीकशतायुतैः ।
आक्रान्ता भूरिभारेण ब्रह्माणं शरणं ययौ ॥१७॥

bhūmir dṛpta-nṛpa-vyāja-
daityānīka-śatāyutaiḥ

ākrāntā bhūri-bhāreṇa
brahmāṇaṁ śaraṇaṁ yayau

bhūmiḥ—mother earth; *dṛpta*—puffed up; *nṛpa-vyāja*—posing as kings, or the supreme power personified in the state; *daitya*—of demons; *anīka*—of military phalanxes of soldiers; *śata-ayutaiḥ*—unlimitedly, by many hundreds of thousands; *ākrāntā*—being overburdened; *bhūri-bhāreṇa*—by a burden of unnecessary fighting power; *brahmāṇam*—unto Lord Brahmā; *śaraṇam*—to take shelter; *yayau*—went.

TRANSLATION

Once when mother earth was overburdened by hundreds of thousands of military phalanxes of various conceited demons dressed like kings, she approached Lord Brahmā for relief.

PURPORT

When the world is overburdened by unnecessary military arrangements and when various demoniac kings are the executive heads of state, this burden causes the appearance of the Supreme Personality of Godhead. As the Lord says in *Bhagavad-gītā* (4.7):

yadā yadā hi dharmasya
glānir bhavati bhārata
abhyutthānam adharmasya
tadātmānaṁ sṛjāmy aham

"Whenever and wherever there is a decline in religious practice, O descendant of Bharata, and a predominant rise of irreligion—at that time I appear Myself." When the residents of this earth become atheistic and godless, they descend to the status of animals like dogs and hogs, and thus their only business is to bark among themselves. This is *dharmasya glāni*, deviation from the goal of life. Human life is meant for attaining the highest perfection of Kṛṣṇa consciousness, but when people are godless and the presidents or kings are unnecessarily puffed up with military power, their business is to fight and increase the military strength of their different states. Nowadays, therefore, it appears that every state is busy manufacturing atomic weapons to prepare for a third world war. Such preparations are certainly unnecessary; they reflect the false pride of the heads of state. The real business of a chief executive is to see to the happiness of the mass of people by training them in Kṛṣṇa consciousness in different divisions of life. *Cātur-varṇyaṁ mayā sṛṣṭaṁ guṇa-karma-vibhāgaśaḥ* (Bg. 4.13). A leader should train the people as *brāhmaṇas, kṣatriyas, vaiśyas* and *śūdras* and engage them in various occupational duties, thus helping them progress toward Kṛṣṇa consciousness. Instead, however, rogues and thieves in the guise of protectors arrange for a voting system, and in the name of democracy they come to power by hook or crook and exploit the citizens. Even long, long ago, *asuras*, persons devoid of God consciousness, became the heads of state, and now this is happening again. The various states of the world are preoccupied with arranging for military strength. Sometimes they spend sixty-five percent of the government's revenue for this purpose. But why should people's hard-earned money be spent in this way? Because of the present world situation, Kṛṣṇa has descended in the form of the Kṛṣṇa consciousness movement. This is quite natural, for without the Kṛṣṇa consciousness movement the world cannot be peaceful and happy.

TEXT 18

गौर्भूत्वाश्रुमुखी खिन्ना क्रन्दन्ती करुणं विभोः ।
उपस्थितान्तिके तस्मै व्यसनं समवोचत ॥१८॥

gaur bhūtvāśru-mukhī khinnā
krandantī karuṇaṁ vibhoḥ
upasthitāntike tasmai
vyasanaṁ samavocata

gauḥ—the shape of a cow; *bhūtvā*—assuming; *aśru-mukhī*—with tears in the eyes; *khinnā*—very much distressed; *krandantī*—weeping; *karuṇam*—piteously; *vibhoḥ*—of Lord Brahmā; *upasthitā*—appeared; *antike*—in front; *tasmai*—unto him (Lord Brahmā); *vyasanam*—her distress; *samavocata*—submitted.

TRANSLATION

Mother earth assumed the form of a cow. Very much distressed, with tears in her eyes, she appeared before Lord Brahmā and told him about her misfortune.

TEXT 19

ब्रह्मा तदुपधार्याथ सह देवैस्तया सह ।
जगाम सत्रिनयनस्तीरं क्षीरपयोनिधेः ॥१९॥

brahmā tad-upadhāryātha
saha devais tayā saha
jagāma sa-tri-nayanas
tīraṁ kṣīra-payo-nidheḥ

brahmā—Lord Brahmā; *tat-upadhārya*—understanding everything rightly; *atha*—thereafter; *saha*—with; *devaiḥ*—the demigods; *tayā saha*—with mother earth; *jagāma*—approached; *sa-tri-nayanaḥ*—with Lord Śiva, who has three eyes; *tīram*—the shore; *kṣīra-payaḥ-nidheḥ*—of the ocean of milk.

TRANSLATION

Thereafter, having heard of the distress of mother earth, Lord Brahmā, with mother earth, Lord Śiva and all the other demigods, approached the shore of the ocean of milk.

PURPORT

After Lord Brahmā understood the precarious condition of the earth, he first visited the demigods headed by Lord Indra, who are in charge of the various affairs of this universe, and Lord Śiva, who is responsible for annihilation. Both maintenance and annihilation go on perpetually, under the order of the Supreme Personality of Godhead. As stated in *Bhagavad-gītā* (4.8), *paritrāṇāya sādhūnāṁ vināśāya ca duṣkṛtām.* Those who are obedient to the laws of God are protected by different servants and demigods, whereas those who are undesirable are vanquished by Lord Śiva. Lord Brahmā first met all the demigods, including Lord

Śiva. Then, along with mother earth, they went to the shore of the ocean of milk, where Lord Viṣṇu lies on a white island, Śvetadvīpa.

TEXT 20

तत्र गत्वा जगन्नाथं देवदेवं वृषाकपिम् ।
पुरुषं पुरुषसूक्तेन उपतस्थे समाहितः ॥२०॥

tatra gatvā jagannāthaṁ
deva-devaṁ vṛṣākapim
puruṣaṁ puruṣa-sūktena
upatasthe samāhitaḥ

tatra—there (on the shore of the ocean of milk); *gatvā*—after going; *jagannātham*—unto the master of the entire universe, the Supreme Being; *deva-devam*—the Supreme God of all gods; *vṛṣākapim*—the Supreme Person, Viṣṇu, who provides for everyone and diminishes everyone's suffering; *puruṣam*—the Supreme Person; *puruṣa-sūktena*—with the Vedic *mantra* known as *Puruṣa-sūkta; upatasthe*—worshiped; *samāhitaḥ*—with full attention.

TRANSLATION

After reaching the shore of the ocean of milk, the demigods worshiped the Supreme Personality of Godhead, Lord Viṣṇu, the master of the whole universe, the supreme God of all gods, who provides for everyone and diminishes everyone's suffering. With great attention, they worshiped Lord Viṣṇu, who lies on the ocean of milk, by reciting the Vedic mantras known as the Puruṣa-sūkta.

PURPORT

The demigods, such as Lord Brahmā, Lord Śiva, King Indra, Candra and Sūrya, are all subordinate to the Supreme Personality of Godhead. Aside from the demigods, even in human society there are many influential personalities supervising various businesses or establishments. Lord Viṣṇu, however, is the God of gods (*parameśvara*). He is *parama-puruṣa*, the Supreme Being, Paramātmā. As confirmed in the

Brahma-saṁhitā (5.1), *īśvaraḥ paramaḥ kṛṣṇaḥ sac-cid-ānanda-vigrahaḥ:* "Kṛṣṇa, known as Govinda, is the supreme controller. He has an eternal, blissful, spiritual body." No one is equal to or greater than the Supreme Personality of Godhead, and therefore He is described here by many words: *jagannātha, deva-deva, vṛṣākapi* and *puruṣa.* The supremacy of Lord Viṣṇu is also confirmed in *Bhagavad-gītā* (10.12) in this statement by Arjuna:

paraṁ brahma paraṁ dhāma
pavitraṁ paramaṁ bhavān
puruṣaṁ śāśvataṁ divyam
ādi-devam ajaṁ vibhum

"You are the Supreme Brahman, the ultimate, the supreme abode and purifier, the Absolute Truth and the eternal divine person. You are the primal God, transcendental and original, and You are the unborn and all-pervading beauty." Kṛṣṇa is *ādi-puruṣa*, the original Personality of Godhead (*govindam ādi-puruṣaṁ tam ahaṁ bhajāmi*). Viṣṇu is a plenary expansion of Lord Kṛṣṇa, and all the *viṣṇu-tattvas* are *parameśvara, deva-deva.*

TEXT 21

गिरं समाधौ गगने समीरितां
निशम्य वेधास्त्रिदशानुवाच ह ।
गां पौरुषीं मे शृणुतामराः पुन-
र्विधीयतामाशु तथैव मा चिरम् ॥२१॥

giraṁ samādhau gagane samīritāṁ
niśamya vedhās tridaśān uvāca ha
gāṁ pauruṣīṁ me śṛṇutāmarāḥ punar
vidhīyatām āśu tathaiva mā ciram

giram—a vibration of words; *samādhau*—in trance; *gagane*—in the sky; *samīritām*—vibrated; *niśamya*—hearing; *vedhāḥ*—Lord Brahmā; *tridaśān*—unto the demigods; *uvāca*—said; *ha*—oh; *gām*—the order;

pauruṣīm—received from the Supreme Person; *me*—from me; *śṛṇuta*—just hear; *amarāḥ*—O demigods; *punaḥ*—again; *vidhīyatām*—execute; *āśu*—immediately; *tathā eva*—just so; *mā*—do not; *ciram*—delay.

TRANSLATION

While in trance, Lord Brahmā heard the words of Lord Viṣṇu vibrating in the sky. Thus he told the demigods: O demigods, hear from me the order of Kṣīrodakaśāyī Viṣṇu, the Supreme Person, and execute it attentively without delay.

PURPORT

It appears that the words of the Supreme Personality of Godhead can be heard in trance by competent persons. Modern science gives us telephones, by which one can hear sound vibrations from a distant place. Similarly, although other persons cannot hear the words of Lord Viṣṇu, Lord Brahmā is able to hear the Lord's words within himself. This is confirmed in the beginning of *Śrīmad-Bhāgavatam* (1.1.1): *tene brahma hṛdā ya ādi-kavaye. Ādi-kavi* is Lord Brahmā. In the beginning of the creation, Lord Brahmā received the instructions of Vedic knowledge from Lord Viṣṇu through the medium of the heart (*hṛdā*). The same principle is confirmed herewith. While Brahmā was in trance, he was able to hear the words of Kṣīrodakaśāyī Viṣṇu, and he carried the Lord's message to the demigods. Similarly, in the beginning, Brahmā first received the Vedic knowledge from the Supreme Personality of Godhead through the core of the heart. In both instances the same process was used in transmitting the message to Lord Brahmā. In other words, although Lord Viṣṇu was invisible even to Lord Brahmā, Lord Brahmā could hear Lord Viṣṇu's words through the heart. The Supreme Personality of Godhead is invisible even to Lord Brahmā, yet He descends on this earth and becomes visible to people in general. This is certainly an act of His causeless mercy, but fools and nondevotees think that Kṛṣṇa is an ordinary historical person. Because they think that the Lord is an ordinary person like them, they are described as *mūḍha* (*avajānanti māṁ mūḍhāḥ*). The causeless mercy of the Supreme Personality of Godhead is neglected by such demoniac persons, who cannot understand the instructions of *Bhagavad-gītā* and who therefore misinterpret them.

TEXT 22

पुरैव पुंसावधृतो धराज्वरो
भवद्भिरंशैर्यदुषूपजन्यताम् ।
स यावदुर्व्या भरमीश्वरेश्वरः
स्वकालशक्त्या क्षपयंश्चरेद् भुवि ॥२२॥

puraiva puṁsāvadhṛto dharā-jvaro
bhavadbhir aṁśair yaduṣūpajanyatām
sa yāvad urvyā bharam īśvareśvaraḥ
sva-kāla-śaktyā kṣapayaṁś cared bhuvi

purā—even before this; *eva*—indeed; *puṁsā*—by the Supreme Personality of Godhead; *avadhṛtaḥ*—was certainly known; *dharā-jvaraḥ*—the distress on the earth; *bhavadbhiḥ*—by your good selves; *aṁśaiḥ*—expanding as plenary portions; *yaduṣu*—in the family of King Yadu; *upajanyatām*—take your birth and appear there; *saḥ*—He (the Supreme Personality of Godhead); *yāvat*—as long as; *urvyāḥ*—of the earth; *bharam*—the burden; *īśvara-īśvaraḥ*—the Lord of lords; *sva-kāla-śaktyā*—by His own potency the time factor; *kṣapayan*—diminishing; *caret*—should move; *bhuvi*—on the surface of the earth.

TRANSLATION

Lord Brahmā informed the demigods: Before we submitted our petition to the Lord, He was already aware of the distress on earth. Consequently, for as long as the Lord moves on earth to diminish its burden by His own potency in the form of time, all of you demigods should appear through plenary portions as sons and grandsons in the family of the Yadus.

PURPORT

As stated in the *Brahma-saṁhitā* (5.39):

rāmādi-mūrtiṣu kalā-niyamena tiṣṭhan
nānāvatāram akarod bhuvaneṣu kintu

kṛṣṇaḥ svayaṁ samabhavat paramaḥ pumān yo
govindam ādi-puruṣaṁ tam ahaṁ bhajāmi

"I worship the Supreme Personality of Godhead, Govinda, who is always situated in various incarnations such as Rāma, Nṛsiṁha and many subincarnations as well, but who is the original Personality of Godhead, known as Kṛṣṇa, and who incarnates personally also."

In this verse from *Śrīmad-Bhāgavatam* we find the words *puraiva puṁsāvadhṛto dharā-jvaraḥ*. The word *puṁsā* refers to Kṛṣṇa, who was already aware of how the whole world was suffering because of the increase of demons. Without reference to the supreme power of the Personality of Godhead, demons assert themselves to be independent kings and presidents, and thus they create a disturbance by increasing their military power. When such disturbances are very prominent, Kṛṣṇa appears. At present also, various demoniac states all over the world are increasing their military power in many ways, and the whole situation has become distressful. Therefore Kṛṣṇa has appeared by His name, in the Hare Kṛṣṇa movement, which will certainly diminish the burden of the world. Philosophers, religionists, and people in general must take to this movement very seriously, for man-made plans and devices will not help bring peace on earth. The transcendental sound Hare Kṛṣṇa is not different from the person Kṛṣṇa.

nāma cintāmaṇiḥ kṛṣṇaś
caitanya-rasa-vigrahaḥ
pūrṇaḥ śuddho nitya-mukto
'bhinnatvān nāma-nāminoḥ
(*Padma Purāṇa*)

There is no difference between the sound Hare Kṛṣṇa and Kṛṣṇa the person.

TEXT 23

वसुदेवगृहे साक्षाद् भगवान् पुरुषः परः ।
जनिष्यते तत्प्रियार्थं सम्भवन्तु सुरस्त्रियः ॥२३॥

vasudeva-gṛhe sākṣād
bhagavān puruṣaḥ paraḥ
janiṣyate tat-priyārthaṁ
sambhavantu sura-striyaḥ

vasudeva-gṛhe—in the house of Vasudeva (who would be the father of Kṛṣṇa when the Lord appeared); *sākṣāt*—personally; *bhagavān*—the Supreme Personality of Godhead, who has full potency; *puruṣaḥ*—the original person; *paraḥ*—who is transcendental; *janiṣyate*—will appear; *tat-priya-artham*—and for His satisfaction; *sambhavantu*—should take birth; *sura-striyaḥ*—all the wives of the demigods.

TRANSLATION

The Supreme Personality of Godhead, Śrī Kṛṣṇa, who has full potency, will personally appear as the son of Vasudeva. Therefore all the wives of the demigods should also appear in order to satisfy Him.

PURPORT

In *Bhagavad-gītā* (4.9) the Lord says, *tyaktvā dehaṁ punar janma naiti mām eti:* after giving up the material body, the devotee of the Lord returns home, back to Godhead. This means that the devotee is first transferred to the particular universe where the Lord is at that time staying to exhibit His pastimes. There are innumerable universes, and the Lord is appearing in one of these universes at every moment. Therefore His pastimes are called *nitya-līlā,* eternal pastimes. The Lord's appearance as a child in the house of Devakī takes place continuously in one universe after another. Therefore, the devotee is first transferred to that particular universe where the pastimes of the Lord are current. As stated in *Bhagavad-gītā,* even if a devotee does not complete the course of devotional service, he enjoys the happiness of the heavenly planets, where the most pious people dwell, and then takes birth in the house of a *śuci* or *śrīmān,* a pious *brāhmaṇa* or a wealthy *vaiśya* (*śucīnāṁ śrīmatāṁ gehe yoga-bhraṣṭo 'bhijāyate*). Thus a pure devotee, even if unable to execute devotional service completely, is transferred to the upper planetary system, where pious people reside. From there, if his devotional service is complete, such a devotee is transferred to the place where the Lord's pastimes are going on. Herein it is said, *sambhavantu sura-striyaḥ. Sura-strī,* the women of the heavenly planets, were thus ordered to appear in the Yadu dynasty in Vṛndāvana to enrich the pastimes of Lord Kṛṣṇa. These *sura-strī,* when further trained to live with Kṛṣṇa, would be transferred to the original Goloka Vṛndāvana. During Lord Kṛṣṇa's pastimes within this world, the *sura-strī* were to appear in different ways in different families to give pleasure to the Lord, just so that they would be fully trained before going to the eternal Goloka Vṛndāvana. With the association of Lord Kṛṣṇa, either at Dvārakā-purī, Mathurā-purī or Vṛndāvana, they would certainly return home, back to Godhead. Among the *sura-strī,* the women of the heavenly planets, there are many devotees, such as the mother of the Upendra incarnation of Kṛṣṇa. It was such devoted women who were called for in this connection.

TEXT 24

वासुदेवकलानन्तः सहस्रवदनः स्वराट् ।
अग्रतो भविता देवो हरेः प्रियचिकीर्षया ॥२४॥

vāsudeva-kalānantaḥ
sahasra-vadanaḥ svarāṭ
agrato bhavitā devo
hareḥ priya-cikīrṣayā

vāsudeva-kalā anantaḥ—the plenary expansion of Lord Kṛṣṇa known as Anantadeva or Saṅkarṣaṇa Ananta, the all-pervasive incarnation of the Supreme Lord; *sahasra-vadanaḥ*—having thousands of hoods; *svarāṭ*—fully independent; *agrataḥ*—previously; *bhavitā*—will appear; *devaḥ*—the Lord; *hareḥ*—of Lord Kṛṣṇa; *priya-cikīrṣayā*—with the desire to act for the pleasure.

TRANSLATION

The foremost manifestation of Kṛṣṇa is Saṅkarṣaṇa, who is known as Ananta. He is the origin of all incarnations within this

material world. Previous to the appearance of Lord Kṛṣṇa, this original Saṅkarṣaṇa will appear as Baladeva, just to please the Supreme Lord Kṛṣṇa in His transcendental pastimes.

PURPORT

Śrī Baladeva is the Supreme Personality of Godhead Himself. He is equal in supremacy to the Supreme Godhead, yet wherever Kṛṣṇa appears, Śrī Baladeva appears as His brother, sometimes elder and sometimes younger. When Kṛṣṇa appears, all His plenary expansions and other incarnations appear with Him. This is elaborately explained in *Caitanya-caritāmṛta.* This time, Baladeva would appear before Kṛṣṇa as Kṛṣṇa's elder brother.

TEXT 25

विष्णोर्माया भगवती यया सम्मोहितं जगत् ।
आदिष्टा प्रभुणांशेन कार्यार्थे सम्भविष्यति ॥२५॥

viṣṇor māyā bhagavatī
yayā sammohitaṁ jagat
ādiṣṭā prabhuṇāṁśena
kāryārthe sambhaviṣyati

viṣṇoḥ māyā—the potency of the Supreme Personality of Godhead, Viṣṇu; *bhagavatī*—as good as Bhagavān and therefore known as Bhagavatī; *yayā*—by whom; *sammohitam*—captivated; *jagat*—all the worlds, both material and spiritual; *ādiṣṭā*—being ordered; *prabhuṇā*—by the master; *aṁśena*—with her different potential factors; *kārya-arthe*—for executing business; *sambhaviṣyati*—would also appear.

TRANSLATION

The potency of the Lord, known as viṣṇu-māyā, who is as good as the Supreme Personality of Godhead, will also appear with Lord Kṛṣṇa. This potency, acting in different capacities, captivates all the worlds, both material and spiritual. At the request of her master, she will appear with her different potencies in order to execute the work of the Lord.

PURPORT

Parāsya śaktir vividhaiva śrūyate (*Śvetāśvatara Upaniṣad* 6.8). In the *Vedas* it is said that the potencies of the Supreme Personality of Godhead are called by different names, such as *yogamāyā* and *mahāmāyā*. Ultimately, however, the Lord's potency is one, exactly as electric potency is one although it can act both to cool and to heat. The Lord's potency acts in both the spiritual and material worlds. In the spiritual world the Lord's potency works as *yogamāyā*, and in the material world the same potency works as *mahāmāyā*, exactly as electricity works in both a heater and a cooler. In the material world, this potency, working as *mahāmāyā*, acts upon the conditioned souls to deprive them more and more of devotional service. It is said, *yayā sammohito jīva ātmānaṁ tri-guṇātmakam*. In the material world the conditioned soul thinks of himself as a product of *tri-guṇa*, the three modes of material nature. This is the bodily conception of life. Because of associating with the three *guṇas* of the material potency, everyone identifies himself with his body. Someone is thinking he is a *brāhmaṇa*, someone a *kṣatriya*, and someone a *vaiśya* or *śūdra*. Actually, however, one is neither a *brāhmaṇa*, a *kṣatriya*, a *vaiśya* nor a *śūdra;* one is part and parcel of the Supreme Lord (*mamaivāṁśaḥ*), but because of being covered by the material energy, *mahāmāyā*, one identifies himself in these different ways. When the conditioned soul becomes liberated, however, he thinks himself an eternal servant of Kṛṣṇa. *Jīvera 'svarūpa' haya—kṛṣṇera 'nitya-dāsa.'* When he comes to that position, the same potency, acting as *yogamāyā*, increasingly helps him become purified and devote his energy to the service of the Lord.

In either case, whether the soul is conditioned or liberated, the Lord is supreme. As stated in *Bhagavad-gītā* (9.10), *mayādhyakṣeṇa prakṛtiḥ sūyate sa-carācaram:* it is by the order of the Supreme Personality of Godhead that the material energy, *mahāmāyā*, works upon the conditioned soul.

prakṛteḥ kriyamāṇāni
guṇaiḥ karmāṇi sarvaśaḥ
ahaṅkāra-vimūḍhātmā
kartāham iti manyate

"The bewildered spirit soul, under the influence of the three modes of material nature, thinks himself to be the doer of activities which are in actuality carried out by nature." (Bg. 3.27) Within conditioned life, no one has freedom, but because one is bewildered, being subject to the rule of *mahāmāyā*, one foolishly thinks himself independent (*ahaṅkāra-vimūḍhātmā kartāham iti manyate*). But when the conditioned soul becomes liberated by executing devotional service, he is given a greater and greater chance to relish a relationship with the Supreme Personality of Godhead in different transcendental statuses, such as *dāsya-rasa, sakhya-rasa, vātsalya-rasa* and *mādhurya-rasa.*

Thus the Lord's potency, *viṣṇu-māyā*, has two features—*āvaraṇikā* and *unmukha.* When the Lord appeared, His potency came with Him and acted in different ways. She acted as *yogamāyā* with Yaśodā, Devakī and other intimate relations of the Lord, and she acted in a different way with Kaṁsa, Śālva and other *asuras.* By the order of Lord Kṛṣṇa, His potency *yogamāyā* came with Him and exhibited different activities according to the time and circumstances. *Kāryārthe sambhaviṣyati. Yogamāyā* acted differently to execute different purposes desired by the Lord. As confirmed in *Bhagavad-gītā* (9.13), *mahātmānas tu māṁ pārtha daivīṁ prakṛtim āśritāḥ.* The *mahātmās*, who fully surrender to the lotus feet of the Lord, are directed by *yogamāyā*, whereas the *durātmās*, those who are devoid of devotional service, are directed by *mahāmāyā.*

TEXT 26

श्रीशुक उवाच

इत्यादिश्यामरगणान् प्रजापतिपतिर्विभुः ।
आश्वास्य च महीं गीर्भिः स्वधाम परमं ययौ ॥२६॥

śrī-śuka uvāca
ity ādiśyāmara-gaṇān
prajāpati-patir vibhuḥ
āśvāsya ca mahīṁ gīrbhiḥ
sva-dhāma paramaṁ yayau

śrī-śukaḥ uvāca—Śrī Śukadeva Gosvāmī said; *iti*—thus; *ādiśya*—after informing; *amara-gaṇān*—all the demigods; *prajāpati-patiḥ*—

Lord Brahmā, the master of the Prajāpatis; *vibhuḥ*—all-powerful; *āśvāsya*—after pacifying; *ca*—also; *mahīm*—mother earth; *gīrbhiḥ*—by sweet words; *sva-dhāma*—his own planet, known as Brahmaloka; *paramam*—the best (within the universe); *yayau*—returned.

TRANSLATION

Śukadeva Gosvāmī continued: After thus advising the demigods and pacifying mother earth, the very powerful Lord Brahmā, who is the master of all other Prajāpatis and is therefore known as Prajāpati-pati, returned to his own abode, Brahmaloka.

TEXT 27

शूरसेनो यदुपतिर्मथुरामावसन् पुरीम् ।
माथुराञ्छूरसेनांश्च विषयान् बुभुजे पुरा ॥२७॥

śūraseno yadupatir
mathurām āvasan purīm
māthurāñ chūrasenāṁś ca
viṣayān bubhuje purā

śūrasenaḥ—King Śūrasena; *yadu-patiḥ*—the chief of the Yadu dynasty; *mathurām*—at the place known as Mathurā; *āvasan*—went to live; *purīm*—in that city; *māthurān*—at the place known as the Māthura district; *śūrasenān ca*—and the place known as Śūrasena; *viṣayān*—such kingdoms; *bubhuje*—enjoyed; *purā*—formerly.

TRANSLATION

Formerly, Śūrasena, the chief of the Yadu dynasty, had gone to live in the city of Mathurā. There he enjoyed the places known as Māthura and Śūrasena.

TEXT 28

राजधानी ततः साभूत् सर्वयादवभूभुजाम् ।
मथुरा भगवान् यत्र नित्यं संनिहितो हरिः ॥२८॥

rājadhānī tataḥ sābhūt
sarva-yādava-bhūbhujām
mathurā bhagavān yatra
nityaṁ sannihito hariḥ

rājadhānī—the capital; *tataḥ*—from that time; *sā*—the country and the city known as Mathurā; *abhūt*—became; *sarva-yādava-bhūbhujām*—of all the kings who appeared in the Yadu dynasty; *mathurā*—the place known as Mathurā; *bhagavān*—the Supreme Personality of Godhead; *yatra*—wherein; *nityam*—eternally; *sannihitaḥ*—intimately connected, living eternally; *hariḥ*—the Lord, the Supreme Personality of Godhead.

TRANSLATION

Since that time, the city of Mathurā had been the capital of all the kings of the Yadu dynasty. The city and district of Mathurā are very intimately connected with Kṛṣṇa, for Lord Kṛṣṇa lives there eternally.

PURPORT

It is understood that Mathurā City is the transcendental abode of Lord Kṛṣṇa; it is not an ordinary material city, for it is eternally connected with the Supreme Personality of Godhead. Vṛndāvana is within the jurisdiction of Mathurā, and it still continues to exist. Because Mathurā and Vṛndāvana are intimately connected with Kṛṣṇa eternally, it is said that Lord Kṛṣṇa never leaves Vṛndāvana (*vṛndāvanaṁ parityajya padam ekaṁ na gacchati*). At present, the place known as Vṛndāvana, in the district of Mathurā, continues its position as a transcendental place, and certainly anyone who goes there becomes transcendentally purified. Navadvīpa-dhāma is also intimately connected with Vrajabhūmi. Śrīla Narottama dāsa Ṭhākura therefore says:

śrī gauḍa-maṇḍala-bhūmi, yebā jāne cintāmaṇi,
tā'ra haya vrajabhūme vāsa

"Vrajabhūmi" refers to Mathurā-Vṛndāvana, and Gauḍa-maṇḍala-bhūmi includes Navadvīpa. These two places are nondifferent. Therefore, anyone living in Navadvīpa-dhāma, knowing Kṛṣṇa and Śrī Caitanya Mahāprabhu to be the same personality, lives in Vrajabhūmi, Mathurā-Vṛndāvana. The Lord has made it convenient for the conditioned soul to live in Mathurā, Vṛndāvana and Navadvīpa and thus be directly connected with the Supreme Personality of Godhead. Simply by living in these places, one can immediately come in contact with the Lord. There are many devotees who vow never to leave Vṛndāvana and Mathurā. This is undoubtedly a good vow, but if one leaves Vṛndāvana, Mathurā or Navadvīpa-dhāma for the service of the Lord, he is not disconnected from the Supreme Personality of Godhead. At any rate, we must understand the transcendental importance of Mathurā-Vṛndāvana and Navadvīpa-dhāma. Anyone who executes devotional service in these places certainly goes back home, back to Godhead, after giving up his body. Thus the words *mathurā bhagavān yatra nityaṁ sannihito hariḥ* are particularly important. A devotee should fully utilize this instruction to the best of his ability. Whenever the Supreme Lord personally appears, He appears in Mathurā because of His intimate connection with this place. Therefore although Mathurā and Vṛndāvana are situated on this planet earth, they are transcendental abodes of the Lord.

TEXT 29

तस्यां तु कर्हिचिच्छौरिर्वसुदेवः कृतोद्वहः ।
देवक्या सूर्यया सार्धं प्रयाणे रथमारुहत् ॥२९॥

tasyāṁ tu karhicic chaurir
vasudevaḥ kṛtodvahaḥ
devakyā sūryayā sārdhaṁ
prayāṇe ratham āruhat

tasyām—in that place known as Mathurā; *tu*—indeed; *karhicit*—some time ago; *śauriḥ*—the demigod, descendant of Śūra; *vasudevaḥ*—who appeared as Vasudeva; *kṛta-udvahaḥ*—after being married; *devakyā*—Devakī; *sūryayā*—his newly married wife; *sārdham*—along with; *prayāṇe*—for returning home; *ratham*—the chariot; *āruhat*—mounted.

TRANSLATION

Some time ago, Vasudeva, who belonged to the demigod family [or to the Śūra dynasty], married Devakī. After the marriage, he mounted his chariot to return home with his newly married wife.

TEXT 30

उग्रसेनसुतः कंसः स्वसुः प्रियचिकीर्षया ।
रश्मीन् हयानां जग्राह रौक्मै रथशतैर्वृतः ॥३०॥

ugrasena-sutaḥ kaṁsaḥ
svasuḥ priya-cikīrṣayā
raśmīn hayānāṁ jagrāha
raukmai ratha-śatair vṛtaḥ

ugrasena-sutaḥ—the son of Ugrasena; *kaṁsaḥ*—by the name Kaṁsa; *svasuḥ*—of his own sister Devakī; *priya-cikīrṣayā*—to please her on the occasion of her marriage; *raśmīn*—the reins; *hayānām*—of the horses; *jagrāha*—took; *raukmaiḥ*—made of gold; *ratha-śataiḥ*—by hundreds of chariots; *vṛtaḥ*—surrounded.

TRANSLATION

Kaṁsa, the son of King Ugrasena, in order to please his sister Devakī on the occasion of her marriage, took charge of the reins of the horses and became the chariot driver. He was surrounded by hundreds of golden chariots.

TEXTS 31–32

चतुःशतं पारिबर्हं गजानां हेममालिनाम् ।
अश्वानामयुतं सार्धं रथानां च त्रिषट्शतम् ॥३१॥
दासीनां सुकुमारीणां द्वे शते समलङ्कृते ।
दुहित्रे देवकः प्रादाद् याने दुहितृवत्सलः ॥३२॥

catuḥ-śataṁ pāribarhaṁ
gajānāṁ hema-mālinām

aśvānām ayutaṁ sārdhaṁ
rathānāṁ ca tri-ṣaṭ-śatam

dāsīnāṁ sukumārīṇāṁ
dve śate samalaṅkṛte
duhitre devakaḥ prādād
yāne duhitṛ-vatsalaḥ

catuḥ-śatam—four hundred; *pāribarham*—dowry; *gajānām*—of elephants; *hema-mālinām*—decorated with garlands of gold; *aśvānām*—of horses; *ayutam*—ten thousand; *sārdham*—along with; *rathānām*—of chariots; *ca*—and; *tri-ṣaṭ-śatam*—three times six hundred (eighteen hundred); *dāsīnām*—of maidservants; *su-kumārīṇām*—very young and beautiful unmarried girls; *dve*—two; *śate*—hundred; *samalaṅkṛte*—fully decorated with ornaments; *duhitre*—unto his daughter; *devakaḥ*—King Devaka; *prādāt*—gave as a gift; *yāne*—while going away; *duhitṛ-vatsalaḥ*—who was very fond of his daughter Devakī.

TRANSLATION

Devakī's father, King Devaka, was very much affectionate to his daughter. Therefore, while she and her husband were leaving home, he gave her a dowry of four hundred elephants nicely decorated with golden garlands. He also gave ten thousand horses, eighteen hundred chariots, and two hundred very beautiful young maidservants, fully decorated with ornaments.

PURPORT

The system of giving a dowry to one's daughter has existed in Vedic civilization for a very long time. Even today, following the same system, a father who has money will give his daughter an opulent dowry. A daughter would never inherit the property of her father, and therefore an affectionate father, during the marriage of his daughter, would give her as much as possible. A dowry, therefore, is never illegal according to the Vedic system. Here, of course, the gift offered as a dowry by Devaka to Devakī was not ordinary. Because Devaka was a king, he gave a dowry quite suitable to his royal position. Even an ordinary man, especially a high-class *brāhmaṇa*, *kṣatriya* or *vaiśya*, is supposed to give his daughter a liberal dowry. Immediately after the marriage, the daughter goes to her husband's house, and it is also a custom for the brother of the bride to accompany his sister and brother-in-law to exhibit affection for her. This system was followed by Kaṁsa. These are all old customs in the society of *varṇāśrama-dharma*, which is now wrongly designated as Hindu. These long-standing customs are nicely described here.

TEXT 33

शङ्खतूर्यमृदङ्गाश्च नेदुर्दुन्दुभयः समम् ।
प्रयाणप्रक्रमे तात वरवध्वोः सुमङ्गलम् ॥३३॥

śaṅkha-tūrya-mṛdaṅgāś ca
nedur dundubhayaḥ samam
prayāṇa-prakrame tāta
vara-vadhvoḥ sumaṅgalam

śaṅkha—conchshells; *tūrya*—bugles; *mṛdaṅgāḥ*—drums; *ca*—also; *neduḥ*—vibrated; *dundubhayaḥ*—kettledrums; *samam*—in concert; *prayāṇa-prakrame*—at the time of departure; *tāta*—O beloved son; *vara-vadhvoḥ*—of the bridegroom and the bride; *su-maṅgalam*—for the purpose of their auspicious departure.

TRANSLATION

O beloved son, Mahārāja Parīkṣit, when the bride and bridegroom were ready to start, conchshells, bugles, drums and kettledrums all vibrated in concert for their auspicious departure.

TEXT 34

पथि प्रग्रहिणं कंसमाभाष्याहाशरीरवाक् ।
अस्यास्त्वामष्टमो गर्भो हन्ता यां वहसेऽबुध ॥३४॥

pathi pragrahiṇaṁ kaṁsam
ābhāṣyāhāśarīra-vāk

asyās tvām aṣṭamo garbho
hantā yāṁ vahase 'budha

pathi—on the way; *pragrahiṇam*—who was managing the reins of the horses; *kaṁsam*—unto Kaṁsa; *ābhāṣya*—addressing; *āha*—said; *a-śarīra-vāk*—a voice coming from someone whose body was invisible; *asyāḥ*—of this girl (Devakī); *tvām*—you; *aṣṭamaḥ*—the eighth; *garbhaḥ*—pregnancy; *hantā*—killer; *yām*—her whom; *vahase*—you are carrying; *abudha*—you foolish rascal.

TRANSLATION

While Kaṁsa, controlling the reins of the horses, was driving the chariot along the way, an unembodied voice addressed him, "You foolish rascal, the eighth child of the woman you are carrying will kill you!"

PURPORT

The omen spoke of *aṣṭamo garbhaḥ*, referring to the eighth pregnancy, but did not clearly say whether the child was to be a son or a daughter. Even if Kaṁsa were to see that the eighth child of Devakī was a daughter, he should have no doubt that the eighth child was to kill him. According to the *Viśva-kośa* dictionary, the word *garbha* means "embryo" and also *arbhaka*, or "child." Kaṁsa was affectionate toward his sister, and therefore he had become the chariot driver to carry her and his brother-in-law to their home. The demigods, however, did not want Kaṁsa to be affectionate toward Devakī, and therefore, from an unseen position, they encouraged Kaṁsa to offend her. Moreover, the six sons of Marīci had been cursed to take birth from the womb of Devakī, and upon being killed by Kaṁsa they would be delivered. When Devakī understood that Kaṁsa would be killed by the Supreme Personality of Godhead, who would appear from her womb, she felt great joy. The word *vahase* is also significant because it indicates that the ominous vibration condemned Kaṁsa for acting just like a beast of burden by carrying his enemy's mother.

TEXT 35

इत्युक्तः स खलः पापो भोजानां कुलपांसनः ।
भगिनीं हन्तुमारब्धं खड्गपाणिः कचेऽग्रहीत् ॥३५॥

ity uktaḥ sa khalaḥ pāpo
bhojānāṁ kula-pāṁsanaḥ
bhaginīṁ hantum ārabdhaṁ
khaḍga-pāṇiḥ kace 'grahīt

iti uktaḥ—thus being addressed; *saḥ*—he (Kaṁsa); *khalaḥ*—envious; *pāpaḥ*—sinful; *bhojānām*—of the Bhoja dynasty; *kula-pāṁsanaḥ*—one who can degrade the reputation of his family; *bhaginīm*—unto his sister; *hantum ārabdham*—being inclined to kill; *khaḍga-pāṇiḥ*—taking a sword in his hand; *kace*—hair; *agrahīt*—took up.

TRANSLATION

Kaṁsa was a condemned personality in the Bhoja dynasty because he was envious and sinful. Therefore, upon hearing this omen from the sky, he caught hold of his sister's hair with his left hand and took up his sword with his right hand to sever her head from her body.

PURPORT

Kaṁsa was driving the chariot and controlling the reins with his left hand, but as soon as he heard the omen that his sister's eighth child would kill him, he gave up the reins, caught hold of his sister's hair, and with his right hand took up a sword to kill her. Before, he had been so affectionate that he was acting as his sister's chariot driver, but as soon as he heard that his self-interest or his life was at risk, he forgot all affection for her and immediately became a great enemy. This is the nature of demons. No one should trust a demon, despite any amount of affection. Aside from this, a king, a politician or a woman cannot be trusted, since they can do anything abominable for their personal interest. Cāṇakya Paṇḍita therefore says, *viśvāso naiva kartavyaḥ strīṣu rāja-kuleṣu ca.*

TEXT 36

तं जुगुप्सितकर्माणं नृशंसं निरपत्रपम् ।
वसुदेवो महाभाग उवाच परिसान्त्वयन् ॥३६॥

taṁ jugupsita-karmāṇaṁ
nṛśaṁsaṁ nirapatrapam
vasudevo mahā-bhāga
uvāca parisāntvayan

tam—unto him (Kaṁsa); *jugupsita-karmāṇam*—who was ready to commit such an offensive act; *nṛśaṁsam*—very cruel; *nirapatrapam*—shameless; *vasudevaḥ*—Vasudeva; *mahā-bhāgaḥ*—the greatly fortunate father of Vāsudeva; *uvāca*—said; *parisāntvayan*—pacifying.

TRANSLATION

Wanting to pacify Kaṁsa, who was so cruel and envious that he was shamelessly ready to kill his sister, the great soul Vasudeva, who was to be the father of Kṛṣṇa, spoke to him in the following words.

PURPORT

Vasudeva, who was to be the father of Kṛṣṇa, is described here as *mahā-bhāga*, a very upright and sober personality, because although Kaṁsa was ready to kill Vasudeva's wife, Vasudeva remained sober and unagitated. In a peaceful attitude, Vasudeva began to address Kaṁsa by putting forward reasonable arguments. Vasudeva was a great personality because he knew how to pacify a cruel person and how to forgive even the bitterest enemy. One who is fortunate is never caught, even by tigers or snakes.

TEXT 37

श्रीवसुदेव उवाच
श्लाघनीयगुणः शूरैर्भवान् भोजयशस्करः ।
स कथं भगिनीं हन्यात् स्त्रियमुद्वाहपर्वणि ॥३७॥

śrī-vasudeva uvāca
ślāghanīya-guṇaḥ śūrair
bhavān bhoja-yaśaskaraḥ
sa kathaṁ bhaginīṁ hanyāt
striyam udvāha-parvaṇi

śrī-vasudevaḥ uvāca—the great personality Vasudeva said; *ślāghanīya-guṇaḥ*—a person who possesses praiseworthy qualities; *śūraiḥ*—by great heroes; *bhavān*—your good self; *bhoja-yaśaḥ-karaḥ*—a brilliant star in the Bhoja dynasty; *saḥ*—one such as your good self; *katham*—how; *bhaginīm*—your sister; *hanyāt*—can kill; *striyam*—especially a woman; *udvāha-parvaṇi*—at the time of the marriage ceremony.

TRANSLATION

Vasudeva said: My dear brother-in-law Kaṁsa, you are the pride of your family, the Bhoja dynasty, and great heroes praise your qualities. How could such a qualified person as you kill a woman, your own sister, especially on the occasion of her marriage?

PURPORT

According to Vedic principles, a *brāhmaṇa*, an old man, a woman, a child or a cow cannot be killed under any circumstances. Vasudeva stressed that Devakī was not only a woman but a member of Kaṁsa's family. Because she was now married to Vasudeva, she was *para-strī*, another man's wife, and if such a woman were killed, not only would Kaṁsa be implicated in sinful activities, but his reputation as king of the Bhoja dynasty would be damaged. Thus Vasudeva tried in many ways to convince Kaṁsa in order to stop him from killing Devakī.

TEXT 38

मृत्युर्जन्मवतां वीर देहेन सह जायते ।
अद्य वाब्दशतान्ते वा मृत्युर्वै प्राणिनां ध्रुवः ॥३८॥

mṛtyur janmavatāṁ vīra
dehena saha jāyate
adya vābda-śatānte vā
mṛtyur vai prāṇināṁ dhruvaḥ

mṛtyuḥ—death; *janma-vatām*—of the living entities who have taken birth; *vīra*—O great hero; *dehena saha*—along with the body; *jāyate*—is born (one who has taken birth is sure to die); *adya*—today; *vā*—

either; *abda-śata*—of hundreds of years; *ante*—at the end; *vā*—or; *mṛtyuḥ*—death; *vai*—indeed; *prāṇinām*—for every living entity; *dhruvaḥ*—is assured.

TRANSLATION

O great hero, one who takes birth is sure to die, for death is born with the body. One may die today or after hundreds of years, but death is sure for every living entity.

PURPORT

Vasudeva wanted to impress upon Kaṁsa that although Kaṁsa feared dying and therefore wanted to kill even a woman, he could not avoid death. Death is sure. Why then should Kaṁsa do something that would be detrimental to his reputation and that of his family? As confirmed in *Bhagavad-gītā* (2.27):

jātasya hi dhruvo mṛtyur
dhruvaṁ janma mṛtasya ca
tasmād aparihārye 'rthe
na tvaṁ śocitum arhasi

"For one who has taken his birth, death is certain; and for one who is dead, birth is certain. Therefore, in the unavoidable discharge of your duty, you should not lament." One should not fear death. Rather, one should prepare oneself for the next birth. One should utilize one's time in this human form to end the process of birth and death. It is not that to save oneself from death one should entangle oneself in sinful activities. This is not good.

TEXT 39

देहे पञ्चत्वमापन्ने देही कर्मानुगोऽवशः ।
देहान्तरमनुप्राप्य प्राक्तनं त्यजते वपुः ॥३९॥

dehe pañcatvam āpanne
dehī karmānugo 'vaśaḥ

dehāntaram anuprāpya
prāktanaṁ tyajate vapuḥ

dehe—when the body; *pañcatvam āpanne*—turns into five elements; *dehī*—the proprietor of the body, the living being; *karma-anugaḥ*—following the reactions of his own fruitive activities; *avaśaḥ*—spontaneously, automatically; *deha-antaram*—another body (made of material elements); *anuprāpya*—receiving as a result; *prāktanam*—the former; *tyajate*—gives up; *vapuḥ*—body.

TRANSLATION

When the present body turns to dust and is again reduced to five elements—earth, water, fire, air and ether—the proprietor of the body, the living being, automatically receives another body of material elements according to his fruitive activities. When the next body is obtained, he gives up the present body.

PURPORT

This is confirmed in *Bhagavad-gītā*, which presents the beginning of spiritual understanding.

dehino 'smin yathā dehe
kaumāraṁ yauvanaṁ jarā
tathā dehāntara-prāptir
dhīras tatra na muhyati

"As the embodied soul continually passes, in this body, from boyhood to youth to old age, the soul similarly passes into another body at death. The self-realized soul is not bewildered by such a change." (Bg. 2.13) A person or an animal is not the material body; rather, the material body is the covering of the living being. *Bhagavad-gītā* compares the body to a dress and elaborately explains how one changes dresses one after another. The same Vedic knowledge is confirmed here. The living being, the soul, is constantly changing bodies one after another. Even in the present life, the body changes from childhood to boyhood, from boyhood to youth, and from youth to old age; similarly, when the body is too old to continue, the living being gives up this body and, by the laws of nature, automatically gets another body according to his fruitive activities, desires and ambitions. The laws of nature control this sequence, and therefore as long as the living entity is under the control of the external, material energy, the process of bodily change takes place automatically, according to one's fruitive activities. Vasudeva therefore wanted to impress upon Kaṁsa that if he committed this sinful act of killing a woman, in his next life he would certainly get a material body still more conditioned to the sufferings of material existence. Thus Vasudeva advised Kaṁsa not to commit sinful activities.

One who commits sinful activities because of ignorance, *tamo-guṇa*, obtains a lower body. *Kāraṇaṁ guṇa-sango 'sya sad-asad-yoni-janmasu* (Bg. 13.22). There are hundreds and thousands of different species of life. Why are there higher and lower bodies? One receives these bodies according to the contaminations of material nature. If in this life one is contaminated by the mode of ignorance and sinful activities (*duṣkṛtī*), in the next life, by the laws of nature, one will certainly get a body full of suffering. The laws of nature are not subservient to the whimsical desires of the conditioned soul. Our endeavor, therefore, should be to associate always with *sattva-guṇa* and not indulge in *rajo-guṇa* or *tamo-guṇa* (*rajas-tamo-bhāvāḥ*). Lusty desires and greed keep the living entity perpetually in ignorance and prevent him from being elevated to the platform of *sattva-guṇa* or *śuddha-sattva-guṇa*. One is advised to be situated in *śuddha-sattva-guṇa*, devotional service, for thus one is immune to the reactions of the three modes of material nature.

TEXT 40

व्रजंस्तिष्ठन् पदैकेन यथैवैकेन गच्छति ।
यथा तृणजलौकैवं देही कर्मगतिं गतः ॥४०॥

vrajaṁs tiṣṭhan padaikena
yathaivaikena gacchati
yathā tṛṇa-jalaukaivaṁ
dehī karma-gatiṁ gataḥ

vrajan—a person, while traveling on the road; *tiṣṭhan*—while standing; *padā ekena*—on one foot; *yathā*—as; *eva*—indeed; *ekena*—by another foot; *gacchati*—goes; *yathā*—as; *tṛṇa-jalaukā*—a worm on a vegetable; *evam*—in this way; *dehī*—the living entity; *karma-gatim*—the reactions of fruitive activities; *gataḥ*—undergoes.

TRANSLATION

Just as a person traveling on the road rests one foot on the ground and then lifts the other, or as a worm on a vegetable transfers itself to one leaf and then gives up the previous one, the conditioned soul takes shelter of another body and then gives up the one he had before.

PURPORT

This is the process of the soul's transmigration from one body to another. At the time of death, according to his mental condition, the living being is carried by the subtle body, consisting of mind, intelligence and ego, to another gross body. When higher authorities have decided what kind of gross body the living entity will have, he is forced to enter such a body, and thus he automatically gives up his previous body. Dull-minded persons who do not have the intelligence to understand this process of transmigration take for granted that when the gross body is finished, one's life is finished forever. Such persons have no brains with which to understand the process of transmigration. At the present moment there is great opposition to the Hare Kṛṣṇa movement, which is being called a "brainwashing" movement. But actually the so-called scientists, philosophers and other leaders in the Western countries have no brains at all. The Hare Kṛṣṇa movement is trying to elevate such foolish persons by enlightening their intelligence so that they will take advantage of the human body. Unfortunately, because of gross ignorance, they regard the Hare Kṛṣṇa movement as a brainwashing movement. They do not know that without God consciousness one is forced to continue transmigrating from one body to another. Because of their devilish brains, they will next be forced to accept an abominable life and practically never be able to liberate themselves from the conditional life of material existence. How this transmigration of the soul takes place is very clearly explained in this verse.

TEXT 41

स्वप्ने यथा पश्यति देहमीदृशं
मनोरथेनाभिनिविष्टचेतनः ।
दृष्टश्रुताभ्यां मनसानुचिन्तयन्
प्रपद्यते तत् किमपि ह्यपस्मृतिः ॥४१॥

svapne yathā paśyati deham īdṛśaṁ
manorathenābhiniviṣṭa-cetanaḥ
dṛṣṭa-śrutābhyāṁ manasānucintayan
prapadyate tat kim api hy apasmṛtiḥ

svapne—in a dream; *yathā*—as; *paśyati*—one sees; *deham*—the kind of body; *īdṛśam*—similarly; *manorathena*—by mental speculation; *abhiniviṣṭa*—is fully absorbed; *cetanaḥ*—he whose consciousness; *dṛṣṭa*—by whatever has been experienced by seeing with the eyes; *śrutābhyām*—and by hearing a description of something else; *manasā*—by the mind; *anucintayan*—thinking, feeling and willing; *prapadyate*—surrenders; *tat*—to that situation; *kim api*—what to speak of; *hi*—indeed; *apasmṛtiḥ*—experiencing forgetfulness of the present body.

TRANSLATION

Having experienced a situation by seeing or hearing about it, one contemplates and speculates about that situation, and thus one surrenders to it, not considering his present body. Similarly, by mental adjustments one dreams at night of living under different circumstances, in different bodies, and forgets his actual position. Under this same process, one gives up his present body and accepts another [tathā dehāntara-prāptiḥ].

PURPORT

Transmigration of the soul is very clearly explained in this verse. One sometimes forgets his present body and thinks of his childhood body, a body of the past, and of how one was playing, jumping, talking and so on. When the material body is no long workable, it becomes dust: "For dust thou art, and unto dust shalt thou return." But when the body again mixes with the five material elements—earth, water, fire, air and ether—the mind continues to work. The mind is the subtle substance in which the body is created, as we actually experience in our dreams and also when we are awake in contemplation. One must understand that the process of mental speculation develops a new type of body that does not actually exist. If one can understand the nature of the mind (*manorathena*) and its thinking, feeling and willing, one can very easily understand how from the mind different types of bodies develop.

The Kṛṣṇa consciousness movement, therefore, offers a process of transcendental activities wherein the mind is fully absorbed in affairs pertaining to Kṛṣṇa. The presence of the soul is perceived by consciousness, and one must purify his consciousness from material to spiritual, or, in other words, to Kṛṣṇa consciousness. That which is spiritual is eternal, and that which is material is temporary. Without Kṛṣṇa consciousness, one's consciousness is always absorbed in temporary things. For everyone, therefore, Kṛṣṇa recommends in *Bhagavad-gītā* (9.34), *man-manā bhava mad-bhakto mad-yājī māṁ namaskuru.* One should always be absorbed in thought of Kṛṣṇa, one should become His devotee, one should always engage in His service and worship Him as the supreme great, and one should always offer Him obeisances. In the material world one is always a servant of a greater person, and in the spiritual world our constitutional position is to serve the Supreme, the greatest, *paraṁ brahma.* This is the instruction of Śrī Caitanya Mahāprabhu. *Jīvera 'svarūpa' haya—kṛṣṇera 'nitya-dāsa'* (Cc. *Madhya* 20.108).

To act in Kṛṣṇa consciousness is the perfection of life and the highest perfection of *yoga.* As Lord Kṛṣṇa says in *Bhagavad-gītā* (6.47):

yoginām api sarveṣāṁ
mad-gatenāntarātmanā
śraddhāvān bhajate yo māṁ
sa me yuktatamo mataḥ

"Of all *yogīs,* he who always abides in Me with great faith, worshiping Me in transcendental loving service, is most intimately united with Me in *yoga* and is the highest of all."

The condition of the mind, which flickers between *saṅkalpa* and *vikalpa,* accepting something and rejecting it, is very important in transferring the soul to another material body at the time of death.

yaṁ yaṁ vāpi smaran bhāvaṁ
tyajaty ante kalevaram
taṁ tam evaiti kaunteya
sadā tad-bhāva-bhāvitaḥ

"Whatever state of being one remembers when he quits his body, that state he will attain without fail." (Bg. 8.6) Therefore one must train the mind in the system of *bhakti-yoga,* as did Mahārāja Ambarīṣa, who kept himself always in Kṛṣṇa consciousness. *Sa vai manaḥ kṛṣṇa-padāravindayoḥ.* One must fix the mind at the lotus feet of Kṛṣṇa twenty-four hours a day. If the mind is fixed upon Kṛṣṇa's lotus feet, the activities of the other senses will be engaged in Kṛṣṇa's service. *Hṛṣīkeṇa hṛṣīkeśa-sevanaṁ bhaktir ucyate:* to serve Hṛṣīkeśa, the master of the senses, with purified senses is called *bhakti.* Those who constantly engage in devotional service are situated in a transcendental state, above the material modes of nature. As Kṛṣṇa says in *Bhagavad-gītā* (14.26):

māṁ ca yo 'vyabhicāreṇa
bhakti-yogena sevate
sa guṇān samatītyaitān
brahma-bhūyāya kalpate

"One who engages in full devotional service, who does not fall down in any circumstance, at once transcends the modes of material nature and thus comes to the level of Brahman." One must learn the secret of success from the Vedic literatures, especially when the cream of Vedic knowledge is presented by *Bhagavad-gītā* as it is.

Because the mind is ultimately controlled by the Supreme Personality of Godhead, Kṛṣṇa, the word *apasmṛtiḥ* is significant. Forgetfulness of one's own identity is called *apasmṛtiḥ.* This *apasmṛtiḥ* can be controlled by the Supreme Lord, for the Lord says, *mattaḥ smṛtir jñānam apohanaṁ ca:* "From Me come remembrance, knowledge and forgetfulness." Instead of allowing one to forget one's real position, Kṛṣṇa can revive one's original identity at the time of one's death, even though the mind may be flickering. Although the mind may work imperfectly at the time of death, Kṛṣṇa gives a devotee shelter at His lotus feet. Therefore when a devotee gives up his body, the mind does not take him to another material body (*tyaktvā dehaṁ punar janma naiti mām eti*); rather, Kṛṣṇa takes the devotee to that place where He is engaged in His pastimes (*mām eti*), as we have already discussed in previous verses. One's consciousness, therefore, must always be absorbed in Kṛṣṇa, and then one's life will be successful. Otherwise the mind will carry the soul to another material body. The soul will be placed in the semen of a father and discharged into the womb of a mother. The semen and ovum create a particular type of body according to the form of the father and mother, and when the body is mature, the soul emerges in that body and begins a new life. This is the process of transmigration of the soul from one body to another (*tathā dehāntara-prāptiḥ*). Unfortunately, those who are less intelligent think that when the body disappears, everything is finished. The entire world is being misled by such fools and rascals. But as stated in *Bhagavad-gītā* (2.20), *na hanyate hanyamāne śarīre*. The soul does not die when the body is destroyed. Rather, the soul takes on another body.

TEXT 42

यतो यतो धावति दैवचोदितं
मनो विकारात्मकमाप पञ्चसु ।
गुणेषु मायारचितेषु देह्यसौ
प्रपद्यमानः सह तेन जायते ॥४२॥

yato yato dhāvati daiva-coditaṁ
mano vikārātmakam āpa pañcasu
guṇeṣu māyā-raciteṣu dehy asau
prapadyamānaḥ saha tena jāyate

yataḥ yataḥ—from one place to another or from one position to another; *dhāvati*—speculates; *daiva-coditam*—impelled by accident or deliberation; *manaḥ*—the mind; *vikāra-ātmakam*—changing from one type of thinking, feeling and willing to another; *āpa*—at the end, he obtains (a mentality); *pañcasu*—at the time of death (when the material body turns totally into matter); *guṇeṣu*—(the mind, not being liberated, becomes attached) to the material qualities; *māyā-raciteṣu*—where the material energy creates a similar body; *dehī*—the spirit soul who accepts such a body; *asau*—he; *prapadyamānaḥ*—being surrendered (to such a condition); *saha*—with; *tena*—a similar body; *jāyate*—takes birth.

TRANSLATION

At the time of death, according to the thinking, feeling and willing of the mind, which is involved in fruitive activities, one receives a particular body. In other words, the body develops according to the activities of the mind. Changes of body are due to the flickering of the mind, for otherwise the soul could remain in its original, spiritual body.

PURPORT

One can very easily understand that the mind is constantly flickering, changing in the quality of its thinking, feeling and willing. This is explained by Arjuna in *Bhagavad-gītā* (6.34):

cañcalaṁ hi manaḥ kṛṣṇa
pramāthi balavad dṛḍham
tasyāhaṁ nigrahaṁ manye
vāyor iva suduṣkaram

The mind is *cañcala*, flickering, and it changes very strongly. Therefore Arjuna admitted that controlling the mind is not at all possible; this would be as difficult as controlling the wind. For example, if one were in a boat moving according to the wind on a river or the sea, and the wind were uncontrollable, the tilting boat would be very much disturbed and extremely difficult to control. It might even capsize. Therefore, in the *bhava-samudra*, the ocean of mental speculation and transmigration to different types of bodies, one must first control the mind.

By regulative practice one can control the mind, and this is the purpose of the *yoga* system (*abhyāsa-yoga-yuktena*). But there is a chance of failure with the *yoga* system, especially in this age of Kali, because the *yoga* system uses artificial means. If the mind is engaged in *bhakti-yoga*, however, by the grace of Kṛṣṇa one can very easily control it. Therefore Śrī Caitanya Mahāprabhu has recommended, *harer nāma harer nāma harer nāmaiva kevalam.* One should chant the holy name of the Lord constantly, for the holy name of the Lord is nondifferent from Hari, the Supreme Person.

By chanting the Hare Kṛṣṇa *mantra* constantly, one can fix the mind on the lotus feet of Kṛṣṇa (*sa vai manaḥ kṛṣṇa-padāravindayoḥ*) and in this way achieve the perfection of *yoga.* Otherwise, the flickering mind will hover on the platform of mental speculation for sense enjoyment, and one will have to transmigrate from one type of body to another because the mind is trained only in relation to the material elements, or, in other words, to sense gratification, which is false. *Māyā-sukhāya bharam udvahato vimūḍhān* (*Bhāg.* 7.9.43). Rascals (*vimūḍhān*), being controlled by mental speculation, make huge arrangements by which to enjoy life temporarily, but they must give up the body at the time of death, when everything is taken away by Kṛṣṇa's external energy (*mṛtyuḥ sarva-haraś cāham*). At that time, whatever one has created in this life is lost, and one must automatically accept a new body by the force of material nature. In this life one may have constructed a very tall skyscraper, but in the next life, because of one's mentality, one may have to accept a body like that of a cat, a dog, a tree or perhaps a demigod. Thus the body is offered by the laws of material nature. *Kāraṇaṁ guṇa-saṅgo 'sya sad-asad-yoni-janmasu* (Bg. 13.22). The spirit soul takes birth in higher and lower species of life only because of his association with the three qualities of material nature.

ūrdhvaṁ gacchanti sattva-sthā
madhye tiṣṭhanti rājasāḥ
jaghanya-guṇa-vṛtti-sthā
adho gacchanti tāmasāḥ

"Those situated in the mode of goodness gradually go upward to the higher planets; those in the mode of passion live on the earthly planets; and those in the mode of ignorance go down to the hellish worlds." (Bg. 14.18)

In conclusion, the Kṛṣṇa consciousness movement offers the topmost welfare activity for human society. The saner section of human society must therefore take this movement very seriously for the benefit of all humanity. To save oneself from the repetition of birth and death, one must purify his consciousness. *Sarvopādhi-vinirmuktaṁ tat-paratvena nirmalam.* One must be freed from all designations—"I am American," "I am Indian," "I am this," "I am that"—and come to the platform of understanding that Kṛṣṇa is the original master and we are His eternal servants. When the senses are purified and engaged in Kṛṣṇa's service, one achieves the highest perfection. *Hṛṣīkeṇa hṛṣīkeśa-sevanaṁ bhaktir ucyate.* The Kṛṣṇa consciousness movement is a movement of *bhakti-yoga. Vairāgya-vidyā-nija-bhakti-yoga.* By following the principles of this movement, one becomes disassociated from material mental concoctions and is established on the original platform of the eternal relationship between the living entity and the Supreme Personality of Godhead as servant and master. This, in summary, is the purpose of the Kṛṣṇa consciousness movement.

TEXT 43

ज्योतिर्यथैवोदकपार्थिवेष्वदः
समीरवेगानुगतं विभाव्यते ।
एवं स्वमायारचितेष्वसौ पुमान्
गुणेषु रागानुगतो विमुह्यति ॥४३॥

jyotir yathaivodaka-pārthiveṣv adaḥ
samīra-vegānugataṁ vibhāvyate
evaṁ sva-māyā-raciteṣv asau pumān
guṇeṣu rāgānugato vimuhyati

jyotiḥ—the luminaries in the sky, such as the sun, the moon and the stars; *yathā*—as; *eva*—indeed; *udaka*—in water; *pārthiveṣu*—or in other liquids, like oil; *adaḥ*—directly; *samīra-vega-anugatam*—being forced by the movements of the wind; *vibhāvyate*—appear in different shapes; *evam*—in this way; *sva-māyā-raciteṣu*—in the situation created by one's mental concoctions; *asau*—the living entity; *pumān*—person; *guṇeṣu*—in the material world, manifested by the modes of nature; *rāga-anugataḥ*—according to his attachment; *vimuhyati*—becomes bewildered by identification.

TRANSLATION

When the luminaries in the sky, such as the moon, the sun and the stars, are reflected in liquids like oil or water, they appear to be of different shapes—sometimes round, sometimes long, and so on—because of the movements of the wind. Similarly, when the living entity, the soul, is absorbed in materialistic thoughts, he accepts various manifestations as his own identity because of ignorance. In other words, one is bewildered by mental concoctions because of agitation from the material modes of nature.

PURPORT

This verse gives a very good example by which to understand the different positions of the eternal spiritual soul in the material world and how the soul takes on different bodies (*dehāntara-prāptiḥ*). The moon is stationary and is one, but when it is reflected in water or oil, it appears to take different shapes because of the movements of the wind. Similarly, the soul is the eternal servant of Kṛṣṇa, the Supreme Personality of Godhead, but when put into the material modes of nature, it takes different bodies, sometimes as a demigod, sometimes a man, a dog, a tree and so on. By the influence of *māyā*, the illusory potency of the Supreme Personality of Godhead, the living entity thinks that he is this person, that person, American, Indian, cat, dog, tree or whatever. This is called *māyā*. When one is freed from this bewilderment and understands that the soul does not belong to any shape of this material world, one is situated on the spiritual platform (*brahma-bhūta*).

This realization is sometimes explained as *nirākāra*, or formlessness. This formlessness, however, does not mean that the soul has no form. The soul has form, but the external, agitating form he has acquired because of material contamination is false. Similarly, God is also described as *nirākāra*, which means that God has no material form but is *sac-cid-ānanda-vigraha*. The living entity is part and parcel of the supreme *sac-cid-ānanda-vigraha*, but his material forms are temporary, or illusory. Both the living entity and the Supreme Lord have original, spiritual forms (*sac-cid-ānanda-vigraha*), but the Lord, the Supreme, does not change His form. The Lord appears as He is, whereas the living entity appears because material nature forces him to accept different forms.

When the living entity receives these different forms, he identifies with them, and not with his original, spiritual form. As soon as the living entity returns to his original, spiritual form and understanding, he immediately surrenders to the supreme form, the Personality of Godhead. This is explained in *Bhagavad-gītā* (7.19). *Bahūnāṁ janmanām ante jñānavān māṁ prapadyate.* When the living entity, after many, many births in different forms, returns to his original form of Kṛṣṇa consciousness, he immediately surrenders unto the lotus feet of the supreme form, Kṛṣṇa. This is liberation. As the Lord says in *Bhagavad-gītā* (18.54):

brahma-bhūtaḥ prasannātmā
na śocati na kāṅkṣati
samaḥ sarveṣu bhūteṣu
mad-bhaktiṁ labhate parām

"One who is thus transcendentally situated at once realizes the Supreme Brahman and becomes fully joyful. He never laments nor desires to have anything; he is equally disposed to every living entity. In that state he attains pure devotional service unto Me." Surrender unto the supreme form is the result of *bhakti*. This *bhakti*, or understanding of one's own position, is the complete liberation. As long as one is under an impersonal understanding of the Absolute Truth, he is not in pure knowledge, but must still struggle for pure knowledge. *Kleśo 'dhikataras teṣām avyaktāsakta-cetasām* (Bg. 12.5). Although one may be spiritually advanced, if one is attached to the impersonal feature of the Absolute Truth one must still work very hard, as indicated by the words *kleśo 'dhikataraḥ*, which mean "greater suffering." A devotee, however, easily attains his original position as a spiritual form and understands the Supreme Personality of Godhead in His original form.

Kṛṣṇa Himself explains the forms of the living entities in the Second Chapter of *Bhagavad-gītā*, where He clearly says to Arjuna that He, Arjuna and all other living entities, who were previously in their original forms, are separate individual identities. They were individuals in the past, they are now situated in individuality, and in the future they will all continue to maintain their individual forms. The only difference is that the conditioned living entity appears in various material forms, whereas Kṛṣṇa appears in His original, spiritual form. Unfortunately, those who are not advanced in spiritual knowledge think that Kṛṣṇa is like one of them and that His form is like their material forms. *Avajānanti māṁ mūḍhā mānuṣīṁ tanum āśritam* (Bg. 9.11). Kṛṣṇa is never puffed up by material knowledge and is therefore called *acyuta*, whereas the living entities fall down and are agitated by material nature. This is the difference between the Supreme Lord and the living entities.

In this connection it is to be noted that Vasudeva, who was situated in a transcendental position, advised Kaṁsa not to commit further sinful activities. Kaṁsa, a representative of the demons, was always ready to kill Kṛṣṇa, or God, whereas Vasudeva represents a transcendentally situated person to whom Kṛṣṇa is born (Vāsudeva is the son of Vasudeva). Vasudeva wanted his brother-in-law Kaṁsa to refrain from the sinful act of killing his sister, since the result of being agitated by material nature would be that Kaṁsa would have to accept a body in which to suffer again and again. Elsewhere in *Śrīmad-Bhāgavatam* (5.5.4), Ṛṣabhadeva also says:

na sādhu manye yata ātmano 'yam
asann api kleśada āsa dehaḥ

As long as the living entity is entangled in the fruitive activities of so-called happiness and distress, he will receive a particular type of body in which to endure the three kinds of suffering due to material nature (*tri-tāpa-yantraṇā*). An intelligent person, therefore, must free himself from the influence of the three modes of material nature and revive his original, spiritual body by engaging in the service of the Supreme Person, Kṛṣṇa. As long as one is materially attached, one must accept the process of birth, death, old age and disease. One is therefore advised that an intelligent person, instead of being entangled in so-called good and bad fruitive activities, should engage his life in advancing in Kṛṣṇa consciousness so that instead of accepting another material body (*tyaktvā dehaṁ punar janma naiti*), he will return home, back to Godhead.

TEXT 44

तस्मान्न कस्यचिद् द्रोहमाचरेत् स तथाविधः ।
आत्मनः क्षेममन्विच्छन् द्रोग्धुर्वै परतो भयम् ॥४४॥

tasmān na kasyacid droham
ācaret sa tathā-vidhaḥ
ātmanaḥ kṣemam anvicchan
drogdhur vai parato bhayam

tasmāt—therefore; *na*—not; *kasyacit*—of anyone; *droham*—envy; *ācaret*—one should act; *saḥ*—a person (Kaṁsa); *tathā-vidhaḥ*—who has been advised in such a way (by Vasudeva); *ātmanaḥ*—his own; *kṣemam*—welfare; *anvicchan*—if he desires; *drogdhuḥ*—of one who is envious of others; *vai*—indeed; *parataḥ*—from others; *bhayam*—there is a cause of fear.

TRANSLATION

Therefore, since envious, impious activities cause a body in which one suffers in the next life, why should one act impiously? Considering one's welfare, one should not envy anyone, for an envious person must always fear harm from his enemies, either in this life or in the next.

PURPORT

Instead of being inimical toward other living entities, one should act piously by engaging in the service of the Supreme Lord, thus avoiding a fearful situation both in this life and in the next. In this regard, the following moral instruction by the great politician Cāṇakya Paṇḍita is very meaningful:

tyaja durjana-saṁsargaṁ
bhaja sādhu-samāgamam
kuru puṇyam aho rātraṁ
smara nityam anityatām

One should give up the company of devils, demons and nondevotees and should always associate with devotees and saintly persons. One should always act piously, thinking that this life is temporary, and not be attached to temporary happiness and distress. The Kṛṣṇa consciousness movement is teaching all of human society this principle of becoming Kṛṣṇa conscious and thus solving the problems of life forever (*tyaktvā dehaṁ punar janma naiti mām eti so 'rjuna*).

TEXT 45

एषा तवानुजा बाला कृपणा पुत्रिकोपमा ।
हन्तुं नार्हसि कल्याणीमिमां त्वं दीनवत्सलः ॥४५॥

eṣā tavānujā bālā
kṛpaṇā putrikopamā
hantuṁ nārhasi kalyāṇīm
imāṁ tvaṁ dīna-vatsalaḥ

eṣā—this; *tava*—your; *anujā*—younger sister; *bālā*—innocent woman; *kṛpaṇā*—completely dependent on you; *putrikā-upamā*—exactly like your own daughter; *hantum*—to kill her; *na*—not; *arhasi*—you deserve; *kalyāṇīm*—who is under your affection; *imām*—her; *tvam*—you; *dīna-vatsalaḥ*—very compassionate to the poor and innocent.

TRANSLATION

As your younger sister, this poor girl Devakī is like your own daughter and deserves to be affectionately maintained. You are merciful, and therefore you should not kill her. Indeed, she deserves your affection.

TEXT 46

श्रीशुक उवाच
एवं स सामभिर्भेदैर्बोध्यमानोऽपि दारुणः ।
न न्यवर्तत कौरव्य पुरुषादाननुव्रतः ॥४६॥

śrī-śuka uvāca
evaṁ sa sāmabhir bhedair
bodhyamāno 'pi dāruṇaḥ
na nyavartata kauravya
puruṣādān anuvrataḥ

śrī-śukaḥ uvāca—Śrī Śukadeva Gosvāmī said; *evam*—in this way; *saḥ*—he (Kaṁsa); *sāmabhiḥ*—by attempts to pacify him (Kaṁsa); *bhedaiḥ*—by moral instructions that one should not be cruel to anyone else; *bodhyamānaḥ api*—even being pacified; *dāruṇaḥ*—he who was the most fiercely cruel; *na nyavartata*—could not be stopped (from the grievous act); *kauravya*—O Mahārāja Parīkṣit; *puruṣa-adān*—the Rākṣasas, man-eaters; *anuvrataḥ*—following in their footsteps.

TRANSLATION

Śukadeva Gosvāmī continued: O best of the Kuru dynasty, Kaṁsa was fiercely cruel and was actually a follower of the Rākṣasas. Therefore he could be neither pacified nor terrified by the good instructions given by Vasudeva. He did not care about the results of sinful activities, either in this life or in the next.

TEXT 47

निर्बन्धं तस्य तं ज्ञात्वा विचिन्त्यानकदुन्दुभिः ।
प्राप्तं कालं प्रतिव्योढुमिदं तत्रान्वपद्यत ॥४७॥

nirbandhaṁ tasya taṁ jñātvā
vicintyānakadundubhiḥ
prāptaṁ kālaṁ prativyoḍhum
idaṁ tatrānvapadyata

nirbandham—determination to do something; *tasya*—of him (Kaṁsa); *tam*—that (determination); *jñātvā*—understanding; *vicintya*—thinking deeply; *ānakadundubhiḥ*—Vasudeva; *prāptam*—had arrived; *kālam*—imminent danger of death; *prativyoḍhum*—to stop him from such activities; *idam*—this; *tatra*—thereupon; *anvapadyata*—thought of other ways.

TRANSLATION

When Vasudeva saw that Kaṁsa was determined to kill his sister Devakī, he thought to himself very deeply. Considering the imminent danger of death, he thought of another plan to stop Kaṁsa.

PURPORT

Although Vasudeva saw the imminent danger that his wife Devakī would be killed, he was convinced of his welfare because at his birth the demigods had played drums and kettledrums. He therefore attempted another way to save Devakī.

TEXT 48

मृत्युर्बुद्धिमतापोह्यो यावद्बुद्धिबलोदयम् ।
यद्यसौ न निवर्तेत नापराधोऽस्ति देहिनः ॥४८॥

mṛtyur buddhimatāpohyo
yāvad buddhi-balodayam
yady asau na nivarteta
nāparādho 'sti dehinaḥ

mṛtyuḥ—death; *buddhi-matā*—by an intelligent person; *apohyaḥ*—should be avoided; *yāvat*—as long as; *buddhi-bala-udayam*—intelligence and bodily strength are present; *yadi*—if; *asau*—that (death); *na nivarteta*—cannot be checked; *na*—not; *aparādhaḥ*—offense; *asti*—there is; *dehinaḥ*—of the person in danger of death.

TRANSLATION

As long as he has intelligence and bodily strength, an intelligent person must try to avoid death. This is the duty of every embodied person. But if death cannot be avoided in spite of one's endeavors, a person facing death commits no offense.

PURPORT

It is natural for a person facing untimely death to try his best to save himself. This is one's duty. Although death is sure, everyone should try to avoid it and not meet death without opposition because every living soul is by nature eternal. Because death is a punishment imposed in the condemned life of material existence, the Vedic culture is based on avoiding death (*tyaktvā dehaṁ punar janma naiti*). Everyone should try to avoid death and rebirth by cultivating spiritual life and should not submit to death without struggling to survive. One who is not trying to stop death is not an intelligent human being. Because Devakī was face to face with imminent death, it was Vasudeva's duty to save her, as he was trying his best to do. He therefore considered another way to approach Kaṁsa so that Devakī would be saved.

TEXTS 49–50

प्रदाय मृत्यवे पुत्रान् मोचये कृपणामिमाम् ।
सुता मे यदि जायेरन् मृत्युर्वा न म्रियेत चेत् ॥४९॥
विपर्ययो वा किं न स्याद् गतिर्धातुर्दुरत्यया ।
उपस्थितो निवर्तेत निवृत्तः पुनरापतेत् ॥५०॥

pradāya mṛtyave putrān
mocaye kṛpaṇām imām
sutā me yadi jāyeran
mṛtyur vā na mriyeta cet

viparyayo vā kiṁ na syād
gatir dhātur duratyayā
upasthito nivarteta
nivṛttaḥ punar āpatet

pradāya—promising to deliver; *mṛtyave*—unto Kaṁsa, who is death personified for Devakī; *putrān*—my sons; *mocaye*—I am releasing her from imminent danger; *kṛpaṇām*—innocent; *imām*—Devakī; *sutāḥ*—sons; *me*—my; *yadi*—whether; *jāyeran*—should take birth; *mṛtyuḥ*—Kaṁsa; *vā*—or; *na*—not; *mriyeta*—should die; *cet*—if; *viparyayaḥ*—just the opposite; *vā*—or; *kim*—whether; *na*—not; *syāt*—it may happen; *gatiḥ*—the movement; *dhātuḥ*—of providence; *duratyayā*—very difficult to understand; *upasthitaḥ*—that which is presently obtained; *nivarteta*—may stop; *nivṛttaḥ*—Devakī's death being stopped; *punaḥ āpatet*—in the future it may happen again (but what can I do).

TRANSLATION

Vasudeva considered: By delivering all my sons to Kaṁsa, who is death personified, I shall save the life of Devakī. Perhaps Kaṁsa will die before my sons take birth, or, since he is already destined

to die at the hands of my son, one of my sons may kill him. For the time being, let me promise to hand over my sons so that Kaṁsa will give up this immediate threat, and if in due course of time Kaṁsa dies, I shall have nothing to fear.

PURPORT

Vasudeva wanted to save the life of Devakī by promising to deliver his sons to Kaṁsa. "In the future," he thought, "Kaṁsa may die, or I may not beget any sons. Even if a son is born and I deliver him to Kaṁsa, Kaṁsa may die at his hands, for by providence anything could happen. It is very difficult to understand how things are managed by providence." Thus Vasudeva decided that he would promise to deliver his sons to the hands of Kaṁsa in order to save Devakī from the imminent danger of death.

TEXT 51

अग्नेर्यथा दारुवियोगयोगयो-
रदृष्टतोऽन्यन्न निमित्तमस्ति ।
एवं हि जन्तोरपि दुर्विभाव्यः
शरीरसंयोगवियोगहेतुः ॥५१॥

agner yathā dāru-viyoga-yogayor
adṛṣṭato 'nyan na nimittam asti
evaṁ hi jantor api durvibhāvyaḥ
śarīra-saṁyoga-viyoga-hetuḥ

agneḥ—of a fire in the forest; *yathā*—as; *dāru*—of wood; *viyoga-yogayoḥ*—of both the escaping and the capturing; *adṛṣṭataḥ*—than unseen providence; *anyat*—some other reason or accident; *na*—not; *nimittam*—a cause; *asti*—there is; *evam*—in this way; *hi*—certainly; *jantoḥ*—of the living being; *api*—indeed; *durvibhāvyaḥ*—cannot be found out; *śarīra*—of the body; *saṁyoga*—of the accepting; *viyoga*—or of the giving up; *hetuḥ*—the cause.

TRANSLATION

When a fire, for some unseen reason, leaps over one piece of wood and sets fire to the next, the reason is destiny. Similarly,

when a living being accepts one kind of body and leaves aside another, there is no other reason than unseen destiny.

PURPORT

When there is a fire in a village, the fire sometimes jumps over one house and burns another. Similarly, when there is a forest fire, the fire sometimes jumps over one tree and catches another. Why this happens, no one can say. One may set forth some imaginary reason why the nearest tree or house did not catch fire whereas a tree or house in a distant place did, but actually the reason is destiny. This reason also applies to the transmigration of the soul, by which a prime minister in one life may become a dog in the next. The work of unseen destiny cannot be ascertained by practical experimental knowledge, and therefore one must be satisfied by reasoning that everything is done by supreme providence.

TEXT 52

एवं विमृश्य तं पापं यावदात्मनिदर्शनम् ।
पूजयामास वै शौरिर्बहुमानपुरःसरम् ॥५२॥

evaṁ vimṛśya taṁ pāpaṁ
yāvad-ātmani-darśanam
pūjayām āsa vai śaurir
bahu-māna-puraḥsaram

evam—in this way; *vimṛśya*—after contemplating; *tam*—unto Kaṁsa; *pāpam*—the most sinful; *yāvat*—as far as possible; *ātmani-darśanam*—with all the intelligence possible within himself; *pūjayām āsa*—praised; *vai*—indeed; *śauriḥ*—Vasudeva; *bahu-māna*—offering all respect; *puraḥsaram*—before him.

TRANSLATION

After thus considering the matter as far as his knowledge would allow, Vasudeva submitted his proposal to the sinful Kaṁsa with great respect.

TEXT 53

प्रसन्नवदनाम्भोजो नृशंसं निरपत्रपम् ।
मनसा दूयमानेन विहसन्निदमब्रवीत् ॥५३॥

prasanna-vadanāmbhojo
nṛśaṁsaṁ nirapatrapam
manasā dūyamānena
vihasann idam abravīt

prasanna-vadana-ambhojaḥ—Vasudeva, who externally presented himself as if very happy; *nṛśaṁsam*—unto the most cruel; *nirapatrapam*—shameless Kaṁsa; *manasā*—with the mind; *dūyamānena*—which was full of anxiety and sorrow; *vihasan*—smiling externally; *idam abravīt*—and spoke as follows.

TRANSLATION

Vasudeva's mind was full of anxiety because his wife was facing danger, but in order to please the cruel, shameless and sinful Kaṁsa, he externally smiled and spoke to him as follows.

PURPORT

Sometimes one must act duplicitously in a dangerous position, as Vasudeva did to save his wife. The material world is complicated, and to execute one's duties, one cannot avoid adopting such diplomacy. Vasudeva did everything possible to save his wife for the sake of begetting Kṛṣṇa. This indicates that one may act duplicitously for the purpose of saving Kṛṣṇa and His interests. According to the arrangement already foretold, Kṛṣṇa was to appear through Vasudeva and Devakī to kill Kaṁsa. Vasudeva, therefore, had to do everything to save the situation. Although all the events were prearranged by Kṛṣṇa, a devotee must try his best to serve the purpose of Kṛṣṇa. Kṛṣṇa Himself is all-powerful, but it is not that a devotee should therefore sit idly and leave everything to Him. This instruction is also found in *Bhagavad-gītā*. Although Kṛṣṇa was doing everything for Arjuna, Arjuna never sat down idly as a nonviolent gentleman. Rather, he tried his best to fight the battle and be victorious.

TEXT 54

श्रीवसुदेव उवाच
न ह्यस्यास्ते भयं सौम्य यद् वै साहाशरीरवाक् ।
पुत्रान् समर्पयिष्येऽस्या यतस्ते भयमुत्थितम् ॥५४॥

śrī-vasudeva uvāca
na hy asyās te bhayaṁ saumya
yad vai sāhāśarīra-vāk
putrān samarpayiṣye 'syā
yatas te bhayam utthitam

śrī-vasudevaḥ uvāca—Śrī Vasudeva said; *na*—not; *hi*—indeed; *asyāḥ*—from Devakī; *te*—of you; *bhayam*—fear; *saumya*—O most sober; *yat*—which; *vai*—indeed; *sā*—that omen; *āha*—dictated; *a-śarīra-vāk*—a vibration without a body; *putrān*—all my sons; *samarpayiṣye*—I shall deliver to you; *asyāḥ*—of her (Devakī); *yataḥ*—from whom; *te*—your; *bhayam*—fear; *utthitam*—has arisen.

TRANSLATION

Vasudeva said: O best of the sober, you have nothing to fear from your sister Devakī because of what you have heard from the unseen omen. The cause of death will be her sons. Therefore I promise that when she gives birth to the sons from whom your fear has arisen, I shall deliver them all unto your hands.

PURPORT

Kaṁsa feared Devakī's existence because after her eighth pregnancy she would give birth to a son who would kill him. Vasudeva, therefore, to assure his brother-in-law the utmost safety, promised to bring him all the sons. He would not wait for the eighth son, but from the very beginning would deliver to the hands of Kaṁsa all the sons to which Devakī would give birth. This was the most liberal proposition offered by Vasudeva to Kaṁsa.

TEXT 55

श्रीशुक उवाच
स्वसुर्वधान्निववृते कंसस्तद्वाक्यसारवित् ।
वसुदेवोऽपि तं प्रीतः प्रशस्य प्राविशद् गृहम् ॥५५॥

śrī-śuka uvāca
svasur vadhān nivavṛte
kaṁsas tad-vākya-sāra-vit
vasudevo 'pi taṁ prītaḥ
praśasya prāviśad gṛham

śrī-śukaḥ uvāca—Śrī Śukadeva Gosvāmī said; *svasuḥ*—of his sister (Devakī); *vadhāt*—from the act of killing; *nivavṛte*—stopped for the time being; *kaṁsaḥ*—Kaṁsa; *tat-vākya*—the words of Vasudeva; *sāra-vit*—knowing to be perfectly correct; *vasudevaḥ*—Vasudeva; *api*—also; *tam*—to him (Kaṁsa); *prītaḥ*—being satisfied; *praśasya*—pacifying more; *prāviśat gṛham*—entered his own house.

TRANSLATION

Śrīla Śukadeva Gosvāmī continued: Kaṁsa agreed to the logical arguments of Vasudeva, and, having full faith in Vasudeva's words, he refrained from killing his sister. Vasudeva, being pleased with Kaṁsa, pacified him further and entered his own house.

PURPORT

Although Kaṁsa was a sinful demon, he believed that Vasudeva would never deviate from his word. The character of a pure devotee like Vasudeva is such that even so great a demon as Kaṁsa firmly believed in his words and was satisfied. *Yasyāsti bhaktir bhagavaty akiñcanā sarvair guṇais tatra samāsate surāḥ* (*Bhāg.* 5.18.12). All good attributes are present in a devotee, so much so that even Kaṁsa believed in Vasudeva's words without a doubt.

TEXT 56

अथ काल उपावृत्ते देवकी सर्वदेवता ।
पुत्रान् प्रसुषुवे चाष्टौ कन्यां चैवानुवत्सरम् ॥५६॥

atha kāla upāvṛtte
devakī sarva-devatā
putrān prasuṣuve cāṣṭau
kanyāṁ caivānuvatsaram

atha—thereafter; *kāle*—in due course of time; *upāvṛtte*—when it was ripe; *devakī*—Devakī, the wife of Vasudeva, Kṛṣṇa's father; *sarva-devatā*—Devakī, to whom all the demigods and God Himself appeared; *putrān*—sons; *prasuṣuve*—gave birth to; *ca*—and; *aṣṭau*—eight; *kanyāṁ ca*—and one daughter named Subhadrā; *eva*—indeed; *anuvatsaram*—year after year.

TRANSLATION

Each year thereafter, in due course of time, Devakī, the mother of God and all the demigods, gave birth to a child. Thus she bore eight sons, one after another, and a daughter named Subhadrā.

PURPORT

The spiritual master is sometimes glorified as *sarva-devamayo guruḥ* (*Bhāg.* 11.7.27). By the grace of the *guru*, the spiritual master, one can understand the different kinds of *devas.* The word *deva* refers to God, the Supreme Personality of Godhead, who is the original source of all the demigods, who are also called *devas.* In *Bhagavad-gītā* (10.2) the Lord says, *aham ādir hi devānām:* "I am the source of all the *devas.*" The Supreme Lord, Viṣṇu, the Original Person, expands in different forms. *Tad aikṣata bahu syām* (*Chāndogya Upaniṣad* 6.2.3). He alone has expanded into many. *Advaitam acyutam anādim ananta-rūpam* (*Brahma-saṁhitā* 5.33). There are different grades of forms, known as *svāṁśa* and *vibhinnāṁśa.* The *svāṁśa* expansions, or *viṣṇu-tattva,* are the Supreme Personality of Godhead, whereas the *vibhinnāṁśa* are *jīva-tattva,* who are part and parcel of the Lord (*mamaivāṁśo jīva-loke jīva-bhūtaḥ sanātanaḥ*). If we accept Kṛṣṇa as the Supreme Personality of Godhead and worship Him, all the parts and expansions of the Lord are automatically worshiped. *Sarvārhaṇam acyutejyā* (*Bhāg.* 4.31.14). Kṛṣṇa is known as Acyuta (*senayor ubhayor madhye rathaṁ sthāpaya me 'cyuta*). By worshiping Acyuta, Kṛṣṇa, one automatically worships all the demigods. There is no need of separately worshiping either the *viṣṇu-tattva* or *jīva-tattva.* If one concentrates upon Kṛṣṇa, one worships everyone. Therefore, because mother Devakī gave birth to Kṛṣṇa, she is described here as *sarva-devatā.*

TEXT 57

कीर्तिमन्तं प्रथमजं कंसायानकदुन्दुभिः ।
अर्पयामास कृच्छ्रेण सोऽनृतादतिविह्वलः ॥५७॥

kīrtimantaṁ prathamajaṁ
kaṁsāyānakadundubhiḥ
arpayām āsa kṛcchreṇa
so 'nṛtād ativihvalaḥ

kīrtimantam—by the name Kīrtimān; *prathama-jam*—the first-born baby; *kaṁsāya*—unto Kaṁsa; *ānakadundubhiḥ*—Vasudeva; *arpayām āsa*—delivered; *kṛcchreṇa*—with great pain; *saḥ*—he (Vasudeva); *anṛtāt*—from the breaking of the promise, or from fear of being a liar; *ati-vihvalaḥ*—was very much disturbed, being afraid.

TRANSLATION

Vasudeva was very much disturbed by fear of becoming a liar by breaking his promise. Thus with great pain he delivered his first-born son, named Kīrtimān, into the hands of Kaṁsa.

PURPORT

In the Vedic system, as soon as a child is born, especially a male child, the father calls for learned *brāhmaṇas,* and according to the description of the child's horoscope, the child is immediately given a name. This ceremony is called *nāma-karaṇa.* There are ten different *saṁskāras,* or reformatory methods, adopted in the system of *varṇāśrama-dharma,* and the name-giving ceremony is one of them. Although Vasudeva's first son was to be delivered into the hands of Kaṁsa, the *nāma-karaṇa* ceremony was performed, and thus the child was named Kīrtimān. Such names are given immediately after birth.

TEXT 58

किं दुःसहं नु साधूनां विदुषां किमपेक्षितम् ।
किमकार्यं कदर्याणां दुस्त्यजं किं धृतात्मनाम् ॥५८॥

kiṁ duḥsahaṁ nu sādhūnāṁ
viduṣāṁ kim apekṣitam
kim akāryaṁ kadaryāṇāṁ
dustyajaṁ kiṁ dhṛtātmanām

kim—what is; *duḥsaham*—painful; *nu*—indeed; *sādhūnām*—for saintly persons; *viduṣām*—of learned persons; *kim apekṣitam*—what is dependence; *kim akāryam*—what is forbidden work; *kadaryāṇām*—of persons in the lowest grade; *dustyajam*—very difficult to give up; *kim*—what is; *dhṛta-ātmanām*—of persons who are self-realized.

TRANSLATION

What is painful for saintly persons who strictly adhere to the truth? How could there not be independence for pure devotees who know the Supreme Lord as the substance? What deeds are forbidden for persons of the lowest character? And what cannot be given up for the sake of Lord Kṛṣṇa by those who have fully surrendered at His lotus feet?

PURPORT

Since the eighth son of Devakī was to kill Kaṁsa, one might ask what the need was for Vasudeva to deliver the first-born child. The answer is that Vasudeva had promised Kaṁsa that he would deliver all the children born of Devakī. Kaṁsa, being an *asura*, did not believe that the eighth child would kill him; he took it for granted that he might be killed by any of the children of Devakī. Vasudeva, therefore, to save Devakī, promised to give Kaṁsa every child, whether male or female. From another point of view, Vasudeva and Devakī were very pleased when they understood that the Supreme Personality of Godhead, Kṛṣṇa, would come as their eighth son. Vasudeva, a pure devotee of the Lord, was eager to see Kṛṣṇa appear as his child from the eighth pregnancy of

Devakī. Therefore he wanted to deliver all the children quickly so that the eighth turn would come and Kṛṣṇa would appear. He begot one child every year so that Kṛṣṇa's turn to appear would come as soon as possible.

TEXT 59

दृष्ट्वा समत्वं तच्छौरेः सत्ये चैव व्यवस्थितिम् ।
कंसस्तुष्टमना राजन् प्रहसन्निदमब्रवीत् ॥५९॥

dṛṣṭvā samatvaṁ tac chaureḥ
satye caiva vyavasthitim
kaṁsas tuṣṭa-manā rājan
prahasann idam abravīt

dṛṣṭvā—by seeing; *samatvam*—being equipoised, undisturbed in distress or happiness; *tat*—that; *śaureḥ*—of Vasudeva; *satye*—in truthfulness; *ca*—indeed; *eva*—certainly; *vyavasthitim*—the firm situation; *kaṁsaḥ*—Kaṁsa; *tuṣṭa-manāḥ*—being very satisfied (with Vasudeva's behavior in delivering the first child to keep his promise); *rājan*—O Mahārāja Parīkṣit; *prahasan*—with a smiling face; *idam*—this; *abravīt*—said.

TRANSLATION

My dear King Parīkṣit, when Kaṁsa saw that Vasudeva, being situated in truthfulness, was completely equipoised in giving him the child, he was very happy. Therefore, with a smiling face, he spoke as follows.

PURPORT

The word *samatvam* is very significant in this verse. *Samatvam* refers to one who is always equipoised, unaffected by either happiness or distress. Vasudeva was so steadily equipoised that he did not seem in the least agitated when delivering his first-born child into the hands of Kaṁsa to be killed. In *Bhagavad-gītā* (2.56) it is said, *duḥkheṣv anudvigna-manāḥ sukheṣu vigata-spṛhaḥ.* In the material world, one should not be very eager to be happy, nor should one be very much disturbed by material distress. Lord Kṛṣṇa advised Arjuna:

mātrā-sparśās tu kaunteya
śītoṣṇa-sukha-duḥkha-dāḥ
āgamāpāyino 'nityās
tāṁs titikṣasva bhārata

"O son of Kuntī, the nonpermanent appearance of happiness and distress, and their disappearance in due course, are like the appearance and disappearance of winter and summer seasons. They arise from sense perception, O scion of Bharata, and one must learn to tolerate them without being disturbed." (Bg. 2.14) The self-realized soul is never disturbed by so-called distress or happiness, and this is especially true of an exalted devotee like Vasudeva, who showed this by his practical example. Vasudeva was not at all disturbed when delivering his first child to Kaṁsa to be killed.

TEXT 60

प्रतियातु कुमारोऽयं न ह्यस्मादस्ति मे भयम् ।
अष्टमाद् युवयोर्गर्भान्मृत्युर्मे विहितः किल ॥६०॥

pratiyātu kumāro 'yaṁ
na hy asmād asti me bhayam
aṣṭamād yuvayor garbhān
mṛtyur me vihitaḥ kila

pratiyātu—my dear Vasudeva, take back your child and go home; *kumāraḥ*—newborn child; *ayam*—this; *na*—not; *hi*—indeed; *asmāt*—from him; *asti*—there is; *me*—my; *bhayam*—fear; *aṣṭamāt*—from the eighth; *yuvayoḥ*—of both you and your wife; *garbhāt*—from the pregnancy; *mṛtyuḥ*—death; *me*—my; *vihitaḥ*—has been ordained; *kila*—indeed.

TRANSLATION

O Vasudeva, you may take back your child and go home. I have no fear of your first child. It is the eighth child of you and Devakī I am concerned with because that is the child by whom I am destined to be killed.

TEXT 61

तथेति सुतमादाय ययावानकदुन्दुभिः ।
नाभ्यनन्दत तद्वाक्यमसतोऽविजितात्मनः ॥६१॥

tatheti sutam ādāya
yayāv ānakadundubhiḥ
nābhyanandata tad-vākyam
asato 'vijitātmanaḥ

tathā—very well; *iti*—thus; *sutam ādāya*—taking back his child; *yayau*—left that place; *ānakadundubhiḥ*—Vasudeva; *na abhyanandata*—did not very much value; *tat-vākyam*—the words (of Kaṁsa); *asataḥ*—who was without character; *avijita-ātmanaḥ*—and without self-control.

TRANSLATION

Vasudeva agreed and took his child back home, but because Kaṁsa had no character and no self-control, Vasudeva knew that he could not rely on Kaṁsa's word.

TEXTS 62–63

नन्दाद्या ये व्रजे गोपा याश्चामीषां च योषितः ।
वृष्णयो वसुदेवाद्या देवक्याद्या यदुस्त्रियः ॥६२॥
सर्वे वै देवताप्राया उभयोरपि भारत ।
ज्ञातयो बन्धुसुहृदो ये च कंसमनुव्रताः ॥६३॥

nandādyā ye vraje gopā
yāś cāmīṣāṁ ca yoṣitaḥ
vṛṣṇayo vasudevādyā
devaky-ādyā yadu-striyaḥ

sarve vai devatā-prāyā
ubhayor api bhārata
jñātayo bandhu-suhṛdo
ye ca kaṁsam anuvratāḥ

nanda-ādyāḥ—beginning from Nanda Mahārāja; *ye*—all of which persons; *vraje*—in Vṛndāvana; *gopāḥ*—the cowherd men; *yāḥ*—which; *ca*—and; *amīṣām*—of all those (inhabitants of Vṛndāvana); *ca*—as well as; *yoṣitaḥ*—the women; *vṛṣṇayaḥ*—members of the Vṛṣṇi family; *vasudeva-ādyāḥ*—headed by Vasudeva; *devakī-ādyāḥ*—headed by Devakī; *yadu-striyaḥ*—all the women of the Yadu dynasty; *sarve*—all of them; *vai*—indeed; *devatā-prāyāḥ*—were inhabitants of heaven; *ubhayoḥ*—of both Nanda Mahārāja and Vasudeva; *api*—indeed; *bhārata*—O Mahārāja Parīkṣit; *jñātayaḥ*—the relatives; *bandhu*—friends; *suhṛdaḥ*—well-wishers; *ye*—all of whom; *ca*—and; *kaṁsam anuvratāḥ*—even though apparently followers of Kaṁsa.

TRANSLATION

The inhabitants of Vṛndāvana, headed by Nanda Mahārāja and including his associate cowherd men and their wives, were none but denizens of the heavenly planets, O Mahārāja Parīkṣit, best of the descendants of Bharata, and so too were the descendants of the Vṛṣṇi dynasty, headed by Vasudeva, and Devakī and the other women of the dynasty of Yadu. The friends, relatives and well-wishers of both Nanda Mahārāja and Vasudeva and even those who externally appeared to be followers of Kaṁsa were all demigods.

PURPORT

As previously discussed, the Supreme Personality of Godhead, Viṣṇu, informed Lord Brahmā that Lord Kṛṣṇa would personally descend to mitigate the suffering on the earth. The Lord ordered all the denizens of the heavenly planets to take birth in different families of the Yadu and Vṛṣṇi dynasties and in Vṛndāvana. Now this verse informs us that all the family and friends of the Yadu dynasty, the Vṛṣṇi dynasty, Nanda Mahārāja and the *gopas* descended from the heavenly planets to see the pastimes of the Lord. As confirmed in *Bhagavad-gītā* (4.8), the Lord's pastimes consist of *paritrāṇāya sādhūnāṁ vināśāya ca duṣkṛtām*—saving the devotees and killing the demons. To demonstrate these activities, the Lord called for devotees from different parts of the universe.

There are many devotees who are elevated to the higher planetary systems.

prāpya puṇya-kṛtāṁ lokān
uṣitvā śāśvatīḥ samāḥ
śucīnāṁ śrīmatāṁ gehe
yoga-bhraṣṭo 'bhijāyate

"The unsuccessful *yogī*, after many, many years of enjoyment on the planets of the pious living entities, is born into a family of righteous people, or into a family of rich aristocracy." (Bg. 6.41) Some devotees, having failed to complete the process of devotional service, are promoted to the heavenly planets, to which the pious are elevated, and after enjoying there they may be directly promoted to the place where the Lord's pastimes are going on. When Lord Kṛṣṇa was to appear, the denizens of the heavenly planets were invited to see the pastimes of the Lord, and thus it is stated here that the members of the Yadu and Vṛṣṇi dynasties and the inhabitants of Vṛndāvana were demigods or almost as good as demigods. Even those who externally helped the activities of Kaṁsa belonged to the higher planetary systems. The imprisonment and release of Vasudeva and the killing of various demons were all manifestations of the pastimes of the Lord, and because the devotees would be pleased to see these activities personally, they were all invited to take birth as friends and relatives of these families. As confirmed in the prayers of Kuntī (*Bhāg.* 1.8.19), *naṭo nāṭya-dharo yathā.* The Lord was to play the part of a demon-killer, and a friend, son and brother to His devotees, and thus these devotees were all summoned.

TEXT 64

एतत् कंसाय भगवाञ्छशंसाभ्येत्य नारदः ।
भूमेर्भारायमाणानां दैत्यानां च वधोद्यमम् ॥६४॥

etat kaṁsāya bhagavāñ
chaśaṁsābhyetya nāradaḥ
bhūmer bhārāyamāṇānāṁ
daityānāṁ ca vadhodyamam

etat—all these words about the Yadu family and Vṛṣṇi family; *kaṁsāya*—unto King Kaṁsa; *bhagavān*—the most powerful representative of the Supreme Personality of Godhead; *śaśaṁsa*—informed (Kaṁsa, who was in doubt); *abhyetya*—after approaching him; *nāradaḥ*—the great sage Nārada; *bhūmeḥ*—on the surface of the earth; *bhārāyamāṇānām*—of those who were a burden; *daityānām ca*—and of the demons; *vadha-udyamam*—the endeavor to kill.

TRANSLATION

Once the great saint Nārada approached Kaṁsa and informed him of how the demoniac persons who were a great burden on the earth were going to be killed. Thus Kaṁsa was placed into great fear and doubt.

PURPORT

It has already been discussed that mother earth implored Lord Brahmā to give her relief from the distress created by the burdensome demons and that Lord Brahmā informed her that Lord Kṛṣṇa Himself was going to appear. Kṛṣṇa says in *Bhagavad-gītā* (4.8):

paritrāṇāya sādhūnāṁ
vināśāya ca duṣkṛtām
dharma-saṁsthāpanārthāya
sambhavāmi yuge yuge

Whenever there is a burden created by the demons and whenever the innocent devotees are distressed by demoniac rulers, the Lord appears in due course of time to kill the demons with the assistance of His real representatives, who are technically called demigods. In the *Upaniṣads* it is stated that the demigods are different parts of the Supreme Personality of Godhead. As it is the duty of the parts of the body to serve the whole, it is the duty of Kṛṣṇa's devotees to serve Kṛṣṇa as He wants. Kṛṣṇa's business is to kill the demons, and therefore this should be a devotee's business also. Because the people of Kali-yuga are fallen, however, Śrī Caitanya Mahāprabhu, out of kindness for them, did not bring any weapon to kill them. Rather, by spreading Kṛṣṇa consciousness, love of Kṛṣṇa, He wanted to kill their nefarious, demoniac activities. This is the purpose of the Kṛṣṇa consciousness movement. Unless the demoniac activities on the surface of the world are diminished or vanquished, no one can be happy. The program for the conditioned soul is fully described in *Bhagavad-gītā*, and one simply has to follow these instructions to become happy. Śrī Caitanya Mahāprabhu has therefore prescribed:

harer nāma harer nāma
harer nāmaiva kevalam
kalau nāsty eva nāsty eva
nāsty eva gatir anyathā

Let people chant the Hare Kṛṣṇa *mantra* constantly. Then their demoniac tendencies will be killed, and they will become first-class devotees, happy in this life and in the next.

TEXTS 65–66

ऋषेर्विनिर्गमे कंसो यदून् मत्वा सुरानिति ।
देवक्या गर्भसम्भूतं विष्णुं च स्ववधं प्रति ॥६५॥
देवकीं वसुदेवं च निगृह्य निगडैर्गृहे ।
जातं जातमहन् पुत्रं तयोरजनशङ्कया ॥६६॥

ṛṣer vinirgame kaṁso
yadūn matvā surān iti
devakyā garbha-sambhūtaṁ
viṣṇuṁ ca sva-vadhaṁ prati

devakīṁ vasudevaṁ ca
nigṛhya nigaḍair gṛhe
jātaṁ jātam ahan putraṁ
tayor ajana-śaṅkayā

ṛṣeḥ—of the great sage Nārada; *vinirgame*—on the departure (after giving information); *kaṁsaḥ*—Kaṁsa; *yadūn*—all the members of the Yadu dynasty; *matvā*—thinking of; *surān*—as demigods; *iti*—thus; *devakyāḥ*—of Devakī; *garbha-sambhūtam*—the children born from the womb; *viṣṇum*—(accepting) as Viṣṇu; *ca*—and; *sva-vadham prati*—fearing his own death from Viṣṇu; *devakīm*—Devakī; *vasudevam ca*—and her husband, Vasudeva; *nigṛhya*—arresting; *nigaḍaiḥ*—by iron shackles; *gṛhe*—confined at home; *jātam jātam*—each one who was born, one after another; *ahan*—killed; *putram*—the sons; *tayoḥ*—of Vasudeva and Devakī; *ajana-śaṅkayā*—with the doubt that they would be Viṣṇu.

TRANSLATION

After the departure of the great saint Nārada, Kaṁsa thought that all the members of the Yadu dynasty were demigods and that any of the children born from the womb of Devakī might be Viṣṇu. Fearing his death, Kaṁsa arrested Vasudeva and Devakī and chained them with iron shackles. Suspecting each of the children to be Viṣṇu, Kaṁsa killed them one after another because of the prophecy that Viṣṇu would kill him.

PURPORT

Śrīla Jīva Gosvāmī, in his notes on this verse, has mentioned how Nārada Muni gave Kaṁsa this information. This incident is described in the *Hari-vaṁśa.* Nārada Muni went to see Kaṁsa by providence, and Kaṁsa received him very well. Nārada, therefore, informed him that any one of the sons of Devakī might be Viṣṇu. Because Viṣṇu was to kill him, Kaṁsa should not spare any of Devakī's children, Nārada Muni advised. Nārada's intention was that Kaṁsa, by killing the children, would increase his sinful activities so that Kṛṣṇa would soon appear to kill him. Upon receiving the instructions of Nārada Muni, Kaṁsa killed all the children of Devakī one after another.

The word *ajana-śaṅkayā* indicates that Lord Viṣṇu never takes birth (*ajana*) and that He therefore appeared as Kṛṣṇa, taking birth just like a human being (*mānuṣīṁ tanum āśritam*). Kaṁsa attempted to kill all the babies born of Devakī and Vasudeva, although he knew that if Viṣṇu were born, He would not be killed. Actually it came to pass that when Viṣṇu appeared as Kṛṣṇa, Kaṁsa could not kill Him; rather, as foretold, it was He who killed Kaṁsa. One should know in truth how Kṛṣṇa, who takes His birth transcendentally, acts to kill the demons but is never killed. When one perfectly understands Kṛṣṇa in this way, through the medium of *śāstra*, one becomes immortal. As the Lord says in *Bhagavad-gītā* (4.9):

janma karma ca me divyam
evaṁ yo vetti tattvataḥ
tyaktvā dehaṁ punar janma
naiti mām eti so 'rjuna

"One who knows the transcendental nature of My appearance and activities does not, upon leaving the body, take his birth again in this material world, but attains My eternal abode, O Arjuna."

TEXT 67

मातरं पितरं भ्रातॄन् सर्वांश्च सुहृदस्तथा ।
घ्नन्ति ह्यसुतृपो लुब्धा राजानः प्रायशो भुवि ॥६७॥

mātaraṁ pitaraṁ bhrātṝn
sarvāṁś ca suhṛdas tathā
ghnanti hy asutṛpo lubdhā
rājānaḥ prāyaśo bhuvi

mātaram—unto the mother; *pitaram*—unto the father; *bhrātṝn*—unto brothers; *sarvān ca*—and anyone else; *suhṛdaḥ*—friends; *tathā*—as well as; *ghnanti*—they kill (as it is practically seen); *hi*—indeed; *asutṛpaḥ*—those who envy the lives of others for their personal sense gratification; *lubdhāḥ*—greedy; *rājānaḥ*—such kings; *prāyaśaḥ*—almost always; *bhuvi*—on the earth.

TRANSLATION

Kings greedy for sense gratification on this earth almost always kill their enemies indiscriminately. To satisfy their own whims, they may kill anyone, even their mothers, fathers, brothers or friends.

PURPORT

We have seen in the history of India that Aurangzeb killed his brother and nephews and imprisoned his father to fulfill political ambitions.

There have been many similar instances, and Kaṁsa was the same type of king. Kaṁsa did not hesitate to kill his nephews and imprison his sister and his father. For demons to do such things is not astonishing. Nonetheless, although Kaṁsa was a demon, he was aware that Lord Viṣṇu cannot be killed, and thus he attained salvation. Even partial understanding of the activities of Lord Viṣṇu makes one eligible for salvation. Kaṁsa knew a little about Kṛṣṇa—that He could not be killed—and therefore he attained salvation although he thought of Viṣṇu, Kṛṣṇa, as an enemy. What then is to be said of one who knows Kṛṣṇa perfectly from the descriptions of *śāstras* like *Bhagavad-gītā?* It is therefore the duty of everyone to read *Bhagavad-gītā* and understand Kṛṣṇa perfectly. This will make one's life successful.

TEXT 68

आत्मानमिह सञ्जातं जानन् प्राग् विष्णुना हतम् ।
महासुरं कालनेमिं यदुभिः स व्यरुध्यत ॥६८॥

ātmānam iha sañjātaṁ
jānan prāg viṣṇunā hatam
mahāsuraṁ kālanemiṁ
yadubhiḥ sa vyarudhyata

ātmānam—personally; *iha*—in this world; *sañjātam*—born again; *jānan*—understanding well; *prāk*—previously, before this birth; *viṣṇunā*—by Lord Viṣṇu; *hatam*—was killed; *mahā-asuram*—a great demon; *kālanemim*—by the name Kālanemi; *yadubhiḥ*—with the members of the Yadu dynasty; *saḥ*—he (Kaṁsa); *vyarudhyata*—acted inimically.

TRANSLATION

In his previous birth, Kaṁsa had been a great demon named Kālanemi and been killed by Viṣṇu. Upon learning this information from Nārada, Kaṁsa became envious of everyone connected with the Yadu dynasty.

PURPORT

Persons who are demons, enemies of the Supreme Personality of Godhead, are called *asuras.* As stated in *Bhagavad-gītā*, the *asuras*, because of their enmity toward the Supreme Personality of Godhead, take birth after birth in *asura* families and therefore glide down to the darkest hellish regions.

TEXT 69

उग्रसेनं च पितरं यदुभोजान्धकाधिपम् ।
स्वयं निगृह्य बुभुजे शूरसेनान् महाबलः ॥६९॥

ugrasenaṁ ca pitaraṁ
yadu-bhojāndhakādhipam
svayaṁ nigṛhya bubhuje
śūrasenān mahā-balaḥ

ugrasenam—unto Ugrasena; *ca*—and; *pitaram*—who was his own father; *yadu*—of the Yadu dynasty; *bhoja*—of the Bhoja dynasty; *andhaka*—of the Andhaka dynasty; *adhipam*—the king; *svayam*—personally; *nigṛhya*—subduing; *bubhuje*—enjoyed; *śūrasenān*—all the states known as Śūrasena; *mahā-balaḥ*—the extremely powerful Kaṁsa.

TRANSLATION

Kaṁsa, the most powerful son of Ugrasena, even imprisoned his own father, the King of the Yadu, Bhoja and Andhaka dynasties, and personally ruled the states known as Śūrasena.

PURPORT

The state known as Mathurā was also included within the states known as Śūrasena.

ADDITIONAL NOTES FOR THIS CHAPTER

Regarding transmigration of the soul, Śrīla Madhvācārya gives the following notes. When one is awake, whatever one sees or hears is impressed upon the mind, which later works in dreams to show one different experiences, although in dreams one appears to accept a different body. For example, when one is awake one does business and talks with customers, and similarly in dreams one meets various customers, talks about business and gives quotations. Madhvācārya says, therefore, that dreams take place according to what one sees, hears and remembers. When one reawakens, of course, one forgets the body of the dream. This forgetfulness is called *apasmṛti.* Thus we are changing bodies because we are sometimes dreaming, sometimes awake and sometimes forgetful. Forgetfulness of our previously created body is called death, and our work in the present body is called life. After death, one cannot remember the activities of one's previous body, whether imaginary or factual.

The agitated mind is compared to agitated water reflecting the sun and the moon. Actually the sun and moon reflected on the water do not exist there; nonetheless, they are reflected according to the movements of the water. Similarly, when our minds are agitated, we wander in different material atmospheres and receive different types of bodies. This is described in *Bhagavad-gītā* as *guṇa-saṅga. Kāraṇaṁ guṇa-saṅgo 'sya.* Madhvācārya says, *guṇānubaddhaḥ san.* And Śrī Caitanya Mahāprabhu says, *brahmāṇḍa bhramite kona bhāgyavān jīva* (Cc. *Madhya* 19.151). The living entity rotates up and down throughout the universe, sometimes in the upper planetary system, sometimes in the middle and lower planetary systems, sometimes as a man, sometimes a god, a dog, a tree and so on. This is all due to the agitation of the mind. The mind must therefore be steadily fixed. As it is said, *sa vai manaḥ kṛṣṇa-padāravindayoḥ.* One should fix one's mind at the lotus feet of Kṛṣṇa, and then one will become free from agitation. This is the instruction of the *Garuḍa Purāṇa*, and in the *Nāradīya Purāṇa* the same process is described. As stated in *Bhagavad-gītā, yānti deva-vratā devān.* The agitated mind goes to different planetary systems because it is attached to different kinds of demigods, but one does not go to the abode of the Supreme Personality of Godhead by worshiping the demigods, for this is not supported by any Vedic literature. Man is the architect of his own fortune. In this human life one has the facility with which to understand one's real situation, and one can decide whether to wander around the universe forever or return home, back to Godhead. This is also confirmed in *Bhagavad-gītā* (*aprāpya māṁ nivartante mṛtyu-saṁsāra-vartmani*).

There is no such thing as chance. When a tree is burning in a forest fire and although the nearest tree is spared a distant tree catches fire, this may appear to be chance. Similarly, one may seem to get different types of bodies by chance, but actually one receives these bodies because of the mind. The mind flickers between accepting and rejecting, and according to the acceptance and rejection of the mind, we receive different types of bodies, although we superficially seem to obtain these bodies by chance. Even if we accept the theory of chance, the immediate cause for the change of body is the agitation of the mind.

Notes on *aṁśa*. This chapter describes that Kṛṣṇa appeared *aṁśena*, with His parts and parcels or His partial manifestation. In this connection, Śrīdhara Svāmī says that Kṛṣṇa is one hundred percent Bhagavān (*kṛṣṇas tu bhagavān svayam*). Because of our imperfections, however, we cannot appreciate Kṛṣṇa in fullness, and therefore whatever Kṛṣṇa exhibited when present on earth was but a partial manifestation of His opulence. Again, Kṛṣṇa appeared with His plenary expansion Baladeva. Kṛṣṇa, however, is full; there is no question of His appearing partially. In the *Vaiṣṇava-toṣaṇī*, Śrīla Sanātana Gosvāmī says that to accept that Kṛṣṇa was partially manifested would contradict the statement *kṛṣṇas tu bhagavān svayam*. Śrīla Jīva Gosvāmī says that the word *aṁśena* means that Kṛṣṇa appeared with all His plenary expansions. The words *aṁśena viṣṇoḥ* do not mean that Kṛṣṇa is a partial representative of Viṣṇu. Rather, Kṛṣṇa appeared in fullness, and He manifests Himself partially in the Vaikuṇṭhalokas. In other words, Lord Viṣṇu is a partial representation of Kṛṣṇa; Kṛṣṇa is not a partial representation of Viṣṇu. In the *Caitanya-caritāmṛta, Ādi-līlā*, Chapter Four, this subject matter is explained very clearly. Śrīla Viśvanātha Cakravartī Ṭhākura also notes that no one can describe Kṛṣṇa in fullness. Whatever descriptions we find in *Śrīmad-Bhāgavatam* are partial explanations of Kṛṣṇa. In conclusion, therefore, the word *aṁśena* indicates that Lord Viṣṇu is a partial representation of Kṛṣṇa, not that Kṛṣṇa is a partial representation of Viṣṇu.

Śrīla Sanātana Gosvāmī's *Vaiṣṇava-toṣaṇī* has explained the word *dharma-śīlasya*. The exact meaning of *dharma-śīla* is "an unadulterated devotee." Real *dharma* consists of full surrender to Kṛṣṇa (*sarva-dharmān parityajya mām ekaṁ śaraṇaṁ vraja*). One who has fully surrendered to Kṛṣṇa is actually religious. One such religious person was Mahārāja Parīkṣit. Anyone who accepts the principle of surrender to the lotus feet of the Lord, giving up all other systems of religion, is actually *dharma-śīla*, perfectly religious.

The word *nivṛtta-tarṣaiḥ* refers to one who no longer has any material desires (*sarvopādhi-vinirmuktam*). One may have many material desires because of contamination in this material world, but when one is completely free from all material desires, he is called *nivṛtta-tṛṣṇa*, which indicates that he no longer has any thirst for material enjoyment. *Svāmin kṛtārtho 'smi varaṁ na yāce* (*Hari-bhakti-sudhodaya*). Materialistic persons want some material profit from executing devotional service, but this is not the purpose of service. The perfection of devotional service lies in complete surrender unto the lotus feet of Kṛṣṇa, with no material desires. One who surrenders in this way is already liberated. *Jīvan-muktaḥ sa ucyate.* One who is always busy serving Kṛṣṇa, in whatever condition he may live, is understood to be liberated even in this life. Such a person, who is a pure devotee, does not need to change his body; indeed, he does not possess a material body, for his body has already been spiritualized. An iron rod kept constantly within a fire will ultimately become fire, and whatever it touches will burn. Similarly, the pure devotee is in the fire of spiritual existence, and therefore his body is *cin-maya;* that is, it is spiritual, not material, because the pure devotee has no desire but the transcendental desire to serve the Lord. In text four the word *upagīyamānāt* is used: *nivṛtta-tarṣair upagīyamānāt.* Who will chant the glories of the Lord unless he is a devotee? Therefore the word *nivṛtta-tarṣaiḥ* indicates the devotee, and no one else. These are the remarks of *ācāryas* like Vīrarāghava Ācārya and Vijayadhvaja. To desire anything other than devotional service will diminish one's freedom from material desires, but when one is free from all such desires one is called *nivṛtta-tarṣaiḥ*.

Vinā paśu-ghnāt. The word *paśu* means "animal." An animal killer, *paśu-ghna*, cannot enter into Kṛṣṇa consciousness. In our Kṛṣṇa consciousness movement, therefore, animal killing is completely prohibited.

Uttamaśloka-guṇānuvādāt. The word *uttamaśloka* means "one who is famous as the best of those who are good." The Lord is good in all circumstances. That is His natural reputation. His goodness is unlimited, and He uses it unlimitedly. A devotee is also sometimes described as *uttamaśloka*, meaning that he is eager to glorify the Supreme Personality of Godhead or the Lord's devotees. Glorifying the Lord and glorifying the Lord's devotees are the same. Or, rather, glorifying the devotee is more important than glorifying the Lord directly. Narottama dāsa Ṭhākura explains this fact: *chāḍiyā vaiṣṇava-sevā, nistāra pāyeche kebā.* One cannot be liberated from material contamination without sincerely serving a devotee of Kṛṣṇa.

Bhavauṣadhāt means "from the universal remedy." Chanting the holy name and glorifying the Supreme Lord are the universal remedy for all the miseries of materialistic life. Persons who desire to be freed from this material world are called *mumukṣu.* Such persons can understand the miseries of materialistic life, and by glorifying the activities of the Lord they can be released from all these miseries. The transcendental sound vibrations concerning the Lord's name, fame, form, qualities and paraphernalia are all nondifferent from the Lord. Therefore the very sound vibration of the Lord's glorification and name are pleasing to the ears, and by understanding the absolute nature of the Lord's name, form and qualities the devotee becomes joyful. Even those who are not devotees, however, enjoy the pleasing narrations of the Lord's transcendental activities. Even ordinary persons not very much advanced in Kṛṣṇa consciousness take pleasure in describing the narrations depicted in *Śrīmad-Bhāgavatam.* When a materialistic person is purified in this way, he engages in hearing and chanting the glories of the Lord. Because glorification of the Lord's pastimes is very pleasing to the ear and heart of the devotee, it is simultaneously his subject and object.

In this world there are three kinds of men: those who are liberated, those trying to be liberated, and those entangled in sense enjoyment. Of these three, those who are already liberated chant and hear the holy name of the Lord, knowing perfectly that to glorify the Lord is the only way to keep oneself in a transcendental position. Those who are trying to be liberated, the second class, may regard the chanting and hearing of the Lord's holy name as a process of liberation, and they too will feel the transcendental pleasure of this chanting. As for *karmīs* and persons engaged in sense gratification, they also may take pleasure in hearing the pastimes of the Lord, like His fighting on the Battlefield of Kurukṣetra and His dancing in Vṛndāvana with the *gopīs.*

The word *uttamaśloka-guṇānuvāda* refers to the transcendental qualities of the Supreme Lord, such as His affection for mother Yaśodā and His friends the cowherd boys and His loving attitude toward the *gopīs*. The Lord's devotees like Mahārāja Yudhiṣṭhira are also described by the qualification *uttamaśloka-guṇānuvāda*. The word *anuvāda* refers to describing the qualities of the Supreme Lord or His devotees. When these qualities are described, other devotees are interested in hearing them. The more one is interested in hearing about these transcendental qualities, the more one transcendentally enjoys. Everyone, therefore, including the *mumukṣus*, the *vimuktas* and the *karmīs*, should chant and hear the glories of the Lord, and in this way everyone will benefit.

Although the sound vibration of the transcendental qualities of the Lord is equally beneficial to all, for those who are *muktas*, liberated, it is especially pleasing. As described in *Śrīmad-Bhāgavatam*, Eighth Canto, Third Chapter, verse twenty, because pure devotees, who no longer have any material desires, surrender fully to the lotus feet of the Lord, they always merge in the ocean of bliss by chanting and hearing the Lord's holy name. According to this verse, devotees like Nārada and other residents of Śvetadvīpa are seen always engaged in chanting the holy name of the Lord because by such chanting they are always externally and internally blissful. The *mumukṣus*, persons desiring to be liberated, do not depend on the pleasures of the senses; instead, they concentrate fully on becoming liberated by chanting the holy name of the Lord. *Karmīs* like to create something pleasing to their ears and hearts, and although they sometimes like to chant or hear the glories of the Lord, they do not do it openly. Devotees, however, always spontaneously hear, chant about and remember the activities of the Lord, and by this process they are fully satisfied, even though these may seem like topics of sense gratification. Simply by hearing the transcendental narrations of the Lord's activities, Parīkṣit Mahārāja was liberated. He was therefore *śrotramano-'bhirāma*; that is, he glorified the process of hearing. This process should be accepted by all living entities.

To distinguish persons who are bereft of these transcendental pleasures, Parīkṣit Mahārāja has used the words *virajyeta pumān*. The word *pumān* refers to any person, whether man, woman or in-between. Because of the bodily conception of life, we are subject to lamentation, but one who has no such bodily conceptions can take pleasure in transcendental hearing and chanting. Therefore a person fully absorbed in the bodily concept of life is surely killing himself by not making spiritual progress. Such a person is called *paśu-ghna*. Especially excluded from spiritual life are the animal hunters, who are not interested in hearing and chanting the holy name of the Lord. Such hunters are always unhappy, both in this life and in the next. It is therefore said that a hunter should neither die nor live because for such persons both living and dying are troublesome. Animal hunters are completely different from ordinary *karmīs*, and thus they have been excluded from the process of hearing and chanting. *Vinā paśu-ghnāt.* They cannot enter into the transcendental pleasure of chanting and hearing the holy name of the Lord.

The word *mahā-ratha* refers to a great hero who can fight alone against eleven thousand other heroes, and the word *atiratha*, as found in text five, refers to one who can fight against an unlimited number. This is mentioned in the *Mahābhārata* as follows:

ekādaśa-sahasrāṇi
yodhayed yas tu dhanvinām
astra-śastra-pravīṇaś ca
mahā-ratha iti smṛtaḥ
amitān yodhayed yas tu
samprokto 'tirathas tu saḥ

This is the description given in the *Bṛhad-vaiṣṇava-toṣaṇī* by Śrīla Sanātana Gosvāmī.

Māyā-manuṣyasya (10.1.17). Because of being covered by *yogamāyā* (*nāhaṁ prakāśaḥ sarvasya yogamāyā-samāvṛtaḥ*), Kṛṣṇa is sometimes called *māyā-manuṣya*, indicating that although He is the Supreme Personality of Godhead, He appears like an ordinary person. A misunderstanding arises because *yogamāyā* covers the vision of the general public. The Lord's position is actually different from that of an ordinary person, for although He appears to act like an ordinary man, He is always transcendental. The word *māyā* also indicates "mercy," and sometimes it also means "knowledge." The Lord is always full of all transcendental knowledge, and therefore although He acts like a human being, He is the Supreme Personality of Godhead, full of knowledge. In His original identity, the Lord is the controller of *māyā* (*mayādhyakṣeṇa prakṛtiḥ sūyate sa-carācaram*). Therefore the Lord may be called *māyā-manuṣya*, or the Supreme Personality of Godhead playing like an ordinary human being, although He is the controller of both the material and spiritual energies. The Lord is the Supreme Person, Puruṣottama, but because we are deluded by *yogamāyā,* He appears to be an ordinary person. Ultimately, however, *yogamāyā* induces even a nondevotee to understand the Lord as the Supreme Person, Puruṣottama. In *Bhagavad-gītā* we find two statements given by the Supreme Personality of Godhead. For the devotees, the Lord says:

teṣāṁ satata-yuktānāṁ
bhajatāṁ prīti-pūrvakam
dadāmi buddhi-yogaṁ taṁ
yena mām upayānti te

"To those who are constantly devoted and worship Me with love, I give the understanding by which they can come to Me." (Bg. 10.10) Thus for the willing devotee the Lord gives intelligence by which to understand Him and return home, back to Godhead. For others, for nondevotees, the Lord says, *mṛtyuḥ sarva-haraś cāham:* "I am all-plundering, inevitable death." A devotee like Prahlāda enjoys the activities of Lord Nṛsiṁhadeva, whereas nondevotees like Prahlāda's father, Hiraṇyakaśipu, meet death before Lord Nṛsiṁhadeva. The Lord therefore acts in two ways, by sending some onto the path of repeated birth and death and sending others back home, back to Godhead.

The word *kāla,* meaning "black," indicates the color of the Supreme Personality of Godhead, Kṛṣṇa. Lord Kṛṣṇa and Lord Rāmacandra, who both look blackish, give liberation and transcendental bliss to Their devotees. Among persons possessing material bodies, sometimes someone is able to subject death to his own will. For such a person, death is almost impossible because no one wants to die. But although Bhīṣmadeva possessed this power, Bhīṣma, by the supreme will of the Lord, died very easily in the Lord's presence. There have also been many demons who had no hope of salvation, yet Kaṁsa attained salvation by the supreme will of the Lord. Not to speak of Kaṁsa, even Pūtanā attained salvation and reached the level of the Lord's mother. Parīkṣit Mahārāja, therefore, was very eager to hear about the Lord, who has inconceivable qualities by which to give liberation to anyone. Parīkṣit Mahārāja, at the point of his death, was certainly interested in his liberation. When such a great and exalted personality as the Lord behaves like an ordinary human being although possessing inconceivable qualities, His behavior is called *māyā*. Therefore the Lord is described as *māyā-manuṣya*. This is the opinion of Śrīla Jīva Gosvāmī. *Mu* refers to *mukti*, or salvation, and *ku* refers to that which is bad or very obnoxious. Thus *muku* refers to the Supreme Personality of Godhead, who saves one from the bad condition of material existence. The Lord is called *mukunda* because He not only saves the devotee from material existence but offers him transcendental bliss in love and service.

As for Keśava, *ka* means Brahmā, and *īśa* means Lord Śiva. The Personality of Godhead captivates both Lord Brahmā and Lord Mahādeva, or Śiva, by His transcendental qualities. Therefore He is called Keśava. This opinion is given by Sanātana Gosvāmī in his *Vaiṣṇava-toṣaṇī* commentary.

It is said that all the demigods, accompanied by Tri-nayana, Lord Śiva, went to the shore of the ocean of milk and offered their prayers through the *mantra* known as *Puruṣa-sūkta*. From this statement it is understood that the demigods cannot directly approach Lord Viṣṇu, who lies on the ocean of milk, or enter His abode. This is also clearly stated in the *Mahābhārata*, *Mokṣa-dharma*, and the next chapter of *Śrīmad-Bhāgavatam*. Kṛṣṇa, the Supreme Personality of Godhead, has His abode in Goloka (*goloka-nāmni nija-dhāmni tale ca tasya*). From Lord Kṛṣṇa come the *catur-vyūha*, the quadruple expansions Saṅkarṣaṇa, Aniruddha, Pradyumna and Vāsudeva. There are innumerable *brahmāṇḍas*, all of which emanate from the pores of Kāraṇodakaśāyī Viṣṇu, and in every *brahmāṇḍa* there is a Garbhodakaśāyī Viṣṇu, who is a partial expansion of Aniruddha. This Aniruddha is a partial expansion of Pradyumna, who is partially represented as Kṣīrodakaśāyī Viṣṇu, the Supersoul of all living entities. These Viṣṇu expansions are different from Kṛṣṇa, who resides in Goloka Vṛndāvana. When it is said that the demigods offered prayers to the Lord by chanting the *Puruṣa-sūkta*, this indicates that they pleased the Lord by enunciating prayers of *bhakti*.

The word *vṛṣākapi* refers to one who satisfies His devotee in every way and frees His devotee from all material anxieties. *Vṛṣa* refers to religious performances like sacrifices. Even without the execution of sacrifices, the Lord can still enjoy the supermost comforts of the heavenly planets. The statement that Puruṣottama, Jagannātha, would appear in the house of

Vasudeva distinguishes the Supreme Personality of Godhead from ordinary persons. The statement that He personally appeared indicates that He did not send His plenary expansion. The word *priyārtham* indicates that the Lord appeared to please Rukmiṇī and Rādhārāṇī. *Priyā* means "the most beloved."

In the commentary of Śrī Vīrarāghava Ācārya, the following extra verse is accepted after text twenty-three:

ṛṣayo 'pi tad-ādeśāt
kalpyantāṁ paśu-rūpiṇaḥ
payo-dāna-mukhenāpi
viṣṇuṁ tarpayituṁ surāḥ

"O demigods, even great sages, following the order of Viṣṇu, appeared in the forms of cows and calves to please the Supreme Personality of Godhead by delivering milk."

Rāmānujācārya sometimes accepts Baladeva as a *śaktyāveśa-avatāra*, but Śrīla Jīva Gosvāmī has explained that Baladeva is an expansion of Kṛṣṇa and that a part of Baladeva is Saṅkarṣaṇa. Although Baladeva is identical with Saṅkarṣaṇa, He is the origin of Saṅkarṣaṇa. Therefore the word *svarāṭ* has been used to indicate that Baladeva always exists in His own independence. The word *svarāṭ* also indicates that Baladeva is beyond the material conception of existence. *Māyā* cannot attract Him, but because He is fully independent, He can appear by His spiritual potency wherever He likes. *Māyā* is fully under the control of Viṣṇu. Because the material potency and *yogamāyā* mingle in the Lord's appearance, they are described as *ekānaṁśā*. Sometimes *ekānaṁśā* is interpreted to mean "without differentiation." Saṅkarṣaṇa and Śeṣa-nāga are identical. As stated by Yamunādevī, "O Rāma, O great-armed master of the world, who have extended Yourself throughout the entire universe by one plenary expansion, it is not possible to understand You fully." Therefore *ekāṁśā* refers to Śeṣa-nāga. In other words, Baladeva, merely by His partial expansion, sustains the entire universe.

The word *kāryārthe* refers to one who attracted the pregnancy of Devakī and bewildered mother Yaśodā. These pastimes are very confidential. The Supreme Personality of Godhead ordered *yogamāyā* to bewilder His associates in His pastimes and bewilder demons like Kaṁsa.

As stated previously, *yogamāyāṁ samādiśat.* To give service to the Lord, *yogamāyā* appeared along with *mahāmāyā. Mahāmāyā* refers to *yayā sammohitaṁ jagat,* "one who bewilders the entire material world." From this statement it is to be understood that *yogamāyā,* in her partial expansion, becomes *mahāmāyā* and bewilders the conditioned souls. In other words, the entire creation has two divisions—transcendental, or spiritual, and material. *Yogamāyā* manages the spiritual world, and by her partial expansion as *mahāmāyā* she manages the material world. As stated in the *Nārada-pañcarātra, mahāmāyā* is a partial expansion of *yogamāyā.* The *Nārada-pañcarātra* clearly states that the Supreme Personality has one potency, which is sometimes described as Durgā. The *Brahma-saṁhitā* says, *chāyeva yasya bhuvanāni bibharti durgā.* Durgā is not different from *yogamāyā.* When one understands Durgā properly, he is immediately liberated, for Durgā is originally the spiritual potency, *hlādinī-śakti,* by whose mercy one can understand the Supreme Personality of Godhead very easily. *Rādhā kṛṣṇa-praṇaya-vikṛtir hlādinī-śaktir asmād.* The *mahāmāyā-śakti,* however, is a covering of *yogamāyā,* and she is therefore called the covering potency. By this covering potency, the entire material world is bewildered (*yayā sammohitaṁ jagat*). In conclusion, bewildering the conditioned souls and liberating the devotees are both functions belonging to *yogamāyā.* Transferring the pregnancy of Devakī and keeping mother Yaśodā in deep sleep were both done by *yogamāyā; mahāmāyā* cannot act upon such devotees, for they are always liberated. But although it is not possible for *mahāmāyā* to control liberated souls or the Supreme Personality of Godhead, she did bewilder Kaṁsa. The action of *yogamāyā* in presenting herself before Kaṁsa was the action of *mahāmāyā,* not *yogamāyā. Yogamāyā* cannot even see or touch such polluted persons as Kaṁsa. In *Caṇḍī,* in the *Mārkaṇḍeya Purāṇa,* Eleventh Chapter, Mahāmāyā says, "During the twenty-eighth *yuga* in the period of Vaivasvata Manu, I shall take birth as the daughter of Yaśodā and be known as Vindhyācala-vāsinī."

The distinction between the two *māyās—yogamāyā* and *mahāmāyā*—is described as follows. Kṛṣṇa's *rāsa-līlā* with the *gopīs* and the *gopīs'* bewilderment in respect to their husbands, fathers-in-law and other such relatives were arrangements of *yogamāyā* in which *mahāmāyā* had no influence. The *Bhāgavatam* gives sufficient evidence of this when it clearly says, *yogamāyām upāśritaḥ*. On the other hand, there were *asuras* headed by Śālva and *kṣatriyas* like Duryodhana who were bereft of devotional service in spite of seeing Kṛṣṇa's carrier Garuḍa and the universal form, and who could not understand Kṛṣṇa to be the Supreme Personality of Godhead. This was also bewilderment, but this bewilderment was due to *mahāmāyā*. Therefore it is to be concluded that the *māyā* which drags a person from the Supreme Personality of Godhead is called *jaḍamāyā*, and the *māyā* which acts on the transcendental platform is called *yogamāyā*. When Nanda Mahārāja was taken away by Varuṇa, he saw Kṛṣṇa's opulence, but nonetheless he thought of Kṛṣṇa as his son. Such feelings of parental love in the spiritual world are acts of *yogamāyā*, not of *jaḍamāyā*, or *mahāmāyā*. This is the opinion of Śrīla Viśvanātha Cakravartī Ṭhākura.

Śūrasenāṁś ca. The son of Kārtavīryārjuna was Śūrasena, and the countries he ruled were also called Śūrasena. This is noted by Sanātana Gosvāmī in his *Vaiṣṇava-toṣaṇī* commentary.

In regard to Mathurā, we find this quotation:

mathyate tu jagat sarvaṁ
brahma-jñānena yena vā
tat-sāra-bhūtaṁ yad yasyāṁ
mathurā sā nigadyate

When a self-realized soul acts in his transcendental position, his situation is called Mathurā. In other words, when one acts in the process of *bhakti-yoga*, he may live anywhere, but actually he lives in Mathurā, Vṛndāvana. Devotion to Kṛṣṇa, the son of Nanda Mahārāja, is the essence of all knowledge, and wherever such knowledge is manifested is called Mathurā. Also, when one establishes *bhakti-yoga*, excluding all other methods, one's situation is called Mathurā. *Yatra nityaṁ sannihito hariḥ:* the place where Hari, the Supreme Personality of Godhead, lives eternally is called Mathurā. The word *nitya* indicates eternality. The Supreme Lord is eternal, and His abode is also eternal. *Goloka eva nivasaty akhilātma-bhūtaḥ.* Although the Lord is always stationed in His abode, Goloka Vṛndāvana, He is present everywhere in fullness. This means that when the Supreme Lord descends on the surface of the world, His original abode is not vacant, for He can remain in His original abode and simultaneously descend upon Mathurā, Vṛndāvana, Ayodhyā and other places. He does not need to descend, since He is already present there; He simply manifests Himself.

Śrīla Śukadeva Gosvāmī has addressed Mahārāja Parīkṣit as *tāta*, or "beloved son." This is due to parental love in the heart of Śukadeva Gosvāmī. Because Kṛṣṇa was soon coming as the son of Vasudeva and Devakī, out of parental affection Śukadeva Gosvāmī addressed Mahārāja Parīkṣit as *tāta*, "my dear son."

In the *Viśva-kośa* dictionary, the word *garbha* is explained: *garbho bhrūṇe arbhake kukṣāv ity ādi.* When Kaṁsa was about to kill Devakī, Vasudeva wanted to dissuade him by the diplomacy of *sāma* and *bheda.* *Sāma* means "pacifying." Vasudeva wanted to pacify Kaṁsa by indicating relations, gain, welfare, identity and glorification. Reference to these five concerns constitutes *sāma*, and Vasudeva's presentation of fear in two situations—in this life and the next—is called *bheda.* Thus Vasudeva used both *sāma* and *bheda* to pacify Kaṁsa. Praising Kaṁsa's qualifications was glorification, and praising him as a descendant of the *bhoja-vaṁśa* appealed to *sambandha*, relationship. Speaking of "your sister" was an appeal to identity. Speaking about killing a woman raises questions about fame and welfare, and arousing fear of the sinful act of killing one's sister during her marriage ceremony is an aspect of *bheda.* The Bhoja dynasty refers to those who were simply interested in sense gratification and were therefore not very aristocratic. Another meaning of *bhoja* is "fighting." These were indications of defamation for Kaṁsa. When Vasudeva addressed Kaṁsa as *dīna-vatsala*, this was excessive praise. Kaṁsa would accept calves as a form of revenue from his poor constituents, and therefore he was called *dīna-vatsala.* Vasudeva knew very well that he could not by force rescue Devakī from the imminent danger. Devakī was actually the daughter of Kaṁsa's uncle, and therefore she is described as *suhṛt*, meaning "relative." It is stated that Kaṁsa refrained from killing his close relation Devakī because if he had killed her, a great fight would have ensued among the other members of the family. Kaṁsa refrained from provoking this great danger of a family fight, for it would have caused many persons to lose their lives.

Formerly an *asura* named Kālanemi had six sons, named Haṁsa, Suvikrama, Krātha, Damana, Ripurmardana and Krodhahantā. They were known as the *ṣaḍ-garbhas*, or six *garbhas*, and they were all equally powerful and expert in military affairs. These *ṣaḍ-garbhas* gave up the association of Hiraṇyakaśipu, their grandfather, and underwent great austerities to satisfy Lord Brahmā, who, upon being satisfied, agreed to give them whatever benediction they might desire. When asked by Lord Brahmā to state what they wanted, the *ṣaḍ-garbhas* replied, "Dear Lord Brahmā, if you want to give us a benediction, give us the blessing that we will not be killed by any demigod, *mahā-roga*, Yakṣa, Gandharva-pati, Siddha, Cāraṇa or human being, nor by great sages who are perfect in their penances and austerities." Brahmā understood their purpose and fulfilled their desire. But when Hiraṇyakaśipu came to know of these events, he was very angry at his grandsons. "You have given up my association and have gone to worship Lord Brahmā," he said, "and therefore I no longer have any affection for you. You have tried to save yourselves from the hands of the demigods, but I curse you in this way: Your father will take birth as Kaṁsa and kill all of you because you will take birth as sons of Devakī." Because of this curse, the grandsons of Hiraṇyakaśipu had to take birth from the womb of Devakī and be killed by Kaṁsa, although he was previously their father. This description is mentioned in the *Hari-vaṁśa*, *Viṣṇu-parva*, Second Chapter. According to the comments of the *Vaiṣṇava-toṣaṇī*, the son of Devakī known as Kīrtimān was the third incarnation. In his first incarnation he was known as Smara and was the son of Marīci, and later he became the son of Kālanemi. This is mentioned in the histories.

An additional verse in this chapter of *Śrīmad-Bhāgavatam* is accepted by the Madhvācārya-sampradāya, represented by Vijayadhvaja Tīrtha. The verse is as follows:

atha kaṁsam upāgamya
nārado brahma-nandanaḥ
ekāntam upasaṅgamya
vākyam etad uvāca ha

atha—in this way; *kaṁsam*—unto Kaṁsa; *upāgamya*—after going; *nāradaḥ*—the great sage Nārada; *brahma-nandanaḥ*—who is the son of Brahmā; *ekāntam upasaṅgamya*—after going to a very solitary place;

vākyam—the following instruction; *etat*—this; *uvāca*—said; *ha*—in the past.

Translation: "Thereafter, Nārada, the mental son of Lord Brahmā, approached Kaṁsa and, in a very solitary place, informed him of the following news."

The great saint Nārada descended from the heavenly planets to the forest of Mathurā and sent his messenger to Kaṁsa. When the messenger approached Kaṁsa and informed him of Nārada's arrival, Kaṁsa, the leader of the *asuras*, was very happy and immediately came out of his palace to receive Nārada, who was as bright as the sun, as powerful as fire, and free from all tinges of sinful activities. Kaṁsa accepted Nārada as his guest, offered him respectful obeisances and gave him a golden seat, brilliant like the sun. Nārada was a friend of the King of heaven, and thus he told Kaṁsa, the son of Ugrasena, "My dear hero, you have satisfied me with a proper reception, and therefore I shall tell you something secret and confidential. While I was coming here from Nandakānana through the Caitraratha forest, I saw a great meeting of the demigods, who followed me to Sumeru Parvata. We traveled through many holy places, and finally we saw the holy Ganges. While Lord Brahmā was consulting the other demigods at the top of Sumeru Hill, I was also present with my stringed instrument, the *vīṇā*. I shall tell you confidentially that the meeting was held just to plan to kill the *asuras*, headed by you. You have a younger sister named Devakī, and it is a fact that her eighth son will kill you." (reference: *Hari-vaṁśa, Viṣṇu-parva* 1.2–16)

No one can blame Nāradajī for encouraging Kaṁsa to kill the sons of Devakī. The saint Nārada is always a well-wisher for human society, and he wanted the Supreme Personality of Godhead, Kṛṣṇa, to descend to this world as soon as possible so that the society of demigods would be pleased and would see Kaṁsa and his friends killed by Kṛṣṇa. Kaṁsa would also attain salvation from his nefarious activities, and this too would very much please the demigods and their followers. Śrīla Viśvanātha Cakravartī Ṭhākura remarks in this connection that Nārada Muni sometimes did things that were beneficial to the demigods and the demons simultaneously. Śrī Vīrarāghava Ācārya, in his commentary, has included the following half-verse in this regard: *asurāḥ sarva evaita lokopadrava-kāriṇaḥ. Asuras* are always disturbing elements for human society.

Thus end the Bhaktivedanta purports of the Tenth Canto, First Chapter, of the Śrīmad-Bhāgavatam, *entitled "The Advent of Lord Kṛṣṇa: Introduction."*

CHAPTER TWO

Prayers by the Demigods for Lord Kṛṣṇa in the Womb

As described in this chapter, when the Supreme Personality of Godhead entered the womb of Devakī to kill Kaṁsa, all the demigods understood that the Lord was living within Devakī's womb, and therefore in veneration they offered Him the *Garbha-stuti* prayers.

Kaṁsa, under the protection of his father-in-law, Jarāsandha, and with the help of his demoniac friends like Pralamba, Baka, Cāṇūra, Tṛṇāvarta, Aghāsura, Muṣṭika, Bāṇa and Bhaumāsura, began oppressing the members of the Yadu dynasty. Therefore, the members of the Yadu dynasty left their homes and sought shelter in such states as Kuru, Pañcāla, Kekaya, Śālva and Vidarbha. Only some of them stayed with Kaṁsa, as nominal friends.

After Kaṁsa killed the *ṣaḍ-garbhas*, the six sons of Devakī, one after another, Anantadeva entered Devakī's womb and was transferred to the womb of Rohiṇī by the manipulation of Yogamāyā, who was following the order of the Supreme Personality of Godhead. The Lord Himself, who was soon to appear as the eighth son of Devakī, ordered Yogamāyā to take birth from the womb of Yaśodādevī. Because Kṛṣṇa and His potency, Yogamāyā, appeared simultaneously as brother and sister, the world is full of Vaiṣṇavas and *śāktas*, and there is certainly some rivalry between them. Vaiṣṇavas worship the Supreme Lord, whereas *śaktas*, according to their desires, worship Yogamāyā in forms like Durgā, Bhadrakālī and Caṇḍikā. Following the orders of the Supreme Personality of Godhead, Yogamāyā transferred Baladeva, Saṅkarṣaṇa, the seventh child of Devakī, from the womb of Devakī to the womb of Rohiṇī. Because Saṅkarṣaṇa appears in order to increase love of Kṛṣṇa, He is known as Baladeva. One may take auspicious strength from Him to become a devotee of the Lord, and therefore He is also known as Balabhadra.

After Yogamāyā transferred the seventh child of Devakī to the womb of Rohiṇī, the Supreme Personality of Godhead appeared within the heart of Vasudeva and transferred Himself into the heart of Devakī. Because the Lord was present in her heart, Devakī, as her pregnancy continued, appeared effulgent. Upon seeing this effulgence, Kaṁsa was full of anxiety, but he could not harm Devakī because of their family relationship. Thus he began indirectly thinking of Kṛṣṇa and became fully Kṛṣṇa conscious.

Meanwhile, because of the Lord's presence within the womb of Devakī, all the demigods came to offer the Lord their prayers. The Supreme Personality of Godhead, they said, is eternally the Absolute Truth. The spiritual soul is more important than the gross body, and the Supersoul, Paramātmā, is still more important than the soul. The Supreme Godhead is absolutely independent, and His incarnations are transcendental. The prayers of the demigods glorify and exalt devotees and explain the fate of persons who superficially consider themselves liberated from the conditions of material nature. A devotee is always safe. When a devotee fully surrenders at the lotus feet of the Lord, he is completely liberated from the fear of material existence. By explaining why the Supreme Personality of Godhead descends, the prayers of the demigods clearly confirm the Lord's statement in *Bhagavad-gītā* (4.7):

yadā yadā hi dharmasya
glānir bhavati bhārata
abhyutthānam adharmasya
tadātmānaṁ sṛjāmy aham

"Whenever and wherever there is a decline in religious practice, O descendant of Bharata, and a predominant rise of irreligion—at that time I descend Myself."

TEXTS 1–2

श्रीशुक उवाच

प्रलम्बबकचाणूरतृणावर्तमहाशनैः ।
मुष्टिकारिष्टद्विविदपूतनाकेशिधेनुकैः ॥ १ ॥
अन्यैश्चासुरभूपालैर्बाणभौमादिभिर्युतः ।
यदूनां कदनं चक्रे बली मागधसंश्रयः ॥ २ ॥

śrī-śuka uvāca
pralamba-baka-cāṇūra-
tṛṇāvarta-mahāśanaiḥ
muṣṭikāriṣṭa-dvivida-
pūtanā-keśi-dhenukaiḥ

anyaiś cāsura-bhūpālair
bāṇa-bhaumādibhir yutaḥ
yadūnāṁ kadanaṁ cakre
balī māgadha-saṁśrayaḥ

śrī-śukaḥ uvāca—Śrī Śukadeva Gosvāmī said; *pralamba*—by the *asura* named Pralamba; *baka*—by the *asura* named Baka; *cāṇūra*—by the *asura* named Cāṇūra; *tṛṇāvarta*—by the *asura* named Tṛṇāvarta; *mahāśanaiḥ*—by Aghāsura; *muṣṭika*—by the *asura* named Muṣṭika; *ariṣṭa*—by the *asura* Ariṣṭa; *dvivida*—by the *asura* named Dvivida; *pūtanā*—by Pūtanā; *keśi*—by Keśī; *dhenukaiḥ*—by Dhenuka; *anyaiḥ ca*—and by many others; *asura-bhūpālaiḥ*—by demoniac kings on the surface of the globe; *bāṇa*—by King Bāṇa; *bhauma*—by Bhaumāsura; *ādibhiḥ*—and by others as well; *yutaḥ*—being assisted; *yadūnām*—of the kings of the Yadu dynasty; *kadanam*—persecution; *cakre*—regularly performed; *balī*—very powerful; *māgadha-saṁśrayaḥ*—under the protection of Jarāsandha, the King of Magadha.

TRANSLATION

Śukadeva Gosvāmī said: Under the protection of Magadharāja, Jarāsandha, the powerful Kaṁsa began persecuting the kings of the Yadu dynasty. In this he had the cooperation of demons like Pralamba, Baka, Cāṇūra, Tṛṇāvarta, Aghāsura, Muṣṭika, Ariṣṭa, Dvivida, Pūtanā, Keśī, Dhenuka, Bāṇāsura, Narakāsura and many other demoniac kings on the surface of the earth.

PURPORT

This verse supports the following statement given by the Lord in *Bhagavad-gītā* (4.7–8):

yadā yadā hi dharmasya
glānir bhavati bhārata
abhyutthānam adharmasya
tadātmānaṁ sṛjāmy aham

paritrāṇāya sādhūnāṁ
vināśāya ca duṣkṛtām
dharma-saṁsthāpanārthāya
sambhavāmi yuge yuge

"Whenever and wherever there is a decline in religious practice, O descendant of Bharata, and a predominant rise of irreligion—at that time I descend Myself. To deliver the pious and to annihilate the miscreants, as well as to reestablish the principles of religion, I advent Myself millennium after millennium."

The Lord's purpose in maintaining this material world is to give everyone a chance to go back home, back to Godhead, but kings and political leaders unfortunately try to hinder the purpose of the Lord, and therefore the Lord appears, either personally or with His plenary portions, to set things right. It is therefore said:

garbhaṁ sañcārya rohiṇyāṁ
devakyā yogamāyayā
tasyāḥ kukṣiṁ gataḥ kṛṣṇo
dvitīyo vibudhaiḥ stutaḥ

"Kṛṣṇa appeared in the womb of Devakī after transferring Baladeva to the womb of Rohiṇī by the power of Yogamāyā." *Yadubhiḥ sa vyarudhyata.* The kings of the Yadu dynasty were all devotees, but there were many powerful demons, such as Śālva, who began to persecute them. At that time, Jarāsandha, who was Kaṁsa's father-in-law, was extremely powerful, and therefore Kaṁsa took advantage of his protection and the help of the demons in persecuting the kings of the Yadu dynasty. The demons naturally appeared more powerful than the demigods, but ultimately, because of help received from the Supreme Personality of Godhead, the demons were defeated and the demigods triumphant.

TEXT 3

ते पीडिता निविविशुः कुरुपञ्चालकेकयान् ।
शाल्वान् विदर्भान् निषधान् विदेहान् कोशलानपि ॥३॥

te pīḍitā niviviśuḥ
kuru-pañcāla-kekayān
śālvān vidarbhān niṣadhān
videhān kośalān api

te—they (the kings of the Yadu dynasty); *pīḍitāḥ*—being persecuted; *niviviśuḥ*—took shelter or entered (the kingdoms); *kuru-pañcāla*—the countries occupied by the Kurus and Pañcālas; *kekayān*—the countries of the Kekayas; *śālvān*—the countries occupied by the Śālvas; *vidarbhān*—the countries occupied by the Vidarbhas; *niṣadhān*—the countries occupied by the Niṣadhas; *videhān*—the country of Videha; *kośalān api*—as well as the countries occupied by the Kośalas.

TRANSLATION

Persecuted by the demoniac kings, the Yadavas left their own kingdom and entered various others, like those of the Kurus, Pañcālas, Kekayas, Śālvas, Vidarbhas, Niṣadhas, Videhas and Kośalas.

TEXTS 4–5

एके तमनुरुन्धाना ज्ञातयः पर्युपासते ।
हतेषु षट्सु बालेषु देवक्या औग्रसेनिना ॥ ४ ॥
सप्तमो वैष्णवं धाम यमनन्तं प्रचक्षते ।
गर्भो बभूव देवक्या हर्षशोकविवर्धनः ॥ ५ ॥

eke tam anurundhānā
jñātayaḥ paryupāsate
hateṣu ṣaṭsu bāleṣu
devakyā augraseninā

saptamo vaiṣṇavaṁ dhāma
yam anantaṁ pracakṣate
garbho babhūva devakyā
harṣa-śoka-vivardhanaḥ

eke—some of them; *tam*—unto Kaṁsa; *anurundhānāḥ*—exactly following his policy; *jñātayaḥ*—relatives; *paryupāsate*—began to agree with him; *hateṣu*—having been killed; *ṣaṭsu*—six; *bāleṣu*—children; *devakyāḥ*—born of Devakī; *augraseninā*—by the son of Ugrasena (Kaṁsa); *saptamaḥ*—the seventh; *vaiṣṇavam*—of Lord Viṣṇu; *dhāma*—a plenary expansion; *yam*—unto whom; *anantam*—by the name Ananta; *pracakṣate*—is celebrated; *garbhaḥ*—embryo; *babhūva*—there was; *devakyāḥ*—of Devakī; *harṣa-śoka-vivardhanaḥ*—simultaneously arousing pleasure and lamentation.

TRANSLATION

Some of their relatives, however, began to follow Kaṁsa's principles and act in his service. After Kaṁsa, the son of Ugrasena, killed the six sons of Devakī, a plenary portion of Kṛṣṇa entered her womb as her seventh child, arousing her pleasure and her lamentation. That plenary portion is celebrated by great sages as Ananta, who belongs to Kṛṣṇa's second quadruple expansion.

PURPORT

Some of the chief devotees, such as Akrūra, stayed with Kaṁsa to satisfy him. This they did for various purposes. They all expected the Supreme Personality of Godhead to appear as the eighth child as soon as Devakī's other children were killed by Kaṁsa, and they were eagerly awaiting His appearance. By remaining in Kaṁsa's association, they would be able to see the Supreme Personality of Godhead take birth and display His childhood pastimes, and Akrūra would later go to Vṛndāvana to bring Kṛṣṇa and Balarāma to Mathurā. The word *paryupāsate* is significant because it indicates that some devotees wanted to stay near Kaṁsa in order to see all these pastimes of the Lord. The six children killed by Kaṁsa had formerly been sons of Marīci, but because of having been cursed by a *brāhmaṇa*, they were obliged to take birth as grandsons of Hiraṇyakaśipu. Kaṁsa had taken birth as Kālanemi, and now he was obliged to kill his own sons. This was a mystery. As soon as the sons of Devakī were killed, they would return to their original place. The devotees wanted to see this also. Generally speaking, no one kills his own nephews, but Kaṁsa was so cruel that he did so without hesitation. Ananta, Saṅkarṣaṇa, belongs to the second *catur-vyūha*, or quadruple expansion. This is the opinion of experienced commentators.

TEXT 6

भगवानपि विश्वात्मा विदित्वा कंसजं भयम् ।
यदूनां निजनाथानां योगमायां समादिशत् ॥ ६ ॥

bhagavān api viśvātmā
viditvā kaṁsajaṁ bhayam
yadūnāṁ nija-nāthānāṁ
yogamāyāṁ samādiśat

bhagavān—Śrī Kṛṣṇa, the Supreme Personality of Godhead; *api*—also; *viśvātmā*—who is the Supersoul of everyone; *viditvā*—understanding the position of the Yadus and His other devotees; *kaṁsa-jam*—because of Kaṁsa; *bhayam*—fear; *yadūnām*—of the Yadus; *nija-nāthānām*—who had accepted Him, the Supreme Lord, as their supreme shelter; *yogamāyām*—unto Yogamāyā, the spiritual potency of Kṛṣṇa; *samādiśat*—ordered as follows.

TRANSLATION

To protect the Yadus, His personal devotees, from Kaṁsa's attack, the Personality of Godhead, Viśvātmā, the Supreme Soul of everyone, ordered Yogamāyā as follows.

PURPORT

The words *bhagavān api viśvātmā viditvā kaṁsajaṁ bhayam* are commented upon by Śrīla Sanātana Gosvāmī. *Bhagavān svayam* is Kṛṣṇa (*kṛṣṇas tu bhagavān svayam*). He is Viśvātmā, the original Supersoul of everyone, because his plenary portion expands as the Supersoul. This is confirmed in *Bhagavad-gītā* (13.3): *kṣetra-jñaṁ cāpi māṁ viddhi sarva-kṣetreṣu bhārata.* Lord Kṛṣṇa is the *kṣetra-jña*, or Supersoul, of all living entities. He is the original source of all expansions of the Personality of Godhead. There are hundreds and thousands of plenary expansions of Viṣṇu, such as Saṅkarṣaṇa, Pradyumna, Aniruddha and Vāsudeva, but here in this material world, the Viśvātmā, the Supersoul for all living entities, is Kṣīrodakaśāyī Viṣṇu. As stated in *Bhagavad-gītā* (18.61), *īśvaraḥ sarva-bhūtānāṁ hṛd-deśe 'rjuna tiṣṭhati:* "The Supreme Lord is situated in the heart of all living entities, O Arjuna." Kṛṣṇa is actually Viśvātmā by His plenary expansion as *viṣṇu-tattva*, yet because of His affection for His devotees, He acts as Supersoul to give them directions (*sarvasya cāhaṁ hṛdi sanniviṣṭo mattaḥ smṛtir jñānam apohanaṁ ca*).

The affairs of the Supersoul pertain to Kṣīrodakaśāyī Viṣṇu, but Kṛṣṇa took compassion on Devakī, His devotee, because He understood her fear of Kaṁsa's persecution. A pure devotee is always fearful of material existence. No one knows what will happen next, for one may have to change his body at any moment (*tathā dehāntara-prāptiḥ*). Knowing this fact, a pure devotee acts in such a way that he will not have his life spoiled by being obliged to accept another body and undergo the tribulations of material existence. This is *bhayam*, or fear. *Bhayaṁ dvitīyābhiniveśataḥ syāt* (*Bhāg.* 11.2.37). This fear is due to material existence. Properly speaking, everyone should always be alert and fearful of material existence, but although everyone is prone to be affected by the ignorance of material existence, the Supreme Personality of Godhead, Kṛṣṇa, is always alert to the protection of His devotees. Kṛṣṇa is so kind and affectionate toward His devotees that He helps them by giving them the intelligence by which to exist in this material world without forgetting Him even for a moment. The Lord says:

teṣām evānukampārtham
aham ajñānajaṁ tamaḥ
nāśayāmy ātma-bhāvastho
jñāna-dīpena bhāsvatā

"Out of compassion for them, I, dwelling in their hearts, destroy with the shining lamp of knowledge the darkness born of ignorance." (Bg. 10.11)

The word *yoga* means "link." Any system of *yoga* is an attempt to reconnect our broken relationship with the Supreme Personality of Godhead. There are different types of *yoga*, of which *bhakti-yoga* is the best. In other *yoga* systems, one must undergo various processes before attaining perfection, but *bhakti-yoga* is direct. The Lord says in *Bhagavad-gītā* (6.47):

yoginām api sarveṣāṁ
mad-gatenāntarātmanā
śraddhāvān bhajate yo māṁ
sa me yuktatamo mataḥ

"Of all *yogīs*, he who always abides in Me with great faith, worshiping Me in transcendental loving service, is most intimately united with Me in *yoga* and is the highest of all." For the *bhakti-yogī*, a human body is guaranteed in his next existence, as stated by Lord Kṛṣṇa (*śucīnāṁ śrīmatāṁ gehe yoga-bhraṣṭo 'bhijāyate*). *Yogamāyā* is the spiritual potency of the Lord. Out of affection for His devotees, the Lord always stays in spiritual touch with them, although otherwise His *māyā* potency is so strong that she bewilders even exalted demigods like Brahmā. Therefore the Lord's potency is called *yogamāyā*. Since the Lord is Viśvātmā, He immediately ordered Yogamāyā to give protection to Devakī.

TEXT 7

गच्छ देवि व्रजं भद्रे गोपगोभिरलङ्कृतम् ।
रोहिणी वसुदेवस्य भार्यास्ते नन्दगोकुले ।
अन्याश्च कंससंविग्ना विवरेषु वसन्ति हि ॥ ७ ॥

gaccha devi vrajaṁ bhadre
gopa-gobhir alaṅkṛtam
rohiṇī vasudevasya
bhāryāste nanda-gokule
anyāś ca kaṁsa-saṁvignā
vivareṣu vasanti hi

gaccha—now go; *devi*—O you who are worshipable for the whole world; *vrajam*—to the land of Vraja; *bhadre*—O you who are auspicious for all living entities; *gopa-gobhiḥ*—with cowherds and cows; *alaṅkṛtam*—decorated; *rohiṇī*—by the name Rohiṇī; *vasudevasya*—of Vasudeva, Kṛṣṇa's father; *bhāryā*—one of the wives; *āste*—is living; *nanda-gokule*—in the estate of Nanda Mahārāja known as Gokula, where hundreds and thousands of cows are maintained; *anyāḥ ca*—and other wives; *kaṁsa-saṁvignāḥ*—being afraid of Kaṁsa; *vivareṣu*—in secluded places; *vasanti*—are living; *hi*—indeed.

TRANSLATION

The Lord ordered Yogamāyā: O My potency, who are worshipable for the entire world and whose nature is to bestow good fortune upon all living entities, go to Vraja, where there live many cowherd men and their wives. In that very beautiful land, where many cows reside, Rohiṇī, the wife of Vasudeva, is living at the home of Nanda Mahārāja. Other wives of Vasudeva are also living there incognito because of fear of Kaṁsa. Please go there.

PURPORT

Nanda-gokula, the residence of King Nanda, was itself very beautiful, and when Yogamāyā was ordered to go there and encourage the devotees with fearlessness, it became even more beautiful and safe. Because Yogamāyā had the ability to create such an atmosphere, the Lord ordered her to go to Nanda-gokula.

TEXT 8

देवक्या जठरे गर्भं शेषाख्यं धाम मामकम् ।
तत् संनिकृष्य रोहिण्या उदरे संनिवेशय ॥ ८ ॥

devakyā jaṭhare garbhaṁ
śeṣākhyaṁ dhāma māmakam
tat sannikṛṣya rohiṇyā
udare sanniveśaya

devakyāḥ—of Devakī; *jaṭhare*—within the womb; *garbham*—the embryo; *śeṣa-ākhyam*—known as Śeṣa, the plenary expansion of Kṛṣṇa;

dhāma—the plenary expansion; *māmakam*—of Me; *tat*—Him; *sannikṛṣya*—attracting; *rohiṇyāḥ*—of Rohiṇī; *udare*—within the womb; *sanniveśaya*—transfer without difficulty.

TRANSLATION

Within the womb of Devakī is My partial plenary expansion known as Saṅkarṣaṇa or Śeṣa. Without difficulty, transfer Him into the womb of Rohiṇī.

PURPORT

The first plenary expansion of Kṛṣṇa is Baladeva, also known as Śeṣa. The Śeṣa incarnation of the Supreme Personality of Godhead supports the entire universe, and the eternal mother of this incarnation is mother Rohiṇī. "Because I am going into the womb of Devakī," the Lord told Yogamāyā, "the Śeṣa incarnation has already gone there and made suitable arrangements so that I may live there. Now He should enter the womb of Rohiṇī, His eternal mother."

In this connection, one may ask how the Supreme Personality of Godhead, who is always situated transcendentally, could enter the womb of Devakī, which had previously been entered by the six *asuras*, the *ṣaḍ-garbhas*. Does this mean that the *ṣaḍ-garbhāsuras* were equal to the transcendental body of the Supreme Personality of Godhead? The following answer is given by Śrīla Viśvanātha Cakravartī Ṭhākura.

The entire creation, as well as its individual parts, is an expansion of the energy of the Supreme Personality of Godhead. Therefore, even though the Lord enters the material world, He does not do so. This is explained by the Lord Himself in *Bhagavad-gītā* (9.4–5):

mayā tatam idaṁ sarvaṁ
jagad avyakta-mūrtinā
mat-sthāni sarva-bhūtāni
na cāhaṁ teṣv avasthitaḥ

na ca mat-sthāni bhūtāni
paśya me yogam aiśvaram

bhūta-bhṛn na ca bhūta-stho
mamātmā bhūta-bhāvanaḥ

"By Me, in My unmanifested form, this entire universe is pervaded. All beings are in Me, but I am not in them. And yet everything that is created does not rest in Me. Behold My mystic opulence! Although I am the maintainer of all living entities, and although I am everywhere, My Self is the very source of creation." *Sarvaṁ khalv idaṁ brahma.* Everything is an expansion of Brahman, the Supreme Personality of Godhead, yet everything is not the Supreme Godhead, and He is not everywhere. Everything rests upon Him and yet does not rest upon Him. This can be explained only through the *acintya-bhedābheda* philosophy. Such truths cannot be understood, however, unless one is a pure devotee, for the Lord says in *Bhagavad-gītā* (18.55), *bhaktyā mām abhijānāti yāvān yaś cāsmi tattvataḥ:* "One can understand the Supreme Personality as He is only by devotional service." Even though the Lord cannot be understood by ordinary persons, this principle should be understood from the statement of the *śāstras.*

A pure devotee is always transcendentally situated because of executing nine different processes of *bhakti-yoga* (*śravaṇaṁ kīrtanaṁ viṣṇoḥ smaraṇaṁ pāda-sevenam/ arcanaṁ vandanaṁ dāsyaṁ sakhyam ātma-nivedanam*). Thus situated in devotional service, a devotee, although in the material world, is not in the material world. Yet a devotee always fears, "Because I am associated with the material world, so many contaminations affect me." Therefore he is always alert in fear, which gradually diminishes his material association.

Symbolically, mother Devakī's constant fear of Kaṁsa was purifying her. A pure devotee should always fear material association, and in this way all the *asuras* of material association will be killed, as the *ṣaḍ-garbhāsuras* were killed by Kaṁsa. It is said that from the mind, Marīci appears. In other words, Marīci is an incarnation of the mind. Marīci has six sons: Kāma, Krodha, Lobha, Moha, Mada and Mātsarya (lust, anger, greed, illusion, madness and envy). The Supreme Personality of Godhead appears in pure devotional service. This is confirmed in the *Vedas: bhaktir evainaṁ darśayati.* Only *bhakti* can bring one in contact with the Supreme Personality of Godhead. The Supreme Personality of Godhead appeared from the womb of Devakī, and therefore Devakī symbolically represents *bhakti*, and Kaṁsa symbolically represents material fear. When a pure devotee always fears material association, his real position of *bhakti* is manifested, and he naturally becomes uninterested in material enjoyment. When the six sons of Marīci are killed by such fear and one is freed from material contamination, within the womb of *bhakti* the Supreme Personality of Godhead appears. Thus the seventh pregnancy of Devakī signifies the appearance of the Supreme Personality of Godhead. After the six sons Kāma, Krodha, Lobha, Moha, Mada and Mātsarya are killed, the Śeṣa incarnation creates a suitable situation for the appearance of the Supreme Personality of Godhead. In other words, when one awakens his natural Kṛṣṇa consciousness, Lord Kṛṣṇa appears. This is the explanation given by Śrīla Viśvanātha Cakravartī Ṭhākura.

TEXT 9

अथाहमंशभागेन देवक्याः पुत्रतां शुभे ।
प्राप्स्यामि त्वं यशोदायां नन्दपत्न्यां भविष्यसि ॥९॥

athāham aṁśa-bhāgena
devakyāḥ putratāṁ śubhe
prāpsyāmi tvaṁ yaśodāyāṁ
nanda-patnyāṁ bhaviṣyasi

atha—therefore; *aham*—I; *aṁśa-bhāgena*—by My plenary expansion; *devakyāḥ*—of Devakī; *putratām*—the son; *śubhe*—O all-auspicious Yogamāyā; *prāpsyāmi*—I shall become; *tvam*—you; *yaśodāyām*—in the womb of mother Yaśodā; *nanda-patnyām*—in the wife of Mahārāja Nanda; *bhaviṣyasi*—shall also appear.

TRANSLATION

O all-auspicious Yogamāyā, I shall then appear with My full six opulences as the son of Devakī, and you will appear as the daughter of mother Yaśodā, the queen of Mahārāja Nanda.

PURPORT

The word *aṁśa-bhāgena* is important in this verse. In *Bhagavad-gītā* (10.42) the Lord says:

athavā bahunaitena
kim jñātena tavārjuna
viṣṭabhyāham idaṁ kṛtsnam
ekāṁśena sthito jagat

"But what need is there, Arjuna, for all this detailed knowledge? With a single fragment of Myself I pervade and support this entire universe." Everything is situated as a part of the Supreme Lord's potency. In regard to Lord Kṛṣṇa's appearance in the womb of Devakī, Brahmā played a part also because on the bank of the milk ocean he requested the Supreme Personality of Godhead to appear. A part was also played by Baladeva, the first expansion of Godhead. Similarly, Yogamāyā, who appeared as the daughter of mother Yaśodā, also played a part. Thus *jīva-tattva, viṣṇu-tattva* and *śakti-tattva* are all integrated with the Supreme Personality of Godhead, and when Kṛṣṇa appears, He appears with all His integrated parts. As explained in previous verses, Yogamāyā was requested to attract Saṅkarṣaṇa, Baladeva, from the womb of Devakī to the womb of Rohiṇī, and this was a very heavy task for her. Yogamāyā naturally could not see how it was possible for her to attract Saṅkarṣaṇa. Therefore Kṛṣṇa addressed her as *śubhe*, auspicious, and said, "Be blessed. Take power from Me, and you will be able to do it." By the grace of the Supreme Personality of Godhead, anyone can do anything, for the Lord is present in everything, all things being His parts and parcels (*aṁśa-bhāgena*) and increasing or decreasing by His supreme will. Balarāma was only fifteen days older than Kṛṣṇa. By the blessings of Kṛṣṇa, Yogamāyā became the daughter of mother Yaśodā, but by the supreme will she was not able to enjoy the parental love of her father and mother. Kṛṣṇa, however, although not actually born from the womb of mother Yaśodā, enjoyed the parental love of mother Yaśodā and Nanda. By the blessings of Kṛṣṇa, Yogamāyā was able to achieve the reputation of being the daughter of mother Yaśodā, who also became famous by the blessings of Kṛṣṇa. Yaśodā means "one who gives fame."

TEXT 10

अर्चिष्यन्ति मनुष्यास्त्वां सर्वकामवरेश्वरीम् ।
धूपोपहारबलिभिः सर्वकामवरप्रदाम् ॥१०॥

arciṣyanti manuṣyās tvāṁ
sarva-kāma-vareśvarīm
dhūpopahāra-balibhiḥ
sarva-kāma-vara-pradām

arciṣyanti—will worship; *manuṣyāḥ*—human society; *tvām*—unto you; *sarva-kāma-vara-īśvarīm*—because you are the best of the demigods who can fulfill all material desires; *dhūpa*—by incense; *upahāra*—by presentations; *balibhiḥ*—by different types of worship through sacrifice; *sarva-kāma*—of all material desires; *vara*—the blessings; *pradām*—one who can bestow.

TRANSLATION

By sacrifices of animals, ordinary human beings will worship you gorgeously, with various paraphernalia, because you are supreme in fulfilling the material desires of everyone.

PURPORT

As stated in *Bhagavad-gītā* (7.20), *kāmais tais tair hṛta-jñānāḥ prapadyante 'nya-devatāḥ:* "Those whose minds are distorted by material desires surrender unto demigods." Therefore the word *manuṣya,* meaning "human being," here refers to one who does not know the actual goal of life. Such a person wants to enjoy the material world by taking birth in a highly elevated family with the benefits of education, beauty and immense wealth, which in this material world are desirable. One who has forgotten the real aim of life may worship goddess Durgā, *māyā-śakti,* under various names, for different purposes, and in different places. As there are many holy places for the worship of Kṛṣṇa, there are also many holy places in India for the worship of Durgādevī, or Māyādevī, who took birth as the daughter of Yaśodā. After cheating Kaṁsa, Māyādevī dispersed herself to various places, especially in Vindhyācala, to accept regular worship from ordinary men. A human being should actually be interested in understanding *ātma-tattva,* the truth of *ātmā,* the spirit soul, and Paramātmā, the supreme soul. Those who are interested in *ātma-tattva* worship the Supreme Personality of Godhead (*yasmin vijñāte sarvam evaṁ vijñātaṁ bhavati*). However, as explained in the next verse of this chapter, those who cannot understand *ātma-tattva* (*apaśyatām ātma-tattvam*) worship Yogamāyā in her different features. Therefore *Śrīmad-Bhāgavatam* (2.1.2) says:

śrotavyādīni rājendra
nṛṇāṁ santi sahasraśaḥ
apaśyatām ātma-tattvaṁ
gṛheṣu gṛha-medhinām

"Those persons who are materially engrossed, being blind to the knowledge of ultimate truth, have many subject matters for hearing in human society, O Emperor." Those who are interested in remaining in this material world and are not interested in spiritual salvation have many duties, but for one who is interested in spiritual salvation, the only duty is to surrender fully unto Kṛṣṇa (*sarva-dharmān parityajya mām ekaṁ śaraṇaṁ vraja*). Such a person is not interested in material enjoyment.

TEXTS 11–12

नामधेयानि कुर्वन्ति स्थानानि च नरा भुवि ।
दुर्गेति भद्रकालीति विजया वैष्णवीति च ॥११॥
कुमुदा चण्डिका कृष्णा माधवी कन्यकेति च ।
माया नारायणीशानी शारदेत्यम्बिकेति च ॥१२॥

nāmadheyāni kurvanti
sthānāni ca narā bhuvi
durgeti bhadrakālīti
vijayā vaiṣṇavīti ca

kumudā caṇḍikā kṛṣṇā
mādhavī kanyaketi ca
māyā nārāyaṇīśānī
śāradety ambiketi ca

nāmadheyāni—different names; *kurvanti*—will give; *sthānāni*—in different places; *ca*—also; *narāḥ*—persons interested in material enjoyment; *bhuvi*—on the surface of the globe; *durgā iti*—the name Durgā; *bhadrakālī iti*—the name Bhadrakālī; *vijayā*—the name Vijayā; *vaiṣṇavī iti*—the name Vaiṣṇavī; *ca*—also; *kumudā*—the name Kumudā; *caṇḍikā*—the name Caṇḍikā; *kṛṣṇā*—the name Kṛṣṇā; *mādhavī*—the name Mādhavī; *kanyakā iti*—the name Kanyakā or Kanyā-kumārī; *ca*—also; *māyā*—the name Māyā; *nārāyaṇī*—the name Nārāyaṇī; *īśānī*—the name Īśānī; *śāradā*—the name Śāradā; *iti*—thus; *ambikā*—the name Ambikā; *iti*—also; *ca*—and.

TRANSLATION

Lord Kṛṣṇa blessed Māyādevī by saying: In different places on the surface of the earth, people will give you different names, such as Durgā, Bhadrakālī, Vijayā, Vaiṣṇavī, Kumudā, Caṇḍikā, Kṛṣṇā, Mādhavī, Kanyakā, Māyā, Nārāyaṇī, Īśānī, Śāradā and Ambikā.

PURPORT

Because Kṛṣṇa and His energy appeared simultaneously, people have generally formed two groups—the *śāktas* and the Vaiṣṇavas—and sometimes there is rivalry between them. Essentially, those who are interested in material enjoyment are *śāktas*, and those interested in spiritual salvation and attaining the spiritual kingdom are Vaiṣṇavas. Because people are generally interested in material enjoyment, they are interested in worshiping Māyādevī, the energy of the Supreme Personality of Godhead. Vaiṣṇavas, however, are *śuddha-śāktas*, or pure *bhaktas*, because the Hare Kṛṣṇa *mahā-mantra* indicates worship of the Supreme Lord's energy, Harā. A Vaiṣṇava prays to the energy of the Lord for the opportunity to serve the Lord along with His spiritual energy. Thus Vaiṣṇavas all worship such Deities as Rādhā-Kṛṣṇa, Sītā-Rāma, Lakṣmī-Nārāyaṇa and Rukmiṇī-Dvārakādhīśa, whereas *durgā-śāktas* worship the material energy under different names.

The names by which Māyādevī is known in different places have been listed by Vallabhācārya as follows. In Vārāṇasī she is known as Durgā, in Avantī she is known as Bhadrakālī, in Orissa she is known as Vijayā, and in Kulahāpura she is known as Vaiṣṇavī or Mahālakṣmī. (The representatives of Mahālakṣmī and Ambikā are present in Bombay.) In the country known as Kāmarūpa she is known as Caṇḍikā, in Northern India as

Śāradā, and in Cape Comorin as Kanyakā. Thus she is distributed according to various names in various places.

Śrīla Vijayadhvaja Tīrthapāda, in his *Pada-ratnāvalī-ṭīkā*, has explained the meanings of the different representations. *Māyā* is known as Durgā because she is approached with great difficulty, as Bhadrā because she is auspicious, and as Kālī because she is deep blue. Because she is the most powerful energy, she is known as Vijayā; because she is one of the different energies of Viṣṇu, she is known as Vaiṣṇavī; and because she enjoys in this material world and gives facilities for material enjoyment, she is known as Kumudā. Because she is very severe to her enemies, the *asuras*, she is known as Caṇḍikā, and because she gives all sorts of material facilities, she is called Kṛṣṇā. In this way the material energy is differently named and situated in different places on the surface of the globe.

TEXT 13

गर्भसंकर्षणात् तं वै प्राहुः संकर्षणं भुवि ।
रामेति लोकरमणाद् बलभद्रं बलोच्छ्रयात् ॥१३॥

garbha-saṅkarṣaṇāt taṁ vai
prāhuḥ saṅkarṣaṇaṁ bhuvi
rāmeti loka-ramaṇād
balabhadraṁ balocchrayāt

garbha-saṅkarṣaṇāt—because He will be taken from the womb of Devakī to that of Rohiṇī; *tam*—Him (Rohiṇī-nandana, the son of Rohiṇī); *vai*—indeed; *prāhuḥ*—people will call; *saṅkarṣaṇam*—by the name Saṅkarṣaṇa; *bhuvi*—in the world; *rāma iti*—He will also be called Rāma; *loka-ramaṇāt*—because of His special mercy in enabling people in general to become devotees; *balabhadram*—He will also be called Balabhadra; *bala-ucchrayāt*—because of extensive bodily strength.

TRANSLATION

The son of Rohiṇī will also be celebrated as Saṅkarṣaṇa because of being sent from the womb of Devakī to the womb of Rohiṇī. He

will be called Rāma because of His ability to please all the inhabitants of Gokula, and He will be known as Balabhadra because of His extensive physical strength.

PURPORT

These are some of the reasons why Balarāma is known as Saṅkarṣaṇa, Balarāma or sometimes Rāma. In the *mahā-mantra*—Hare Kṛṣṇa, Hare Kṛṣṇa, Kṛṣṇa Kṛṣṇa, Hare Hare/ Hare Rāma, Hare Rāma, Rāma Rāma, Hare Hare—people sometimes object when Rāma is accepted as Balarāma. But although devotees of Lord Rāma may object, they should know that there is no difference between Balarāma and Lord Rāma. Here *Śrīmad-Bhāgavatam* clearly states that Balarāma is also known as Rāma (*rāmeti*). Therefore, it is not artificial for us to speak of Lord Balarāma as Lord Rāma. Jayadeva Gosvāmī also speaks of three Rāmas: Paraśurāma, Raghupati Rāma and Balarāma. All of them are Rāmas.

TEXT 14

सन्दिष्टैवं भगवता तथेत्योमिति तद्वचः ।
प्रतिगृह्य परिक्रम्य गां गता तत् तथाकरोत् ॥१४॥

sandiṣṭaivaṁ bhagavatā
tathety om iti tad-vacaḥ
pratigṛhya parikramya
gāṁ gatā tat tathākarot

sandiṣṭā—having been ordered; *evam*—thus; *bhagavatā*—by the Supreme Personality of Godhead; *tathā iti*—so be it; *oṁ*—affirmation by the mantra *oṁ; iti*—thus; *tat-vacaḥ*—His words; *pratigṛhya*—accepting the order; *parikramya*—after circumambulating Him; *gām*—to the surface of the globe; *gatā*—she immediately went; *tat*—the order, as given by the Supreme Personality of Godhead; *tathā*—just so; *akarot*—executed.

TRANSLATION

Thus instructed by the Supreme Personality of Godhead, Yogamāyā immediately agreed. With the Vedic mantra oṁ, she

confirmed that she would do what He asked. Thus having accepted the order of the Supreme Personality of Godhead, she circumambulated Him and started for the place on earth known as Nanda-gokula. There she did everything just as she had been told.

PURPORT

After receiving the orders of the Supreme Personality of Godhead, Yogamāyā twice confirmed her acceptance by saying, "Yes, sir, I shall do as You order," and then saying *oṁ*. Śrīla Viśvanātha Cakravartī Ṭhākura comments that *oṁ* signifies Vedic confirmation. Thus Yogamāyā very faithfully received the Lord's order as a Vedic injunction. It is a fact that whatever is spoken by the Supreme Personality of Godhead is a Vedic injunction that no one should neglect. In Vedic injunctions there are no mistakes, illusions, cheating or imperfection. Unless one understands the authority of the Vedic version, there is no purpose in quoting *śāstra*. No one should violate the Vedic injunctions. Rather, one should strictly execute the orders given in the *Vedas*. As stated in *Bhagavad-gītā* (16.24):

tasmāc chāstraṁ pramāṇaṁ te
kāryākārya-vyavasthitau
jñātvā śāstra-vidhānoktaṁ
karma kartum ihārhasi

"One should understand what is duty and what is not duty by the regulations of the scriptures. Knowing such rules and regulations, one should act so that one may gradually be elevated."

TEXT 15

गर्भे प्रणीते देवक्या रोहिणीं योगनिद्रया ।
अहो विस्रंसितो गर्भ इति पौरा विचुक्रुशुः ॥१५॥

garbhe praṇīte devakyā
rohiṇīṁ yoga-nidrayā
aho visraṁsito garbha
iti paurā vicukruśuḥ

garbhe—when the embryo; *praṇīte*—was carried from the womb; *devakyāḥ*—of Devakī; *rohiṇīm*—to the womb of Rohiṇī; *yoga-nidrayā*—by the spiritual energy called Yogamāyā; *aho*—alas; *visraṁsitaḥ*—is lost; *garbhaḥ*—the embryo; *iti*—thus; *paurāḥ*—all the inhabitants of the house; *vicukruśuḥ*—lamented.

TRANSLATION

When the child of Devakī was attracted and transferred into the womb of Rohiṇī by Yogamāyā, Devakī seemed to have a miscarriage. Thus all the inhabitants of the palace loudly lamented, "Alas, Devakī has lost her child!"

PURPORT

"All the inhabitants of the palace" includes Kaṁsa. When everyone lamented, Kaṁsa joined in compassion, thinking that perhaps because of drugs or some other external means, Devakī had undergone this abortion. The real story of what happened after Yogamāyā attracted the child of Devakī into the womb of Rohiṇī in the seventh month of Rohiṇī's pregnancy is described as follows in the *Hari-vaṁśa.* At midnight, while Rohiṇī was deeply sleeping, she experienced, as if in a dream, that she had undergone a miscarriage. After some time, when she awoke, she saw that this had indeed happened, and she was in great anxiety. But Yogamāyā then informed her, "O auspicious lady, your child is now being replaced. I am attracting a child from the womb of Devakī, and therefore your child will be known as Saṅkarṣaṇa."

The word *yoga-nidrā* is significant. When one is spiritually reconnected through self-realization, one regards his material life as having been like a dream. As stated in *Bhagavad-gītā* (2.69):

yā niśā sarva-bhūtānāṁ
tasyāṁ jāgarti saṁyamī
yasyāṁ jāgrati bhūtāni
sā niśā paśyato muneḥ

"What is night for all beings is the time of awakening for the self-controlled; and the time of awakening for all beings is night for the introspective sage." The stage of self-realization is called *yoga-nidrā*. All material activities appear to be a dream when one is spiritually awakened. Thus *yoga-nidrā* may be explained to be Yogamāyā.

TEXT 16

भगवानपि विश्वात्मा भक्तानामभयङ्करः ।
आविवेशांशभागेन मन आनकदुन्दुभेः ॥१६॥

bhagavān api viśvātmā
bhaktānām abhayaṅkaraḥ
āviveśāṁśa-bhāgena
mana ānakadundubheḥ

bhagavān—the Supreme Personality of Godhead; *api*—also; *viśvātmā*—the Supersoul of all living entities; *bhaktānām*—of His devotees; *abhayam-karaḥ*—always killing the causes of fear; *āviveśa*—entered; *aṁśa-bhāgena*—with all of His potential opulences (*ṣaḍ-aiśvarya-pūrṇa*); *manaḥ*—in the mind; *ānakadundubheḥ*—of Vasudeva.

TRANSLATION

Thus the Supreme Personality of Godhead, who is the Supersoul of all living entities and who vanquishes all the fear of His devotees, entered the mind of Vasudeva in full opulence.

PURPORT

The word *viśvātmā* refers to one who is situated in everyone's heart (*īśvaraḥ sarva-bhūtānāṁ hṛd-deśe 'rjuna tiṣṭhati*). Another meaning of *viśvātmā* is "the only lovable object for everyone." Because of forgetfulness of this object, people are suffering in this material world, but if one fortunately revives his old consciousness of loving Kṛṣṇa and connects with Viśvātmā, one becomes perfect. The Lord is described in the Third Canto (3.2.15) as follows: *parāvareśo mahad-aṁśa-yukto hy ajo 'pi jāto bhagavān.* Although unborn, the Lord, the master of everything, appears like a born child by entering the mind of a devotee. The Lord is already there within the mind, and consequently it is not astonishing for Him to appear as if born from a devotee's body. The word *āviveśa* signifies that the Lord appeared within the mind of Vasudeva. There was no need for a discharge of semen. That is the opinion of Śrīpāda Śrīdhara Svāmī and Śrīla Viśvanātha Cakravartī Ṭhākura. In the *Vaiṣṇava-toṣaṇī*, Śrīla Sanātana Gosvāmī says that consciousness was awakened within the mind of Vasudeva. Śrīla Vīrarāghava Ācārya also says that Vasudeva was one of the demigods and that within his mind the Supreme Personality of Godhead appeared as an awakening of consciousness.

TEXT 17

स बिभ्रत् पौरुषं धाम भ्राजमानो यथा रविः ।
दुरासदोऽतिदुर्धर्षो भूतानां सम्बभूव ह ॥१७॥

sa bibhrat pauruṣaṁ dhāma
bhrājamāno yathā raviḥ
durāsado 'tidurdharṣo
bhūtānāṁ sambabhūva ha

saḥ—he (Vasudeva); *bibhrat*—carried; *pauruṣam*—pertaining to the Supreme Person; *dhāma*—the spiritual effulgence; *bhrājamānaḥ*—illuminating; *yathā*—as; *raviḥ*—the sunshine; *durāsadaḥ*—very difficult even to look at, difficult to understand by sensory perception; *ati-durdharṣaḥ*—approachable with great difficulty; *bhūtānām*—of all living entities; *sambabhūva*—so he became; *ha*—positively.

TRANSLATION

While carrying the form of the Supreme Personality of Godhead within the core of his heart, Vasudeva bore the Lord's transcendentally illuminating effulgence, and thus he became as bright as the sun. He was therefore very difficult to see or approach through sensory perception. Indeed, he was unapproachable and unperceivable even for such formidable men as Kaṁsa, and not only for Kaṁsa but for all living entities.

PURPORT

The word *dhāma* is significant. *Dhāma* refers to the place where the Supreme Personality of Godhead resides. In the beginning of *Śrīmad-Bhāgavatam* (1.1.1) it is said, *dhāmnā svena sadā nirasta-kuhakaṁ satyaṁ paraṁ dhīmahi.* In the abode of the Supreme Personality of Godhead, there is no influence of material energy (*dhāmnā svena sadā nirasta-kuhakam*). Any place where the Supreme Personality of Godhead is present by His name, form, qualities or paraphernalia immediately becomes a *dhāma.* For example, we speak of Vṛndāvana-dhāma, Dvārakā-dhāma and Mathurā-dhāma because in these places the name, fame, qualities and paraphernalia of the Supreme Godhead are always present. Similarly, if one is empowered by the Supreme Personality of Godhead to do something, the core of his heart becomes a *dhāma,* and thus he becomes so extraordinarily powerful that not only his enemies but also people in general are astonished to observe his activities. Because he is unapproachable, his enemies are simply struck with wonder, as explained here by the words *durāsado 'tidurdharṣaḥ.*

The words *pauruṣaṁ dhāma* have been explained by various *ācāryas.* Śrī Vīrarāghava Ācārya says that these words refer to the effulgence of the Supreme Personality of Godhead. Vijayadhvaja says that they signify *viṣṇu-tejas,* and Śukadeva says *bhagavat-svarūpa.* The *Vaiṣṇava-toṣaṇī* says that these words indicate the influence of the Supreme Lord's effulgence, and Viśvanātha Cakravartī Ṭhākura says that they signify the appearance of the Supreme Personality of Godhead.

TEXT 18

ततो जगन्मङ्गलमच्युतांशं
समाहितं शूरसुतेन देवी ।
दधार सर्वात्मकमात्मभूतं
काष्ठा यथानन्दकरं मनस्तः ॥१८॥

tato jagan-maṅgalam acyutāṁśaṁ
samāhitaṁ śūra-sutena devī
dadhāra sarvātmakam ātma-bhūtaṁ
kāṣṭhā yathānanda-karaṁ manastaḥ

tataḥ—thereafter; *jagat-maṅgalam*—auspiciousness for all living entities in all the universes of the creation; *acyuta-aṁśam*—the Supreme Personality of Godhead, who is never bereft of the six opulences, all of which are present in all His plenary expansions; *samāhitam*—fully transferred; *śūra-sutena*—by Vasudeva, the son of Śūrasena; *devī*—Devakī-devī; *dadhāra*—carried; *sarva-ātmakam*—the Supreme Soul of everyone; *ātma-bhūtam*—the cause of all causes; *kāṣṭhā*—the east; *yathā*—just as; *ānanda-karam*—the blissful (moon); *manastaḥ*—being placed within the mind.

TRANSLATION

Thereafter, accompanied by plenary expansions, the fully opulent Supreme Personality of Godhead, who is all-auspicious for the entire universe, was transferred from the mind of Vasudeva to the mind of Devakī. Devakī, having thus been initiated by Vasudeva, became beautiful by carrying Lord Kṛṣṇa, the original consciousness for everyone, the cause of all causes, within the core of her heart, just as the east becomes beautiful by carrying the rising moon.

PURPORT

As indicated here by the word *manastaḥ*, the Supreme Personality of Godhead was transferred from the core of Vasudeva's mind or heart to the core of the heart of Devakī. We should note carefully that the Lord was transferred to Devakī not by the ordinary way for a human being, but by *dīkṣā*, initiation. Thus the importance of initiation is mentioned here. Unless one is initiated by the right person, who always carries within his heart the Supreme Personality of Godhead, one cannot acquire the power to carry the Supreme Godhead within the core of one's own heart.

The word *acyutāṁśam* is used because the Supreme Personality of Godhead is *ṣaḍ-aiśvarya-pūrṇa*, full in the opulences of wealth, strength, fame, knowledge, beauty and renunciation. The Supreme Godhead is never separated from His personal opulences. As stated in the *Brahma-saṁhitā* (5.39), *rāmādi-mūrtiṣu kalā-niyamena tiṣṭhan:* the Lord is always situated with all His plenary expansions, such as Rāma, Nṛsiṁha and Varāha. Therefore the word *acyutāṁśam* is specifically used here, signifying that the Lord is always present with His plenary expansions and opulences. There is no need to think of the Lord artificially as *yogīs* do. *Dhyānāvasthita-tad-gatena manasā paśyanti yaṁ yoginaḥ* (*Bhāg.* 12.13.1). *Yogīs* meditate upon the Supreme Person within the mind. For a devotee, however, the Lord is present, and His presence need only be awakened through initiation by a bona fide spiritual master. The Lord did not need to live within the womb of Devakī, for His presence within the core of her heart was sufficient to carry Him. One is here forbidden to think that Kṛṣṇa was begotten by Vasudeva within the womb of Devakī and that she carried the child within her womb.

When Vasudeva was sustaining the form of the Supreme Personality of Godhead within his heart, he appeared just like the glowing sun, whose shining rays are always unbearable and scorching to the common man. The form of the Lord situated in the pure, unalloyed heart of Vasudeva is not different from the original form of Kṛṣṇa. The appearance of the form of Kṛṣṇa anywhere, and specifically within the heart, is called *dhāma. Dhāma* refers not only to Kṛṣṇa's form, but to His name, His form, His quality and His paraphernalia. Everything becomes manifest simultaneously.

Thus the eternal form of the Supreme Personality of Godhead with full potencies was transferred from the mind of Vasudeva to the mind of Devakī, exactly as the setting sun's rays are transferred to the full moon rising in the east.

Kṛṣṇa, the Supreme Personality of Godhead, entered the body of Devakī from the body of Vasudeva. He was beyond the conditions of the ordinary living entity. When Kṛṣṇa is there, it is to be understood that all His plenary expansions, such as Nārāyaṇa, and incarnations like Lord Nṛsiṁha and Varāha, are with Him, and they are not subject to the conditions of material existence. In this way, Devakī became the residence of the Supreme Personality of Godhead, who is one without a second and the cause of all creation. Devakī became the residence of the Absolute Truth, but because she was within the house of Kaṁsa, she looked just like a suppressed fire, or like misused education. When fire is covered by the walls of a pot or is kept in a jug, the illuminating rays of the fire cannot be very much appreciated. Similarly, misused knowledge, which does not benefit the people in general, is not very much appreciated. So Devakī was kept within the prison walls of Kaṁsa's palace, and no one could see her transcendental beauty, which resulted from her conceiving the Supreme Personality of Godhead.

Commenting upon this verse, Śrī Vīrarāghava Ācārya writes, *vasudeva-devakī-jaṭharayor hṛdayayor bhagavataḥ sambandhaḥ*. The Supreme Lord's entrance into the womb of Devakī from the heart of Vasudeva was a heart-to-heart relationship.

TEXT 19

सा देवकी सर्वजगन्निवास-
निवासभूता नितरां न रेजे ।
भोजेन्द्रगेहेऽग्निशिखेव रुद्धा
सरस्वती ज्ञानखले यथा सती ॥१९॥

sā devakī sarva-jagan-nivāsa-
nivāsa-bhūtā nitarāṁ na reje
bhojendra-gehe 'gni-śikheva ruddhā
sarasvatī jñāna-khale yathā satī

sā devakī—that Devakīdevī; *sarva-jagat-nivāsa*—of the Supreme Personality of Godhead, the sustainer of all the universes (*mat-sthāni sarva-bhūtāni*); *nivāsa-bhūtā*—the womb of Devakī has now become the residence; *nitarām*—extensively; *na*—not; *reje*—became illuminated; *bhojendra-gehe*—within the limits of the house of Kaṁsa; *agni-śikhā iva*—like the flames of a fire; *ruddhā*—covered; *sarasvatī*—knowledge; *jñāna-khale*—in a person known as *jñāna-khala*, one who possesses knowledge but cannot distribute it; *yathā*—or just as; *satī*—so being.

TRANSLATION

Devakī then kept within herself the Supreme Personality of Godhead, the cause of all causes, the foundation of the entire cosmos, but because she was under arrest in the house of Kaṁsa, she was like the flames of a fire covered by the walls of a pot, or like a person who has knowledge but cannot distribute it to the world for the benefit of human society.

PURPORT

In this verse the word *jñāna-khala* is most significant. Knowledge is meant for distribution. Although there is already much scientific knowledge, whenever scientists or philosophers awaken to a particular type of knowledge, they try to distribute it throughout the world, for otherwise the knowledge gradually dries up and no one benefits from it. India has the knowledge of *Bhagavad-gītā*, but unfortunately, for some reason or other, this sublime knowledge of the science of God was not distributed throughout the world, although it is meant for all of human society. Therefore Kṛṣṇa Himself appeared as Śrī Caitanya Mahāprabhu and ordered all Indians to take up the cause of distributing the knowledge of *Bhagavad-gītā* throughout the entire world.

yāre dekha, tāre kaha 'kṛṣṇa'-upadeśa
āmāra ājñāya guru hañā tāra' ei deśa

"Instruct everyone to follow the orders of Lord Śrī Kṛṣṇa as they are given in *Bhagavad-gītā* and *Śrīmad-Bhāgavatam.* In this way become a spiritual master and try to liberate everyone in this land." (Cc. *Madhya* 7.128) Although India has the sublime knowledge of *Bhagavad-gītā*, Indians have not done their proper duty of distributing it. Now, therefore, the Kṛṣṇa consciousness movement has been set up to distribute this knowledge as it is, without distortion. Although previously there were attempts to distribute the knowledge of *Bhagavad-gītā*, these attempts involved distortion and compromise with mundane knowledge. But now the Kṛṣṇa consciousness movement, without mundane compromises, is distributing *Bhagavad-gītā* as it is, and people are deriving the benefits of awakening to Kṛṣṇa consciousness and becoming devotees of Lord Kṛṣṇa. Therefore the proper distribution of knowledge has begun by which not only will the whole world benefit, but India's glory will be magnified in human society. Kaṁsa tried to arrest Kṛṣṇa consciousness within his house (*bhojendra-gehe*), with the result that Kaṁsa, with all his opulences, was later vanquished. Similarly, the real knowledge of *Bhagavad-gītā* was being choked by unscrupulous Indian leaders, with the result that India's culture, and knowledge of the Supreme were being lost. Now, however, because Kṛṣṇa consciousness is spreading, the proper use of *Bhagavad-gītā* is being attempted.

TEXT 20

तां वीक्ष्य कंसः प्रभयाजितान्तरां
विरोचयन्तीं भवनं शुचिस्मिताम् ।
आहैष मे प्राणहरो हरिर्गुहां
ध्रुवं श्रितो यन्न पुरेयमीदृशी ॥२०॥

tāṁ vīkṣya kaṁsaḥ prabhayājitāntarāṁ
virocayantīṁ bhavanaṁ śuci-smitām
āhaiṣa me prāṇa-haro harir guhāṁ
dhruvaṁ śrito yan na pureyam īdṛśī

tām—her (Devakī); *vīkṣya*—after seeing; *kaṁsaḥ*—her brother Kaṁsa; *prabhayā*—with the enhancement of her beauty and influence; *ajita-antarām*—because of keeping Ajita, the Supreme Personality of Godhead, Viṣṇu, within herself; *virocayantīm*—illuminating; *bhavanam*—the whole atmosphere of the house; *śuci-smitām*—smiling and brilliant; *āha*—said to himself; *eṣaḥ*—this (Supreme Person); *me*—my; *prāṇa-haraḥ*—who will kill me; *hariḥ*—Lord Viṣṇu; *guhām*—within the womb of Devakī; *dhruvam*—certainly; *śritaḥ*—has taken shelter; *yat*—because; *na*—was not; *purā*—formerly; *iyam*—Devakī; *īdṛśī*—like this.

TRANSLATION

Because the Supreme Personality of Godhead was within her womb, Devakī illuminated the entire atmosphere in the place where she was confined. Seeing her jubilant, pure and smiling, Kaṁsa thought, "The Supreme Personality of Godhead, Viṣṇu, who is now within her, will kill me. Devakī has never before looked so brilliant and jubilant."

PURPORT

The Lord says in *Bhagavad-gītā* (4.7):

yadā yadā hi dharmasya
glānir bhavati bhārata

abhyutthānam adharmasya
tadātmānaṁ sṛjāmy aham

"Whenever and wherever there is a decline in religious practice, O descendant of Bharata, and a predominant rise of irreligion—at that time I descend Myself." In this age, at the present moment, there are inordinate discrepancies in the discharge of human duties. Human life is meant for God realization, but unfortunately the materialistic civilization is stressing only the senses of the body, not understanding the living force within the body. As clearly stated in *Bhagavad-gītā* (*dehino 'smin yathā dehe*), within the body is the body's proprietor, the living force, which is more important. But human society has become so fallen that instead of understanding the living force within the body, people have become busy with external things. This is a discrepancy in human duties. Therefore Kṛṣṇa has taken birth or taken shelter within the womb of the Kṛṣṇa consciousness movement. Men of Kaṁsa's class, therefore, are very much afraid and are busy trying to stop this movement, especially in the Western countries. One politician has remarked that the Kṛṣṇa consciousness movement is spreading like an epidemic and that if not checked immediately, within ten years it may capture governmental power. There is, of course, such potency in the Kṛṣṇa consciousness movement. As stated by authorities (Cc. *Ādi* 17.22), *kali-kāle nāma-rūpe kṛṣṇa-avatāra:* in this age, Kṛṣṇa has appeared in the Hare Kṛṣṇa *mahā-mantra.* The Kṛṣṇa consciousness movement is spreading like wildfire all over the world, and it will go on doing so. Men who are like Kaṁsa are very much afraid of the movement's progress and acceptance by the younger generation, but as Kṛṣṇa could not be killed by Kaṁsa, this movement cannot be checked by men of Kaṁsa's class. The movement will go on increasing more and more, provided the leaders of the movement remain firmly Kṛṣṇa conscious by following the regulative principles and the primary activities of chanting the Hare Kṛṣṇa *mantra* regularly.

TEXT 21

किमद्य तस्मिन् करणीयमाशु मे
यदर्थतन्त्रो न विहन्ति विक्रमम् ।

स्त्रियाः स्वसुर्गुरुमत्या वधोऽयं
यशः श्रियं हन्त्यनुकालमायुः ॥२१॥

kim adya tasmin karaṇīyam āśu me
yad artha-tantro na vihanti vikramam
striyāḥ svasur gurumatyā vadho 'yaṁ
yaśaḥ śriyaṁ hanty anukālam āyuḥ

kim—what; *adya*—now, immediately; *tasmin*—in this situation; *karaṇīyam*—is to be done; *āśu*—without delay; *me*—my duty; *yat*—because; *artha-tantraḥ*—the Supreme Personality of Godhead, who is always determined to protect the *sādhus* and kill the *asādhus; na*—does not; *vihanti*—give up; *vikramam*—His prowess; *striyāḥ*—of a woman; *svasuḥ*—of my sister; *guru-matyāḥ*—especially when she is pregnant; *vadhaḥ ayam*—the killing; *yaśaḥ*—fame; *śriyam*—opulence; *hanti*—will vanquish; *anukālam*—forever; *āyuḥ*—and the duration of life.

TRANSLATION

Kaṁsa thought: What is my duty now? The Supreme Lord, who knows His purpose [paritrāṇāya sādhūnāṁ vināśāya ca duṣkṛtām], will not give up His prowess. Devakī is a woman, she is my sister, and moreover she is now pregnant. If I kill her, my reputation, opulence and duration of life will certainly be vanquished.

PURPORT

According to Vedic principles, a woman, a *brāhmaṇa*, an old man, a child and a cow should never be killed. It appears that Kaṁsa, although a great enemy of the Supreme Personality of Godhead, was aware of the Vedic culture and conscious of the fact that the soul transmigrates from one body to another and that one suffers in the next life according to the *karmas* of this life. Therefore he was afraid of killing Devakī, since she was a woman, she was his sister, and she was pregnant. A *kṣatriya* becomes famous by performing heroic acts. But what would be heroic about killing a woman who, while confined in his custody, was under his shelter? Therefore, he did not want to act drastically by killing Devakī. Kaṁsa's enemy was within Devakī's womb, but killing an enemy in such a nescient state would not be an exhibition of prowess. According to *kṣatriya* rules, an enemy should be fought face to face and with proper weapons. Then if the enemy is killed, the victor becomes famous. Kaṁsa very conscientiously deliberated upon these facts and therefore refrained from killing Devakī, although he was completely confident that his enemy had already appeared within her womb.

TEXT 22

स एष जीवन् खलु सम्परेतो
वर्तेत योऽत्यन्तनृशंसितेन ।
देहे मृते तं मनुजाः शपन्ति
गन्ता तमोऽन्धं तनुमानिनो ध्रुवम् ॥२२॥

sa eṣa jīvan khalu sampareto
varteta yo 'tyanta-nṛśaṁsitena
dehe mṛte taṁ manujāḥ śapanti
gantā tamo 'ndhaṁ tanu-mānino dhruvam

saḥ—he; *eṣaḥ*—that jealous person; *jīvan*—while living; *khalu*—even; *samparetaḥ*—is dead; *varteta*—continues to live; *yaḥ*—anyone who; *atyanta*—very much; *nṛśaṁsitena*—by executing cruel activities; *dehe*—when the body; *mṛte*—is finished; *tam*—him; *manujāḥ*—all human beings; *śapanti*—condemn; *gantā*—he will go; *tamaḥ andham*—to hellish life; *tanu-māninaḥ*—of a person in the bodily concept of life; *dhruvam*—without a doubt.

TRANSLATION

A person who is very cruel is regarded as dead even while living, for while he is living or after his death, everyone condemns him. And after the death of a person in the bodily concept of life, he is undoubtedly transferred to the hell known as Andhatama.

PURPORT

Kaṁsa considered that if he killed his sister, while living he would be condemned by everyone, and after death he would go to the darkest region of hellish life because of his cruelty. It is said that a cruel person like a butcher is advised not to live and not to die. While living, a cruel person creates a hellish condition for his next birth, and therefore he should not live; but he is also advised not to die, because after death he must go to the darkest region of hell. Thus in either circumstance he is condemned. Kaṁsa, therefore, having good sense about the science of the soul's transmigration, deliberately refrained from killing Devakī.

In this verse the words *gantā tamo 'ndhaṁ tanu-mānino dhruvam* are very important and require extensive understanding. Śrīla Jīva Gosvāmī, in his *Vaiṣṇava-toṣaṇī-ṭīkā*, says: *tatra tanu-māninaḥ pāpina iti dehātma-buddhyaiva pāpābhiniveśo bhavati.* One who lives in the bodily concept, thinking, "I am this body," involves himself, by the very nature of this conception, in a life of sinful activities. Anyone living in such a conception is to be considered a candidate for hell.

adānta-gobhir viśatāṁ tamisraṁ
punaḥ punaś carvita-carvaṇānām
(*Bhāg.* 7.5.30)

One who is in a bodily concept of life has no control over sense gratification. Such a person can do anything sinful to eat, drink, be merry and enjoy a life of sense gratification, not knowing of the soul's transmigration from one body to another. Such a person does whatever he likes, whatever he imagines, and therefore, being subject to the laws of nature, he suffers miserably again and again in different material bodies.

yāvat kriyās tāvad idaṁ mano vai
karmātmakaṁ yena śarīra-bandhaḥ
(*Bhāg.* 5.5.5)

In the bodily concept of life, a person is *karmānubandha,* or conditioned by *karma,* and as long as the mind is absorbed in *karma,* one must accept a material body. *Śarīra-bandha,* bondage to the material body, is a source of misery (*kleśa-da*).

na sādhu manye yata ātmano 'yam
asann api kleśada āsa dehaḥ

Although the body is temporary, it always gives one trouble in many ways, but human civilization is now unfortunately based on *tanu-mānī*, the bodily concept of life, by which one thinks, "I belong to this nation," "I belong to this group," "I belong to that group," and so on. Each of us has his own ideas, and we are becoming increasingly involved, individually, socially, communally and nationally, in the complexities of *karmānubandha*, sinful activities. For the maintenance of the body, men are killing so many other bodies and becoming implicated in *karmānubandha*. Therefore Śrīla Jīva Gosvāmī says that *tanu-mānī*, those in the bodily concept of life, are *pāpī*, sinful persons. For such sinful persons, the ultimate destination is the darkest region of hellish life (*gantā tamo 'ndham*). In particular, a person who wants to maintain his body by killing animals is most sinful and cannot understand the value of spiritual life. In *Bhagavad-gītā* (16.19–20) the Lord says:

tān ahaṁ dviṣataḥ krūrān
saṁsāreṣu narādhamān
kṣipāmy ajasram aśubhān
āsurīṣv eva yoniṣu

āsurīṁ yonim āpannā
mūḍhā janmani janmani
mām aprāpyaiva kaunteya
tato yānty adhamāṁ gatim

"Those who are envious and mischievous, who are the lowest among men, are cast by Me into the ocean of material existence, into various demoniac species of life. Attaining repeated birth among the species of demoniac life, such persons can never approach Me. Gradually they sink down to the most abominable type of existence." A human being is meant to understand the value of human life, which is a boon obtained after many, many births. Therefore one must free oneself from *tanu-mānī*, the bodily concept of life, and realize the Supreme Personality of Godhead.

TEXT 23

इति घोरतमाद् भावात् सन्निवृत्तः स्वयं प्रभुः ।
आस्ते प्रतीक्षंस्तज्जन्म हरेर्वैरानुबन्धकृत् ॥२३॥

iti ghoratamād bhāvāt
sannivṛttaḥ svayaṁ prabhuḥ
āste pratīkṣaṁs taj-janma
harer vairānubandha-kṛt

iti—thus (thinking in the above-mentioned way); *ghora-tamāt bhāvāt*—from the most ghastly contemplation of how to kill his sister; *sannivṛttaḥ*—refrained; *svayam*—personally deliberating; *prabhuḥ*—one who was in full knowledge (Kaṁsa); *āste*—remained; *pratīkṣan*—awaiting the moment; *tat-janma*—until the birth of Him; *hareḥ*—of the Supreme Personality of Godhead, Hari; *vaira-anubandha-kṛt*—determined to continue such enmity.

TRANSLATION

Śukadeva Gosvāmī said: Deliberating in this way, Kaṁsa, although determined to continue in enmity toward the Supreme Personality of Godhead, refrained from the vicious killing of his sister. He decided to wait until the Lord was born and then do what was needed.

TEXT 24

आसीनः संविशंस्तिष्ठन् भुञ्जानः पर्यटन् महीम् ।
चिन्तयानो हृषीकेशमपश्यत् तन्मयं जगत् ॥२४॥

āsīnaḥ saṁviśaṁs tiṣṭhan
bhuñjānaḥ paryaṭan mahīm
cintayāno hṛṣīkeśam
apaśyat tanmayaṁ jagat

āsīnaḥ—while sitting comfortably in his sitting room or on the throne; *saṁviśan*—or lying on his bed; *tiṣṭhan*—or staying anywhere; *bhuñjānaḥ*—while eating; *paryaṭan*—while walking or moving; *mahīm*—on the ground, going hither and thither; *cintayānaḥ*—always inimically thinking of; *hṛṣīkeśam*—the Supreme Personality of Godhead, the controller of everything; *apaśyat*—observed; *tat-mayam*—consisting of Him (Kṛṣṇa), and nothing more; *jagat*—the entire world.

TRANSLATION

While sitting on his throne or in his sitting room, while lying on his bed, or, indeed, while situated anywhere, and while eating, sleeping or walking, Kaṁsa saw only his enemy, the Supreme Lord, Hṛṣīkeśa. In other words, by thinking of his all-pervading enemy, Kaṁsa became unfavorably Kṛṣṇa conscious.

PURPORT

Śrīla Rūpa Gosvāmī has described the finest pattern of devotional service as *ānukūlyena kṛṣṇānuśīlanam,* or cultivating Kṛṣṇa consciousness favorably. Kaṁsa, of course, was also Kṛṣṇa conscious, but because he regarded Kṛṣṇa as his enemy, even though he was fully absorbed in Kṛṣṇa consciousness, his Kṛṣṇa consciousness was not favorable for his existence. Kṛṣṇa consciousness, favorably cultivated, makes one completely happy, so much so that a Kṛṣṇa conscious person does not consider *kaivalya-sukham,* or merging into the existence of Kṛṣṇa, to be a great gain. *Kaivalyaṁ narakāyate.* For a Kṛṣṇa conscious person, even merging into the existence of Kṛṣṇa, or Brahman, as impersonalists aspire to do, is uncomfortable. *Kaivalyaṁ narakāyate tridaśa-pūr ākāśa-puṣpāyate. Karmīs* hanker to be promoted to the heavenly planets, but a Kṛṣṇa conscious person considers such promotion a will-o'-the-wisp, good for nothing. *Durdāntendriya-kāla-sarpa-paṭalī protkhāta-daṁṣṭrāyate. Yogīs* try to control their senses and thus become happy, but a Kṛṣṇa conscious person neglects the methods of *yoga.* He is unconcerned with the greatest of enemies, the senses, which are compared to snakes. For a Kṛṣṇa conscious person who is cultivating Kṛṣṇa consciousness favorably, the happiness conceived by the *karmīs, jñānīs* and *yogīs* is treated as less than a fig. Kaṁsa, however, because of cultivating Kṛṣṇa consciousness in a different way—that is, inimically—was uncomfortable in all the affairs of his life; whether sitting, sleeping, walking or eating, he was always in danger. This is the difference between a devotee and a nondevotee. A nondevotee or atheist also cultivates God consciousness—by trying to avoid God in everything. For example, so-called scientists who want to create life by a combination of chemicals regard the external, material elements as supreme. Such scientists do not like the idea that life is part and parcel of the Supreme Lord. As clearly stated in *Bhagavad-gītā* (*mamaivāṁśo jīva-loke jīva-bhūtaḥ*), the living entities do not arise from a combination of material elements, such as earth, water, air and fire, but are separated portions of the Supreme Personality of Godhead. If one can understand the position of the living entity as a separated portion of the Supreme Personality of Godhead, by studying the nature of the living entity one can understand the nature of the Supreme Godhead, since the living entity is a fragmental sample of the Godhead. But because atheists are not interested in God consciousness, they try to be happy by cultivating Kṛṣṇa consciousness in various unfavorable ways.

Although Kaṁsa was always absorbed in thoughts of Hari, the Supreme Personality of Godhead, he was not happy. A devotee, however, whether sitting on a throne or beneath a tree, is always happy. Śrīla Rūpa Gosvāmī resigned from office as a government minister to sit beneath a tree, yet he was happy. *Tyaktvā tūrṇam aśeṣa-maṇḍalapati-śreṇīṁ sadā tucchavat* (*Ṣaḍ-gosvāmy-aṣṭaka* 4). He did not care for his comfortable position as minister; he was happy even beneath a tree in Vṛndāvana, favorably serving the Supreme Personality of Godhead. This is the difference between a devotee and a nondevotee. For a nondevotee, the world is full of problems, whereas for a devotee the entire world is full of happiness.

> *viśvaṁ pūrṇa-sukhāyate vidhi-mahendrādiś ca kīṭāyate*
> *yat-kāruṇya-kaṭākṣa-vaibhavavatāṁ taṁ gauram eva stumaḥ*
> (*Caitanya-candrāmṛta* 95)

This comfortable position of a devotee can be established by the mercy of Lord Caitanya Mahāprabhu. *Yasmin sthito na duḥkhena guruṇāpi vicālyate* (Bg. 6.22). Even when a devotee is superficially put into great difficulty, he is never disturbed.

TEXT 25

ब्रह्मा भवश्च तत्रैत्य मुनिभिर्नारदादिभिः ।
देवैः सानुचरैः साकं गीर्भिर्वृषणमैडयन् ॥२५॥

brahmā bhavaś ca tatraitya
munibhir nāradādibhiḥ
devaiḥ sānucaraiḥ sākaṁ
gīrbhir vṛṣaṇam aiḍayan

brahmā—the supreme four-headed demigod; *bhavaḥ ca*—and Lord Śiva; *tatra*—there; *etya*—arriving; *munibhiḥ*—accompanied by great sages; *nārada-ādibhiḥ*—by Nārada and others; *devaiḥ*—and by demigods like Indra, Candra and Varuṇa; *sa-anucaraiḥ*—with their followers; *sākam*—all together; *gīrbhiḥ*—by their transcendental prayers; *vṛṣaṇam*—the Supreme Personality of Godhead, who can bestow blessings upon everyone; *aiḍayan*—pleased.

TRANSLATION

Lord Brahmā and Lord Śiva, accompanied by great sages like Nārada, Devala and Vyāsa and by other demigods like Indra, Candra and Varuṇa, invisibly approached the room of Devakī, where they all joined in offering their respectful obeisances and prayers to please the Supreme Personality of Godhead, who can bestow blessings upon everyone.

PURPORT

Dvau bhūta-sargau loke 'smin daiva āsura eva ca (*Padma Purāṇa*). There are two classes of men—the *daivas* and the *asuras*— and there is a great difference between them. Kaṁsa, being an *asura*, was always planning how to kill the Supreme Personality of Godhead or His mother, Devakī. Thus he was also Kṛṣṇa conscious. But devotees are Kṛṣṇa conscious favorably (*viṣṇu-bhaktaḥ smṛto daivaḥ*). Brahmā is so powerful that he is in charge of creating an entire universe, yet he personally came to receive the Supreme Personality of Godhead. Bhava, Lord Śiva, is always jubilant in chanting the holy name of the Lord. And what to speak of Nārada? *Nārada-muni, bājāya vīṇā, rādhikā-ramaṇa-nāme.* Nārada Muni is always chanting the glories of the Lord, and his engagement is to travel all over the universe and find a devotee or make someone a devotee. Even a hunter was made a devotee by the grace of Nārada. Śrīla Sanātana Gosvāmī, in his *Toṣaṇī*, says that the word *nārada-ādibhiḥ* means that Nārada and the demigods were accompanied by other saintly persons, like Sanaka and Sanātana, all of whom came to congratulate or welcome the Supreme Personality of Godhead. Even though Kaṁsa was planning to kill Devakī, he too awaited the arrival of the Supreme Personality of Godhead (*pratīkṣaṁs taj-janma*).

TEXT 26

सत्यव्रतं सत्यपरं त्रिसत्यं
सत्यस्य योनिं निहितं च सत्ये ।
सत्यस्य सत्यमृतसत्यनेत्रं
सत्यात्मकं त्वां शरणं प्रपन्नाः ॥२६॥

satya-vrataṁ satya-paraṁ tri-satyaṁ
satyasya yoniṁ nihitaṁ ca satye
satyasya satyam ṛta-satya-netraṁ
satyātmakaṁ tvāṁ śaraṇaṁ prapannāḥ

satya-vratam—the Personality of Godhead, who never deviates from His vow;* *satya-param*—who is the Absolute Truth (as stated in the beginning of *Śrīmad-Bhāgavatam, satyaṁ paraṁ dhīmahi*); *tri-satyam*—He is always present as the Absolute Truth, before the creation of this cosmic manifestation, during its maintenance, and even after its annihilation; *satyasya*—of all relative truths, which are emanations from the Absolute Truth, Kṛṣṇa; *yonim*—the cause; *nihitam*—entered;† *ca*—and; *satye*—in the factors that create this material world (namely, the five elements—earth, water, fire, air and ether); *satyasya*—of all that is accepted as the truth; *satyam*—the Lord is the original truth; *ṛta-satya-netram*—He is the origin of whatever truth is pleasing (*sunetram*); *satya-ātmakam*—everything pertaining to the Lord is truth (*sac-cid-ānanda:* His body is truth, His knowledge is truth,

*The Lord vows: *yadā yadā hi dharmasya glānir bhavati bhārata/ abhyutthānam adharmasya tadātmānaṁ sṛjāmy aham* (Bg. 4.7). To honor this vow, the Lord appeared.

†The Lord enters everything, even the atom: *aṇḍāntara-stha-paramāṇu-cayāntara-stham* (*Brahma-saṁhitā* 5.44). Therefore He is called *antaryāmī*, the inner force.

and His pleasure is truth); *tvām*—unto You, O Lord; *śaraṇam*—offering our full surrender; *prapannāḥ*—we are completely under Your protection.

TRANSLATION

The demigods prayed: O Lord, You never deviate from Your vow, which is always perfect because whatever You decide is perfectly correct and cannot be stopped by anyone. Being present in the three phases of cosmic manifestation—creation, maintenance and annihilation—You are the Supreme Truth. Indeed, unless one is completely truthful, one cannot achieve Your favor, which therefore cannot be achieved by hypocrites. You are the active principle, the real truth, in all the ingredients of creation, and therefore you are known as antaryāmī, the inner force. You are equal to everyone, and Your instructions apply for everyone, for all time. You are the beginning of all truth. Therefore, offering our obeisances, we surrender unto You. Kindly give us protection.

PURPORT

The demigods or devotees know perfectly well that the Supreme Personality of Godhead is the true substance, whether within this material world or in the spiritual world. *Śrīmad-Bhāgavatam* begins, therefore, with the words *oṁ namo bhagavate vāsudevāya . . . satyaṁ paraṁ dhīmahi.* Vāsudeva, Kṛṣṇa, is the *paraṁ satyam,* the Supreme Truth. The Supreme Truth can be approached or understood by the supreme method, as declared by the Supreme Truth: *bhaktyā mām abhijānāti yāvān yaś cāsmi tattvataḥ* (Bg. 18.55). *Bhakti,* devotional service, is the only way to understand the Absolute Truth. For protection, therefore, the demigods surrender to the Supreme Truth, not to the relative truth. There are persons who worship various demigods, but the Supreme Truth, Kṛṣṇa, declares in *Bhagavad-gītā* (7.23), *antavat tu phalaṁ teṣāṁ tad bhavaty alpa-medhasām:* "Men of small intelligence worship the demigods, and their fruits are limited and temporary." Worship of demigods may be useful for a limited time, but the result is *antavat,* perishable. This material world is impermanent, the demigods are impermanent, and the benedictions derived from the demigods are also impermanent, whereas the living entity is eternal (*nityo nityānāṁ cetanaś cetanānām*). Every living entity, therefore, must search for eternal happiness, not temporary happiness. The words *satyaṁ paraṁ dhīmahi* indicate that one should search for the Absolute Truth, not the relative truth.

While offering prayers to the Supreme Personality of Godhead, Nṛsiṁhadeva, Prahlāda Mahārāja said:

bālasya neha śaraṇaṁ pitarau nṛsiṁha
nārtasya cāgadam udanvati majjato nauḥ

Generally it is understood that the protectors for a child are his parents, but this is not actually the fact. The real protector is the Supreme Personality of Godhead.

taptasya tat-pratividhir ya ihāñjaseṣṭas
tāvad vibho tanu-bhṛtāṁ tvad-upekṣitānām
(*Bhāg.* 7.9.19)

If neglected by the Supreme Personality of Godhead, a child, despite the presence of his parents, will suffer, and a diseased person, despite all medical help, will die. In this material world, where there is a struggle for existence, men have invented many means for protection, but these are useless if the Supreme Personality of Godhead rejects them. Therefore the demigods purposefully say, *satyātmakaṁ tvāṁ śaraṇaṁ prapannāḥ:* "Real protection can be obtained from You, O Lord, and therefore we surrender unto You."

The Lord demands that one surrender unto Him (*sarva-dharmān parityajya mām ekaṁ śaraṇaṁ vraja*), and He further says:

sakṛd eva prapanno yas
tavāsmīti ca yācate
abhayaṁ sarvadā tasmai
dadāmy etad vrataṁ mama

"If one surrenders unto Me sincerely, saying, 'My Lord, from this day I am fully surrendered unto You,' I always give him protection. That is My vow." (*Rāmāyaṇa, Yuddha-kāṇḍa* 18.33) The demigods offered their prayers to the Supreme Personality of Godhead because He had now appeared in the womb of His devotee Devakī to protect all the devotees harassed by Kaṁsa and his lieutenants. Thus the Lord acts as *satya-vrata.* The protection given by the Supreme Personality of Godhead cannot be compared to the protection given by the demigods. It is said that Rāvaṇa was a great devotee of Lord Śiva, but when Lord Rāmacandra went to kill him, Lord Śiva could not give him protection.

Lord Brahmā and Lord Śiva, accompanied by great sages like Nārada and followed by many other demigods, had now invisibly appeared in the house of Kaṁsa. They began to pray for the Supreme Personality of Godhead in select prayers which are very pleasing to the devotees and which award fulfillment of devotional desires. The first words they spoke acclaimed that the Lord is true to His vow. As stated in the *Bhagavad-gītā,* Kṛṣṇa descends upon this material world just to protect the pious and destroy the impious. That is His vow. The demigods could understand that the Lord had taken His residence within the womb of Devakī to fulfill this vow. They were very glad that the Lord was appearing to fulfill His mission, and they addressed Him as *satyaṁ param,* or the Supreme Absolute Truth.

Everyone is searching after the truth. That is the philosophical way of life. The demigods give information that the Supreme Absolute Truth is Kṛṣṇa. One who becomes fully Kṛṣṇa conscious can attain the Absolute Truth. Kṛṣṇa is the Absolute Truth. Relative truth is not truth in all the three phases of eternal time. Time is divided into past, present and future. Kṛṣṇa is Truth always, past, present and future. In the material world, everything is being controlled by supreme time, in the course of past, present and future. But before the creation, Kṛṣṇa was existing, and when there is creation, everything is resting in Kṛṣṇa, and when this creation is finished, Kṛṣṇa will remain. Therefore, He is Absolute Truth in all circumstances. If there is any truth within this material world, it emanates from the Supreme Truth, Kṛṣṇa. If there is any opulence within this material world, the cause of the opulence is Kṛṣṇa. If there is any reputation within this material world, the cause of the reputation is Kṛṣṇa. If there is any strength within this material world, the cause of such strength is Kṛṣṇa. If there is any wisdom and education within this material world, the cause of such wisdom and education is Kṛṣṇa. Therefore Kṛṣṇa is the source of all relative truths.

Devotees, therefore, following in the footsteps of Lord Brahmā, pray, *govindam ādi-puruṣaṁ tam ahaṁ bhajāmi,* worshiping the *ādi-puruṣa,* the supreme truth, Govinda. Everything, everywhere, is performed in terms of three principles, *jñāna-bala-kriyā*—knowledge, strength and activity. In every field, if there is not full knowledge, full strength and full activity, an endeavor is never successful. Therefore, if one wants success in everything, one must be backed by these three principles. In the *Vedas* (*Śvetāśvatara Upaniṣad* 6.8) there is this statement about the Supreme Personality of Godhead:

na tasya kāryaṁ karaṇaṁ ca vidyate
na tat samaś cābhyadhikaś ca dṛśyate
parāsya śaktir vividhaiva śrūyate
svābhāvikī jñāna-bala-kriyā ca

The Supreme Personality of Godhead does not need to do anything personally, for He has such potencies that anything He wants done will be done perfectly well through the control of material nature (*svābhāvikī jñāna-bala-kriyā ca*). Similarly, those who are engaged in the service of the Lord are not meant to struggle for existence. The devotees who are fully engaged in spreading the Kṛṣṇa consciousness movement, more than ten thousand men and women all over the world, have no steady or permanent occupation, yet we actually see that they are maintained very opulently. The Lord says in *Bhagavad-gītā* (9.22):

ananyāś cintayanto māṁ
ye janāḥ paryupāsate
teṣāṁ nityābhiyuktānāṁ
yoga-kṣemaṁ vahāmy aham

"For those who worship Me with devotion, meditating on My transcendental form, I carry to them what they lack and preserve what they have." The devotees have no anxiety over what will happen next, where they will stay or what they will eat, for everything is maintained and supplied by the Supreme Personality of Godhead, who has promised, *kaunteya pratijānīhi na me bhaktaḥ praṇaśyati:* "O son of Kuntī, declare it boldly that My devotee never perishes." (Bg. 9.31) From all angles of vision, therefore, in all circumstances, if one fully surrenders unto the Supreme Personality of Godhead, there is no question of one's struggling for existence. In this connection, the commentary by Śrīpāda Madhvācārya, who quotes from the *Tantra-bhāgavata,* is very meaningful:

sac-chadba uttamaṁ brūyād
ānandantīti vai vadet
yetijñānaṁ samuddiṣṭaṁ
pūrṇānanda-dṛśis tataḥ

. . .

attṛtvāc ca tadā dānāt
satyāttya cocyate vibhuḥ

Explaining the words *satyasya yonim,* Śrīla Viśvanātha Cakravartī Ṭhākura says that Kṛṣṇa is the *avatārī,* the origin of all incarnations. All incarnations are the Absolute Truth, yet the Supreme Personality of Godhead Kṛṣṇa is the origin of all incarnations. *Dīpārcir eva hi daśāntaram abhyupetya dīpāyate* (*Brahma-saṁhitā* 5.46). There may be many lamps, all equal in power, yet there is a first lamp, a second lamp, a third lamp and so on. Similarly, there are many incarnations, who are compared to lamps, but the first lamp, the original Personality of Godhead, is Kṛṣṇa. *Govindam ādi-puruṣaṁ tam ahaṁ bhajāmi.*

The demigods must offer worship in obedience to the Supreme Personality of Godhead, but one might argue that since the Supreme Godhead was within the womb of Devakī, He was also coming in a material body. Why then should He be worshiped? Why should one make a distinction between an ordinary living entity and the Supreme Personality of Godhead? These questions are answered in the following verses.

TEXT 27

एकायनोऽसौ द्विफलस्त्रिमूल-
श्चतूरसः पञ्चविधः षडात्मा ।

सप्तत्वगष्टविटपो नवाक्षो
दशच्छदी द्विखगो ह्यादिवृक्षः ॥२७॥

ekāyano 'sau dvi-phalas tri-mūlaś
catū-rasaḥ pañca-vidhaḥ ṣaḍ-ātmā
sapta-tvag aṣṭa-viṭapo navākṣo
daśa-cchadī dvi-khago hy ādi-vṛkṣaḥ

eka-ayanaḥ—the body of an ordinary living being is fully dependent on the material elements; *asau*—that; *dvi-phalaḥ*—in this body we are subject to material happiness and distress, which result from *karma; tri-mūlaḥ*—having three roots, the three modes of nature (goodness, passion and ignorance), upon which the body is created; *catuḥ-rasaḥ*—four *rasas*, or tastes;* *pañca-vidhaḥ*—consisting of five senses for acquiring knowledge (the eyes, ears, nose, tongue and touch); *ṣaṭ-ātmā*—six circumstances (lamentation, illusion, old age, death, hunger and thirst); *sapta-tvak*—having seven coverings (skin, blood, muscle, fat, bone, marrow and semen); *aṣṭa-viṭapaḥ*—eight branches (the five gross elements—earth, water, fire, air and ether—and also the mind, intelligence and ego); *nava-akṣaḥ*—nine holes; *daśa-chadī*—ten kinds of life air, resembling the leaves of a tree; *dvi-khagaḥ*—two birds (the individual soul and the Supersoul); *hi*—indeed; *ādi-vṛkṣaḥ*—this is the original tree or construction of the material body, whether individual or universal.

TRANSLATION

The body [the total body and the individual body are of the same composition] may figuratively be called "the original tree." From this tree, which fully depends on the ground of material nature, come two kinds of fruit—the enjoyment of happiness and the suffering of distress. The cause of the tree, forming its three roots, is association with the three modes of material nature—goodness,

*As the root of a tree extracts water (*rasa*) from the earth, the body tastes *dharma, artha, kāma* and *mokṣa*—religion, economic development, sense gratification and liberation. These are four kinds of *rasa*, or taste.

passion and ignorance. The fruits of bodily happiness have four tastes—religiosity, economic development, sense gratification and liberation—which are experienced through five senses for acquiring knowledge in the midst of six circumstances: lamentation, illusion, old age, death, hunger and thirst. The seven layers of bark covering the tree are skin, blood, muscle, fat, bone, marrow and semen, and the eight branches of the tree are the five gross and three subtle elements—earth, water, fire, air, ether, mind, intelligence and false ego. The tree of the body has nine hollows—the eyes, the ears, the nostrils, the mouth, the rectum and the genitals—and ten leaves, the ten airs passing through the body. In this tree of the body there are two birds: one is the individual soul, and the other is the Supersoul.

PURPORT

This material world is composed of five principal elements—earth, water, fire, air and ether—all of which are emanations from Kṛṣṇa. Although materialistic scientists may accept these five primary elements as the cause of the material manifestation, these elements in their gross and subtle states are produced by Kṛṣṇa, whose marginal potency also produces the living entities working within this material world. The Seventh Chapter of *Bhagavad-gītā* clearly states that the entire cosmic manifestation is a combination of two of Kṛṣṇa's energies—the superior energy and the inferior energy. The living entities are the superior energy, and the inanimate material elements are His inferior energy. In the dormant stage, everything rests in Kṛṣṇa.

Material scientists cannot give such a thorough analysis of the material structure of the body. The analysis of the material scientists concerns itself only with inanimate matter, but this is inadequate because the living entity is completely separate from the material bodily structure. In *Bhagavad-gītā* (7.5) the Lord says:

apareyam itas tv anyāṁ
prakṛtiṁ viddhi me parām
jīva-bhūtāṁ mahā-bāho
yayedaṁ dhāryate jagat

"Besides this inferior nature, O mighty-armed Arjuna, there is a superior energy of Mine, which consists of all the living entities who are struggling with material nature and are sustaining the universe." Although the material elements emanate from the Supreme Personality of Godhead, Kṛṣṇa, they are separated elements and are sustained by the living elements.

As indicated by the word *dvi-khagaḥ*, the living elements within the body resemble two birds in a tree. *Kha* means "sky," and *ga* means "one who flies." Thus the word *dvi-khagaḥ* refers to birds. In the tree of the body there are two birds, or two living elements, and they are always different. In *Bhagavad-gītā* (13.3), the Lord says, *kṣetra-jñaṁ cāpi māṁ viddhi sarva-kṣetreṣu bhārata:* "O scion of Bharata, you should understand that I am also the knower in all bodies." The *kṣetra-jña*, the owner of the body, is also called the *khaga*, the living entity. Within the body there are two such *kṣetra-jñas*—the individual soul and the Supersoul. The individual soul is the owner of his individual body, but the Supersoul is present within the bodies of all living entities. Such a thorough analysis and understanding of the bodily structure cannot be obtained anywhere but in the Vedic literature.

When two birds enter a tree, one may foolishly think that the birds become one or merge with the tree, but actually they do not. Rather, each bird keeps its individual identity. Similarly, the individual soul and the Supersoul do not become one, nor do they merge with matter. The living entity lives close to matter, but this does not mean that he merges or mixes with it (*asaṅgo hy ayaṁ puruṣaḥ*), although material scientists mistakenly see the organic and inorganic, or animate and inanimate, to be mixed.

Vedic knowledge has been kept imprisoned or concealed, but every human being needs to understand it in truth. The modern civilization of ignorance is simply engaged in analyzing the body, and thus people come to the erroneous conclusion that the living force within the body is generated under certain material conditions. People have no information of the soul, but this verse gives the perfect explanation that there are two living forces (*dvi-khaga*): the individual soul and the Supersoul. The Supersoul is present in every body (*īśvaraḥ sarva-bhūtānāṁ hṛd-deśe 'rjuna tiṣṭhati*), whereas the individual soul is situated only in his own body (*dehī*) and is transmigrating from one body to another.

TEXT 28

त्वमेक एवास्य सतः प्रसूति-
स्त्वं सन्निधानं त्वमनुग्रहश्च ।
त्वन्मायया संवृतचेतसस्त्वां
पश्यन्ति नाना न विपश्चितो ये ॥२८॥

tvam eka evāsya sataḥ prasūtis
tvaṁ sannidhānaṁ tvam anugrahaś ca
tvan-māyayā saṁvṛta-cetasas tvāṁ
paśyanti nānā na vipaścito ye

tvam—You (O Lord); *ekaḥ*—being one without a second, You are everything; *eva*—indeed; *asya sataḥ*—of this cosmic manifestation now visible; *prasūtiḥ*—the original source; *tvam*—Your Lordship; *sannidhānam*—the conservation of all such energy when everything is annihilated; *tvam*—Your Lordship; *anugrahaḥ ca*—and the maintainer; *tvat-māyayā*—by Your illusory, external energy; *saṁvṛta-cetasaḥ*—those whose intelligence is covered by such illusory energy; *tvām*—unto You; *paśyanti*—observe; *nānā*—many varieties; *na*—not; *vipaścitaḥ*—learned scholars or devotees; *ye*—who are.

TRANSLATION

The efficient cause of this material world, manifested with its many varieties as the original tree, is You, O Lord. You are also the maintainer of this material world, and after annihilation You are the one in whom everything is conserved. Those who are covered by Your external energy cannot see You behind this manifestation, but theirs is not the vision of learned devotees.

PURPORT

Various demigods, beginning from Lord Brahmā, Lord Śiva and even Viṣṇu, are supposed to be the creator, maintainer and annihilator of this material world, but actually they are not. The fact is that everything is the Supreme Personality of Godhead, manifested in varieties of energy. *Ekam evādvitīyaṁ brahma.* There is no second existence. Those who are truly *vipaścit,* learned, are those who have reached the platform of understanding and observing the Supreme Personality of Godhead in any condition of life. *Premāñjana-cchurita-bhakti-vilocanena santaḥ sadaiva hṛdayeṣu vilokayanti* (*Brahma-saṁhitā* 5.38). Learned devotees accept even conditions of distress as representing the presence of the Supreme Lord. When a devotee is in distress, he sees that the Lord has appeared as distress just to relieve or purify the devotee from the contamination of the material world. While one is within this material world, one is in various conditions, and therefore a devotee sees a condition of distress as but another feature of the Lord. *Tat te 'nukampāṁ susamīkṣamāṇaḥ* (*Bhāg.* 10.14.8). A devotee, therefore, regards distress as a great favor of the Lord because he understands that he is being cleansed of contamination. *Teṣām ahaṁ samuddhartā mṛtyu-saṁsāra-sāgarāt* (Bg. 12.7). The appearance of distress is a negative process intended to give the devotee relief from this material world, which is called *mṛtyu-saṁsāra,* or the constant repetition of birth and death. To save a surrendered soul from repeated birth and death, the Lord purifies him of contamination by offering him a little distress. This cannot be understood by a nondevotee, but a devotee can see this because he is *vipaścit,* or learned. A nondevotee, therefore, is perturbed in distress, but a devotee welcomes distress as another feature of the Lord. *Sarvaṁ khalv idaṁ brahma.* A devotee can actually see that there is only the Supreme Personality of Godhead and no second entity. *Ekam evādvitīyam.* There is only the Lord, who presents Himself in different energies.

Persons who are not in real knowledge think that Brahmā is the creator, Viṣṇu the maintainer and Śiva the annihilator and that the different demigods are intended to fulfill diverse purposes. Thus they create diverse purposes and worship various demigods to have these purposes fulfilled (*kāmais tais tair hṛta-jñānāḥ prapadyante 'nya-devatāḥ*). A devotee, however, knows that these various demigods are but different parts of the Supreme Personality of Godhead and that these parts need not be worshiped. As the Lord says in *Bhagavad-gītā* (9.23):

ye 'py anya-devatā bhaktā
yajante śraddhayānvitāḥ
te 'pi mām eva kaunteya
yajanty avidhi-pūrvakam

"Whatever a man may sacrifice to other gods, O son of Kuntī, is really meant for Me alone, but it is offered without true understanding." There is no need to worship the demigods, for this is *avidhi,* not in order. Simply by surrendering oneself at the lotus feet of Kṛṣṇa, one can completely discharge one's duties; there is no need to worship various deities or demigods. These various divinities are observed by the *mūḍhas,* fools, who are bewildered by the three modes of material nature (*tribhir guṇamayair bhāvair ebhiḥ sarvam idaṁ jagat*). Such fools cannot understand that the real source of everything is the Supreme Personality of Godhead (*mohitaṁ nābhijānāti mām ebhyaḥ param avyayam*). Not being disturbed by the Lord's various features, one should concentrate upon and worship the Supreme Lord (*mām ekaṁ śaraṇaṁ vraja*). This should be the guiding principle of one's life.

TEXT 29

बिभर्षि रूपाण्यवबोध आत्मा
क्षेमाय लोकस्य चराचरस्य ।
सत्त्वोपपन्नानि सुखावहानि
सतामभद्राणि मुहुः खलानाम् ॥२९॥

bibharṣi rūpāṇy avabodha ātmā
kṣemāya lokasya carācarasya
sattvopapannāni sukhāvahāni
satām abhadrāṇi muhuḥ khalānām

bibharṣi—You accept; *rūpāṇi*—varieties of forms, such as Matsya, Kūrma, Varāha, Rāma and Nṛsiṁha; *avabodhaḥ ātmā*—in spite of having different incarnations, You remain the Supreme, full of knowledge; *kṣemāya*—for the benefit of everyone, and especially the devotees; *lokasya*—of all living entities; *cara-acarasya*—moving and nonmoving; *sattva-upapannāni*—all such incarnations are transcendental (*śuddha-sattva*); *sukha-avahāni*—full of transcendental bliss; *satām*—of the devotees; *abhadrāṇi*—all inauspiciousness or annihilation; *muhuḥ*—again and again; *khalānām*—of the nondevotees.

TRANSLATION

O Lord, You are always in full knowledge, and to bring all good fortune to all living entities, You appear in different incarnations, all of them transcendental to the material creation. When You appear in these incarnations, You are pleasing to the pious and religious devotees, but for nondevotees You are the annihilator.

PURPORT

This verse explains why the Supreme Personality of Godhead appears as an incarnation again and again. The incarnations of the Supreme Personality of Godhead all function differently, but their main purpose is *paritrāṇāya sādhūnāṁ vināśāya ca duṣkṛtām*—to protect the devotees and annihilate the miscreants. Yet even though the *duṣkṛtīs*, or miscreants, are annihilated, this is ultimately good for them.

TEXT 30

त्वय्यम्बुजाक्षाखिलसत्त्वधाम्नि
समाधिनावेशितचेतसैके ।
त्वत्पादपोतेन महत्कृतेन
कुर्वन्ति गोवत्सपदं भवाब्धिम् ॥३०॥

tvayy ambujākṣākhila-sattva-dhāmni
samādhināveśita-cetasaike
tvat-pāda-potena mahat-kṛtena
kurvanti govatsa-padaṁ bhavābdhim

tvayi—in You; *ambhuja-akṣa*—O lotus-eyed Lord; *akhila-sattva-dhāmni*—who are the original cause of all existence, from whom everything emanates and in whom all potencies reside; *samādhinā*—by constant meditation and complete absorption (in thoughts of You, the Supreme Personality of Godhead); *āveśita*—fully absorbed, fully engaged; *cetasā*—but by such a mentality; *eke*—the one process of always thinking of Your lotus feet; *tvat-pāda-potena*—by boarding such a boat as Your lotus feet; *mahat-kṛtena*—by that action which is considered the most powerful original existence or which is executed by *mahājanas; kurvanti*—they make; *govatsa-padam*—like the hoofprint of a calf; *bhava-abdhim*—the great ocean of nescience.

TRANSLATION

O lotus-eyed Lord, by concentrating one's meditation on Your lotus feet, which are the reservoir of all existence, and by accepting those lotus feet as the boat by which to cross the ocean of nescience, one follows in the footsteps of mahājanas [great saints, sages and devotees]. By this simple process, one can cross the ocean of nescience as easily as one steps over the hoofprint of a calf.

PURPORT

The true mission in life is to cross the ocean of nescience, of repeated birth and death. Those in the darkness of ignorance, however, do not know this mission. Instead, being carried away by the waves of material nature (*prakṛteḥ kriyamāṇāni guṇaiḥ karmāṇi sarvaśaḥ*), they are undergoing the tribulations of *mṛtyu-saṁsāra-vartmani*, repeated birth and death. But persons who have achieved knowledge by the association of devotees follow the *mahājanas* (*mahat-kṛtena*). Such a person always concentrates his mind upon the lotus feet of the Lord and executes one or more of the nine varieties of devotional service (*śravaṇaṁ kīrtanaṁ viṣṇoḥ smaraṇaṁ pāda-sevanam*). Simply by this process, one can cross the insurmountable ocean of nescience.

Devotional service is powerful in any form. *Śrī-viṣṇoḥ śravaṇe parīkṣid abhavad vaiyāsakiḥ kīrtane* (*Bhakti-rasāmṛta-sindhu* 1.2.265). According to this verse, Mahārāja Parīkṣit became liberated by fully concentrating his mind on hearing the Lord's holy name, attributes and pastimes. Similarly, Śukadeva Gosvāmī simply glorified the Lord, and by speaking on the subject matters of Kṛṣṇa that constitute the entire *Śrīmad-Bhāgavatam*, he too was liberated. One may also be liberated simply by *sakhya*, friendly behavior with the Lord. Such is the power of devotional service, as we learn from the examples set by the Lord's many pure devotees.

svayambhūr nāradaḥ śambhuḥ
kumāraḥ kapilo manuḥ
prahlādo janako bhīṣmo
balir vaiyāsakir vayam
(*Bhāg.* 6.3.20)

We have to follow in the footsteps of such devotees, for by this one easy process one can cross the great ocean of nescience just as one might cross a small hole created by the hoof of a calf.

Here the Lord is described as *ambujākṣa*, or lotus-eyed. By seeing the eyes of the Lord, which are compared to lotus flowers, one becomes so satisfied that one does not want to turn his eyes to anything else. Simply by seeing the transcendental form of the Lord, a devotee is at once fully absorbed in the Lord in his heart. This absorption is called *samādhi. Dhyānāvasthita-tad-gatena manasā paśyanti yaṁ yoginaḥ* (*Bhāg.* 12.13.1). A *yogī* is fully absorbed in thoughts of the Supreme Personality of Godhead, for he has no other business than to think of the Lord always within the heart. It is also said:

samāśritā ye pada-pallava-plavaṁ
mahat-padaṁ puṇya-yaśo murāreḥ
bhavāmbudhir vatsa-padaṁ paraṁ padaṁ
padaṁ padaṁ yad vipadāṁ na teṣām

"For one who has accepted the boat of the lotus feet of the Lord, who is the shelter of the cosmic manifestation and is famous as Murāri, the enemy of the demon Mura, the ocean of the material world is like the water contained in a calf's hoofprint. His goal is *paraṁ padam*, or Vaikuṇṭha, the place where there are no material miseries, not the place where there is danger at every step." (*Bhāg.* 10.14.58) This process is recommended here by authorities like Lord Brahmā and Lord Śiva (*svayambhūr nāradaḥ śambhuḥ*), and therefore we must take to this process in order to transcend nescience. This is very easy, but we must follow in the footsteps of great personalities, and then success will be possible.

In regard to the word *mahat-kṛtena*, it is also significant that the process shown by great devotees is not only for them but also for others. If things are made easy, this affords facility for the person who has made them easy and also for others who follow the same principles. The process recommended in this verse for crossing the ocean of nescience is easy not only for the devotee but also for common persons who follow the devotee (*mahājano yena gataḥ sa panthāḥ*).

TEXT 31

स्वयं समुत्तीर्य सुदुस्तरं द्युमन्
भवार्णवं भीममदभ्रसौहृदाः ।
भवत्पदाम्भोरुहनावमत्र ते
निधाय याताः सदनुग्रहो भवान् ॥३१॥

svayaṁ samuttīrya sudustaraṁ dyuman
bhavārṇavaṁ bhīmam adabhra-sauhṛdāḥ
bhavat-padāmbhoruha-nāvam atra te
nidhāya yātāḥ sad-anugraho bhavān

svayam—personally; *samuttīrya*—perfectly crossing; *su-dustaram*—which is very difficult to cross; *dyuman*—O Lord, who appear exactly like the sun, illuminating the darkness of this world of ignorance; *bhava-arṇavam*—the ocean of nescience; *bhīmam*—which is extremely fierce; *adabhra-sauhṛdāḥ*—devotees who are incessantly friendly to the fallen souls; *bhavat-pada-ambhoruha*—Your lotus feet; *nāvam*—the boat for crossing; *atra*—in this world; *te*—they (the Vaiṣṇavas); *nidhāya*—leaving behind; *yātāḥ*—on to the ultimate destination, Vaikuṇṭha; *sat-anugrahaḥ*—who are always kind and merciful to the devotees; *bhavān*—You.

TRANSLATION

O Lord, who resemble the shining sun, You are always ready to fulfill the desire of Your devotee, and therefore You are known as a desire tree [vāñchā-kalpataru]. When ācāryas completely take shelter under Your lotus feet in order to cross the fierce ocean of nescience, they leave behind on earth the method by which they

cross, and because You are very merciful to Your other devotees, You accept this method to help them.

PURPORT

This statement reveals how the merciful *ācāryas* and the merciful Supreme Personality of Godhead together help the serious devotee who wants to return home, back to Godhead. Śrī Caitanya Mahāprabhu, in His teachings to Rūpa Gosvāmī, said:

brahmāṇḍa bhramite kona bhāgyavān jīva
guru-kṛṣṇa-prasāde pāya bhakti-latā-bīja
(Cc. *Madhya* 19.151)

One can achieve the seed of *bhakti-latā*, devotional service, by the mercy of *guru* and Kṛṣṇa. The duty of the *guru* is to find the means, according to the time, the circumstances and the candidate, by which one can be induced to render devotional service, which Kṛṣṇa accepts from a candidate who wants to be successful in going back home, back to Godhead. After wandering throughout the universe, a fortunate person within this material world seeks shelter of such a *guru*, or *ācārya*, who trains the devotee in the suitable ways to render service according to the circumstances so that the Supreme Personality of Godhead will accept the service. This makes it easier for the candidate to reach the ultimate destination. The *ācārya's* duty, therefore, is to find the means by which devotees may render service according to references from *śāstra*. Rūpa Gosvāmī, for example, in order to help subsequent devotees, published such devotional books as *Bhakti-rasāmṛta-sindhu*. Thus it is the duty of the *ācārya* to publish books that will help future candidates take up the method of service and become eligible to return home, back to Godhead, by the mercy of the Lord. In our Kṛṣṇa consciousness movement, this same path is being prescribed and followed. Thus the devotees have been advised to refrain from four sinful activities—illicit sex, intoxication, meat-eating and gambling—and to chant sixteen rounds a day. These are bona fide instructions. Because in the Western countries constant chanting is not possible, one should not artificially imitate Haridāsa Ṭhākura, but should follow this method. Kṛṣṇa will accept a devotee who strictly follows the regulative principles and the method prescribed in the various books and literatures published by the authorities. The *ācārya* gives the suitable method for crossing the ocean of nescience by accepting the boat of the Lord's lotus feet, and if this method is strictly followed, the followers will ultimately reach the destination, by the grace of the Lord. This method is called *ācārya-sampradāya.* It is therefore said, *sampradāya-vihīnā ye mantrās te niṣphalā matāḥ* (*Padma Purāṇa*). The *ācārya-sampradāya* is strictly bona fide. Therefore one must accept the *ācārya-sampradāya;* otherwise one's endeavor will be futile. Śrīla Narottama dāsa Ṭhākura therefore sings:

tāṅdera caraṇa sevi bhakta sane vāsa
janame janame haya, ei abhilāṣa

One must worship the lotus feet of the *ācārya* and live within the society of devotees. Then one's endeavor to cross over nescience will surely be successful.

TEXT 32

येऽन्येऽरविन्दाक्ष विमुक्तमानिन-
स्त्वय्यस्तभावादविशुद्धबुद्धयः ।
आरुह्य कृच्छ्रेण परं पदं ततः
पतन्त्यधोऽनादृतयुष्मदङ्घ्रयः ॥३२॥

ye 'nye 'ravindākṣa vimukta-māninas
tvayy asta-bhāvād aviśuddha-buddhayaḥ
āruhya kṛcchreṇa paraṁ padaṁ tataḥ
patanty adho 'nādṛta-yuṣmad-aṅghrayaḥ

ye anye—anyone, or all others; *aravinda-akṣa*—O lotus-eyed one; *vimukta-māninaḥ*—falsely considering themselves free from the bondage of material contamination; *tvayi*—unto You; *asta-bhāvāt*—speculating in various ways but not knowing or desiring more information of Your lotus feet; *aviśuddha-buddhayaḥ*—whose intelligence is still not purified and who do not know the goal of life; *āruhya*—even though achieving; *kṛcchreṇa*—by undergoing severe austerities, penances and hard labor; *param padam*—the highest position (according to their imagination and speculation); *tataḥ*—from that position; *patanti*—they fall; *adhaḥ*—down into material existence again; *anādṛta*—neglecting devotion to; *yuṣmat*—Your; *aṅghrayaḥ*—lotus feet.

TRANSLATION

[Someone may say that aside from devotees, who always seek shelter at the Lord's lotus feet, there are those who are not devotees but who have accepted different processes for attaining salvation. What happens to them? In answer to this question, Lord Brahmā and the other demigods said:] O lotus-eyed Lord, although nondevotees who accept severe austerities and penances to achieve the highest position may think themselves liberated, their intelligence is impure. They fall down from their position of imagined superiority because they have no regard for Your lotus feet.

PURPORT

Aside from devotees, there are many others, nondevotees, known as *karmīs*, *jñānīs* or *yogīs*, philanthropists, altruists, politicians, impersonalists and voidists. There are many varieties of nondevotees who have their respective ways of liberation, but simply because they do not know the shelter of the Lord's lotus feet, although they falsely think that they have been liberated and elevated to the highest position, they fall down. As clearly stated by the Lord Himself in *Bhagavad-gītā* (9.3):

aśraddadhānāḥ puruṣā
dharmasyāsya parantapa
aprāpya māṁ nivartante
mṛtyu-saṁsāra-vartmani

"Those who are not faithful on the path of devotional service cannot attain Me, O conqueror of foes, but return to birth and death in this material world." It doesn't matter whether one is a *karmī*, *jñānī*, *yogī*, philanthropist, politician or whatever; if one has no love for the lotus feet of the Lord, one falls down. That is the verdict given by Lord Brahmā in this verse.

There are persons who advocate accepting any process and who say that whatever process one accepts will lead to the same goal, but that is refuted in this verse, where such persons are referred to as *vimukta-māninaḥ*, signifying that although they think they have attained the highest perfection, in fact they have not. In the present day, big, big politicians all over the world think that by scheming they can occupy the highest political post, that of president or prime minister, but we actually see that even in this life such big prime ministers, presidents and other politicians, because of being nondevotees, fall down (*patanty adhaḥ*). To become president or prime minister is not easy; one must work very hard (*āruhya kṛcchreṇa*) to achieve the post. And even though one may reach his goal, at any moment one may be kicked down by material nature. In human society there have been many instances in which great, exalted politicians have fallen from government and become lost in historical oblivion. The cause of this is *aviśuddha-buddhayah:* their intelligence is impure. The *śāstra* says, *na te viduḥ svārtha-gatiṁ hi viṣṇum* (*Bhāg.* 7.5.31). One achieves the perfection of life by becoming a devotee of Viṣṇu, but people do not know this. Therefore, as stated in *Bhagavad-gītā* (12.5), *kleśo 'dhikataras teṣām avyaktāsakta-cetasām.* Persons who do not ultimately accept the Supreme Personality of Godhead and take to devotional service, but who instead are attached to impersonalism and voidism, must undergo great labor to achieve their goals.

śreyaḥ-sṛtiṁ bhaktim udasya te vibho
kliśyanti ye kevala-bodha-labdhaye
(*Bhāg.* 10.14.4)

To achieve understanding, such persons work very hard and undergo severe austerities, but their hard labor and austerities themselves are their only achievement, for they do not actually achieve the real goal of life.

Dhruva Mahārāja at first wanted to achieve the greatest material kingdom and greater material possessions than his father, but when he was actually favored by the Lord, who appeared before him to give him the benediction he desired, Dhruva Mahārāja refused it, saying, *svāmin kṛtārtho 'smi varaṁ na yāce:* "Now I am fully satisfied. I do not want any material benediction." (*Hari-bhakti-sudhodaya* 7.28) This is the perfection of life. *Yaṁ labdhvā cāparaṁ lābhaṁ manyate nādhikaṁ tataḥ* (Bg. 6.22). If one achieves the shelter of the Lord's lotus feet, one is fully satisfied and does not need to ask for any material benediction.

At night, no one can see a lotus, for lotuses blossom only during the daytime. Therefore the word *aravindākṣa* is significant. One who is not captivated by the lotus eyes or transcendental form of the Supreme Lord is in darkness, exactly like one who cannot see a lotus. One who has not come to the point of seeing the lotus eyes and transcendental form of Śyāmasundara is a failure. *Premāñjana-cchurita-bhakti-vilocanena santaḥ sadaiva hṛdayeṣu vilokayanti.* Those who are attached to the Supreme Personality of Godhead in love always see the Lord's lotus eyes and lotus feet, whereas others cannot see the Lord's beauty and are therefore classified as *anādṛta-yuṣmad-aṅghrayaḥ*, or neglectful of the Lord's personal form. Those who neglect the Lord's form are surely failures on every path in life, but if one develops even a little love for the Supreme Personality of Godhead, one is liberated without difficulty (*svalpam apy asya dharmasya trāyate mahato bhayāt*). Therefore the Supreme Personality of Godhead recommends in *Bhagavad-gītā* (9.34), *man-manā bhava mad-bhakto mad-yājī māṁ namaskuru:* "Simply think of Me, become My devotee, worship Me and offer some slight homage to Me." Simply by this process, one is guaranteed to return home, back to Godhead, and thus attain the highest perfection. The Lord further affirms in *Bhagavad-gītā* (18.54–55):

brahma-bhūtaḥ prasannātmā
na śocati na kāṅkṣati
samaḥ sarveṣu bhūteṣu
mad-bhaktiṁ labhate parām

bhaktyā mām abhijānāti
yāvān yaś cāsmi tattvataḥ
tato māṁ tattvato jñātvā
viśate tad-anantaram

"One who is thus transcendentally situated at once realizes the Supreme Brahman and becomes fully joyful. He never laments nor desires to have anything; he is equally disposed to every living entity. In that state he attains pure devotional service unto Me. One can understand the Supreme Personality as He is only by devotional service. And when one is in full consciousness of the Supreme Lord by such devotion, he can enter into the kingdom of God."

TEXT 33

तथा न ते माधव तावकाः क्वचिद्
भ्रश्यन्ति मार्गात्त्वयि बद्धसौहृदाः ।
त्वयाभिगुप्ता विचरन्ति निर्भया
विनायकानीकपमूर्धसु प्रभो ॥३३॥

tathā na te mādhava tāvakāḥ kvacid
bhraśyanti mārgāt tvayi baddha-sauhṛdāḥ
tvayābhiguptā vicaranti nirbhayā
vināyakānīkapa-mūrdhasu prabho

tathā—like them (the nondevotees); *na*—not; *te*—they (the devotees); *mādhava*—O Lord, husband of the goddess of fortune; *tāvakāḥ*—the followers of the devotional path, the devotees; *kvacit*—in any circumstances; *bhraśyanti*—fall down; *mārgāt*—from the path of devotional service; *tvayi*—unto You; *baddha-sauhṛdāḥ*—because of being fully attached to Your lotus feet; *tvayā*—by You; *abhiguptāḥ*—always protected from all dangers; *vicaranti*—they move; *nirbhayāḥ*—without fear; *vināyaka-anīkapa*—the enemies who maintain paraphernalia to oppose the *bhakti* cult; *mūrdhasu*—on their heads; *prabho*—O Lord.

TRANSLATION

O Mādhava, Supreme Personality of Godhead, Lord of the goddess of fortune, if devotees completely in love with You sometimes fall from the path of devotion, they do not fall like nondevotees, for You still protect them. Thus they fearlessly traverse the heads of their opponents and continue to progress in devotional service.

PURPORT

Devotees generally do not fall down, but if circumstantially they do, the Lord, because of their strong attachment to Him, gives them protection in all circumstances. Thus even if devotees fall down, they are still strong enough to traverse the heads of their enemies. We have actually seen that our Kṛṣṇa consciousness movement has many opponents, such as the "deprogrammers," who instituted a strong legal case against the devotees. We thought that this case would take a long time to settle, but because the devotees were protected by the Supreme Personality of Godhead, we unexpectedly won the case in one day. Thus a case that was expected to continue for years was settled in a day because of the protection of the Supreme Personality of Godhead, who has promised in *Bhagavad-gītā* (9.31), *kaunteya pratijānīhi na me bhaktaḥ praṇaśyati:* "O son of Kuntī, declare it boldly that My devotee never perishes." In history there are many instances of devotees like Citraketu, Indradyumna and Mahārāja Bharata who circumstantially fell down but were still protected. Mahārāja Bharata, for example, because of his attachment to a deer, thought of the deer at the time of death, and therefore in his next life he became a deer (*yaṁ yaṁ vāpi smaran bhāvaṁ tyajaty ante kalevaram*). Because of protection by the Supreme Personality of Godhead, however, the deer remembered his relationship with the Lord and next took birth in a good brahminical family and performed devotional service (*śucīnāṁ śrīmatāṁ gehe yoga-bhraṣṭo 'bhijāyate*). Similarly, Citraketu fell down and became a demon, Vṛtrāsura, but he too was protected. Thus even if one falls down from the path of *bhakti-yoga*, one is ultimately saved. If a devotee is strongly situated in devotional service, the Supreme Personality of Godhead has promised to protect him (*kaunteya pratijānīhi na me bhaktaḥ praṇaśyati*). But even if a devotee circumstantially falls down, he is protected by Mādhava.

The word Mādhava is significant. *Mā*, mother Lakṣmī, the mother of all opulences, is always with the Supreme Personality of Godhead, and if a devotee is in touch with the Supreme Personality of Godhead, all the opulences of the Lord are ready to help him.

yatra yogeśvaraḥ kṛṣṇo
yatra pārtho dhanur-dharaḥ

tatra śrīr vijayo bhūtir
dhruvā nītir matir mama
(Bg. 18.78)

Wherever there is the Supreme Personality of Godhead, Kṛṣṇa, and His devotee Arjuna, Pārtha, there is victory, opulence, extraordinary power and morality. The opulences of a devotee are not a result of *karma-kāṇḍa-vicāra.* A devotee is always protected by all of the Supreme Lord's opulences, of which no one can deprive him (*teṣāṁ nityābhiyuktānāṁ yoga-kṣemaṁ vahāmy aham*). Thus a devotee cannot be defeated by any opponents. A devotee, therefore, should not deviate knowingly from the path of devotion. The adherent devotee is assured all protection from the Supreme Personality of Godhead.

TEXT 34

सत्त्वं विशुद्धं श्रयते भवान् स्थितौ
शरीरिणां श्रेयउपायनं वपुः ।
वेदक्रियायोगतपःसमाधिभि-
स्तवार्हणं येन जनः समीहते ॥३४॥

sattvaṁ viśuddhaṁ śrayate bhavān sthitau
śarīriṇāṁ śreya-upāyanaṁ vapuḥ
veda-kriyā-yoga-tapaḥ-samādhibhis
tavārhaṇaṁ yena janaḥ samīhate

sattvam—existence; *viśuddham*—transcendental, beyond the three modes of material nature; *śrayate*—accepts; *bhavān*—Your Lordship; *sthitau*—during the maintenance of this material world; *śarīriṇām*—of all living entities; *śreyaḥ*—of supreme auspiciousness; *upāyanam*—for the benefit; *vapuḥ*—a transcendental form or body; *veda-kriyā*—by ritualistic ceremonies according to the directions of the *Vedas; yoga*—by practice of devotion; *tapaḥ*—by austerities; *samādhibhiḥ*—by becoming absorbed in transcendental existence; *tava*—Your; *arhaṇam*—worship; *yena*—by such activities; *janaḥ*—human society; *samīhate*—offers (its obligation unto You).

TRANSLATION

O Lord, during the time of maintenance You manifest several incarnations, all with transcendental bodies, beyond the material modes of nature. When You appear in this way, You bestow all good fortune upon the living entities by teaching them to perform Vedic activities such as ritualistic ceremonies, mystic yoga, austerities, penances, and ultimately samādhi, ecstatic absorption in thoughts of You. Thus You are worshiped by the Vedic principles.

PURPORT

As stated in *Bhagavad-gītā* (18.3), *yajña-dāna-tapaḥ-karma na tyājyam:* the Vedic ritualistic ceremonies, charity, austerity and all such prescribed duties are never to be given up. *Yajño dānaṁ tapaś caiva pāvanāni manīṣiṇām* (18.5): even one who is very much advanced in spiritual realization must still execute the Vedic principles. Even in the lowest stage, the *karmīs* are advised to work for the sake of the Lord.

yajñārthāt karmaṇo 'nyatra
loko 'yaṁ karma-bandhanaḥ

"Work done as a sacrifice for Viṣṇu has to be performed, otherwise work binds one to this material world." (Bg. 3.9) The words *yajñārthāt karmaṇaḥ* indicate that while performing all kinds of duties, one should remember that these duties should be performed to satisfy the Supreme Lord (*sva-karmaṇā tam abhyarcya*). According to Vedic principles, there must be divisions of human society (*cātur-varṇyaṁ mayā sṛṣṭam*). There should be *brāhmaṇas, kṣatriyas, vaiśyas* and *śūdras*, and everyone should learn to worship the Supreme Personality of Godhead (*tam abhyarcya*). This is real human society, and without this system we are left with animal society.

The modern activities of human society are described in *Śrīmad-Bhāgavatam* as the activities of *go-khara,* cows and asses (*sa eva gokharaḥ*). Everyone is acting in a bodily concept of life involving society, friendship and love for the improvement of economic and political conditions, and thus all activities are enacted in ignorance. The Supreme

Personality therefore comes to teach us how to act according to the Vedic principles. In this age of Kali, the Supreme Personality of Godhead appeared as Śrī Caitanya Mahāprabhu and preached that in this age the Vedic activities cannot be systematically performed because people are so fallen. He gave this recommendation from the *śāstras:*

harer nāma harer nāma
harer nāmaiva kevalam
kalau nāsty eva nāsty eva
nāsty eva gatir anyathā

"In this age of quarrel and hypocrisy the only means of deliverance is chanting the holy name of the Lord. There is no other way. There is no other way. There is no other way." The Kṛṣṇa consciousness movement is therefore teaching people all over the world how to chant the Hare Kṛṣṇa *mantra*, and this has proved very much effective in all places at all times. The Supreme Personality of Godhead appears in order to teach us Vedic principles intended for understanding Him (*vedaiś ca sarvair aham eva vedyaḥ*). We should always know that when Kṛṣṇa and Lord Caitanya appeared, They appeared in *śuddha-sattva* bodies. One should not mistake the body of Kṛṣṇa or Caitanya Mahāprabhu to be a material body like ours, for Kṛṣṇa and Caitanya Mahāprabhu appeared as needed for the benefit of the entire human society. Out of causeless mercy, the Lord appears in different ages in His original *śuddha-sattva* transcendental body to elevate human society to the spiritual platform upon which they can truly benefit. Unfortunately, modern politicians and other leaders stress the bodily comforts of life (*yasyātma-buddhiḥ kuṇape tri-dhātuke*) and concentrate on the activities of this ism and that ism, which they describe in different kinds of flowery language. Essentially such activities are the activities of animals (*sa eva go-kharaḥ*). We should learn how to act from *Bhagavad-gītā*, which explains everything for human understanding. Thus we can become happy even in this age of Kali.

TEXT 35

सत्त्वं न चेद्धातरिदं निजं भवेद्
विज्ञानमज्ञानभिदापमार्जनम् ।

गुणप्रकाशैरनुमीयते भवान्
प्रकाशते यस्य च येन वा गुणः ॥३५॥

sattvaṁ na ced dhātar idaṁ nijaṁ bhaved
vijñānam ajñāna-bhidāpamārjanam
guṇa-prakāśair anumīyate bhavān
prakāśate yasya ca yena vā guṇaḥ

sattvam—*śuddha-sattva*, transcendental; *na*—not; *cet*—if; *dhātaḥ*—O reservoir of all energies, cause of all causes; *idam*—this; *nijam*—personal, spiritual; *bhavet*—could have been; *vijñānam*—transcendental knowledge; *ajñāna-bhidā*—which drives away the ignorance of the material modes; *apamārjanam*—completely vanquished; *guṇa-prakāśaiḥ*—by the awakening of such transcendental knowledge; *anumīyate*—becomes manifested; *bhavān*—Your Lordship; *prakāśate*—exhibit; *yasya*—whose; *ca*—and; *yena*—by which; *vā*—either; *guṇaḥ*—quality or intelligence.

TRANSLATION

O Lord, cause of all causes, if Your transcendental body were not beyond the modes of material nature, one could not understand the difference between matter and transcendence. Only by Your presence can one understand the transcendental nature of Your Lordship, who are the controller of material nature. Your transcendental nature is very difficult to understand unless one is influenced by the presence of Your transcendental form.

PURPORT

It is said, *traiguṇya-viṣayā vedā nistraiguṇyo bhavārjuna.* Unless one is situated in transcendence, one cannot understand the transcendental nature of the Lord. As stated in *Śrīmad-Bhāgavatam* (10.14.29):

athāpi te deva padāmbuja-dvaya-
prasāda-leśānugṛhīta eva hi
jānāti tattvaṁ bhagavan-mahimno
na cānya eko 'pi ciraṁ vicinvan

Only by the mercy of the Supreme Personality of Godhead can one understand Him. Those who are in the modes of material nature, although speculating for thousands of years, cannot understand Him. The Lord has innumerable forms (*rāmādi-mūrtiṣu kalā-niyamena tiṣṭhan*), and unless these forms, such as Lord Rāmacandra, Nṛsiṁhadeva, Kṛṣṇa and Balarāma, were transcendental, how could they be worshiped by devotees since time immemorial? *Bhaktyā mām abhijānāti yāvān yaś cāsmi tattvataḥ* (Bg. 18.55). Devotees who awaken their transcendental nature in the presence of the Lord and who follow the rules and regulations of devotional service can understand Lord Kṛṣṇa, Lord Rāmacandra and other incarnations, who are not of this material world but who come from the spiritual world for the benefit of people in general. If one does not take to this process, one imagines or manufactures some form of God according to material qualities and can never awaken a real understanding of the Supreme Personality of Godhead. The words *bhaktyā mām abhijānāti yāvān yaś cāsmi tattvataḥ* signify that unless one worships the Lord according to the regulative devotional principles, one cannot awaken the transcendental nature. Deity worship, even in the absence of the Supreme Personality of Godhead, awakens the transcendental nature of the devotee, who thus becomes increasingly attached to the Lord's lotus feet.

The appearance of Kṛṣṇa is the answer to all imaginative iconography of the Supreme Personality of Godhead. Everyone imagines the form of the Supreme Personality of Godhead according to his mode of material nature. In the *Brahma-saṁhitā* it is said that the Lord is the oldest person. Therefore a section of religionists imagine that God must be very old, and therefore they depict a form of the Lord like a very old man. But in the same *Brahma-saṁhitā*, that is contradicted; although He is the oldest of all living entities, He has His eternal form as a fresh youth. The exact words used in this connection in the *Śrīmad-Bhāgavatam* are *vijñānam ajñāna-bhidāpamārjanam*. *Vijñāna* means transcendental knowledge of the Supreme Personality; *vijñāna* is also experienced knowledge. Transcendental knowledge has to be accepted by the descending process of disciplic succession as Brahmā presents the knowledge of Kṛṣṇa in the *Brahma-saṁhitā*. *Brahma-saṁhitā* is *vijñāna* as realized by Brahmā's transcendental experience, and in that way he presented the form and the pastimes of Kṛṣṇa in the transcendental abode.

Ajñāna-bhidā means "that which can match all kinds of speculation." In ignorance, people are imagining the form of the Lord; sometimes He has no form and sometimes He has form, according to their different imaginations. But the presentation of Kṛṣṇa in the *Brahma-saṁhitā* is *vijñāna*—scientific, experienced knowledge given by Lord Brahmā and accepted by Lord Caitanya. There is no doubt about it. Śrī Kṛṣṇa's form, Śrī Kṛṣṇa's flute, Kṛṣṇa's color—everything is reality. Here it is said that this *vijñānam* is always defeating all kinds of speculative knowledge. "Therefore," the demigods prayed, "without Your appearing as Kṛṣṇa, as You are, neither *ajñāna-bhidā* (the nescience of speculative knowledge) nor *vijñānam* would be realized. *Ajñāna-bhidāpamārjanam*—by Your appearance the speculative knowledge of ignorance will be vanquished, and the real, experienced knowledge of authorities like Lord Brahmā will be established. Men influenced by the three modes of material nature imagine their own God according to the modes of material nature. In this way God is presented in various ways, but Your appearance will establish what the real form of God is."

The highest blunder committed by the impersonalist is to think that when the incarnation of God comes, He accepts a form of matter in the mode of goodness. Actually the form of Kṛṣṇa or Nārāyaṇa is transcendental to any material idea. Even the greatest impersonalist, Śaṅkarācārya, has admitted, *nārāyaṇaḥ paro 'vyaktāt:* the material creation is caused by the *avyakta*, the impersonal manifestation of matter or the nonphenomenal total reservoir of matter, and Kṛṣṇa is transcendental to that material conception. This is expressed in the *Śrīmad-Bhāgavatam* as *śuddha-sattva*, or transcendental. The Lord does not belong to the material mode of goodness, for He is above the position of material goodness. He belongs to the transcendental, eternal status of bliss and knowledge.

"Dear Lord," the demigods prayed, "when You appear in Your different incarnations, You take different names and forms according to different situations. Lord Kṛṣṇa is Your name because You are all-attractive; You are called Śyāmasundara because of Your transcendental beauty. *Śyāma* means blackish, yet they say that You are more beautiful than thousands of cupids. *Kandarpa-koṭi-kamanīya.* Although You appear in a color which is compared to that of a blackish cloud, You are the transcendental Absolute, and therefore Your beauty is many, many times more attractive than the delicate body of Cupid. Sometimes You are called Giridhārī because You lifted the hill known as Govardhana. You are sometimes called Nanda-nandana or Vāsudeva or Devakī-nandana because You appear as the son of Mahārāja Nanda or Devakī or Vasudeva. Impersonalists think that Your many names or forms are according to a particular type of work and quality because they accept You from the position of a material observer.

"Our dear Lord, the way of understanding is not to study Your absolute nature, form and activities by mental speculation. One must engage himself in devotional service; then one can understand Your absolute nature and Your transcendental form, name and quality. Actually, only a person who has a little taste for the service of Your lotus feet can understand Your transcendental nature or form and quality. Others may go on speculating for millions of years, but it is not possible for them to understand even a single part of Your actual position." In other words, the Supreme Personality of Godhead, Kṛṣṇa, cannot be understood by the nondevotees because there is a curtain of *yogamāyā* which covers Kṛṣṇa's actual features. As confirmed in the *Bhagavad-gītā* (7.25), *nāhaṁ prakāśaḥ sarvasya.* The Lord says, "I am not exposed to anyone and everyone." When Kṛṣṇa came, He was actually present on the battlefield of Kurukṣetra, and everyone saw Him. But not everyone could understand that He was the Supreme Personality of Godhead. Still, everyone who died in His presence attained complete liberation from material bondage and was transferred to the spiritual world.

Because foolish *mūḍhas* do not awaken their spiritual nature, they do not understand Kṛṣṇa or Rāma (*avajānanti māṁ mūḍhā mānuṣīṁ tanum āśritam*). Even big academic scholars, not considering the endeavors of the *ācāryas* who have recommended devotional service in many elaborate commentaries and notes, think that Kṛṣṇa is fictitious. This is due to a lack of transcendental knowledge and a failure to awaken Kṛṣṇa consciousness. One should have the common sense to ask why, if Kṛṣṇa or Rāma were fictitious, stalwart scholars like Śrīdhara Svāmī, Rūpa Gosvāmī, Sanātana Gosvāmī, Vīrarāghava, Vijayadhvaja, Vallabhācārya and many other recognized *ācāryas* would have spent so much time to write about Kṛṣṇa in notes and commentaries on *Śrīmad-Bhāgavatam.*

TEXT 36

न नामरूपे गुणजन्मकर्मभि-
र्निरूपितव्ये तव तस्य साक्षिणः ।
मनोवचोभ्यामनुमेयवर्त्मनो
देव क्रियायां प्रतियन्त्यथापि हि ॥३६॥

na nāma-rūpe guṇa-janma-karmabhir
nirūpitavye tava tasya sākṣiṇaḥ
mano-vacobhyām anumeya-vartmano
deva kriyāyāṁ pratiyanty athāpi hi

na—not; *nāma-rūpe*—the name and form; *guṇa*—with attributes; *janma*—appearance; *karmabhiḥ*—activities or pastimes; *nirūpitavye*—are not able to be ascertained; *tava*—Your; *tasya*—of Him; *sākṣiṇaḥ*—who is the direct observer; *manaḥ*—of the mind; *vacobhyām*—words; *anumeya*—hypothesis; *vartmanaḥ*—the path; *deva*—O Lord; *kriyāyām*—in devotional activities; *pratiyanti*—they realize; *atha api*—still; *hi*—indeed (You can be realized by the devotees).

TRANSLATION

O Lord, Your transcendental name and form are not ascertained by those who merely speculate on the path of imagination. Your name, form and attributes can be ascertained only through devotional service.

PURPORT

As stated in the *Padma Purāṇa:*

ataḥ śrī-kṛṣṇa-nāmādi
na bhaved grāhyam indriyaiḥ
sevonmukhe hi jihvādau
svayam eva sphuraty adaḥ

"One cannot understand the transcendental nature of the name, form, quality and pastimes of Śrī Kṛṣṇa through one's materially contaminated senses. Only when one becomes spiritually saturated by transcendental service to the Lord are the transcendental name, form, quality and pastimes of the Lord revealed to him." Since Kṛṣṇa and His transcendental name, form and activities are all of a transcendental nature, ordinary persons or those who are only slightly advanced cannot understand them. Even big scholars who are nondevotees think that Kṛṣṇa is fictitious. Yet although so-called scholars and commentators do not believe that Kṛṣṇa was factually a historical person whose presence on the Battlefield of Kurukṣetra is recorded in the history of *Mahābhārata*, they feel compelled to write commentaries on *Bhagavad-gītā* and other historical records. *Sevonmukhe hi jihvādau svayam eva sphuraty adaḥ:* Kṛṣṇa's transcendental name, form, attributes and activities can be revealed only when one engages in His service in full consciousness. This confirms Kṛṣṇa's own words in *Bhagavad-gītā* (18.55):

bhaktyā mām abhijānāti
yāvān yaś cāsmi tattvataḥ
tato māṁ tattvato jñātvā
viśate tad-anantaram

"One can understand the Supreme Personality of Godhead as He is only by devotional service. And when one is in full consciousness of the Supreme Lord by such devotion, he can enter into the kingdom of God." Only by *sevonmukha*, by engaging oneself in the Lord's service, can one realize the name, form and qualities of the Supreme Personality of Godhead.

"O Lord," the demigods say, "the impersonalists, who are nondevotees, cannot understand that Your name is identical with Your form." Since the Lord is absolute, there is no difference between His name and His actual form. In the material world there is a difference between form and name. The mango fruit is different from the name of the mango. One cannot taste the mango fruit simply by chanting, "Mango, mango, mango." But the devotee who knows that there is no difference between the name and the form of the Lord chants Hare Kṛṣṇa, Hare Kṛṣṇa, Kṛṣṇa Kṛṣṇa, Hare Hare/ Hare Rāma, Hare Rāma, Rāma Rāma, Hare Hare, and realizes that he is always in Kṛṣṇa's company.

For persons who are not very advanced in absolute knowledge of the

Supreme, Lord Kṛṣṇa exhibits His transcendental pastimes. They can simply think of the pastimes of the Lord and get the full benefit. Since there is no difference between the transcendental name and form of the Lord, there is no difference between the transcendental pastimes and the form of the Lord. For those who are less intelligent (like women, laborers or the mercantile class), the great sage Vyāsadeva wrote *Mahābhārata.* In the *Mahābhārata,* Kṛṣṇa is present in His different activities. *Mahābhārata* is history, and simply by studying, hearing, and memorizing the transcendental activities of Kṛṣṇa, the less intelligent can also gradually rise to the standard of pure devotees.

The pure devotees, who are always absorbed in the thought of the transcendental lotus feet of Kṛṣṇa and who are always engaged in devotional service in full Kṛṣṇa consciousness, are never to be considered to be in the material world. Śrīla Rūpa Gosvāmī has explained that those who are always engaged in Kṛṣṇa consciousness by body, mind and activities are to be considered liberated even within this body. This is also confirmed in the *Bhagavad-gītā:* those who are engaged in the devotional service of the Lord have already transcended the material position.

Kṛṣṇa appears in order to give a chance to both the devotees and the nondevotees for realization of the ultimate goal of life. The devotees get the direct chance to see Him and worship Him. Those who are not on that platform get the chance to become acquainted with His activities and thus become elevated to the same position.

The *Brahma-saṁhitā* (5.38) says:

premāñjana-cchurita-bhakti-vilocanena
santaḥ sadaiva hṛdayeṣu vilokayanti
yaṁ śyāmasundaram acintya-guṇa-svarūpaṁ
govindam ādi-puruṣaṁ tam ahaṁ bhajāmi

Although Kṛṣṇa's transcendental form is presented as black, devotees who are in love with the Supreme Personality of Godhead appreciate the Lord as Śyāmasundara, having a very beautiful blackish form. The Lord's form is so beautiful that the *Brahma-saṁhitā* (5.30) also states:

veṇuṁ kvaṇantam aravinda-dalāyatākṣaṁ
barhāvataṁsam asitāmbuda-sundarāṅgam

kandarpa-koṭi-kamanīya-viśeṣa-śobhaṁ
govindam ādi-puruṣaṁ tam ahaṁ bhajāmi

"I worship Govinda, the primeval Lord, who plays on His transcendental flute. His eyes are like lotus flowers, He is decorated with peacock plumes, and His bodily color resembles the color of a fresh black cloud, although His bodily features are more beautiful than millions of Cupids." This beauty of the Supreme Lord can be seen by devotees who are in love with Him, devotees whose eyes are anointed with love of Godhead (*premāñjana-cchurita-bhakti-vilocanena*).

The Lord is also known as Giridhārī or Girivara-dhārī. Because Kṛṣṇa, for the sake of His devotees, lifted Govardhana Hill, the devotees appreciate the Lord's inconceivable strength; but nondevotees, in spite of directly perceiving the Lord's inconceivable strength and power, regard the Lord's activities as fictitious. This is the difference between a devotee and a nondevotee. Nondevotees cannot give any nomenclature for the Supreme Personality of Godhead, yet the Lord is known as Śyāmasundara and Giridhārī. Similarly, the Lord is known as Devakī-nandana and Yaśodā-nandana because He accepted the role of son for mother Devakī and mother Yaśodā, and He is known as Gopāla because He enjoyed the sport of maintaining the cows and calves. Therefore, although He has no mundane name, He is addressed by devotees as Devakī-nandana, Yaśodā-nandana, Gopāla and Śyāmasundara. These are all transcendental names that only devotees can appreciate and nondevotees cannot.

The history of Kṛṣṇa the person has been openly seen by everyone, yet only those who are in love with the Supreme Personality of Godhead can appreciate this history, whereas nondevotees, who have not developed their loving qualities, think that the activities, form and attributes of the Supreme Personality of Godhead are fictitious. Therefore this verse explains, *na nāma-rūpe guṇa-janma-karmabhir nirūpitavye tava tasya sākṣiṇaḥ*. In this connection, Śrīla Viśvanātha Cakravartī Ṭhākura has given the example that persons suffering from jaundice cannot taste the sweetness of sugar candy, although everyone knows that sugar candy is sweet. Similarly, because of the material disease, nondevotees cannot understand the transcendental name, form, attributes and activities of the Supreme Personality of Godhead, although they actually see the

Lord's activities, either through authority or through history. The *Purāṇas* are old, authentic histories, but nondevotees cannot understand them, especially *Śrīmad-Bhāgavatam*, which is the essence of Vedic knowledge. Nondevotees cannot understand even the preliminary study of transcendental knowledge, *Bhagavad-gītā*. They simply speculate and present commentaries with absurd distortions. In conclusion, unless one elevates himself to the transcendental platform by practicing *bhakti-yoga*, one cannot understand the Supreme Personality of Godhead or His name, form, attributes or activities. But if by chance, by the association of devotees, one can actually understand the Lord and His features, one immediately becomes a liberated person. As the Lord says in *Bhagavad-gītā* (4.9):

janma karma ca me divyam
evaṁ yo vetti tattvataḥ
tyaktvā dehaṁ punar janma
naiti mām eti so 'rjuna

"One who knows the transcendental nature of My appearance and activities does not, upon leaving the body, take his birth again in this material world, but attains My eternal abode, O Arjuna."

Śrīla Rūpa Gosvāmī has therefore said that by affection and love for the Supreme Personality of Godhead, devotees can express their mind to Him with their words. Others, however, cannot do this, as confirmed in *Bhagavad-gītā* (*bhaktyā mām abhijānāti yāvān yaś cāsmi tattvataḥ*).

TEXT 37

शृण्वन् गृणन् संस्मरयंश्च चिन्तयन्
नामानि रूपाणि च मङ्गलानि ते ।
क्रियासु यस्त्वच्चरणारविन्दयो-
राविष्टचेता न भवाय कल्पते ॥३७॥

śṛṇvan gṛṇan saṁsmarayaṁś ca cintayan
nāmāni rūpāṇi ca maṅgalāni te

kriyāsu yas tvac-caraṇāravindayor
āviṣṭa-cetā na bhavāya kalpate

śṛṇvan—constantly hearing about the Lord (*śravaṇaṁ kīrtanaṁ viṣṇoḥ*); *gṛṇan*—chanting or reciting (the holy name of the Lord and His activities); *saṁsmarayan*—remembering (constantly thinking of the Lord's lotus feet and His form); *ca*—and; *cintayan*—contemplating (the transcendental activities of the Lord); *nāmāni*—His transcendental names; *rūpāṇi*—His transcendental forms; *ca*—also; *maṅgalāni*—which are all transcendental and therefore auspicious; *te*—of Your Lordship; *kriyāsu*—in being engaged in the devotional service; *yaḥ*—he who; *tvat-caraṇa-aravindayoḥ*—at Your lotus feet; *āviṣṭa-cetāḥ*—the devotee who is completely absorbed (in such activities); *na*—not; *bhavāya*—for the material platform; *kalpate*—is fit.

TRANSLATION

Even while engaged in various activities, devotees whose minds are completely absorbed at Your lotus feet, and who constantly hear, chant, contemplate and cause others to remember Your transcendental names and forms, are always on the transcendental platform, and thus they can understand the Supreme Personality of Godhead.

PURPORT

How *bhakti-yoga* can be practiced is explained in this verse. Śrīla Rūpa Gosvāmī has said that anyone who has dedicated his life to the service of the Lord (*īhā yasya harer dāsye*) by his activities, his mind and his words (*karmaṇā manasā girā*) may stay in any condition of life (*nikhilāsv apy avasthāsu*) and yet is no longer actually conditioned but is liberated (*jīvan-muktaḥ sa ucyate*). Even though such a devotee is in a material body, he has nothing to do with this body, for he is transcendentally situated. *Nārāyaṇa-parāḥ sarve na kutaścana bibhyati:* because a devotee is engaged in transcendental activities, he is not afraid of being materially embodied. (*Bhāg.* 6.17.28) Illustrating this liberated position, Śrī Caitanya Mahāprabhu prayed, *mama janmani janmanīśvare bhava-*

tād bhaktir ahaitukī tvayi: "All I want is Your causeless devotional service in My life, birth after birth." (*Śikṣāṣṭaka* 4) Even if a devotee, by the supreme will of the Lord, takes birth in this material world, he continues his devotional service. When King Bharata made a mistake and in his next life became a deer, his devotional service did not stop, although some slight chastisement was given to him because of his negligence. Nārada Muni says that even if one falls from the platform of devotional service, he is not lost, whereas nondevotees are lost entirely because they are not engaged in service. *Bhagavad-gītā* (9.14) therefore recommends that one always engage at least in chanting the Hare Kṛṣṇa *mahā-mantra:*

satataṁ kīrtayanto māṁ
yatantaś ca dṛḍha-vratāḥ
namasyantaś ca māṁ bhaktyā
nitya-yuktā upāsate

"Always chanting My glories, endeavoring with great determination, bowing down before Me, the great souls perpetually worship Me with devotion."

One should not give up the process of devotional service, which is performed in nine different ways (*śravaṇaṁ kīrtanaṁ viṣṇoḥ smaraṇaṁ pāda-sevanam,* etc.). The most important process is hearing (*śravaṇam*) from the *guru, sādhu* and *śāstra*—the spiritual master, the saintly *ācāryas* and the Vedic literature. *Sādhu-śāstra-guru-vākya, cittete kariyā aikya.* We should not hear the commentaries and explanations of nondevotees, for this is strictly forbidden by Śrīla Sanātana Gosvāmī, who quotes from the *Padma Purāṇa:*

avaiṣṇava-mukhodgīrṇaṁ
pūtaṁ hari-kathāmṛtam
śravaṇaṁ naiva kartavyaṁ
sarpocchiṣṭaṁ yathā payaḥ

We should strictly follow this injunction and never try to hear from Māyāvādīs, impersonalists, voidists, politicians or so-called scholars.

Strictly avoiding such inauspicious association, we should simply hear from pure devotees. Śrīla Rūpa Gosvāmī therefore recommends, *śrī-guru-padāśrayaḥ:* one must seek shelter at the lotus feet of a pure devotee who can be one's *guru.* Caitanya Mahāprabhu advises that a *guru* is one who strictly follows the instructions of *Bhagavad-gītā: yare dekha, tare kaha, 'kṛṣṇa'—upadeśa* (Cc. *Madhya* 7.128). A juggler, a magician or one who speaks nonsense as an academic career is not a *guru.* Rather, a *guru* is one who presents *Bhagavad-gītā,* Kṛṣṇa's instructions, as it is. *Śravaṇa* is very important; one must hear from the Vaiṣṇava *sādhu, guru* and *śāstra.*

The word *kriyāsu,* meaning "by manual labor" or "by work," is important in this verse. One should engage in practical service to the Lord. In our Kṛṣṇa consciousness movement, all our activities are concentrated upon distributing Kṛṣṇa literature. This is very important. One may approach any person and induce him to read Kṛṣṇa literature so that in the future he also may become a devotee. Such activities are recommended in this verse. *Kriyāsu yas tvac-caraṇāravindayoḥ.* Such activities will always remind the devotees of the Lord's lotus feet. By fully concentrating on distributing books for Kṛṣṇa, one is fully absorbed in Kṛṣṇa. This is *samādhi.*

TEXT 38

दिष्ट्या हरेऽस्या भवतः पदो भुवो
भारोऽपनीतस्तव जन्मनेशितुः ।
दिष्ट्याङ्कितां त्वत्पदकैः सुशोभनै-
र्द्रक्ष्याम गां द्यां च तवानुकम्पिताम् ॥३८॥

diṣṭyā hare 'syā bhavataḥ pado bhuvo
bhāro 'panītas tava janmaneśituḥ
diṣṭyāṅkitāṁ tvat-padakaiḥ suśobhanair
drakṣyāma gāṁ dyāṁ ca tavānukampitām

diṣṭyā—by fortune; *hare*—O Lord; *asyāḥ*—of this (world); *bhavataḥ*—of Your Lordship; *padaḥ*—of the place; *bhuvaḥ*—on this earth; *bhāraḥ*—the burden created by the demons; *apanītaḥ*—now removed; *tava*—of Your Lordship; *janmanā*—by appearance as an incarnation; *īśituḥ*—You, the controller of everything; *diṣṭyā*—and by fortune; *aṅkitām*—marked; *tvat-padakaiḥ*—by Your lotus feet; *su-śobhanaiḥ*—which are transcendentally decorated with the marks of conchshell, disc, lotus and club; *drakṣyāma*—we shall surely observe; *gām*—upon this earth; *dyām ca*—in heaven also; *tava anukampitām*—due to Your causeless mercy upon us.

TRANSLATION

O Lord, we are fortunate because the heavy burden of the demons upon this earth is immediately removed by Your appearance. Indeed, we are certainly fortunate, for we shall be able to see upon this earth and in the heavenly planets the marks of lotus, conchshell, club and disc that adorn Your lotus feet.

PURPORT

The soles of the Lord's lotus feet are marked with *śaṅkha-cakra-gadā-padma*—conchshell, disc, club and lotus—and also by a flag and a thunderbolt. When Kṛṣṇa walks on this earth or in the heavenly planets, these marks are visible wherever He goes. Vṛndāvana-dhāma is a transcendental place because of Kṛṣṇa's walking on this land frequently. The inhabitants of Vṛndāvana were fortunate to see these marks here and there. When Akrūra went to Vṛndāvana to take Kṛṣṇa and Balarāma away to the festival arranged by Kaṁsa, upon seeing the marks of the Lord's lotus feet on the ground of Vṛndāvana, he fell down and began to groan. These marks are visible to devotees who receive the causeless mercy of the Supreme Personality of Godhead (*tavānukampitām*). The demigods were jubilant not only because the appearance of the Supreme Lord would do away with the burdensome demons, but also because they would be able to see upon the ground the transcendental marks from the soles of the Lord's lotus feet. The *gopīs* always thought of the Lord's lotus feet when He was walking in the pasturing grounds, and, as described in the previous verse, simply by thinking of the Lord's lotus feet, the *gopīs* were fully absorbed in transcendence (*āviṣṭa-cetā na bhavāya kalpate*). Like the *gopīs*, one who is always absorbed in thought of the Lord is beyond the material platform and will not remain in this material world. It is our duty, therefore, always to hear, chant and think about the Lord's lotus feet, as actually done by Vaiṣṇavas who have decided to live in Vṛndāvana always and think of the Lord's lotus feet twenty-four hours a day.

TEXT 39

न तेऽभवस्येश भवस्य कारणं
विना विनोदं बत तर्कयामहे ।
भवो निरोधः स्थितिरप्यविद्यया
कृता यतस्त्वय्यभयाश्रयात्मनि ॥३९॥

na te 'bhavasyeśa bhavasya kāraṇaṁ
vinā vinodaṁ bata tarkayāmahe
bhavo nirodhaḥ sthitir apy avidyayā
kṛtā yatas tvayy abhayāśrayātmani

na—not; *te*—of Your Lordship; *abhavasya*—of whom there is no birth, death or maintenance as for an ordinary being; *īśa*—O Supreme Lord; *bhavasya*—of Your appearance, Your birth; *kāraṇam*—the cause; *vinā*—without; *vinodam*—the pastimes (despite what is said, You are not forced to come to this world by any cause); *bata*—however; *tarkayāmahe*—we cannot argue (but must simply understand that these are Your pastimes); *bhavaḥ*—birth; *nirodhaḥ*—death; *sthitiḥ*—maintenance; *api*—also; *avidyayā*—by the external, illusory energy; *kṛtāḥ*—done; *yataḥ*—because; *tvayi*—unto You; *abhaya-āśraya*—O fearless shelter of all; *ātmani*—of the ordinary living entity.

TRANSLATION

O Supreme Lord, You are not an ordinary living entity appearing in this material world as a result of fruitive activities. Therefore Your appearance or birth in this world has no other cause than Your pleasure potency. Similarly, the living entities, who are part of You, have no cause for miseries like birth, death

and old age, except when these living entities are conducted by Your external energy.

PURPORT

As stated in *Bhagavad-gītā* (15.7), *mamaivaṁśo jīva-loke jīva-bhūtaḥ sanātanaḥ:* the living entities are parts and parcels of the Supreme Lord, and thus they are qualitatively one with the Lord. We can understand that when the Supreme Lord appears or disappears as an incarnation, there is no other cause than His pleasure potency. We cannot force the Supreme Personality of Godhead to appear. As He says in *Bhagavad-gītā* (4.7):

yadā yadā hi dharmasya
glānir bhavati bhārata
abhyutthānam adharmasya
tadātmānaṁ sṛjāmy aham

"Whenever and wherever there is a decline in religious practice, O descendant of Bharata, and a predominant rise of irreligion—at that time I descend Myself." When there is a need to diminish a burden created by the demons, the Supreme Godhead can do it in many ways because He has multifarious energies. There is no need for Him to come as an incarnation, since He is not forced to do anything like ordinary living entities. The living entities come to this material world in the spirit of enjoyment, but because they want to enjoy without Kṛṣṇa (*kṛṣṇa-bahirmukha haiyā bhoja-vāñchā kare*), they suffer birth, death, old age and disease under the control of the illusory energy. When the Supreme Personality of Godhead appears, however, no such causes are involved; His descent is an act of His pleasure potency. We should always remember this distinction between the Lord and the ordinary living entity and not uselessly argue that the Lord cannot come. There are philosophers who do not believe in the Lord's incarnation and who ask, "Why should the Supreme Lord come?" But the answer is, "Why should He not come? Why should He be controlled by the desire of the living entity?" The Lord is free to do whatever He likes. Therefore this verse says, *vinā vinodaṁ bata tarkayāmahe.* It is only for His pleasure that He comes although He does not need to come.

When the living entities come to this world for material enjoyment, they are entangled in *karma* and *karma-phala* by the Lord's illusory energy. But if one seeks shelter at the Lord's lotus feet, one is again situated in his original, liberated state. As stated here, *kṛtā yatas tvayy abhayāśrayātmani:* one who seeks shelter at the lotus feet of the Lord is always fearless. Because we are dependent on the Supreme Personality of Godhead, we should give up the idea that without Kṛṣṇa we can enjoy freedom in this material world. This idea is the reason we have become entangled. Now it is our duty to seek shelter again at the Lord's lotus feet. This shelter is described as *abhaya*, or fearless. Since Kṛṣṇa is not subject to birth, death, old age or disease, and since we are part and parcel of Kṛṣṇa, we also are not subject to birth, death, old age and disease, but we have become subject to these illusory problems because of our forgetfulness of Kṛṣṇa and our position as His eternal servants (*jīvera 'svarūpa' haya—kṛṣṇera 'nitya-dāsa'*). Therefore, if we practice devotional service by always thinking of the Lord, always glorifying Him and always chanting about Him, as described in text 37 (*śṛṇvan gṛṇan saṁsmarayaṁś ca cintayan*), we will be reinstated in our original, constitutional position and thus be saved. The demigods, therefore, encouraged Devakī not to fear Kaṁsa, but to think of the Supreme Personality of Godhead, who was already within her womb.

TEXT 40

मत्स्याश्वकच्छपनृसिंहवराहहंस-
राजन्यविप्रविबुधेषु कृतावतारः ।
त्वं पासि नस्त्रिभुवनं च यथाधुनेश
भारं भुवो हर यदूत्तम वन्दनं ते ॥४०॥

matsyāśva-kacchapa-nṛsiṁha-varāha-haṁsa-
rājanya-vipra-vibudheṣu kṛtāvatāraḥ
tvaṁ pāsi nas tri-bhuvanaṁ ca yathādhuneśa
bhāraṁ bhuvo hara yadūttama vandanaṁ te

matsya—the fish incarnation; *aśva*—the horse incarnation; *kacchapa*—the tortoise incarnation; *nṛsiṁha*—the Narasiṁha incarnation;

varāha—the Varāha incarnation; *haṁsa*—the swan incarnation; *rājanya*—incarnations as Lord Rāmacandra and other *kṣatriyas; vipra*—incarnations as *brāhmaṇas* like Vāmanadeva; *vibudheṣu*—among the demigods; *kṛta-avatāraḥ*—appeared as incarnations; *tvam*—Your Lordship; *pāsi*—please save; *naḥ*—us; *tri-bhuvanam ca*—and the three worlds; *yathā*—as well as; *adhunā*—now; *īśa*—O Supreme Lord; *bhāram*—burden; *bhuvaḥ*—of the earth; *hara*—please diminish; *yadu-uttama*—O Lord Kṛṣṇa, best of the Yadus; *vandanam te*—we offer our prayers unto You.

TRANSLATION

O supreme controller, Your Lordship previously accepted incarnations as a fish, a horse, a tortoise, Narasiṁhadeva, a boar, a swan, Lord Rāmacandra, Paraśurāma and, among the demigods, Vāmanadeva, to protect the entire world by Your mercy. Now please protect us again by Your mercy by diminishing the disturbances in this world. O Kṛṣṇa, best of the Yadus, we respectfully offer our obeisances unto You.

PURPORT

In every incarnation, the Supreme Personality of Godhead has a particular mission to execute, and this was true in His appearance as the son of Devakī in the family of the Yadus. Thus all the demigods offered their prayers to the Lord, bowing down before Him, and requested the Lord to do the needful. We cannot order the Supreme Personality of Godhead to do anything for us. We can simply offer Him our obeisances, as advised in *Bhagavad-gītā* (*man-manā bhava mad-bhakto mad-yājī māṁ namaskuru*), and pray to Him for annihilation of dangers.

TEXT 41

दिष्ट्याम्ब ते कुक्षिगतः परः पुमा-
नंशेन साक्षाद् भगवान् भवाय नः ।
माभूद् भयं भोजपतेर्मुमूर्षो-
र्गोप्ता यदूनां भविता तवात्मजः ॥४१॥

diṣṭyāmba te kukṣi-gataḥ paraḥ pumān
aṁśena sākṣād bhagavān bhavāya naḥ
mābhūd bhayaṁ bhoja-pater mumūrṣor
goptā yadūnāṁ bhavitā tavātmajaḥ

diṣṭyā—by fortune; *amba*—O mother; *te*—your; *kukṣi-gataḥ*—in the womb; *paraḥ*—the Supreme; *pumān*—Personality of Godhead; *aṁśena*—with all His energies, His parts and parcels; *sākṣāt*—directly; *bhagavān*—the Supreme Personality of Godhead; *bhavāya*—for the auspiciousness; *naḥ*—of all of us; *mā abhūt*—never be; *bhayam*—fearful; *bhoja-pateḥ*—from Kaṁsa, King of the Bhoja dynasty; *mumūrṣoḥ*—who has decided to be killed by the Lord; *goptā*—the protector; *yadūnām*—of the Yadu dynasty; *bhavitā*—will become; *tava ātmajaḥ*—your son.

TRANSLATION

O mother Devakī, by your good fortune and ours, the Supreme Personality of Godhead Himself, with all His plenary portions, such as Baladeva, is now within your womb. Therefore you need not fear Kaṁsa, who has decided to be killed by the Lord. Your eternal son, Kṛṣṇa, will be the protector of the entire Yadu dynasty.

PURPORT

The words *paraḥ pumān aṁśena* signify that Kṛṣṇa is the original Supreme Personality of Godhead. This is the verdict of the *śāstra* (*kṛṣṇas tu bhagavān svayam*). Thus the demigods assured Devakī, "Your son is the Supreme Personality of Godhead, and He is appearing with Baladeva, His plenary portion. He will give you all protection and kill Kaṁsa, who has decided to continue his enmity toward the Lord and thus be killed by Him."

TEXT 42

श्रीशुक उवाच

इत्यभिष्टूय पुरुषं यद्रूपमनिदं यथा ।
ब्रह्मेशानौ पुरोधाय देवाः प्रतिययुर्दिवम् ॥४२॥

śrī-śuka uvāca
ity abhiṣṭūya puruṣaṁ
yad-rūpam anidaṁ yathā
brahmeśānau purodhāya
devāḥ pratiyayur divam

śrī-śukaḥ uvāca—Śrī Śukadeva Gosvāmī said; *iti*—in this way; *abhiṣṭūya*—offering prayers; *puruṣam*—unto the Supreme Personality; *yat-rūpam*—whose form; *anidam*—transcendental; *yathā*—as; *brahma*—Lord Brahmā; *īśānau*—and Lord Śiva; *purodhāya*—keeping them in front; *devāḥ*—all the demigods; *pratiyayuḥ*—returned; *divam*—to their heavenly homes.

TRANSLATION

After thus offering prayers to the Supreme Personality of Godhead, Lord Viṣṇu, the Transcendence, all the demigods, with Lord Brahmā and Lord Śiva before them, returned to their homes in the heavenly planets.

PURPORT

It is said:

adyāpiha caitanya e saba līlā kare
yāṅ'ra bhāgye thāke, se dekhaye nirantare
(*Caitanya-bhāgavata, Madhya* 23.513)

The incarnations of the Supreme Personality of Godhead appear continuously, like the waves of a river or an ocean. There is no limit to the Lord's incarnations, but they can be perceived only by devotees who are fortunate. The *devatās*, the demigods, fortunately understood the incarnation of the Supreme Personality of Godhead, and thus they offered their prayers. Then Lord Śiva and Lord Brahmā led the demigods in returning to their homes.

The word *kukṣi-gataḥ*, meaning "within the womb of Devakī," has been discussed by Śrī Jīva Gosvāmī in his *Krama-sandarbha* commentary. Since it was said at first that Kṛṣṇa was present within the heart of Vasudeva and was transferred to the heart of Devakī, Śrī Jīva Gosvāmī writes, how is it that Kṛṣṇa was now in the womb? He replies that there is no contradiction. From the heart the Lord can go to the womb, or from the womb He can go to the heart. Indeed, He can go or stay anywhere. As confirmed in the *Brahma-saṁhitā* (5.35), *aṇḍāntara-stha-paramāṇu-cayāntara-sthaṁ govindam ādi-puruṣaṁ tam ahaṁ bhajāmi.* The Lord can stay wherever He likes. Devakī, therefore, in accordance with the desire of her former life, now had the opportunity to seek the benediction of having the Supreme Personality of Godhead as her son, Devakī-nandana.

Thus end the Bhaktivedanta purports of the Tenth Canto, Second Chapter, of the Śrīmad-Bhāgavatam, *entitled "Prayers by the Demigods for Lord Kṛṣṇa in the Womb."*

CHAPTER THREE

The Birth of Lord Kṛṣṇa

As described in this chapter, the Supreme Personality of Godhead, Kṛṣṇa, Hari in His original form, appeared as Viṣṇu so that His father and mother could understand that their son was the Supreme Personality of Godhead. Because they were afraid of Kaṁsa, when the Lord appeared as an ordinary child they took Him to Gokula, the home of Nanda Mahārāja.

Mother Devakī, being fully transcendental, *sac-cid-ānanda,* does not belong to this material world. Thus the Supreme Personality of Godhead appeared with four hands, as if born from her womb. Upon seeing the Lord in that Viṣṇu form, Vasudeva was struck with wonder, and in transcendental happiness he and Devakī mentally gave ten thousand cows in charity to the *brāhmaṇas.* Vasudeva then offered prayers to the Lord, addressing Him as the Supreme Person, Parabrahman, the Supersoul, who is beyond duality and who is internally and externally all-pervading. The Lord, the cause of all causes, is beyond material existence, although He is the creator of this material world. When He enters this world as Paramātmā, He is all-pervading (*aṇḍāntara-stha-paramāṇu-cayāntara-stham*), yet He is transcendentally situated. For the creation, maintenance and annihilation of this material world, the Lord appears as the *guṇa-avatāras*—Brahmā, Viṣṇu and Maheśvara. Thus Vasudeva offered prayers full of meaning to the Supreme Personality of Godhead. Devakī followed her husband by offering prayers describing the transcendental nature of the Lord. Fearing Kaṁsa and desiring that the Lord not be understood by atheistic and materialistic nondevotees, she prayed that the Lord withdraw His transcendental four-armed form and appear like an ordinary child with two hands.

The Lord reminded Vasudeva and Devakī of two other incarnations in which He had appeared as their son. He had appeared as Pṛśnigarbha and Vāmanadeva, and now this was the third time He was appearing as the son of Devakī to fulfill their desire. The Lord then decided to leave the residence of Vasudeva and Devakī, in the prison house of Kaṁsa, and at this very time, Yogamāyā took birth as the daughter of Yaśodā. By the arrangement of Yogamāyā, Vasudeva was able to leave the prison house and save the child from the hands of Kaṁsa. When Vasudeva brought Kṛṣṇa to the house of Nanda Mahārāja, he saw that by Yogamāyā's arrangement, Yaśodā, as well as everyone else, was deeply asleep. Thus he exchanged the babies, taking Yogamāyā from Yaśodā's lap and placing Kṛṣṇa there instead. Then Vasudeva returned to his own place, having taken Yogamāyā as his daughter. He placed Yogamāyā on Devakī's bed and prepared to be a prisoner as before. In Gokula, Yaśodā could not understand whether she had given birth to a male or a female child.

TEXTS 1–5

श्रीशुक उवाच
अथ सर्वगुणोपेतः कालः परमशोभनः ।
यर्ह्येवाजनजन्मर्क्षं शान्तर्क्षग्रहतारकम् ॥ १ ॥
दिशः प्रसेदुर्गगनं निर्मलोडुगणोदयम् ।
मही मङ्गलभूयिष्ठपुरग्रामव्रजाकरा ॥ २ ॥
नद्यः प्रसन्नसलिला ह्रदा जलरुहश्रियः ।
द्विजालिकुलसंनादस्तवका वनराजयः ॥ ३ ॥
ववौ वायुः सुखस्पर्शः पुण्यगन्धवहः शुचिः ।
अग्नयश्च द्विजातीनां शान्तास्तत्र समिन्धत ॥ ४ ॥
मनांस्यासन् प्रसन्नानि साधूनामसुरद्रुहाम् ।
जायमानेऽजने तस्मिन् नेदुर्दुन्दुभयः समम् ॥ ५ ॥

śrī-śuka uvāca
atha sarva-guṇopetaḥ
kālaḥ parama-śobhanaḥ
yarhy evājana-janmarkṣaṁ
śāntarkṣa-graha-tārakam

diśaḥ prasedur gaganaṁ
nirmaloḍu-gaṇodayam

mahī maṅgala-bhūyiṣṭha-
pura-grāma-vrajākarā

nadyaḥ prasanna-salilā
hradā jalaruha-śriyaḥ
dvijāli-kula-sannāda-
stavakā vana-rājayaḥ

vavau vāyuḥ sukha-sparśaḥ
puṇya-gandhavahaḥ śuciḥ
agnayaś ca dvijātīnāṁ
śāntās tatra samindhata

manāṁsy āsan prasannāni
sādhūnām asura-druhām
jāyamāne 'jane tasmin
nedur dundubhayaḥ samam

śrī-śukaḥ uvāca—Śrī Śukadeva Gosvāmī said; *atha*—on the occasion of the Lord's appearance; *sarva*—all around; *guṇa-upetaḥ*—endowed with material attributes or facilities; *kālaḥ*—a favorable time; *parama-śobhanaḥ*—all-auspicious and very favorable from all points of view; *yarhi*—when; *eva*—certainly; *ajana-janma-ṛkṣam*—the constellation of stars known as Rohiṇī; *śānta-ṛkṣa*—none of the constellations were fierce (all of them were peaceful); *graha-tārakam*—and the planets and stars like Aśvinī; *diśaḥ*—all directions; *praseduḥ*—appeared very auspicious and peaceful; *gaganam*—all of outer space or the sky; *nirmala-uḍu-gaṇa-udayam*—in which all the auspicious stars were visible (in the upper strata of the universe); *mahī*—the earth; *maṅgala-bhūyiṣṭha-pura-grāma-vraja-ākarāḥ*—whose many cities, towns, pasturing grounds and mines became auspicious and very neat and clean; *nadyaḥ*—the rivers; *prasanna-salilāḥ*—the waters became clear; *hradāḥ*—the lakes or large reservoirs of water; *jalaruha-śriyaḥ*—appeared very beautiful because of blooming lotuses all around; *dvija-ali-kula-sannāda-stavakāḥ*—the birds, especially the cuckoos, and swarms of bees began to chant in sweet voices, as if praying to the Supreme

Personality of Godhead; *vana-rājayaḥ*—the green trees and plants were also very pleasing to see; *vavau*—blew; *vāyuḥ*—the breeze; *sukha-sparśaḥ*—very pleasing to the touch; *puṇya-gandha-vahaḥ*—which was full of fragrance; *śuciḥ*—without pollution by dust; *agnayaḥ ca*—and the fires (at the places of sacrifice); *dvijātīnām*—of the *brāhmaṇas; śāntāḥ*—undisturbed, steady, calm and quiet; *tatra*—there; *samindhata*—blazed; *manāṁsi*—the minds of the *brāhmaṇas* (who because of Kaṁsa had always been afraid); *āsan*—became; *prasannāni*—fully satisfied and free from disturbances; *sādhūnām*—of the *brāhmaṇas*, who were all Vaiṣṇava devotees; *asura-druhām*—who had been oppressed by Kaṁsa and other demons disturbing the discharge of religious rituals; *jāyamāne*—because of the appearance or birth; *ajane*—of Lord Viṣṇu, who is always unborn; *tasmin*—in that situation; *neduḥ*—resounded; *dundubhayaḥ*—kettledrums; *samam*—simultaneously (from the upper planets).

TRANSLATION

Thereafter, at the auspicious time for the appearance of the Lord, the entire universe was surcharged with all the qualities of goodness, beauty and peace. The constellation Rohiṇī appeared, as did stars like Aśvinī. The sun, the moon and the other stars and planets were very peaceful. All directions appeared extremely pleasing, and the beautiful stars twinkled in the cloudless sky. Decorated with towns, villages, mines and pasturing grounds, the earth seemed all-auspicious. The rivers flowed with clear water, and the lakes and vast reservoirs, full of lilies and lotuses, were extraordinarily beautiful. In the trees and green plants, full of flowers and leaves, pleasing to the eyes, birds like cuckoos and swarms of bees began chanting with sweet voices for the sake of the demigods. A pure breeze began to blow, pleasing the sense of touch and bearing the aroma of flowers, and when the brāhmaṇas engaging in ritualistic ceremonies ignited their fires according to Vedic principles, the fires burned steadily, undisturbed by the breeze. Thus when the birthless Lord Viṣṇu, the Supreme Personality of Godhead, was about to appear, the saints and brāhmaṇas, who had always been disturbed by demons like Kaṁsa

and his men, felt peace within the core of their hearts, and kettledrums simultaneously vibrated from the upper planetary system.

PURPORT

As stated in the *Bhagavad-gītā,* the Lord says that His appearance, birth, and activities are all transcendental and that one who factually understands them is immediately eligible to be transferred to the spiritual world. The Lord's appearance or birth is not like that of an ordinary man, who is forced to accept a material body according to his past deeds. The Lord's appearance is explained in the previous chapter: He appears out of His own sweet pleasure.

When the time was mature for the appearance of the Lord, the constellations became very auspicious. The astrological influence of the constellation known as Rohiṇī was also predominant because this constellation is considered very auspicious. Rohiṇī is under the direct supervision of Brahmā, who is born of Viṣṇu, and it appears at the birth of Lord Viṣṇu, who in fact is birthless. According to the astrological conclusion, besides the proper situation of the stars, there are auspicious and inauspicious moments due to the different situations of the different planetary systems. At the time of Kṛṣṇa's birth, the planetary systems were automatically adjusted so that everything became auspicious.

At that time, in all directions, east, west, south, north, everywhere, there was an atmosphere of peace and prosperity. Auspicious stars were visible in the sky, and on the surface in all towns and villages or pasturing grounds and within the mind of everyone there were signs of good fortune. The rivers were flowing full of water, and the lakes were beautifully decorated with lotus flowers. The forests were full with beautiful birds and peacocks. All the birds within the forests began to sing with sweet voices, and the peacocks began to dance with their consorts. The wind blew very pleasantly, carrying the aroma of different flowers, and the sensation of bodily touch was very pleasing. At home, the *brāhmaṇas,* who were accustomed to offer sacrifices in the fire, found their homes very pleasant for offerings. Because of disturbances created by the demoniac kings, the sacrificial fire had been almost stopped in the houses of *brāhmaṇas,* but now they could find the opportunity to start the fire peacefully. Being forbidden to offer sacrifices, the *brāhmaṇas* were very distressed in mind, intelligence and activities. But just on the point of Kṛṣṇa's appearance, automatically their minds became full of joy because they could hear loud vibrations in the sky of transcendental sounds proclaiming the appearance of the Supreme Personality of Godhead.

On the occasion of Lord Kṛṣṇa's birth, seasonal changes took place throughout the entire universe. Kṛṣṇa was born during the month of September, yet it appeared like springtime. The atmosphere, however, was very cool, although not chilly, and the rivers and reservoirs appeared just as they would in *śarat*, the fall. Lotuses and lilies blossom during the day, but although Kṛṣṇa appeared at twelve o'clock midnight, the lilies and lotuses were in bloom, and thus the wind blowing at that time was full of fragrance. Because of Kaṁsa's disturbances, the Vedic ritualistic ceremonies had almost stopped. The *brāhmaṇas* and saintly persons could not execute the Vedic rituals with peaceful minds. But now the *brāhmaṇas* were very pleased to perform their daily ritualistic ceremonies undisturbed. The business of the *asuras* is to disturb the *suras*, the devotees and *brāhmaṇas*, but at the time of Kṛṣṇa's appearance these devotees and *brāhmaṇas* were undisturbed.

TEXT 6

जगुः किन्नरगन्धर्वास्तुष्टुवुः सिद्धचारणाः ।
विद्याधर्यश्च ननृतुरप्सरोभिः समं मुदा ॥ ६ ॥

jaguḥ kinnara-gandharvās
tuṣṭuvuḥ siddha-cāraṇāḥ
vidyādharyaś ca nanṛtur
apsarobhiḥ samaṁ mudā

jaguḥ—recited auspicious songs; *kinnara-gandharvāḥ*—the Kinnaras and Gandharvas, inhabitants of various planets in the heavenly planetary system; *tuṣṭuvuḥ*—offered their respective prayers; *siddha-cāraṇāḥ*—the Siddhas and Cāraṇas, other inhabitants of the heavenly planets; *vidyādharyaḥ ca*—and the Vidyādharīs, another group of inhabitants of the heavenly planets; *nanṛtuḥ*—danced in transcendental bliss; *apsa-*

robhiḥ—the Apsarās, beautiful dancers in the heavenly kingdom; *samam*—along with; *mudā*—in great jubilation.

TRANSLATION

The Kinnaras and Gandharvas began to sing auspicious songs, the Siddhas and Cāraṇas offered auspicious prayers, and the Vidyādharīs, along with the Apsarās, began to dance in jubilation.

TEXTS 7–8

मुमुचुर्मुनयो देवाः सुमनांसि मुदान्विताः ।
मन्दं मन्दं जलधरा जगर्जुरनुसागरम् ॥ ७ ॥
निशीथे तमउद्भूते जायमाने जनार्दने ।
देवक्यां देवरूपिण्यां विष्णुः सर्वगुहाशयः ।
आविरासीद् यथा प्राच्यां दिशीन्दुरिव पुष्कलः ॥ ८ ॥

mumucur munayo devāḥ
sumanāṁsi mudānvitāḥ
mandaṁ mandaṁ jaladharā
jagarjur anusāgaram

niśīthe tama-udbhūte
jāyamāne janārdane
devakyāṁ deva-rūpiṇyāṁ
viṣṇuḥ sarva-guhā-śayaḥ
āvirāsīd yathā prācyāṁ
diśīndur iva puṣkalaḥ

mumucuḥ—showered; *munayaḥ*—all the great sages and saintly persons; *devāḥ*—and the demigods; *sumanāṁsi*—very beautiful and fragrant flowers; *mudā anvitāḥ*—being joyous in their attitude; *mandam mandam*—very mildly; *jala-dharāḥ*—the clouds; *jagarjuḥ*—vibrated; *anusāgaram*—following the vibrations of the sea waves; *niśīthe*—late at night; *tamaḥ-udbhūte*—when it was densely dark; *jāyamāne*—on the appearance of; *janārdane*—the Supreme Personality of Godhead, Viṣṇu; *devakyām*—in the womb of Devakī; *deva-rūpiṇyām*—who was in the same category as the Supreme Personality of Godhead (*ānanda-cinmaya-rasa-pratibhāvitābhiḥ*); *viṣṇuḥ*—Lord Viṣṇu, the Supreme Lord; *sarva-guhā-śayaḥ*—who is situated in the core of everyone's heart; *āvirāsīt*—appeared; *yathā*—as; *prācyām diśi*—in the east; *induḥ iva*—like the full moon; *puṣkalaḥ*—complete in every respect.

TRANSLATION

The demigods and great saintly persons showered flowers in a joyous mood, and clouds gathered in the sky and very mildly thundered, making sounds like those of the ocean's waves. Then the Supreme Personality of Godhead, Viṣṇu, who is situated in the core of everyone's heart, appeared from the heart of Devakī in the dense darkness of night, like the full moon rising on the eastern horizon, because Devakī was of the same category as Śrī Kṛṣṇa.

PURPORT

As stated in the *Brahma-saṁhitā* (5.37):

ānanda-cinmaya-rasa-pratibhāvitābhis
tābhir ya eva nija-rūpatayā kalābhiḥ
goloka eva nivasaty akhilātma-bhūto
govindam ādi-puruṣaṁ tam ahaṁ bhajāmi

This verse indicates that Kṛṣṇa and His entourage are of the same spiritual potency (*ānanda-cinmaya-rasa*). Kṛṣṇa's father, His mother, His friends the cowherd boys, and the cows are all expansions of Kṛṣṇa, as will be explained in the *brahma-vimohana-līlā*. When Brahmā took away Kṛṣṇa's associates to test the supremacy of Lord Kṛṣṇa, the Lord expanded Himself again in the forms of the many cowherd boys and calves, all of whom, as Brahmā saw, were *viṣṇu-mūrtis*. Devakī is also an expansion of Kṛṣṇa, and therefore this verse says, *devakyāṁ deva-rūpiṇyāṁ viṣṇuḥ sarva-guhā-śayaḥ*.

At the time for the Lord's appearance, the great sages and the demigods, being pleased, began to shower flowers. At the seashore, there was the sound of mild waves, and above the sea there were clouds in the sky which began to thunder very pleasingly.

When things were adjusted like this, Lord Viṣṇu, who is residing within the heart of every living entity, appeared in the darkness of night as the Supreme Personality of Godhead before Devakī, who appeared as one of the demigoddesses. The appearance of Lord Viṣṇu at that time could be compared to the rising of the full moon in the sky on the eastern horizon. The objection may be raised that since Lord Kṛṣṇa appeared on the eighth day of the waning moon, there could be no rising of the full moon. In answer to this it may be said that Lord Kṛṣṇa appeared in the dynasty which is in the hierarchy of the moon; therefore, although the moon was incomplete on that night, because of the Lord's appearance in the dynasty wherein the moon is himself the original person, the moon was in an overjoyous condition, so by the grace of Kṛṣṇa he could appear as a full moon. To welcome the Supreme Personality of Godhead, the waning moon became a full moon in jubilation.

Instead of *deva-rūpiṇyām*, some texts of *Śrīmad-Bhāgavatam* clearly say *viṣṇu-rūpiṇyām*. In either case, the meaning is that Devakī has the same spiritual form as the Lord. The Lord is *sac-cid-ānanda-vigraha*, and Devakī is also *sac-cid-ānanda-vigraha*. Therefore no one can find any fault in the way the Supreme Personality of Godhead, *sac-cid-ānanda-vigraha*, appeared from the womb of Devakī.

Those who are not in full knowledge that the appearance and disappearance of the Lord are transcendental (*janma karma ca me divyam*) are sometimes surprised that the Supreme Personality of Godhead can take birth like an ordinary child. Actually, however, the Lord's birth is never ordinary. The Supreme Personality of Godhead is already situated within the core of everyone's heart as *antaryāmī*, the Supersoul. Thus because He was present in full potency in Devakī's heart, He was also able to appear outside her body.

One of the twelve great personalities is Bhīṣmadeva (*svayambhūr nāradaḥ śambhuḥ kumāraḥ kapilo manuḥ prahlādo janako bhīṣmaḥ*). In *Śrīmad-Bhāgavatam* (1.9.42), Bhīṣma, a great authority to be followed by devotees, says that the Supreme Personality of Godhead is situated in the core of everyone's heart, just as the sun may be on everyone's head. Yet although the sun may be on the heads of millions and millions of people, this does not mean that the sun is variously situated.

Similarly, because the Supreme Personality of Godhead has inconceivable potencies, He can be within everyone's heart and yet not be situated variously. *Ekatvam anupaśyataḥ* (*Īśopaniṣad* 7). The Lord is one, but He can appear in everyone's heart by His inconceivable potency. Thus although the Lord was within the heart of Devakī, He appeared as her child. According to the *Viṣṇu Purāṇa*, therefore, as quoted in the *Vaiṣṇava-toṣaṇī*, the Lord appeared like the sun (*anugrahāsaya*). The *Brahma-saṁhitā* (5.35) confirms that the Lord is situated even within the atom (*aṇḍāntara-stha-paramāṇu-cayāntara-stham*). He is situated in Mathurā, in Vaikuṇṭha and in the core of the heart. Therefore one should clearly understand that He did not live like an ordinary child in the heart or the womb of Devakī. Nor did He appear like an ordinary human child, although He seemed to do so in order to bewilder *asuras* like Kaṁsa. The *asuras* wrongly think that Kṛṣṇa took birth like an ordinary child and passed away from this world like an ordinary man. Such asuric conceptions are rejected by persons in knowledge of the Supreme Personality of Godhead. *Ajo 'pi sann avyayātmā bhūtānām īśvaro 'pi san* (Bg. 4.6). As stated in *Bhagavad-gītā*, the Lord is *aja*, unborn, and He is the supreme controller of everything. Nonetheless, He appeared as the child of Devakī. This verse describes the inconceivable potency of the Lord, who appeared like the full moon. Understanding the special significance of the appearance of the Supreme Godhead, one should never regard Him as having taken birth like an ordinary child.

TEXTS 9–10

तमद्भुतं बालकमम्बुजेक्षणं
चतुर्भुजं शङ्खगदाद्युदायुधम् ।
श्रीवत्सलक्ष्मं गलशोभिकौस्तुभं
पीताम्बरं सान्द्रपयोदसौभगम् ॥ ९ ॥
महार्हवैदूर्यकिरीटकुण्डल-
त्विषा परिष्वक्तसहस्रकुन्तलम् ।
उद्दामकाञ्च्यङ्गदकङ्कणादिभि-
र्विरोचमानं वसुदेव ऐक्षत ॥१०॥

tam adbhutaṁ bālakam ambujekṣaṇaṁ
catur-bhujaṁ śaṅkha-gadādy-udāyudham
śrīvatsa-lakṣmaṁ gala-śobhi-kaustubhaṁ
pītāmbaraṁ sāndra-payoda-saubhagam

mahārha-vaidūrya-kirīṭa-kuṇḍala-
tviṣā pariṣvakta-sahasra-kuntalam
uddāma-kāñcy-aṅgada-kaṅkaṇādibhir
virocamānaṁ vasudeva aikṣata

tam—that; *adbhutam*—wonderful; *bālakam*—child; *ambuja-īkṣaṇam*—with eyes resembling lotuses; *catuḥ-bhujam*—with four hands; *śaṅkha-gadā-ādi*—bearing a conchshell, club, disc and lotus (in those four hands); *udāyudham*—different weapons; *śrīvatsa-lakṣmam*—decorated with a particular type of hair called Śrīvatsa, which is visible only on the chest of the Supreme Personality of Godhead; *gala-śobhi-kaustubham*—on His neck was the Kaustubha gem, which is particularly available in Vaikuṇṭhaloka; *pīta-ambaram*—His garments were yellow; *sāndra-payoda-saubhagam*—very beautiful, being present with the hue of blackish clouds; *mahā-arha-vaidūrya-kirīṭa-kuṇḍala*—of His helmet and earrings, which were studded with very valuable Vaidūrya gems; *tviṣā*—by the beauty; *pariṣvakta-sahasra-kuntalam*—brilliantly illuminated by scattered, fully grown hair; *uddāma-kāñcī-aṅgada-kaṅkaṇa-ādibhiḥ*—with a brilliant belt on His waist, armbands on His arms, bracelets on His wrists, etc.; *virocamānam*—very beautifully decorated; *vasudevaḥ*—Vasudeva, the father of Kṛṣṇa; *aikṣata*—saw.

TRANSLATION

Vasudeva then saw the newborn child, who had very wonderful lotuslike eyes and who bore in His four hands the four weapons śaṅkha, cakra, gadā and padma. On His chest was the mark of Śrīvatsa and on His neck the brilliant Kaustubha gem. Dressed in yellow, His body blackish like a dense cloud, His scattered hair fully grown, and His helmet and earrings sparkling uncommonly with the valuable gem Vaidūrya, the child, decorated with a brilliant belt, armlets, bangles and other ornaments, appeared very wonderful.

PURPORT

To support the word *adbhutam*, meaning "wonderful," the decorations and opulences of the newborn child are fully described. As confirmed in the *Brahma-saṁhitā* (5.30), *barhāvataṁsam asitāmbuda-sundarāṅgam:* the hue of the Lord's beautiful form resembles the blackish color of dense clouds (*asita* means "blackish," and *ambuda* means "cloud"). It is clear from the word *catur-bhujam* that Kṛṣṇa first appeared with four hands, as Lord Viṣṇu. No ordinary child in human society has ever been born with four hands. And when is a child born with fully grown hair? The descent of the Lord, therefore, is completely distinct from the birth of an ordinary child. The Vaidūrya gem, which sometimes appears bluish, sometimes yellow and sometimes red, is available in Vaikuṇṭhaloka. The Lord's helmet and earrings were decorated with this particular gem.

TEXT 11

स विस्मयोत्फुल्लविलोचनो हरिं
सुतं विलोक्यानकदुन्दुभिस्तदा ।
कृष्णावतारोत्सवसम्भ्रमोऽस्पृशन्
मुदा द्विजेभ्योऽयुतमाप्लुतो गवाम् ॥११॥

sa vismayotphulla-vilocano hariṁ
sutaṁ vilokyānakadundubhis tadā
kṛṣṇāvatārotsava-sambhramo 'spṛśan
mudā dvijebhyo 'yutam āpluto gavām

saḥ—he (Vasudeva, also known as Ānakadundubhi); *vismaya-utphulla-vilocanaḥ*—his eyes being struck with wonder at the beautiful appearance of the Supreme Personality of Godhead; *harim*—Lord Hari, the Supreme Personality of Godhead; *sutam*—as his son; *vilokya*—observing; *ānakadundubhiḥ*—Vasudeva; *tadā*—at that time; *kṛṣṇa-avatāra-utsava*—for a festival to be observed because of Kṛṣṇa's appearance; *sambhramaḥ*—wishing to welcome the Lord with great respect; *aspṛśat*—took advantage by distributing; *mudā*—with great jubilation; *dvijebhyaḥ*—to the *brāhmaṇas; ayutam*—ten thousand; *āplutaḥ*—overwhelmed, surcharged; *gavām*—cows.

TRANSLATION

When Vasudeva saw his extraordinary son, his eyes were struck with wonder. In transcendental jubilation, he mentally collected ten thousand cows and distributed them among the brāhmaṇas as a transcendental festival.

PURPORT

Śrīla Viśvanātha Cakravartī Ṭhākura has analyzed the wonder of Vasudeva upon seeing his extraordinary child. Vasudeva was shivering with wonder to see a newborn child decorated so nicely with valuable garments and gems. He could immediately understand that the Supreme Personality of Godhead had appeared, not as an ordinary child but in His original, fully decorated, four-handed form. The first wonder was that the Lord was not afraid to appear within the prison house of Kaṁsa, where Vasudeva and Devakī were interned. Second, although the Lord, the Supreme Transcendence, is all-pervading, He had appeared from the womb of Devakī. The third point of wonder, therefore, was that a child could take birth from the womb so nicely decorated. Fourth, the Supreme Personality of Godhead was Vasudeva's worshipable Deity yet had taken birth as his son. For all these reasons, Vasudeva was transcendentally jubilant, and he wanted to perform a festival, as *kṣatriyas* do to celebrate the birth of a child, but because of his imprisonment he was unable to do it externally, and therefore he performed the festival within his mind. This was just as good. If one cannot externally serve the Supreme Personality of Godhead, one can serve the Lord within one's mind, since the activities of the mind are as good as those of the other senses. This is called the nondual or absolute situation (*advaya-jñāna*). People generally perform ritualistic ceremonies for the birth of a child. Why then should Vasudeva not have performed such a ceremony when the Supreme Lord appeared as his son?

TEXT 12

अथैनमस्तौदवधार्य पूरुषं
परं नताङ्गः कृतधीः कृताञ्जलिः ।
स्वरोचिषा भारत सूतिकागृहं
विरोचयन्तं गतभीः प्रभाववित् ॥१२॥

athainam astaud avadhārya pūruṣaṁ
paraṁ natāṅgaḥ kṛta-dhīḥ kṛtāñjaliḥ
sva-rociṣā bhārata sūtikā-gṛhaṁ
virocayantaṁ gata-bhīḥ prabhāva-vit

atha—thereafter; *enam*—to the child; *astaut*—offered prayers; *avadhārya*—understanding surely that the child was the Supreme Personality of Godhead; *pūruṣam*—the Supreme Person; *param*—transcendental; *nata-aṅgaḥ*—falling down; *kṛta-dhīḥ*—with concentrated attention; *kṛta-añjaliḥ*—with folded hands; *sva-rociṣā*—by the brilliance of His personal beauty; *bhārata*—O Mahārāja Parīkṣit, descendant of Mahārāja Bharata; *sūtikā-gṛham*—the place where the Lord was born; *virocayantam*—illuminating all around; *gata-bhīḥ*—all his fear disappeared; *prabhāva-vit*—he could now understand the influence (of the Supreme Personality of Godhead).

TRANSLATION

O Mahārāja Parīkṣit, descendant of King Bharata, Vasudeva could understand that this child was the Supreme Personality of Godhead, Nārāyaṇa. Having concluded this without a doubt, he became fearless. Bowing down with folded hands and concentrating his attention, he began to offer prayers to the child, who illuminated His birthplace by His natural influence.

PURPORT

Struck with such great wonder, Vasudeva now concentrated his attention on the Supreme Personality of Godhead. Understanding the influence of the Supreme Lord, he was surely fearless, since he understood that the Lord had appeared to give him protection (*gata-bhīḥ prabhāva-vit*). Understanding that the Supreme Personality of Godhead was present, he appropriately offered prayers as follows.

TEXT 13

श्रीवसुदेव उवाच
विदितोऽसि भवान् साक्षात् पुरुषः प्रकृतेः परः।
केवलानुभवानन्दस्वरूपः सर्वबुद्धिदृक् ॥१३॥

śrī-vasudeva uvāca
vidito 'si bhavān sākṣāt
puruṣaḥ prakṛteḥ paraḥ
kevalānubhavānanda-
svarūpaḥ sarva-buddhi-dṛk

śrī-vasudevaḥ uvāca—Śrī Vasudeva prayed; *viditaḥ asi*—now I am fully conscious of You; *bhavān*—Your Lordship; *sākṣāt*—directly; *puruṣaḥ*—the Supreme Person; *prakṛteḥ*—to material nature; *paraḥ*—transcendental, beyond everything material; *kevala-anubhava-ānanda-svarūpaḥ*—Your form is *sac-cid-ānanda-vigraha,* and whoever perceives You becomes transcendentally blissful; *sarva-buddhi-dṛk*—the supreme observer, the Supersoul, the intelligence of everyone.

TRANSLATION

Vasudeva said: My Lord, You are the Supreme Person, beyond material existence, and You are the Supersoul. Your form can be perceived by transcendental knowledge, by which You can be understood as the Supreme Personality of Godhead. I now understand Your position perfectly.

PURPORT

Within Vasudeva's heart, affection for his son and knowledge of the Supreme Lord's transcendental nature both awakened. In the beginning Vasudeva thought, "Such a beautiful child has been born, but now Kaṁsa will come and kill Him." But when he understood that this was not an ordinary child but the Supreme Personality of Godhead, he became fearless. Regarding his son as the Supreme Lord, wonderful in everything, he began offering prayers appropriate for the Supreme Lord. Completely free from fear of Kaṁsa's atrocities, he accepted the child simultaneously as an object of affection and as an object of worship by prayers.

TEXT 14

स एव स्वप्रकृत्येदं सृष्ट्वाग्रे त्रिगुणात्मकम् ।
तदनु त्वं ह्यप्रविष्टः प्रविष्ट इव भाव्यसे ॥१४॥

sa eva svaprakṛtyedaṁ
sṛṣṭvāgre tri-guṇātmakam
tad anu tvaṁ hy apraviṣṭaḥ
praviṣṭa iva bhāvyase

saḥ—He (the Supreme Personality of Godhead); *eva*—indeed; *sva-prakṛtyā*—by Your personal energy (*mayādhyakṣeṇa prakṛtiḥ sūyate sa-carācaram*); *idam*—this material world; *sṛṣṭvā*—after creating; *agre*—in the beginning; *tri-guṇa-ātmakam*—made of three modes of energy (*sattva-rajas-tamo-guṇa*); *tat anu*—thereafter; *tvam*—Your Lordship; *hi*—indeed; *apraviṣṭaḥ*—although You did not enter; *praviṣṭaḥ iva*—You appear to have entered; *bhāvyase*—are so understood.

TRANSLATION

My Lord, You are the same person who in the beginning created this material world by His personal external energy. After the creation of this world of three guṇas [sattva, rajas and tamas], You appear to have entered it, although in fact You have not.

PURPORT

In *Bhagavad-gītā* (7.4) the Supreme Personality of Godhead clearly explains:

bhūmir āpo 'nalo vāyuḥ
khaṁ mano buddhir eva ca
ahaṅkāra itīyaṁ me
bhinnā prakṛtir aṣṭadhā

This material world of three modes of nature—*sattva-guṇa, rajo-guṇa* and *tamo-guṇa*—is a composition of earth, water, fire, air, mind, intelligence and false ego, all of which are energies coming from Kṛṣṇa, yet Kṛṣṇa, being always transcendental, is aloof from this material world. Those who are not in pure knowledge think that Kṛṣṇa is a product of matter and that His body is material like ours (*avajānanti māṁ mūḍhāḥ*). In fact, however, Kṛṣṇa is always aloof from this material world.

In the Vedic literature, we find the creation described in relationship to Mahā-Viṣṇu. As stated in the *Brahma-saṁhitā* (5.35):

eko 'py asau racayituṁ jagad-aṇḍa-koṭiṁ
yac-chaktir asti jagad-aṇḍa-cayā yad-antaḥ
aṇḍāntara-stha-paramāṇu-cayāntara-sthaṁ
govindam ādi-puruṣaṁ tam ahaṁ bhajāmi

"I worship the primeval Lord, Govinda, the original Personality of Godhead. By His partial plenary expansion as Mahā-Viṣṇu, He enters into material nature. Then He enters every universe as Garbhodakaśāyī Viṣṇu, and He enters all the elements, including every atom of matter, as Kṣīrodakaśāyī Viṣṇu. Such manifestations of cosmic creation are innumerable, both in the universes and in the individual atoms." Govinda is partially exhibited as *antaryāmī*, the Supersoul, who enters this material world (*aṇḍāntara-stha*) and who is also within the atom. The *Brahma-saṁhitā* (5.48) further says:

yasyaika-niśvasita-kālam athāvalambya
jīvanti loma-vilajā jagad-aṇḍa-nāthāḥ
viṣṇur mahān sa iha yasya kalā-viśeṣo
govindam ādi-puruṣaṁ tam ahaṁ bhajāmi

This verse describes Mahā-Viṣṇu as a plenary expansion of Kṛṣṇa. Mahā-Viṣṇu lies on the Causal Ocean, and when He exhales, millions of *brahmāṇḍas*, or universes, come from the pores of His body. Then, when Mahā-Viṣṇu inhales, all these *brahmāṇḍas* disappear. Thus the millions of *brahmāṇḍas* controlled by the Brahmās and other demigods come and go in this material world through the breathing of Mahā-Viṣṇu.

Foolish persons think that when Kṛṣṇa appears as the son of Vasudeva, He is limited like an ordinary child. But Vasudeva was aware that although the Lord had appeared as his son, the Lord had not entered Devakī's womb and then come out. Rather, the Lord was always there. The Supreme Lord is all-pervading, present within and without. *Praviṣṭa iva bhāvyase:* He only seemed to have entered the womb of Devakī and to have now appeared as Vasudeva's child. The expression of this knowledge by Vasudeva indicates that Vasudeva knew how these events took place. Vasudeva was certainly a devotee of the Lord in full knowledge, and we must learn from devotees like him. *Bhagavad-gītā* (4.34) therefore recommends:

tad viddhi praṇipātena
paripraśnena sevayā
upadekṣyanti te jñānaṁ
jñāninas tattva-darśinaḥ

"Just try to learn the truth by approaching a spiritual master. Inquire from him submissively and render service unto him. The self-realized soul can impart knowledge unto you because he has seen the truth." Vasudeva begot the Supreme Personality of Godhead, yet he was in full knowledge of how the Supreme Lord appears and disappears. He was therefore *tattva-darśī*, a seer of the truth, because he personally saw how the Supreme Absolute Truth appeared as his son. Vasudeva was not in ignorance, thinking that because the Supreme Godhead had appeared as his son, the Lord had become limited. The Lord is unlimitedly existing and all-pervading, inside and outside. Thus there is no question of His appearance or disappearance.

TEXTS 15–17

यथेमेऽविकृता भावास्तथा ते विकृतैः सह ।
नानावीर्याः पृथग्भूता विराजं जनयन्ति हि ॥१५॥
सन्निपत्य समुत्पाद्य दृश्यन्तेऽनुगता इव ।
प्रागेव विद्यमानत्वान्न तेषामिह सम्भवः ॥१६॥
एवं भवान् बुद्ध्यनुमेयलक्षणै-
ग्राह्यैर्गुणैः सन्नपि तद्गुणाग्रहः ।
अनावृतत्वाद् बहिरन्तरं न ते
सर्वस्य सर्वात्मन आत्मवस्तुनः ॥१७॥

yatheme 'vikṛtā bhāvās
tathā te vikṛtaiḥ saha
nānā-vīryāḥ pṛthag-bhūtā
virājaṁ janayanti hi

sannipatya samutpādya
dṛśyante 'nugatā iva
prāg eva vidyamānatvān
na teṣām iha sambhavaḥ

evaṁ bhavān buddhy-anumeya-lakṣaṇair
grāhyair guṇaiḥ sann api tad-guṇāgrahaḥ
anāvṛtatvād bahir antaraṁ na te
sarvasya sarvātmana ātma-vastunaḥ

yathā—as; *ime*—these material creations, made of material energy; *avikṛtāḥ*—actually not disintegrated; *bhāvāḥ*—with such a conception; *tathā*—similarly; *te*—they; *vikṛtaiḥ saha*—association with these different elements coming from the total material energy; *nānā-vīryāḥ*—every element is full of different energies; *pṛthak*—separated; *bhūtāḥ*—becoming; *virājam*—the whole cosmic manifestation; *janayanti*—create; *hi*—indeed; *sannipatya*—because of association with the spiritual energy; *samutpādya*—after being created; *dṛśyante*—they appear; *anugatāḥ*—entered within it; *iva*—as if; *prāk*—from the very beginning, before the creation of this cosmic manifestation; *eva*—indeed; *vidyamānatvāt*—due to the existence of the Supreme Personality of Godhead; *na*—not; *teṣām*—of these material elements; *iha*—in this matter of creation; *sambhavaḥ*—entering would have been possible; *evam*—in this way; *bhavān*—O my Lord; *buddhi-anumeya-lakṣaṇaiḥ*—by real intelligence and by such symptoms; *grāhyaiḥ*—with the objects of the senses; *guṇaiḥ*—with the modes of material nature; *san api*—although in touch; *tat-guṇa-agrahaḥ*—are not touched by the material qualities; *anāvṛtatvāt*—because of being situated everywhere; *bahiḥ antaram*—within the external and internal; *na te*—there is no such thing for You; *sarvasya*—of everything; *sarva-ātmanaḥ*—You are the root of everything; *ātma-vastunaḥ*—everything belongs to You, but You are outside and inside of everything.

TRANSLATION

The mahat-tattva, the total material energy, is undivided, but because of the material modes of nature, it appears to separate into earth, water, fire, air and ether. Because of the living energy

[jīva-bhūta], these separated energies combine to make the cosmic manifestation visible, but in fact, before the creation of the cosmos, the total energy is already present. Therefore, the total material energy never actually enters the creation. Similarly, although You are perceived by our senses because of Your presence, You cannot be perceived by the senses, nor experienced by the mind or words [avāṅ-mānasa-gocara]. With our senses we can perceive some things, but not everything; for example, we can use our eyes to see, but not to taste. Consequently, You are beyond perception by the senses. Although in touch with the modes of material nature, You are unaffected by them. You are the prime factor in everything, the all-pervading, undivided Supersoul. For You, therefore, there is no external or internal. You never entered the womb of Devakī; rather, You existed there already.

PURPORT

This same understanding is explained by the Lord Himself in *Bhagavad-gītā* (9.4):

mayā tatam idaṁ sarvaṁ
jagad-avyakta-mūrtinā
mat-sthāni sarva-bhūtāni
na cāhaṁ teṣv avasthitaḥ

"By Me, in My unmanifested form, this entire universe is pervaded. All beings are in Me, but I am not in them."

The Supreme Personality of Godhead is not perceivable through the gross material senses. It is said that Lord Śrī Kṛṣṇa's name, fame, pastimes, etc., cannot be understood by material senses. Only to one who is engaged in pure devotional service under proper guidance is He revealed. As stated in *Brahma-saṁhitā* (5.38):

premāñjana-cchurita-bhakti-vilocanena
santaḥ sadaiva hṛdayeṣu vilokayanti

One can see the Supreme Personality of Godhead, Govinda, always, within oneself and outside oneself, if one has developed the transcendental loving attitude toward Him. Thus for people in general, He is not visible. In the above-mentioned verse from *Bhagavad-gītā*, therefore, it is said that although He is all-pervading, everywhere present, He is not conceivable by the material senses. But actually, although we cannot see Him, everything is resting in Him. As discussed in the Seventh Chapter of *Bhagavad-gītā*, the entire material cosmic manifestation is only a combination of His two different energies, the superior, spiritual energy and the inferior, material energy. Just as the sunshine is spread all over the universe, the energy of the Lord is spread all over the creation, and everything is resting in that energy.

Yet one should not conclude that because He is spread all over He has lost His personal existence. To refute such arguments, the Lord says, "I am everywhere, and everything is in Me, but still I am aloof." For example, a king heads a government which is but the manifestation of the king's energy; the different governmental departments are nothing but the energies of the king, and each department is resting on the king's power. But still one cannot expect the king to be present in every department personally. That is a crude example. Similarly, all the manifestations that we see, and everything that exists, both in this material world and in the spiritual world, are resting on the energy of the Supreme Personality of Godhead. The creation takes place by the diffusion of His different energies, and, as stated in the *Bhagavad-gītā*, He is everywhere present by His personal representation, the diffusion of His different energies.

One may argue that the Supreme Personality of Godhead, who creates the whole cosmic manifestation simply by His glance, cannot come within the womb of Devakī, the wife of Vasudeva. To eradicate this argument, Vasudeva said, "My dear Lord, it is not very wonderful that You appeared within the womb of Devakī, for the creation was also made in that way. You were lying in the Causal Ocean as Mahā-Viṣṇu, and by Your breathing, innumerable universes came into existence. Then You entered into each of the universes as Garbhodakaśāyī Viṣṇu. Then again You expanded Yourself as Kṣīrodakaśāyī Viṣṇu and entered into the heart of all living entities and entered even within the atoms. Therefore Your entrance into the womb of Devakī is understandable in the same way. You appear to have entered, but You are simultaneously all-pervading. We can understand Your entrance and nonentrance from material examples.

The total material energy remains intact even after being divided into sixteen elements. The material body is nothing but a combination of the five gross elements—namely earth, water, fire, air and ether. Whenever there is a material body, it appears that such elements are newly created, but actually the elements are always existing outside of the body. Similarly, although You appear as a child in the womb of Devakī, You are also existing outside. You are always in Your abode, but still You can simultaneously expand Yourself into millions of forms.

"One has to understand Your appearance with great intelligence because the material energy is also emanating from You. You are the original source of the material energy, just as the sun is the source of the sunshine. The sunshine cannot cover the sun globe, nor can the material energy—being an emanation from You—cover You. You appear to be in the three modes of material energy, but actually the three modes of material energy cannot cover You. This is understood by the highly intellectual philosophers. In other words, although You appear to be within the material energy, You are never covered by it."

We hear from the Vedic version that the Supreme Brahman exhibits His effulgence and therefore everything is illuminated. We can understand from *Brahma-saṁhitā* that the *brahmajyoti*, or the Brahman effulgence, emanates from the body of the Supreme Lord. And from the Brahman effulgence, all creation takes place. It is further stated in the *Bhagavad-gītā* that the Lord is the support of the Brahman effulgence. Originally He is the root cause of everything. But persons who are less intelligent think that when the Supreme Personality of Godhead comes within this material world, He accepts material qualities. Such conclusions are not mature, but are made by the less intelligent.

TEXT 18

य आत्मनो दृश्यगुणेषु सन्निति
व्यवस्यते स्वव्यतिरेकतोऽबुधः ।
विनानुवादं न च तन्मनीषितं
सम्यग् यतस्त्यक्तमुपाददत् पुमान् ॥१८॥

ya ātmano dṛśya-guṇeṣu sann iti
vyavasyate sva-vyatirekato 'budhaḥ

vinānuvādaṁ na ca tan manīṣitaṁ
samyag yatas tyaktam upādadat pumān

yaḥ—anyone who; *ātmanaḥ*—of his own real identity, the soul; *dṛśya-guṇeṣu*—among the visible objects, beginning with the body; *san*—being situated in that position; *iti*—thus; *vyavasyate*—continues to act; *sva-vyatirekataḥ*—as if the body were independent of the soul; *abudhaḥ*—a rascal; *vinā anuvādam*—without proper analytical study; *na*—not; *ca*—also; *tat*—the body and other visible objects; *manīṣitam*—such considerations having been discussed; *samyak*—fully; *yataḥ*—because he is a fool; *tyaktam*—are rejected; *upādadat*—accepts this body as reality; *pumān*—a person.

TRANSLATION

One who considers his visible body, which is a product of the three modes of nature, to be independent of the soul is unaware of the basis of existence, and therefore he is a rascal. Those who are learned have rejected his conclusion because one can understand through full discussion that with no basis in soul, the visible body and senses would be insubstantial. Nonetheless, although his conclusion has been rejected, a foolish person considers it a reality.

PURPORT

Without the basic principle of soul, the body cannot be produced. So-called scientists have tried in many ways to produce a living body in their chemical laboratories, but no one has been able to do it because unless the spirit soul is present, a body cannot be prepared from material elements. Since scientists are now enamored of theories about the chemical composition of the body, we have challenged many scientists to make even a small egg. The chemicals in eggs can be found very easily. There is a white substance and a yellow substance, covered by a shell, and modern scientists should very easily be able to duplicate all this. But even if they were to prepare such an egg and put it in an incubator, this man-made chemical egg would not produce a chicken. The soul must be added because there is no question of a chemical combination for life. Those who think that life can exist wihout the soul have therefore been described here as *abudhaḥ*, foolish rascals.

Again, there are those who reject the body, regarding it as insubstantial. They are of the same category of fools. One can neither reject the body nor accept it as substantial. The substance is the Supreme Personality of Godhead, and both the body and the soul are energies of the Supreme Godhead, as described by the Lord Himself in *Bhagavad-gītā* (7.4–5):

bhūmir āpo 'nalo vāyuḥ
khaṁ mano buddhir eva ca
ahaṅkāra itīyaṁ me
bhinnā prakṛtir aṣṭadhā

apareyam itas tv anyāṁ
prakṛtiṁ viddhi me parām
jīva-bhūtāṁ mahā-bāho
yayedaṁ dhāryate jagat

"Earth, water, fire, air, ether, mind, intelligence and false ego—all together these eight comprise My separated material energies. But besides this inferior nature, O mighty-armed Arjuna, there is a superior energy of Mine, which consists of all living entities who are struggling with material nature and are sustaining the universe."

The body, therefore, has a relationship with the Supreme Personality of Godhead, just as the soul does. Since both of them are energies of the Lord, neither of them is false, because they come from the reality. One who does not know this secret of life is described as *abudhaḥ.* According to the Vedic injunctions, *aitadātmyam idaṁ sarvam, sarvaṁ khalv idaṁ brahma:* everything is the Supreme Brahman. Therefore, both the body and the soul are Brahman, since matter and spirit emanate from Brahman.

Not knowing the conclusions of the *Vedas,* some people accept the material nature as substance, and others accept the spirit soul as substance, but actually Brahman is the substance. Brahman is the cause of all causes. The ingredients and the immediate cause of this manifested material world are Brahman, and we cannot make the ingredients of this world independent of Brahman. Furthermore, since the ingredients and the immediate cause of this material manifestation are Brahman, both of them are truth, *satya;* there is no validity to the expression *brahma satyaṁ jagan mithyā.* The world is not false.

Jñānīs reject this world, and foolish persons accept this world as reality, and in this way they are both misguided. Although the body is not as important as the soul, we cannot say that it is false. Yet the body is temporary, and only foolish, materialistic persons, who do not have full knowledge of the soul, regard the temporary body as reality and engage in decorating this body. Both of these pitfalls—rejection of the body as false and acceptance of the body as all in all—can be avoided when one is fully situated in Kṛṣṇa consciousness. If we regard this world as false, we fall into the category of *asuras,* who say that this world is unreal, with no foundation and no God in control (*asatyam apratiṣṭhaṁ te jagad āhur anīśvaram*). As described in the Sixteenth Chapter of *Bhagavad-gītā,* this is the conclusion of demons.

TEXT 19

त्वत्तोऽस्य जन्मस्थितिसंयमान् विभो
वदन्त्यनीहादगुणादविक्रियात् ।
त्वयीश्वरे ब्रह्मणि नो विरुध्यते
त्वदाश्रयत्वादुपचर्यते गुणैः ॥१९॥

tvatto 'sya janma-sthiti-saṁyamān vibho
vadanty anīhād aguṇād avikriyāt
tvayīśvare brahmaṇi no virudhyate
tvad-āśrayatvād upacaryate guṇaiḥ

tvattaḥ—are from Your Lordship; *asya*—of the entire cosmic manifestation; *janma*—the creation; *sthiti*—maintenance; *saṁyamān*—and annihilation; *vibho*—O my Lord; *vadanti*—the learned Vedic scholars conclude; *anīhāt*—who are free from endeavor; *aguṇāt*—who are unaffected by the modes of material nature; *avikriyāt*—who are unchanging in Your spiritual situation; *tvayi*—in You; *īśvare*—the Supreme Personality of Godhead; *brahmaṇi*—who are Parabrahman, the Supreme Brahman; *no*—not; *virudhyate*—there is a contradiction; *tvat-āśrayatvāt*—because of being controlled by You; *upacaryate*—

things are going on automatically; *guṇaiḥ*—by the operation of the material modes.

TRANSLATION

O my Lord, learned Vedic scholars conclude that the creation, maintenance and annihilation of the entire cosmic manifestation are performed by You, who are free from endeavor, unaffected by the modes of material nature, and changeless in Your spiritual situation. There are no contradictions in You, who are the Supreme Personality of Godhead, Parabrahman. Because the three modes of material nature—sattva, rajas and tamas—are under Your control, everything takes place automatically.

PURPORT

As stated in the *Vedas:*

na tasya kāryaṁ karaṇaṁ ca vidyate
na tat-samaś cābhyadhikaś ca dṛśyate
parāsya śaktir vividhaiva śrūyate
svābhāvikī jñāna-bala-kriyā ca

"The Supreme Lord has nothing to do, and no one is found to be equal to or greater than Him, for everything is done naturally and systematically by His multifarious energies." (*Śvetāśvatara Upaniṣad* 6.8) Creation, maintenance and annihilation are all conducted personally by the Supreme Personality of Godhead, and this is confirmed in *Bhagavad-gītā* (*mayādhyakṣeṇa prakṛtiḥ sūyate sa-carācaram*). Yet ultimately the Lord does not need to do anything, and therefore He is *nirvikāra*, changeless. Because everything is done under His direction, He is called *sṛṣṭi-kartā*, the master of creation. Similarly, He is the master of annihilation. When a master sits in one place while his servants work in different duties, whatever the servants are doing is ultimately an activity of the master, although he is doing nothing (*na tasya kāryaṁ karaṇaṁ ca vidyate*). The Lord's potencies are so numerous that everything is nicely done. Therefore, He is naturally still and is not directly the doer of anything in this material world.

TEXT 20

स त्वं त्रिलोकस्थितये स्वमायया
बिभर्षि शुक्लं खलु वर्णमात्मनः ।
सर्गाय रक्तं रजसोपबृंहितं
कृष्णं च वर्णं तमसा जनात्यये ॥२०॥

sa tvaṁ tri-loka-sthitaye sva-māyayā
bibharṣi śuklaṁ khalu varṇam ātmanaḥ
sargāya raktaṁ rajasopabṛṁhitaṁ
kṛṣṇaṁ ca varṇaṁ tamasā janātyaye

saḥ tvam—Your Lordship, who are the same person, the Transcendence; *tri-loka-sthitaye*—to maintain the three worlds, the upper, middle and lower planetary systems; *sva-māyayā*—by Your personal energy (*ātma-māyayā*); *bibharṣi*—assume; *śuklam*—the white form of Viṣṇu in goodness; *khalu*—as well as; *varṇam*—color; *ātmanaḥ*—of the same category as You (*viṣṇu-tattva*); *sargāya*—for the creation of the entire world; *raktam*—the reddish color of *rajo-guṇa; rajasā*—with the quality of passion; *upabṛṁhitam*—being charged; *kṛṣṇam ca*—and the quality of darkness; *varṇam*—the color; *tamasā*—which is surrounded by ignorance; *jana-atyaye*—for the ultimate destruction of the entire creation.

TRANSLATION

My Lord, Your form is transcendental to the three material modes, yet for the maintenance of the three worlds, You assume the white color of Viṣṇu in goodness; for creation, which is surrounded by the quality of passion, You appear reddish; and at the end, when there is a need for annihilation, which is surrounded by ignorance, You appear blackish.

PURPORT

Vasudeva prayed to the Lord, "You are called *śuklam. Śuklam,* or 'whiteness,' is the symbolic representation of the Absolute Truth because it is unaffected by the material qualities. Lord Brahmā is called *rakta,* or red, because Brahmā represents the qualities of passion for creation. Darkness is entrusted to Lord Śiva because he annihilates the cosmos. The creation, annihilation and maintenance of this cosmic manifestation are conducted by Your potencies, yet You are always unaffected by those qualities." As confirmed in the *Vedas, harir hi nirguṇaḥ sākṣāt:* the Supreme Personality of Godhead is always free from all material qualities. It is also said that the qualities of passion and ignorance are nonexistent in the person of the Supreme Lord.

In this verse, the three colors mentioned—*śukla, rakta* and *kṛṣṇa*—are not to be understood literally, in terms of what we experience with our senses, but rather as representatives of *sattva-guṇa, rajo-guṇa* and *tamo-guṇa.* After all, sometimes we see that a duck is white, although it is in *tamo-guṇa,* the mode of ignorance. Illustrating the logic called *bakāndha-nyāya,* the duck is such a fool that it runs after the testicles of a bull, thinking them to be a hanging fish that can be taken when it drops. Thus the duck is always in darkness. Vyāsadeva, however, the compiler of the Vedic literature, is blackish, but this does not mean that he is in *tamo-guṇa;* rather, he is in the highest position of *sattva-guṇa,* beyond the material modes of nature. Sometimes these colors (*śukla-raktas tathā pītaḥ*) are used to designate the *brāhmaṇas, kṣatriyas, vaiśyas* and *śūdras.* Lord Kṣīrodakaśāyī Viṣṇu is celebrated as possessing a blackish color, Lord Śiva is whitish, and Lord Brahmā is reddish, but according to Śrīla Sanātana Gosvāmī in the *Vaiṣṇava-toṣaṇī-ṭīkā,* this exhibition of colors is not what is referred to here.

The real understanding of *śukla, rakta* and *kṛṣṇa* is as follows. The Lord is always transcendental, but for the sake of creation He assumes the color *rakta* as Lord Brahmā. Again, sometimes the Lord becomes angry. As He says in *Bhagavad-gītā* (16.19):

tān ahaṁ dviṣataḥ krūrān
saṁsāreṣu narādhamān
kṣipāmy ajasram aśubhān
āsurīṣv eva yoniṣu

"Those who are envious and mischievous, who are the lowest among men, are cast by Me into the ocean of material existence, into various demoniac species of life." To destroy the demons, the Lord becomes angry, and therefore He assumes the form of Lord Śiva. In summary, the Supreme Personality of Godhead is always beyond the material qualities, and we should not be misled into thinking otherwise simply because of sense perception. One must understand the position of the Lord through the authorities, or *mahājanas*. As stated in *Śrīmad-Bhāgavatam* (1.3.28), *ete cāṁśa-kalāḥ puṁsaḥ kṛṣṇas tu bhagavān svayam.*

TEXT 21

त्वमस्य लोकस्य विभो रिरक्षिषु-
गृहेऽवतीर्णोऽसि ममाखिलेश्वर ।
राजन्यसंज्ञासुरकोटियूथपै-
र्निर्व्यूह्यमाना निहनिष्यसे चमूः ॥२१॥

tvam asya lokasya vibho rirakṣiṣur
gṛhe 'vatīrṇo 'si mamākhileśvara
rājanya-saṁjñāsura-koṭi-yūthapair
nirvyūhyamānā nihaniṣyase camūḥ

tvam—Your Lordship; *asya*—of this world; *lokasya*—especially of this *martya-loka*, the planet earth; *vibho*—O Supreme; *rirakṣiṣuḥ*—desiring protection (from the disturbance of the *asuras*); *gṛhe*—in this house; *avatīrṇaḥ asi*—have now appeared; *mama*—my; *akhila-īśvara*—although You are the proprietor of the entire creation; *rājanya-saṁjña-asura-koṭi-yūtha-paiḥ*—with millions of demons and their followers in the roles of politicians and kings; *nirvyūhyamānāḥ*—which are moving here and there all over the world; *nihaniṣyase*—will kill; *camūḥ*—the armies, paraphernalia, soldiers and retinues.

TRANSLATION

O my Lord, proprietor of all creation, You have now appeared in my house, desiring to protect this world. I am sure that You will kill all the armies that are moving all over the world under the leadership of politicians who are dressed as kṣatriya rulers but who are factually demons. They must be killed by You for the protection of the innocent public.

PURPORT

Kṛṣṇa appears in this world for two purposes, *paritrāṇāya sādhūnāṁ vināśāya ca duṣkṛtām:* to protect the innocent, religious devotees of the Lord and to annihilate all the uneducated, uncultured *asuras*, who unnecessarily bark like dogs and fight among themselves for political power. It is said, *kali-kāle nāma-rūpe kṛṣṇa avatāra*. The Hare Kṛṣṇa movement is also an incarnation of Kṛṣṇa in the form of the holy name (*nāma-rūpe*). Every one of us who is actually afraid of the asuric rulers and politicians must welcome this incarnation of Kṛṣṇa: Hare Kṛṣṇa, Hare Kṛṣṇa, Kṛṣṇa Kṛṣṇa, Hare Hare/ Hare Rāma, Hare Rāma, Rāma Rāma, Hare Hare. Then we will surely be protected from the harassment of asuric rulers. At the present moment these rulers are so powerful that by hook or by crook they capture the highest posts in government and harass countless numbers of people on the plea of national security or some emergency. Then again, one *asura* defeats another *asura*, but the public continues to suffer. Therefore the entire world is in a precarious condition, and the only hope is this Hare Kṛṣṇa movement. Lord Nṛsiṁhadeva appeared when Prahlāda was excessively harassed by his asuric father. Because of such asuric fathers—that is, the ruling politicians—it is very difficult to press forward the Hare Kṛṣṇa movement, but because Kṛṣṇa has now appeared in His holy name through this movement, we can hope that these asuric fathers will be annihilated and the kingdom of God established all over the world. The entire world is now full of many *asuras* in the guise of politicians, *gurus*, *sādhus*, *yogīs* and incarnations, and they are misleading the general public away from Kṛṣṇa consciousness, which can offer true benefit to human society.

TEXT 22

अयं त्वसभ्यस्तव जन्म नौ गृहे
श्रुत्वाग्रजांस्ते न्यवधीत् सुरेश्वर ।
स तेऽवतारं पुरुषैः समर्पितं
श्रुत्वाधुनैवाभिसरत्युदायुधः ॥२२॥

ayaṁ tv asabhyas tava janma nau gṛhe
śrutvāgrajāṁs te nyavadhīt sureśvara

sa te 'vatāraṁ puruṣaiḥ samarpitaṁ
śrutvādhunaivābhisaraty udāyudhaḥ

ayam—this (rascal); *tu*—but; *asabhyaḥ*—who is not civilized at all (*asura* means "uncivilized," and *sura* means "civilized"); *tava*—of Your Lordship; *janma*—the birth; *nau*—our; *gṛhe*—into the home; *śrutvā*—after hearing; *agrajān te*—all the brothers born before You; *nyavadhīt*—killed; *sura-īśvara*—O Lord of the *suras*, the civilized persons; *saḥ*—he (that uncivilized Kaṁsa); *te*—Your; *avatāram*—appearance; *puruṣaiḥ*—by his lieutenants; *samarpitam*—being informed of; *śrutvā*—after hearing; *adhunā*—now; *eva*—indeed; *abhisarati*—will come immediately; *udāyudhaḥ*—with raised weapons.

TRANSLATION

O my Lord, Lord of the demigods, after hearing the prophecy that You would take birth in our home and kill him, this uncivilized Kaṁsa killed so many of Your elder brothers. As soon as he hears from his lieutenants that You have appeared, he will immediately come with weapons to kill You.

PURPORT

Kaṁsa has here been described as *asabhya*, meaning "uncivilized" or "most heinous," because he killed the many children of his sister. When he heard the prophecy that he would be killed by her eighth son, this uncivilized man, Kaṁsa, was immediately ready to kill his innocent sister on the occasion of her marriage. An uncivilized man can do anything for the satisfaction of his senses. He can kill children, he can kill cows, he can kill *brāhmaṇas*, he can kill old men; he has no mercy for anyone. According to the Vedic civilization, cows, women, children, old men and *brāhmaṇas* should be excused if they are at fault. But *asuras*, uncivilized men, do not care about that. At the present moment, the killing of cows and the killing of children is going on unrestrictedly, and therefore this civilization is not at all human, and those who are conducting this condemned civilization are uncivilized *asuras*.

Such uncivilized men are not in favor of the Kṛṣṇa consciousness movement. As public officers, they declare without hesitation that the chanting of the Hare Kṛṣṇa movement is a nuisance, although *Bhagavad-gītā* clearly says, *satataṁ kīrtayanto māṁ yatantaś ca dṛḍha-vratāḥ*. According to this verse, it is the duty of the *mahātmās* to chant the Hare Kṛṣṇa *mantra* and try to spread it all over the world to the best of their ability. Unfortunately, society is in such an uncivilized state that there are so-called *mahātmās* who are prepared to kill cows and children and stop the Hare Kṛṣṇa movement. Such uncivilized activities were actually demonstrated in opposition to the Hare Kṛṣṇa movement's Bombay center, Hare Kṛṣṇa Land. As Kaṁsa was not expected to kill the beautiful child of Devakī and Vasudeva, the uncivilized society, although unhappy about the advancement of the Kṛṣṇa consciousness movement, cannot be expected to stop it. Yet we must face many difficulties in many different ways. Although Kṛṣṇa cannot be killed, Vasudeva, as the father of Kṛṣṇa, was trembling because in affection he thought that Kaṁsa would immediately come and kill his son. Similarly, although the Kṛṣṇa consciousness movement and Kṛṣṇa are not different and no *asuras* can check it, we are afraid that at any moment the *asuras* can stop this movement in any part of the world.

TEXT 23

श्रीशुक उवाच
अथैनमात्मजं वीक्ष्य महापुरुषलक्षणम् ।
देवकी तमुपाधावत् कंसाद् भीता सुविस्मिता ॥२३॥

śrī-śuka uvāca
athainam ātmajaṁ vīkṣya
mahā-puruṣa-lakṣaṇam
devakī tam upādhāvat
kaṁsād bhītā suvismitā

śrī-śukaḥ uvāca—Śrī Śukadeva Gosvāmī said; *atha*—after this offering of prayers by Vasudeva; *enam*—this Kṛṣṇa; *ātmajam*—their son; *vīkṣya*—observing; *mahā-puruṣa-lakṣaṇam*—with all the symptoms of the Supreme Personality of Godhead, Viṣṇu; *devakī*—Kṛṣṇa's mother; *tam*—unto Him (Kṛṣṇa); *upādhāvat*—offered prayers; *kaṁsāt*—of

Kaṁsa; *bhītā*—being afraid; *su-vismitā*—and also being astonished by seeing such a wonderful child.

TRANSLATION

Śukadeva Gosvāmī continued: Thereafter, having seen that her child had all the symptoms of the Supreme Personality of Godhead, Devakī, who was very much afraid of Kaṁsa and unusually astonished, began to offer prayers to the Lord.

PURPORT

The word *suvismitā*, meaning "astonished," is significant in this verse. Devakī and her husband, Vasudeva, were assured that their child was the Supreme Personality of Godhead and could not be killed by Kaṁsa, but because of affection, as they thought of Kaṁsa's previous atrocities, they were simultaneously afraid that Kṛṣṇa would be killed. This is why the word *suvismitā* has been used. Similarly, we are also astounded upon thinking of whether this movement will be killed by the *asuras* or will continue to advance without fear.

TEXT 24

श्रीदेवक्युवाच
रूपं यत् तत् प्राहुरव्यक्तमाद्यं
ब्रह्म ज्योतिर्निर्गुणं निर्विकारम् ।
सत्तामात्रं निर्विशेषं निरीहं
स त्वं साक्षाद् विष्णुरध्यात्मदीपः ॥२४॥

śrī-devaky uvāca
rūpaṁ yat tat prāhur avyaktam ādyaṁ
brahma jyotir nirguṇaṁ nirvikāram
sattā-mātraṁ nirviśeṣaṁ nirīhaṁ
sa tvaṁ sākṣād viṣṇur adhyātma-dīpaḥ

śrī-devakī uvāca—Śrī Devakī said; *rūpam*—form or substance; *yat tat*—because You are the same substance; *prāhuḥ*—You are sometimes called; *avyaktam*—not perceivable by the material senses (*ataḥ śrī-kṛṣṇa-nāmādi na bhaved grāhyam indriyaiḥ*); *ādyam*—You are the original cause; *brahma*—You are known as Brahman; *jyotiḥ*—light; *nirguṇam*—without material qualities; *nirvikāram*—without change, the same form of Viṣṇu perpetually; *sattā-mātram*—the original substance, the cause of everything; *nirviśeṣam*—You are present everywhere as the Supersoul (within the heart of a human being and within the heart of an animal, the same substance is present); *nirīham*—without material desires; *saḥ*—that Supreme Person; *tvam*—Your Lordship; *sākṣāt*—directly; *viṣṇuḥ*—Lord Viṣṇu; *adhyātma-dīpaḥ*—the light for all transcendental knowledge (knowing You, one knows everything: *yasmin vijñāte sarvam evaṁ vijñātaṁ bhavati*).

TRANSLATION

Śrī Devakī said: My dear Lord, there are different Vedas, some of which describe You as unperceivable through words and the mind. Yet You are the origin of the entire cosmic manifestation. You are Brahman, the greatest of everything, full of effulgence like the sun. You have no material cause, You are free from change and deviation, and You have no material desires. Thus the Vedas say that You are the substance. Therefore, my Lord, You are directly the origin of all Vedic statements, and by understanding You, one gradually understands everything. You are different from the light of Brahman and Paramātmā, yet You are not different from them. Everything emanates from You. Indeed, You are the cause of all causes, Lord Viṣṇu, the light of all transcendental knowledge.

PURPORT

Viṣṇu is the origin of everything, and there is no difference between Lord Viṣṇu and Lord Kṛṣṇa because both of Them are *viṣṇu-tattva*. From the *Ṛg Veda* we understand, *oṁ tad viṣṇoḥ paramaṁ padam:* the original substance is the all-pervading Lord Viṣṇu, who is also Paramātmā and the effulgent Brahman. The living entities are also part and parcel of Viṣṇu, who has various energies (*parāsya śaktir vividhaiva śrūyate svābhāvikī jñāna-bala-kriyā ca*). Viṣṇu, or Kṛṣṇa, is therefore everything. Lord Kṛṣṇa says in the *Bhagavad-gītā* (10.8), *ahaṁ sarvasya prabhavo mattaḥ sarvaṁ pravartate:* "I am the source of all spiritual and material worlds. Everything emanates from Me." Kṛṣṇa, therefore, is the original cause of everything (*sarva-kāraṇa-kāraṇam*). When Viṣṇu expands in His all-pervading aspect, we should understand Him to be the *nirākāra-nirviśeṣa-brahmajyoti.*

Although everything emanates from Kṛṣṇa, He is ultimately a person. *Aham ādir hi devānām:* He is the origin of Brahmā, Viṣṇu and Maheśvara, and from them many other demigods are manifested. Kṛṣṇa therefore says in *Bhagavad-gītā* (14.27), *brahmaṇo hi pratiṣṭhāham:* "Brahman rests upon Me." The Lord also says:

ye 'py anya-devatā-bhaktā
yajante śraddhayānvitāḥ
te 'pi mām eva kaunteya
yajanty avidhi-pūrvakam

"Whatever a man may sacrifice to other gods, O son of Kuntī, is really meant for Me alone, but it is offered without true understanding." (Bg. 9.23) There are many persons who worship different demigods, considering all of them to be separate gods, which in fact they are not. The fact is that every demigod, and every living entity, is part and parcel of Kṛṣṇa (*mamaivāṁśo jīva-loke jīva-bhūtaḥ*). The demigods are also in the category of living entities; they are not separate gods. But men whose knowledge is immature and contaminated by the modes of material nature worship various demigods, according to their intelligence. Therefore they are rebuked in *Bhagavad-gītā* (*kāmais tais tair hṛta-jñānāḥ prapadyante 'nya-devatāḥ*). Because they are unintelligent and not very advanced and have not properly considered the truth, they take to the worship of various demigods or speculate according to various philosophies, such as the Māyāvāda philosophy.

Kṛṣṇa, Viṣṇu, is the actual origin of everything. As stated in the *Vedas, yasya bhāṣā sarvam idaṁ vibhāti.* The Absolute Truth is described later in the *Śrīmad-Bhāgavatam* (10.28.15) as *satyaṁ jñānam anantam yad brahma-jyotiḥ sānatanam.* The *brahmajyoti* is *sanātana,* eternal, yet it is dependent on Kṛṣṇa (*brahmaṇo hi pratiṣṭhāham*). The

Brahma-saṁhitā states that the Lord is all-pervading. *Aṇḍāntara-stha-paramāṇu-cayāntara-stham:* He is within this universe, and He is within the atom as Paramātmā. *Yasya prabhā prabhavato jagad-aṇḍa-koṭi-koṭiṣv aśeṣa-vasudhādi-vibhūti-bhinnam:* Brahman is also not independent of Him. Therefore whatever a philosopher may describe is ultimately Kṛṣṇa, or Lord Viṣṇu (*sarvaṁ khalv idaṁ brahma, paraṁ brahma paraṁ dhāma pavitraṁ paramaṁ bhavān*). According to different phases of understanding, Lord Viṣṇu is differently described, but in fact He is the origin of everything.

Because Devakī was an unalloyed devotee, she could understand that the same Lord Viṣṇu had appeared as her son. Therefore, after the prayers of Vasudeva, Devakī offered her prayers. She was very frightened because of her brother's atrocities. Devakī said, "My dear Lord, Your eternal forms, like Nārāyaṇa, Lord Rāma, Śeṣa, Varāha, Nṛsiṁha, Vāmana, Baladeva, and millions of similar incarnations emanating from Viṣṇu, are described in the Vedic literature as original. You are original because all Your forms as incarnations are outside of this material creation. Your form was existing before this cosmic manifestation was created. Your forms are eternal and all-pervading. They are self-effulgent, changeless and uncontaminated by the material qualities. Such eternal forms are evercognizant and full of bliss; they are situated in transcendental goodness and are always engaged in different pastimes. You are not limited to a particular form only; all such transcendental, eternal forms are self-sufficient. I can understand that You are the Supreme Lord Viṣṇu." We may conclude, therefore, that Lord Viṣṇu is everything, although He is also different from everything. This is the *acintya-bhedābheda-tattva* philosophy.

TEXT 25

नष्टे लोके द्विपरार्धावसाने
महाभूतेष्वादिभूतं गतेषु ।
व्यक्तेऽव्यक्तं कालवेगेन याते
भवानेकः शिष्यतेऽशेषसंज्ञः ॥२५॥

naṣṭe loke dvi-parārdhāvasāne
mahā-bhūteṣv ādi-bhūtaṁ gateṣu

vyakte 'vyaktaṁ kāla-vegena yāte
bhavān ekaḥ śiṣyate 'śeṣa-saṁjñaḥ

naṣṭe—after the annihilation; *loke*—of the cosmic manifestation; *dvi-parārdha-avasāne*—after millions and millions of years (the life of Brahmā); *mahā-bhūteṣu*—when the five primary elements (earth, water, fire, air and ether); *ādi-bhūtam gateṣu*—enter within the subtle elements of sense perception; *vyakte*—when everything manifested; *avyaktam*—into the unmanifested; *kāla-vegena*—by the force of time; *yāte*—enters; *bhavān*—Your Lordship; *ekaḥ*—only one; *śiṣyate*—remains; *aśeṣa-saṁjñaḥ*—the same one with different names.

TRANSLATION

After millions of years, at the time of cosmic annihilation, when everything, manifested and unmanifested, is annihilated by the force of time, the five gross elements enter into the subtle conception, and the manifested categories enter into the unmanifested substance. At that time, You alone remain, and You are known as Ananta Śeṣa-nāga.

PURPORT

At the time of annihilation, the five gross elements—earth, water, fire, air and ether—enter into the mind, intelligence and false ego (*ahaṅkāra*), and the entire cosmic manifestation enters into the spiritual energy of the Supreme Personality of Godhead, who alone remains as the origin of everything. The Lord is therefore known as Śeṣa-nāga, as Ādi-puruṣa and by many other names.

Devakī therefore prayed, "After many millions of years, when Lord Brahmā comes to the end of his life, the annihilation of the cosmic manifestation takes place. At that time the five elements—namely earth, water, fire, air and ether—enter into the *mahat-tattva.* The *mahat-tattva* again enters, by the force of time, into the nonmanifested total material energy; the total material energy enters into the energetic *pradhāna,* and the *pradhāna* enters into You. Therefore after the annihilation of the whole cosmic manifestation, You alone remain with Your transcendental name, form, quality and paraphernalia.

"My Lord, I offer my respectful obeisances unto You because You are the director of the unmanifested total energy, and the ultimate reservoir of the material nature. My Lord, the whole cosmic manifestation is under the influence of time, beginning from the moment up to the duration of the year. All act under Your direction. You are the original director of everything and the reservoir of all potent energies."

TEXT 26

योऽयं कालस्तस्य तेऽव्यक्तबन्धो
चेष्टामाहुश्चेष्टते येन विश्वम् ।
निमेषादिर्वत्सरान्तो महीयां-
स्तं त्वेशानं क्षेमधाम प्रपद्ये ॥२६॥

yo 'yaṁ kālas tasya te 'vyakta-bandho
ceṣṭām āhuś ceṣṭate yena viśvam
nimeṣādir vatsarānto mahīyāṁs
taṁ tveśānaṁ kṣema-dhāma prapadye

yaḥ—that which; *ayam*—this; *kālaḥ*—time (minutes, hours, seconds); *tasya*—of Him; *te*—of You; *avyakta-bandho*—O my Lord, You are the inaugurator of the unmanifested (the original *mahat-tattva* or *prakṛti*); *ceṣṭām*—attempt or pastimes; *āhuḥ*—it is said; *ceṣṭate*—works; *yena*—by which; *viśvam*—the entire creation; *nimeṣa-ādiḥ*—beginning with minute parts of time; *vatsara-antaḥ*—up to the limit of a year; *mahīyān*—powerful; *tam*—unto Your Lordship; *tvā īśānam*—unto You, the supreme controller; *kṣema-dhāma*—the reservoir of all auspiciousness; *prapadye*—I offer full surrender.

TRANSLATION

O inaugurator of the material energy, this wonderful creation works under the control of powerful time, which is divided into seconds, minutes, hours and years. This element of time, which extends for many millions of years, is but another form of Lord Viṣṇu. For Your pastimes, You act as the controller of time, but

You are the reservoir of all good fortune. Let me offer my full surrender unto Your Lordship.

PURPORT

As stated in the *Brahma-saṁhitā* (5.52):

yac-cakṣur eṣa savitā sakala-grahāṇāṁ
rājā samasta-sura-mūrtir aśeṣa-tejāḥ
yasyājñayā bhramati saṁbhṛta-kāla-cakro
govindam ādi-puruṣaṁ tam ahaṁ bhajāmi

"The sun is the king of all planetary systems and has unlimited potency in heat and light. I worship Govinda, the primeval Lord, the Supreme Personality of Godhead, under whose control even the sun, which is considered to be the eye of the Lord, rotates within the fixed orbit of eternal time." Although we see the cosmic manifestation as gigantic and wonderful, it is within the limitations of *kāla*, the time factor. This time factor is also controlled by the Supreme Personality of Godhead, as confirmed in *Bhagavad-gītā* (*mayādhyakṣeṇa prakṛtiḥ sūyate sa-carācaram*). *Prakṛti,* the cosmic manifestation, is under the control of time. Indeed, everything is under the control of time, and time is controlled by the Supreme Personality of Godhead. Therefore the Supreme Lord has no fear of the onslaughts of time. Time is estimated according to the movements of the sun (*savitā*). Every minute, every second, every day, every night, every month and every year of time can be calculated according to the sun's movements. But the sun is not independent, for it is under time's control. *Bhramati saṁbhṛta-kāla-cakraḥ:* the sun moves within the *kāla-cakra,* the orbit of time. The sun is under the control of time, and time is controlled by the Supreme Personality of Godhead. Therefore the Lord has no fear of time.

The Lord is addressed here as *avyakta-bandhu,* or the inaugurator of the movements of the entire cosmic manifestation. Sometimes the cosmic manifestation is compared to a potter's wheel. When a potter's wheel is spinning, who has set it in motion? It is the potter, of course, although sometimes we can see only the motion of the wheel and cannot see the potter himself. Therefore the Lord, who is behind the motion of the cosmos, is called *avyakta-bandhu.* Everything is within the limits of time, but time moves under the direction of the Lord, who is therefore not within time's limit.

TEXT 27

मर्त्यो मृत्युव्यालभीतः पलायन्
लोकान् सर्वान्निर्भयं नाध्यगच्छत् ।
त्वत्पादाब्जं प्राप्य यदृच्छयाद्य
सुस्थः शेते मृत्युरस्मादपैति ॥२७॥

martyo mṛtyu-vyāla-bhītaḥ palāyan
lokān sarvān nirbhayaṁ nādhyagacchat
tvat-pādābjaṁ prāpya yadṛcchayādya
susthaḥ śete mṛtyur asmād apaiti

martyaḥ—the living entities who are sure to die; *mṛtyu-vyāla-bhītaḥ*—afraid of the serpent of death; *palāyan*—running (as soon as a serpent is seen, everyone runs away, fearing immediate death); *lokān*—to the different planets; *sarvān*—all; *nirbhayam*—fearlessness; *na adhyagacchat*—do not obtain; *tvat-pāda-abjam*—of Your lotus feet; *prāpya*—obtaining the shelter; *yadṛcchayā*—by chance, by the mercy of Your Lordship and Your representative, the spiritual master (*guru-kṛpā, kṛṣṇa-kṛpā*); *adya*—presently; *su-sthaḥ*—being undisturbed and mentally composed; *śete*—are sleeping; *mṛtyuḥ*—death; *asmāt*—from those persons; *apaiti*—flees.

TRANSLATION

No one in this material world has become free from the four principles birth, death, old age and disease, even by fleeing to various planets. But now that You have appeared, My Lord, death is fleeing in fear of You, and the living entities, having obtained shelter at Your lotus feet by Your mercy, are sleeping in full mental peace.

PURPORT

There are different categories of living entities, but everyone is afraid of death. The highest aim of the *karmīs* is to be promoted to the higher, heavenly planets, where the duration of life is very long. As stated in *Bhagavad-gītā* (8.17), *sahasra-yuga-paryantam ahar yad brahmaṇo viduḥ:* one day of Brahmā equals 1,000 *yugas*, and each *yuga* consists of 4,300,000 years. Similarly, Brahmā has a night of 1,000 times 4,300,000 years. In this way, we may calculate Brahmā's month and year, but even Brahmā, who lives for millions and millions of years (*dvi-parārdha-kāla*), also must die. According to Vedic *śāstra*, the inhabitants of the higher planetary systems live for 10,000 years, and just as Brahmā's day is calculated to equal 4,300,000,000 of our years, one day in the higher planetary systems equals six of our months. *Karmīs*, therefore, try for promotion to the higher planetary systems, but this cannot free them from death. In this material world, everyone from Brahmā to the insignificant ant must die. Therefore this world is called *martya-loka.* As Kṛṣṇa says in *Bhagavad-gītā* (8.16), *ābrahma-bhuvanāl lokāḥ punar āvartino 'rjuna:* as long as one is within this material world, either on Brahmaloka or on any other *loka* within this universe, one must undergo the *kāla-cakra* of one life after another (*bhūtvā bhūtvā pralīyate*). But if one returns to the Supreme Personality of Godhead (*yad gatvā na nivartante*), one need not reenter the limits of time. Therefore, devotees who have taken shelter of the lotus feet of the Supreme Lord can sleep very peacefully with this assurance from the Supreme Personality of Godhead. As confirmed in *Bhagavad-gītā* (4.9), *tyaktvā dehaṁ punar janma naiti:* after giving up the present body, a devotee who has understood Kṛṣṇa as He is need not return to this material world.

The constitutional position for the living entity is eternity (*na hanyate hanyamāne śarīre, nityaḥ śāśvato 'yam*). Every living entity is eternal. But because of having fallen into this material world, one wanders within the universe, continually changing from one body to another. Caitanya Mahāprabhu says:

brahmāṇḍa bhramite kona bhāgyavān jīva
guru-kṛṣṇa prasāde pāya bhakti-latā-bīja
(Cc. *Madhya* 19.151)

Everyone is wandering up and down within this universe, but one who is sufficiently fortunate comes in contact with Kṛṣṇa consciousness, by the mercy of the spiritual master, and takes to the path of devotional service. Then one is assured of eternal life, with no fear of death. When Kṛṣṇa appears, everyone is freed from fear of death, yet Devakī felt, "We are still afraid of Kaṁsa, although You have appeared as our son." She was more or less bewildered as to why this should be so, and she appealed to the Lord to free her and Vasudeva from this fear.

In this connection, it may be noted that the moon is one of the heavenly planets. From the Vedic literature we understand that one who goes to the moon receives a life with a duration of ten thousand years in which to enjoy the fruits of pious activities. If our so-called scientists are going to the moon, why should they come back here? We must conclude without a doubt that they have never gone to the moon. To go to the moon, one must have the qualification of pious activities. Then one may go there and live. If one has gone to the moon, why should he return to this planet, where life is of a very short duration?

TEXT 28

स त्वं घोरादुग्रसेनात्मजान्न-
त्राहि त्रस्तान् भृत्यवित्रासहासि ।
रूपं चेदं पौरुषं ध्यानधिष्ण्यं
मा प्रत्यक्षं मांसदृशां कृषीष्ठाः ॥२८॥

sa tvaṁ ghorād ugrasenātmajān nas
trāhi trastān bhṛtya-vitrāsa-hāsi
rūpaṁ cedaṁ pauruṣaṁ dhyāna-dhiṣṇyaṁ
mā pratyakṣaṁ māṁsa-dṛśāṁ kṛṣīṣṭhāḥ

saḥ—Your Lordship; *tvam*—You; *ghorāt*—terribly fierce; *ugrasena-ātmajāt*—from the son of Ugrasena; *naḥ*—us; *trāhi*—kindly protect; *trastān*—who are very much afraid (of him); *bhṛtya-vitrāsa-hā asi*—You are naturally the destroyer of the fear of Your servants; *rūpam*—in Your Viṣṇu form; *ca*—also; *idam*—this; *pauruṣam*—as the Supreme Personality of Godhead; *dhyāna-dhiṣṇyam*—who is appreciated by meditation; *mā*—not; *pratyakṣam*—directly visible; *māṁsa-dṛśām*—to those who see with their material eyes; *kṛṣīṣṭhāḥ*—please be.

TRANSLATION

My Lord, because You dispell all the fear of Your devotees, I request You to save us and give us protection from the terrible fear of Kaṁsa. Your form as Viṣṇu, the Supreme Personality of Godhead, is appreciated by yogīs in meditation. Please make this form invisible to those who see with material eyes.

PURPORT

The word *dhyāna-dhiṣṇyam* is significant in this verse because the form of Lord Viṣṇu is meditated upon by *yogīs* (*dhyānāvasthita-tad-gatena manasā paśyanti yaṁ yoginaḥ*). Devakī requested the Lord, who had appeared as Viṣṇu, to conceal that form, for she wanted to see the Lord as an ordinary child, like a child appreciated by persons who have material eyes. Devakī wanted to see whether the Supreme Personality of Godhead had factually appeared or she was dreaming the Viṣṇu form. If Kaṁsa were to come, she thought, upon seeing the Viṣṇu form he would immediately kill the child, but if he saw a human child, he might reconsider. Devakī was afraid of Ugrasena-ātmaja; that is, she was afraid not of Ugrasena and his men, but of the son of Ugrasena. Thus she requested the Lord to dissipate that fear, since He is always ready to give protection (*abhayam*) to His devotees. "My Lord," she prayed, "I request You to save me from the cruel hands of the son of Ugrasena, Kaṁsa. I am praying to Your Lordship to please rescue me from this fearful condition because You are always ready to give protection to Your servitors." The Lord has confirmed this statement in the *Bhagavad-gītā* by assuring Arjuna, "You may declare to the world, My devotee shall never be vanquished."

While thus praying to the Lord for rescue, mother Devakī expressed her motherly affection: "I understand that this transcendental form is generally perceived in meditation by the great sages, but I am still afraid because as soon as Kaṁsa understands that You have appeared, he might harm You. So I request that for the time being You become invisible to our material eyes." In other words, she requested the Lord to assume the form of an ordinary child. "My only cause of fear from my brother Kaṁsa is due to Your appearance. My Lord Madhusūdana, Kaṁsa may know that You are already born. Therefore I request You to conceal this four-armed form of Your Lordship, which holds the four symbols of Viṣṇu—namely the conchshell, the disc, the club and the lotus flower. My dear Lord, at the end of the annihilation of the cosmic manifestation, You put the whole universe within Your abdomen; still, by Your unalloyed mercy, You have appeared in my womb. I am surprised that You imitate the activities of ordinary human beings just to please Your devotee."

Devakī was so afraid of Kaṁsa that she could not believe that Kaṁsa would be unable to kill Lord Viṣṇu, who was personally present. Out of motherly affection, therefore, she requested the Supreme Personality of Godhead to disappear. Although because of the Lord's disappearance Kaṁsa would harass her more and more, thinking that the child born of her was hidden somewhere, she did not want the transcendental child to be harassed and killed. Therefore she requested Lord Viṣṇu to disappear. Later, when harassed, she would think of Him within her mind.

TEXT 29

जन्म ते मय्यसौ पापो मा विद्यान्मधुसूदन ।
समुद्विजे भवद्धेतोः कंसादहमधीरधीः ॥२९॥

janma te mayy asau pāpo
mā vidyān madhusūdana
samudvije bhavad-dhetoḥ
kaṁsād aham adhīra-dhīḥ

janma—the birth; *te*—of Your Lordship; *mayi*—in my (womb); *asau*—that Kaṁsa; *pāpaḥ*—extremely sinful; *mā vidyāt*—may be unable to understand; *madhusūdana*—O Madhusūdana; *samudvije*—I am full of anxiety; *bhavat-hetoḥ*—because of Your appearance; *kaṁsāt*—because of Kaṁsa, with whom I have had such bad experience; *aham*—I; *adhīra-dhīḥ*—have become more and more anxious.

TRANSLATION

O Madhusūdana, because of Your appearance, I am becoming more and more anxious in fear of Kaṁsa. Therefore, please arrange for that sinful Kaṁsa to be unable to understand that You have taken birth from my womb.

PURPORT

Devakī addressed the Supreme Personality of Godhead as Madhusūdana. She was aware that the Lord had killed many demons like Madhu who were hundreds and thousands of times more powerful than Kaṁsa, yet because of affection for the transcendental child, she believed that Kaṁsa could kill Him. Instead of thinking of the unlimited power of the Lord, she thought of the Lord with affection, and therefore she requested the transcendental child to disappear.

TEXT 30

उपसंहर विश्वात्मन्नदो रूपमलौकिकम् ।
शङ्खचक्रगदापद्मश्रिया जुष्टं चतुर्भुजम् ॥३०॥

upasaṁhara viśvātmann
ado rūpam alaukikam
śaṅkha-cakra-gadā-padma-
śriyā juṣṭaṁ catur-bhujam

upasaṁhara—withdraw; *viśvātman*—O all-pervading Supreme Personality of Godhead; *adaḥ*—that; *rūpam*—form; *alaukikam*—which is unnatural in this world; *śaṅkha-cakra-gadā-padma*—of the conchshell, disc, club and lotus; *śriyā*—with these opulences; *juṣṭam*—decorated; *catuḥ-bhujam*—four hands.

TRANSLATION

O my Lord, You are the all-pervading Supreme Personality of Godhead, and Your transcendental four-armed form, holding conchshell, disc, club and lotus, is unnatural for this world. Please

withdraw this form [and become just like a natural human child so that I may try to hide You somewhere].

PURPORT

Devakī was thinking of hiding the Supreme Personality of Godhead and not handing Him over to Kaṁsa as she had all her previous children. Although Vasudeva had promised to hand over every child to Kaṁsa, this time he wanted to break his promise and hide the child somewhere. But because of the Lord's appearance in this surprising four-armed form, He would be impossible to hide.

TEXT 31

विश्वं यदेतत् स्वतनौ निशान्ते
यथावकाशं पुरुषः परो भवान् ।
बिभर्ति सोऽयं मम गर्भगोऽभू-
दहो नृलोकस्य विडम्बनं हि तत् ॥३१॥

viśvaṁ yad etat sva-tanau niśānte
yathāvakāśaṁ puruṣaḥ paro bhavān
bibharti so 'yaṁ mama garbhago 'bhūd
aho nṛ-lokasya viḍambanaṁ hi tat

viśvam—the entire cosmic manifestation; *yat etat*—containing all moving and nonmoving creations; *sva-tanau*—within Your body; *niśā-ante*—at the time of devastation; *yathā-avakāśam*—shelter in Your body without difficulty; *puruṣaḥ*—the Supreme Personality of Godhead; *paraḥ*—transcendental; *bhavān*—Your Lordship; *bibharti*—keep; *saḥ*—that (Supreme Personality of Godhead); *ayam*—this form; *mama*—my; *garbha-gaḥ*—came within my womb; *abhūt*—it so happened; *aho*—alas; *nṛ-lokasya*—within this material world of living entities; *viḍambanam*—it is impossible to think of; *hi*—indeed; *tat*—that (kind of conception).

TRANSLATION

At the time of devastation, the entire cosmos, containing all created moving and nonmoving entities, enters Your transcendental

body and is held there without difficulty. But now this transcendental form has taken birth from my womb. People will not be able to believe this, and I shall become an object of ridicule.

PURPORT

As explained in *Caitanya-caritāmṛta*, loving service to the Personality of Godhead is of two different kinds: *aiśvarya-pūrṇa*, full of opulence, and *aiśvarya-śīthila*, without opulence. Real love of Godhead begins with *aiśvarya-śīthila*, simply on the basis of pure love.

premāñjana-cchurita-bhakti-vilocanena
santaḥ sadaiva hṛdayeṣu vilokayanti
yaṁ śyāmasundaram acintya-guṇa-svarūpaṁ
govindam ādi-puruṣaṁ tam ahaṁ bhajāmi
(*Brahma-saṁhitā* 5.38)

Pure devotees, whose eyes are anointed with the ointment of *premā*, love, want to see the Supreme Personality of Godhead as Śyāmasundara, Muralīdhara, with a flute swaying in His two hands. This is the form available to the inhabitants of Vṛndāvana, who are all in love with the Supreme Personality of Godhead as Śyāmasundara, not as Lord Viṣṇu, Nārāyaṇa, who is worshiped in Vaikuṇṭha, where the devotees admire His opulence. Although Devakī is not on the Vṛndāvana platform, she is near the Vṛndāvana platform. On the Vṛndāvana platform the mother of Kṛṣṇa is mother Yaśodā, and on the Mathurā and Dvārakā platform the mother of Kṛṣṇa is Devakī. In Mathurā and Dvārakā the love for the Lord is mixed with appreciation of His opulence, but in Vṛndāvana the opulence of the Supreme Personality of Godhead is not exhibited.

There are five stages of loving service to the Supreme Personality of Godhead—*śānta, dāsya, sakhya, vātsalya* and *mādhurya.* Devakī is on the platform of *vātsalya.* She wanted to deal with her eternal son, Kṛṣṇa, in that stage of love, and therefore she wanted the Supreme Personality of Godhead to withdraw His opulent form of Viṣṇu. Śrīla Viśvanātha Cakravartī Ṭhākura illuminates this fact very clearly in his explanation of this verse.

Bhakti, bhagavān and *bhakta* do not belong to the material world. This is confirmed in *Bhagavad-gītā* (14.26):

māṁ ca yo 'vyabhicāreṇa
bhakti-yogena sevate
sa guṇān samatītyaitān
brahma-bhūyāya kalpate

"One who engages in the spiritual activities of unalloyed devotional service immediately transcends the modes of material nature and is elevated to the spiritual platform." From the very beginning of one's transactions in *bhakti*, one is situated on the transcendental platform. Vasudeva and Devakī, therefore, being situated in a completely pure devotional state, are beyond this material world and are not subject to material fear. In the transcendental world, however, because of pure devotion, there is a similar conception of fear, which is due to intense love.

As stated in *Bhagavad-gītā* (*bhaktyā mām abhijānāti yāvān yaś cāsmi tattvataḥ*) and as confirmed in *Śrīmad-Bhāgavatam* (*bhaktyāham ekayā grāhyaḥ*), without *bhakti* one cannot understand the spiritual situation of the Lord. *Bhakti* may be considered in three stages, called *guṇī-bhūta, pradhānī-bhūta* and *kevala*, and according to these stages there are three divisions, which are called *jñāna, jñānamayī* and *rati*, or *premā*—that is, simple knowledge, love mixed with knowledge, and pure love. By simple knowledge, one can perceive transcendental bliss without variety. This perception is called *māna-bhūti*. When one comes to the stage of *jñānamayī*, one realizes the transcendental opulences of the Personality of Godhead. But when one reaches pure love, one realizes the transcendental form of the Lord as Lord Kṛṣṇa or Lord Rāma. This is what is wanted. Especially in the *mādhurya-rasa*, one becomes attached to the Personality of Godhead (*śrī-vigraha-niṣṭha-rūpādi*). Then loving transactions between the Lord and the devotee begin.

The special significance of Kṛṣṇa's bearing a flute in His hands in Vrajabhūmi, Vṛndāvana, is described as *mādhurī . . . virājate*. The form of the Lord with a flute in His hands is most attractive, and the one who is most sublimely attracted is Śrīmatī Rādhārāṇī, Rādhikā. She enjoys supremely blissful association with Kṛṣṇa. Sometimes people cannot understand why Rādhikā's name is not mentioned in *Śrīmad-Bhāgavatam*. Actually, however, Rādhikā can be understood from the word *ārādhana*, which indicates that She enjoys the highest loving affairs with Kṛṣṇa.

Not wanting to be ridiculed for having given birth to Viṣṇu, Devakī wanted Kṛṣṇa, with two hands, and therefore she requested the Lord to change His form.

TEXT 32

श्रीभगवानुवाच
त्वमेव पूर्वसर्गेऽभूः पृश्निः स्वायम्भुवे सति ।
तदायं सुतपा नाम प्रजापतिरकल्मषः ॥३२॥

śrī-bhagavān uvāca
tvam eva pūrva-sarge 'bhūḥ
pṛśniḥ svāyambhuve sati
tadāyaṁ sutapā nāma
prajāpatir akalmaṣaḥ

śrī-bhagavān uvāca—the Supreme Personality of Godhead said to Devakī; *tvam*—you; *eva*—indeed; *pūrva-sarge*—in a previous millennium; *abhūḥ*—became; *pṛśniḥ*—by the name Pṛśni; *svāyambhuve*—the millennium of Svāyambhuva Manu; *sati*—O supremely chaste; *tadā*—at that time; *ayam*—Vasudeva; *sutapā*—Sutapā; *nāma*—by the name; *prajāpatiḥ*—a Prajāpati; *akalmaṣaḥ*—a spotlessly pious person.

TRANSLATION

The Supreme Personality of Godhead replied: My dear mother, best of the chaste, in your previous birth, in the Svāyambhuva millennium, you were known as Pṛśni, and Vasudeva, who was the most pious Prajāpati, was named Sutapā.

PURPORT

The Supreme Personality of Godhead made it clear that Devakī had not become His mother only now; rather, she had been His mother previously also. Kṛṣṇa is eternal, and His selection of a father and mother from among His devotees takes place eternally. Previously also, Devakī had been the Lord's mother and Vasudeva the Lord's father, and they were named Pṛśni and Sutapā. When the Supreme Personality of Godhead appears, He accepts His eternal father and mother, and they accept

Kṛṣṇa as their son. This pastime takes place eternally and is therefore called *nitya-līlā.* Thus there was no cause for surprise or ridicule. As confirmed by the Lord Himself in *Bhagavad-gītā* (4.9):

janma karma ca me divyam
evaṁ yo vetti tattvataḥ
tyaktvā dehaṁ punar janma
naiti mām eti so 'rjuna

"One who knows the transcendental nature of My appearance and activities does not, upon leaving the body, take his birth again in this material world, but attains My eternal abode, O Arjuna." One should try to understand the appearance and disappearance of the Supreme Personality of Godhead from Vedic authorities, not from imagination. One who follows his imaginations about the Supreme Personality of Godhead is condemned.

avajānanti māṁ mūḍhā
mānuṣīṁ tanum āśritam
paraṁ bhāvam ajānanto
mama bhūta-maheśvaram
(Bg. 9.11)

The Lord appears as the son of His devotee by His *paraṁ bhāvam.* The word *bhāva* refers to the stage of pure love, which has nothing to do with material transactions.

TEXT 33

युवां वै ब्रह्मणादिष्टौ प्रजासर्गे यदा ततः ।
सन्नियम्येन्द्रियग्रामं तेपाथे परमं तपः ॥३३॥

yuvāṁ vai brahmaṇādiṣṭau
prajā-sarge yadā tataḥ
sanniyamyendriya-grāmaṁ
tepāthe paramaṁ tapaḥ

yuvām—both of you (Pṛśni and Sutapā); *vai*—indeed; *brahmaṇā ādiṣṭau*—ordered by Lord Brahmā (who is known as Pitāmaha, the father of the Prajāpatis); *prajā-sarge*—in the creation of progeny; *yadā*—when; *tataḥ*—thereafter; *sanniyamya*—keeping under full control; *indriya-grāmam*—the senses; *tepāthe*—underwent; *paramam*—very great; *tapaḥ*—austerity.

TRANSLATION

When both of you were ordered by Lord Brahmā to create progeny, you first underwent severe austerities by controlling your senses.

PURPORT

Here is an instruction about how to use one's senses to create progeny. According to Vedic principles, before creating progeny one must fully control the senses. This control takes place through the *garbhādhāna-saṁskāra.* In India there is great agitation for birth control in various mechanical ways, but birth cannot be mechanically controlled. As stated in *Bhagavad-gītā* (13.9), *janma-mṛtyu-jarā-vyādhi-duḥkha-doṣānu-darśanam:* birth, death, old age and disease are certainly the primary distresses of the material world. People are trying to control birth, but they are not able to control death; and if one cannot control death, one cannot control birth either. In other words, artificially controlling birth is not any more feasible than artificially controlling death.

According to Vedic civilization, procreation should not be contrary to religious principles, and then the birthrate will be controlled. As stated in *Bhagavad-gītā* (7.11), *dharmāviruddho bhūteṣu kāmo 'smi:* sex not contrary to religious principles is a representation of the Supreme Lord. People should be educated in how to give birth to good children through *saṁskāras*, beginning with the *garbhādhāna-saṁskāra;* birth should not be controlled by artificial means, for this will lead to a civilization of animals. If one follows religious principles, he automatically practices birth control because if one is spiritually educated he knows that the aftereffects of sex are various types of misery (*bahu-duḥkha-bhāja*). One who is spiritually advanced does not indulge in uncontrolled sex. Therefore, instead of being forced to refrain from sex or refrain from giving birth to many children, people should be spiritually educated, and then birth control will automatically follow.

If one is determined to make spiritual advancement, he will not beget a child unless able to make that child a devotee. As stated in *Śrīmad-Bhāgavatam* (5.5.18), *pitā na sa syāt:* one should not become a father unless one is able to protect his child from *mṛtyu,* the path of birth and death. But where is there education about this? A responsible father never begets children like cats and dogs. Instead of being encouraged to adopt artificial means of birth control, people should be educated in Kṛṣṇa consciousness because only then will they understand their responsibility to their children. If one can beget children who will be devotees and be taught to turn aside from the path of birth and death (*mṛtyu-saṁsāra-vartmani*), there is no need of birth control. Rather, one should be encouraged to beget children. Artificial means of birth control have no value. Whether one begets children or does not, a population of men who are like cats and dogs will never make human society happy. It is therefore necessary for people to be educated spiritually so that instead of begetting children like cats and dogs, they will undergo austerities to produce devotees. This will make their lives successful.

TEXTS 34–35

वर्षवातातपहिमघर्मकालगुणाननु ।
सहमानौ श्वासरोधविनिर्धूतमनोमलौ ॥३४॥
शीर्णपर्णानिलाहारावुपशान्तेन चेतसा ।
मत्तः कामानभीप्सन्तौ मदाराधनमीहतुः ॥३५॥

varṣa-vātātapa-hima-
gharma-kāla-guṇān anu
sahamānau śvāsa-rodha-
vinirdhūta-mano-malau

śīrṇa-parṇānilāhārāv
upaśāntena cetasā
mattaḥ kāmān abhīpsantau
mad-ārādhanam īhatuḥ

varṣa—the rain; *vāta*—strong wind; *ātapa*—strong sunshine; *hima*—severe cold; *gharma*—heat; *kāla-guṇān anu*—according to seasonal changes; *sahamānau*—by enduring; *śvāsa-rodha*—by practicing *yoga,* controlling the breath; *vinirdhūta*—the dirty things accumulated in the mind were completely washed away; *manaḥ-malau*—the mind became clean, free from material contamination; *śīrṇa*—rejected, dry; *parṇa*—leaves from the trees; *anila*—and air; *āhārau*—eating; *upaśāntena*—peaceful; *cetasā*—with a fully controlled mind; *mattaḥ*—from Me; *kāmān abhīpsantau*—desiring to beg some benediction; *mat*—My; *ārādhanam*—worship; *īhatuḥ*—you both executed.

TRANSLATION

My dear father and mother, you endured rain, wind, strong sun, scorching heat and severe cold, suffering all sorts of inconvenience according to different seasons. By practicing prāṇāyāma to control the air within the body through yoga, and by eating only air and dry leaves fallen from the trees, you cleansed from your minds all dirty things. In this way, desiring a benediction from Me, you worshiped Me with peaceful minds.

PURPORT

Vasudeva and Devakī did not obtain the Supreme Personality of Godhead as their son very easily, nor does the Supreme Godhead accept merely anyone as His father and mother. Here we can see how Vasudeva and Devakī obtained Kṛṣṇa as their eternal son. In our own lives, we are meant to follow the principles indicated herewith for getting good children. Of course, it is not possible for everyone to get Kṛṣṇa as his son, but at least one can get very good sons and daughters for the benefit of human society. In *Bhagavad-gītā* it is said that if human beings do not follow the spiritual way of life, there will be an increase of *varṇa-saṅkara* population, population begotten like cats and dogs, and the entire world will become like hell. Not practicing Kṛṣṇa consciousness but simply encouraging artificial means to check the population will be futile; the population will increase, and it will consist of *varṇa-saṅkara,* unwanted progeny. It is better to teach people how to beget children not like hogs and dogs, but in controlled life.

Human life is meant not for becoming a hog or dog, but for *tapo divyam,* transcendental austerity. Everyone should be taught to undergo austerity, *tapasya.* Although it may not be possible to undergo *tapasya* like that of Pṛśni and Sutapā, the *śāstra* has given an opportunity for a method of *tapasya* very easy to perform—the *saṅkīrtana* movement. One cannot expect to undergo *tapasya* to get Kṛṣṇa as one's child, yet simply by chanting the Hare Kṛṣṇa *mahā-mantra* (*kīrtanād eva kṛṣṇasya*), one can become so pure that one becomes free from all the contamination of this material world (*mukta-saṅgaḥ*) and goes back home, back to Godhead (*paraṁ vrajet*). The Kṛṣṇa consciousness movement, therefore, is teaching people not to adopt artificial means of happiness, but to take the real path of happiness as prescribed in the *śāstra*—the chanting of the Hare Kṛṣṇa *mantra*—and become perfect in every aspect of material existence.

TEXT 36

एवं वां तप्यतोस्तीव्रं तपः परमदुष्करम् ।
दिव्यवर्षसहस्राणि द्वादशेयुर्मदात्मनोः ॥३६॥

evaṁ vāṁ tapyatos tīvraṁ
tapaḥ parama-duṣkaram
divya-varṣa-sahasrāṇi
dvādaśeyur mad-ātmanoḥ

evam—in this way; *vām*—for both of you; *tapyatoḥ*—executing austerities; *tīvram*—very severe; *tapaḥ*—austerity; *parama-duṣkaram*—extremely difficult to execute; *divya-varṣa*—celestial years, or years counted according to the higher planetary system; *sahasrāṇi*—thousand; *dvādaśa*—twelve; *īyuḥ*—passed; *mat-ātmanoḥ*—simply engaged in consciousness of Me.

TRANSLATION

Thus you spent twelve thousand celestial years performing difficult activities of tapasya in consciousness of Me [Kṛṣṇa consciousness].

TEXTS 37–38

तदा वां परितुष्टोऽहममुना वपुषानघे ।
तपसा श्रद्धया नित्यं भक्त्या च हृदि भावितः ॥३७॥

प्रादुरासं वरदराड् युवयोः कामदित्सया ।
व्रियतां वर इत्युक्ते मादृशो वां वृतः सुतः ॥३८॥

tadā vāṁ paritușṭo 'ham
amunā vapușānaghe
tapasā śraddhayā nityaṁ
bhaktyā ca hṛdi bhāvitaḥ

prādurāsaṁ varada-rāḍ
yuvayoḥ kāma-ditsayā
vriyatāṁ vara ity ukte
mādṛśo vāṁ vṛtaḥ sutaḥ

tadā—then (after the expiry of twelve thousand celestial years); *vām*—with both of you; *parituṣṭaḥ aham*—I was very much satisfied; *amunā*—by this; *vapuṣā*—in this form as Kṛṣṇa; *anaghe*—O My dear sinless mother; *tapasā*—by austerity; *śraddhayā*—by faith; *nityam*—constantly (engaged); *bhaktyā*—by devotional service; *ca*—as well as; *hṛdi*—within the core of the heart; *bhāvitaḥ*—fixed (in determination); *prādurāsam*—appeared before you (in the same way); *vara-da-rāṭ*—the best of all who can bestow benedictions; *yuvayoḥ*—of both of you; *kāma-ditsayā*—wishing to fulfill the desire; *vriyatām*—asked you to open your minds; *varaḥ*—for a benediction; *iti ukte*—when you were requested in this way; *mādṛśaḥ*—exactly like Me; *vām*—of both of you; *vṛtaḥ*—was asked; *sutaḥ*—as Your son (you wanted a son exactly like Me).

TRANSLATION

O sinless mother Devakī, after the expiry of twelve thousand celestial years, in which you constantly contemplated Me within the core of your heart with great faith, devotion and austerity, I was very much satisfied with you. Since I am the best of all bestowers of benediction, I appeared in this same form as Kṛṣṇa to ask you to take from Me the benediction you desired. You then expressed your desire to have a son exactly like Me.

PURPORT

Twelve thousand years on the celestial planets is not a very long time for those who live in the upper planetary system, although it may be very long for those who live on this planet. Sutapā was the son of Brahmā, and as we have already understood from *Bhagavad-gītā* (8.17), one day of Brahmā equals many millions of years according to our calculation (*sahasra-yuga-paryantam ahar yad brahmaṇo viduḥ*). We should be careful to understand that to get Kṛṣṇa as one's son, one must undergo such great austerities. If we want to get the Supreme Personality of Godhead to become one of us in this material world, this requires great penance, but if we want to go back to Kṛṣṇa (*tyaktvā dehaṁ punar janma naiti mām eti so 'rjuna*), we need only understand Him and love Him. Through love only, we can very easily go back home, back to Godhead. Śrī Caitanya Mahāprabhu therefore declared, *premā pum-artho mahān:* love of Godhead is the highest achievement for anyone.

As we have explained, in worship of the Lord there are three stages—*jñāna, jñānamayī* and *rati,* or love. Sutapā and his wife, Pṛśni, inaugurated their devotional activities on the basis of full knowledge. Gradually they developed love for the Supreme Personality of Godhead, and when this love was mature, the Lord appeared as Viṣṇu, although Devakī then requested Him to assume the form of Kṛṣṇa. To love the Supreme Personality of Godhead more, we want a form of the Lord like Kṛṣṇa or Rāma. We can engage in loving transactions with Kṛṣṇa especially.

In this age, we are all fallen, but the Supreme Personality of Godhead has appeared as Caitanya Mahāprabhu to bestow upon us love of Godhead directly. This was appreciated by the associates of Śrī Caitanya Mahāprabhu. Rūpa Gosvāmī said:

namo mahā-vadānyāya
kṛṣṇa-prema-pradāya te
kṛṣṇāya kṛṣṇa-caitanya-
nāmne gaura-tviṣe namaḥ

In this verse, Śrī Caitanya Mahāprabhu is described as *mahā-vadānya,* the most munificent of charitable persons, because He gives Kṛṣṇa so easily that one can attain Kṛṣṇa simply by chanting the Hare Kṛṣṇa *mahā-mantra.* We should therefore take advantage of the benediction given by Śrī Caitanya Mahāprabhu, and when by chanting the Hare Kṛṣṇa *mantra* we are cleansed of all dirty things (*ceto-darpaṇa-mārjanam*), we shall be able to understand very easily that Kṛṣṇa is the only object of love (*kīrtanād eva kṛṣṇasya mukta-saṅgaḥ paraṁ vrajet*).

Therefore, one need not undergo severe penances for many thousands of years; one need only learn how to love Kṛṣṇa and be always engaged in His service (*sevonmukhe hi jihvādau svayam eva sphuraty adaḥ*). Then one can very easily go back home, back to Godhead. Instead of bringing the Lord here for some material purpose, to have a son or whatever else, if we go back home, back to Godhead, our real relationship with the Lord is revealed, and we eternally engage in our eternal relationship. By chanting the Hare Kṛṣṇa *mantra*, we gradually develop our eternal relationship with the Supreme Person and thus attain the perfection called *svarūpa-siddhi*. We should take advantage of this benediction and go back home, back to Godhead. Śrīla Narottama dāsa Ṭhākura has therefore sung, *patita-pāvana-hetu tava avatāra:* Caitanya Mahāprabhu appeared as an incarnation to deliver all fallen souls like us and directly bestow upon us love of Godhead. We must take advantage of this great benediction of the great Personality of Godhead.

TEXT 39

अजुष्टग्राम्यविषयावनपत्यौ च दम्पती ।
न वव्राथेऽपवर्गं मे मोहितौ देवमायया ॥३९॥

ajuṣṭa-grāmya-viṣayāv
anapatyau ca dam-patī
na vavrāthe 'pavargaṁ me
mohitau deva-māyayā

ajuṣṭa-grāmya-viṣayau—for sex life and to beget a child like Me; *anapatyau*—because of possessing no son; *ca*—also; *dam-patī*—both husband and wife; *na*—never; *vavrāthe*—asked for (any other benediction); *apavargam*—liberation from this world; *me*—from Me; *mohitau*—being so much attracted; *deva-māyayā*—by transcendental love for Me (desiring Me as your beloved son).

TRANSLATION

Being husband and wife but always sonless, you were attracted by sexual desires, for by the influence of devamāyā, transcendental

love, you wanted to have Me as your son. Therefore you never desired to be liberated from this material world.

PURPORT

Vasudeva and Devakī had been *dam-patī*, husband and wife, since the time of Sutapā and Pṛśni, and they wanted to remain husband and wife in order to have the Supreme Personality of Godhead as their son. This attachment came about by the influence of *devamāyā*. Loving Kṛṣṇa as one's son is a Vedic principle. Vasudeva and Devakī never desired anything but to have the Lord as their son, yet for this purpose they apparently wanted to live like ordinary *gṛhasthas* for sexual indulgence. Although this was a transaction of spiritual potency, their desire appears like attachment for sex in conjugal life. If one wants to return home, back to Godhead, one must give up such desires. This is possible only when one develops intense love for the Supreme Personality of Godhead. Śrī Caitanya Mahāprabhu has said:

niṣkiñcanasya bhagavad-bhajanonmukhasya
pāraṁ paraṁ jigamiṣor bhava-sāgarasya
(Cc. *Madhya* 11.8)

If one wants to go back home, back to Godhead, one must be *niṣkiñcana*, free from all material desires. Therefore, instead of desiring to have the Lord come here and become one's son, one should desire to become free from all material desires (*anyābhilāṣitā-śūnyam*) and go back home, back to Godhead. Śrī Caitanya Mahāprabhu teaches us in His *Śikṣāṣṭaka:*

na dhanaṁ na janaṁ na sundarīṁ
kavitāṁ vā jagad-īśa kāmaye
mama janmani janmanīśvare
bhavatād bhaktir ahaitukī tvayi

"O almighty Lord, I have no desire to accumulate wealth, nor do I desire beautiful women, nor do I want any number of followers. I only want Your causeless devotional service, birth after birth." One should not ask the Lord to fulfill any materially tainted desires.

TEXT 40

गते मयि युवां लब्ध्वा वरं मत्सदृशं सुतम् ।
ग्राम्यान् भोगानभुञ्जाथां युवां प्राप्तमनोरथौ ॥४०॥

gate mayi yuvāṁ labdhvā
varaṁ mat-sadṛśaṁ sutam
grāmyān bhogān abhuñjāthāṁ
yuvāṁ prāpta-manorathau

gate mayi—after My departure; *yuvām*—both of you (husband and wife); *labdhvā*—after receiving; *varam*—the benediction of (having a son); *mat-sadṛśam*—exactly like Me; *sutam*—a son; *grāmyān bhogān*—engagement in sex; *abhuñjāthām*—enjoyed; *yuvām*—both of you; *prāpta*—having been achieved; *manorathau*—the desired result of your aspirations.

TRANSLATION

After you received that benediction and I disappeared, you engaged yourselves in sex to have a son like Me, and I fulfilled your desire.

PURPORT

According to the Sanskrit dictionary *Amara-kośa*, sex life is also called *grāmya-dharma*, material desire, but in spiritual life this *grāmya-dharma*, the material desire for sex, is not very much appreciated. If one has a tinge of attachment for the material enjoyments of eating, sleeping, mating and defending, one is not *niṣkiñcana*. But one really should be *niṣkiñcana*. Therefore, one should be free from the desire to beget a child like Kṛṣṇa by sexual enjoyment. This is indirectly hinted at in this verse.

TEXT 41

अदृष्ट्वान्यतमं लोके शीलौदार्यगुणैः समम् ।
अहं सुतो वामभवं पृश्निगर्भ इति श्रुतः ॥४१॥

adṛṣṭvānyatamaṁ loke
śīlaudārya-guṇaiḥ samam
ahaṁ suto vām abhavaṁ
pṛśnigarbha iti śrutaḥ

adṛṣṭvā—not finding; *anyatamam*—anyone else; *loke*—in this world; *śīla-audārya-guṇaiḥ*—with the transcendental qualities of good character and magnanimity; *samam*—equal to you; *aham*—I; *sutaḥ*—the son; *vām*—of both of you; *abhavam*—became; *pṛśni-garbhaḥ*—celebrated as born of Pṛśni; *iti*—thus; *śrutaḥ*—I am known.

TRANSLATION

Since I found no one else as highly elevated as you in simplicity and other qualities of good character, I appeared in this world as Pṛśnigarbha, or one who is celebrated as having taken birth from Pṛśni.

PURPORT

In the Tretā-yuga the Lord appeared as Pṛśnigarbha. Śrīla Viśvanātha Cakravartī Ṭhākura says, *pṛśnigarbha iti so 'yaṁ tretā-yugāvatāro lakṣyate.*

TEXT 42

तयोर्वां पुनरेवाहमदित्यामास कश्यपात् ।
उपेन्द्र इति विख्यातो वामनत्वाच्च वामनः ॥४२॥

tayor vāṁ punar evāham
adityām āsa kaśyapāt
upendra iti vikhyāto
vāmanatvāc ca vāmanaḥ

tayoḥ—of you two, husband and wife; *vām*—in both of you; *punaḥ eva*—even again; *aham*—I Myself; *adityām*—in the womb of Aditi; *āsa*—appeared; *kaśyapāt*—by the semen of Kaśyapa Muni; *upendraḥ*—by the name Upendra; *iti*—thus; *vikhyātaḥ*—celebrated; *vāmanatvāt ca*—and because of being a dwarf; *vāmanaḥ*—I was known as Vāmana.

TRANSLATION

In the next millennium, I again appeared from the two of you, who appeared as My mother, Aditi, and My father, Kaśyapa. I was known as Upendra, and because of being a dwarf, I was also known as Vāmana.

TEXT 43

तृतीयेऽस्मिन् भवेऽहं वै तेनैव वपुषाथ वाम् ।
जातो भूयस्तयोरेव सत्यं मे व्याहृतं सति ॥४३॥

tṛtīye 'smin bhave 'haṁ vai
tenaiva vapuṣātha vām
jāto bhūyas tayor eva
satyaṁ me vyāhṛtaṁ sati

tṛtīye—for the third time; *asmin bhave*—in this appearance (as Kṛṣṇa); *aham*—I Myself; *vai*—indeed; *tena*—with the same personality; *eva*—in this way; *vapuṣā*—by the form; *atha*—as; *vām*—of both of you; *jātaḥ*—born; *bhūyaḥ*—again; *tayoḥ*—of both of you; *eva*—indeed; *satyam*—take as truth; *me*—My; *vyāhṛtam*—words; *sati*—O supremely chaste.

TRANSLATION

O supremely chaste mother, I, the same personality, have now appeared of you both as your son for the third time. Take My words as the truth.

PURPORT

The Supreme Personality of Godhead chooses a mother and father from whom to take birth again and again. The Lord took birth originally from Sutapā and Pṛśni, then from Kaśyapa and Aditi, and again from the same father and mother, Vasudeva and Devakī. "In other appearances also," the Lord said, "I took the form of an ordinary child just to become your son so that we could reciprocate eternal love." Jīva Gosvāmī has explained this verse in his *Kṛṣṇa-sandarbha*, Ninety-sixth Chapter, where he notes that in text 37 the Lord says, *amunā vapuṣa*, meaning "by this same form." In other words, the Lord told Devakī, "This time I have appeared in My original form as Śrī Kṛṣṇa." Śrīla Jīva Gosvāmī says that the other forms were partial expansions of the Lord's original form, but because of the intense love developed by Pṛśni and Sutapā, the Lord appeared from Devakī and Vasudeva in His full opulence as Śrī Kṛṣṇa. In this verse the Lord confirms, "I am the same Supreme Personality of Godhead, but I appear in full opulence as Śrī Kṛṣṇa." This is the purport of the words *tenaiva vapuṣā.* When the Lord mentioned the birth of Pṛśnigarbha, He did not say *tenaiva vapuṣā,* but He assured Devakī that in the third birth the Supreme Personality of Godhead Kṛṣṇa had appeared, not His partial expansion. Pṛśnigarbha and Vāmana were partial expansions of Kṛṣṇa, but in this third birth Kṛṣṇa Himself appeared. This is the explanation given in *Śrī Kṛṣṇa-sandarbha* by Śrīla Jīva Gosvāmī.

TEXT 44

एतद् वां दर्शितं रूपं प्राग्जन्मस्मरणाय मे ।
नान्यथा मद्भवं ज्ञानं मर्त्यलिङ्गेन जायते ॥४४॥

etad vāṁ darśitaṁ rūpaṁ
prāg-janma-smaraṇāya me
nānyathā mad-bhavaṁ jñānaṁ
martya-liṅgena jāyate

etat—this form of Viṣṇu; *vām*—unto both of you; *darśitam*—has been shown; *rūpam*—My form as the Supreme Personality of Godhead with four hands; *prāk-janma*—of My previous appearances; *smaraṇāya*—just to remind you; *me*—My; *na*—not; *anyathā*—otherwise; *mat-bhavam*—Viṣṇu's appearance; *jñānam*—this transcendental knowledge; *martya-liṅgena*—by taking birth like a human child; *jāyate*—does arise.

TRANSLATION

I have shown you this form of Viṣṇu just to remind you of My previous births. Otherwise, if I appeared like an ordinary human child, you would not believe that the Supreme Personality of Godhead, Viṣṇu, has indeed appeared.

PURPORT

Devakī did not need to be reminded that the Supreme Personality of Godhead, Lord Viṣṇu, had appeared as her son; she already accepted this. Nonetheless, she was anxious, thinking that if her neighbors heard that Viṣṇu had appeared as her son, none of them would believe it. Therefore she wanted Lord Viṣṇu to transform Himself into a human child. On the other hand, the Supreme Lord was also anxious, thinking that if He appeared as an ordinary child, she would not believe that Lord Viṣṇu had appeared. Such are the dealings between devotees and the Lord. The Lord deals with His devotees exactly like a human being, but this does not mean that the Lord is one of the human beings, for this is the conclusion of nondevotees (*avajānanti māṁ mūḍhā mānuṣīṁ tanum āśritam*). Devotees know the Supreme Personality of Godhead under any circumstances. This is the difference between a devotee and a nondevotee. The Lord says, *man-manā bhava mad-bhakto mad-yājī māṁ namaskuru:* "Engage your mind always in thinking of Me, become My devotee, offer obeisances and worship Me." A nondevotee cannot believe that simply by thinking of one person, one can achieve liberation from this material world and go back home, back to Godhead. But this is a fact. The Lord comes as a human being, and if one becomes attached to the Lord on the platform of loving service, one's promotion to the transcendental world is assured.

TEXT 45

युवां मां पुत्रभावेन ब्रह्मभावेन चासकृत् ।
चिन्तयन्तौ कृतस्नेहौ यास्येथे मद्गतिं पराम् ॥४५॥

yuvāṁ māṁ putra-bhāvena
brahma-bhāvena cāsakṛt
cintayantau kṛta-snehau
yāsyethe mad-gatiṁ parām

yuvām—both of you (husband and wife); *mām*—unto Me; *putra-bhāvena*—as your son; *brahma-bhāvena*—knowing that I am the Supreme Personality of Godhead; *ca*—and; *asakṛt*—constantly; *cintayantau*—thinking like that; *kṛta-snehau*—dealing with love and affection; *yāsyethe*—shall both obtain; *mat-gatim*—My supreme abode; *parām*—which is transcendental, beyond this material world.

TRANSLATION

Both of you, husband and wife, constantly think of Me as your son, but always know that I am the Supreme Personality of Godhead. By thus thinking of Me constantly with love and affection, you will achieve the highest perfection: returning home, back to Godhead.

PURPORT

This instruction by the Supreme Personality of Godhead to His father and mother, who are eternally connected with Him, is especially intended for persons eager to return home, back to Godhead. One should never think of the Supreme Personality of Godhead as an ordinary human being, as nondevotees do. Kṛṣṇa, the Supreme Personality of Godhead, personally appeared and left His instructions for the benefit of all human society, but fools and rascals unfortunately think of Him as an ordinary human being and twist the instructions of *Bhagavad-gītā* for the satisfaction of their senses. Practically everyone commenting on *Bhagavad-gītā* interprets it for sense gratification. It has become especially fashionable for modern scholars and politicians to interpret *Bhagavad-gītā* as if it were something fictitious, and by their wrong interpretations they are spoiling their own careers and the careers of others. The Kṛṣṇa consciousness movement, however, is fighting against this principle of regarding Kṛṣṇa as a fictitious person and of accepting that there was no Battle of Kurukṣetra, that everything is symbolic, and that nothing in *Bhagavad-gītā* is true. In any case, if one truly wants to be successful, one can do so by reading the text of *Bhagavad-gītā* as it is. Śrī Caitanya Mahāprabhu especially stressed the instructions of *Bhagavad-gītā: yāre dekha, tāre kaha 'kṛṣṇa'-upadeśa.* If one wants to achieve the highest success in life, one must accept *Bhagavad-gītā* as spoken by the Supreme Lord. By accepting *Bhagavad-gītā* in this way, all of human society can become perfect and happy.

It is to be noted that because Vasudeva and Devakī would be separated from Kṛṣṇa when He was carried to Gokula, the residence of Nanda

Mahārāja, the Lord personally instructed them that they should always think of Him as their son and as the Supreme Personality of Godhead. That would keep them in touch with Him. After eleven years, the Lord would return to Mathurā to be their son, and therefore there was no question of separation.

TEXT 46

श्रीशुक उवाच
इत्युक्त्वासीद्धरिस्तूष्णीं भगवानात्ममायया ।
पित्रोः सम्पश्यतोः सद्यो बभूव प्राकृतः शिशुः ॥४६॥

śrī-śuka uvāca
ity uktvāsīd dharis tūṣṇīṁ
bhagavān ātma-māyayā
pitroḥ sampaśyatoḥ sadyo
babhūva prākṛtaḥ śiśuḥ

śrī-śukaḥ uvāca—Śrī Śukadeva Gosvāmī said; *iti uktvā*—after instructing in this way; *āsīt*—remained; *hariḥ*—the Supreme Personality of Godhead; *tūṣṇīm*—silent; *bhagavān*—Lord Viṣṇu, the Supreme Personality of Godhead; *ātma-māyayā*—by acting in His own spiritual energy; *pitroḥ sampaśyatoḥ*—while His father and mother were factually seeing Him; *sadyaḥ*—immediately; *babhūva*—He became; *prākṛtaḥ*—like an ordinary human being; *śiśuḥ*—a child.

TRANSLATION

Śukadeva Gosvāmī said: After thus instructing His father and mother, the Supreme Personality of Godhead, Kṛṣṇa, remained silent. In their presence, by His internal energy, He then transformed Himself into a small human child. [In other words, He transformed Himself into His original form: kṛṣṇas tu bhagavān svayam.]

PURPORT

As stated in *Bhagavad-gītā* (4.6), *sambhavāmy ātma-māyayā:* whatever is done by the Supreme Personality of Godhead is done by His spiritual energy; nothing is forced upon Him by the material energy. This is the difference between the Lord and an ordinary living being. The *Vedas* say:

parāsya śaktir vividhaiva śrūyate
svābhāvikī jñāna-bala-kriyā ca
(*Śvetāśvatara Upaniṣad* 6.8)

It is natural for the Lord to be untinged by material qualities, and because everything is perfectly present in His spiritual energy, as soon as He desires something, it is immediately done. The Lord is not a *prākṛta-śiśu*, a child of this world, but by His personal energy He appeared like one. Ordinary people may have difficulty accepting the supreme controller, God, as a human being because they forget that He can do everything by spiritual energy (*ātma-māyayā*). Nonbelievers say, "How can the supreme controller descend as an ordinary being?" This sort of thinking is materialistic. Śrīla Jīva Gosvāmī says that unless we accept the energy of the Supreme Personality of Godhead as inconceivable, beyond the conception of our words and mind, we cannot understand the Supreme Lord. Those who doubt that the Supreme Personality of Godhead can come as a human being and turn Himself into a human child are fools who think that Kṛṣṇa's body is material, that He is born and that He therefore also dies.

In *Śrīmad-Bhāgavatam*, Third Canto, Fourth Chapter, verses 28 and 29, there is a description of Kṛṣṇa's leaving His body. Mahārāja Parīkṣit inquired from Śukadeva Gosvāmī, "When all the members of the Yadu dynasty met their end, Kṛṣṇa also put an end to Himself, and the only member of the family who remained alive was Uddhava. How was this possible?" Śukadeva Gosvāmī answered that Kṛṣṇa, by His own energy, destroyed the entire family and then thought of making His own body disappear. In this connection, Śukadeva Gosvāmī described how the Lord gave up His body. But this was not the destruction of Kṛṣṇa's body; rather, it was the disappearance of the Supreme Lord by His personal energy.

Actually, the Lord does not give up His body, which is eternal, but as He can change His body from the form of Viṣṇu to that of an ordinary human child, He can change His body to any form He likes. This does not mean that He gives up His body. By spiritual energy, the Lord can appear in a body made of wood or stone. He can change His body into anything because everything is His energy (*parāsya śaktir vividhaiva śrūyate*). As clearly said in *Bhagavad-gītā* (7.4), *bhinnā prakṛtir aṣṭadhā:* the material elements are separated energies of the Supreme Lord. If He transforms Himself into the *arcā-mūrti,* the worshipable Deity, which we see as stone or wood, He is still Kṛṣṇa. Therefore the *śāstra* warns, *arcye viṣṇau śilā-dhīr guruṣu nara-matiḥ.* One who thinks that the worshipable Deity in the temple is made of wood or stone, one who sees a Vaiṣṇava *guru* as an ordinary human being, or one who materially conceives of a Vaiṣṇava as belonging to a particular caste is *nārakī,* a resident of hell. The Supreme Personality of Godhead can appear before us in many forms, as he likes, but we must know the true facts: *janma karma ca me divyam evaṁ yo vetti tattvataḥ* (Bg. 4.9). By following the instructions of *sādhu, guru* and *śāstra*—the saintly persons, the spiritual master and the authoritative scriptures—one can understand Kṛṣṇa, and then one makes his life successful by returning home, back to Godhead.

TEXT 47

ततश्च शौरिर्भगवत्प्रचोदितः
सुतं समादाय स सूतिकागृहात् ।
यदा बहिर्गन्तुमियेष तर्ह्यजा
या योगमायाजनि नन्दजायया ॥४७॥

tataś ca śaurir bhagavat-pracoditaḥ
sutaṁ samādāya sa sūtikā-gṛhāt
yadā bahir gantum iyeṣa tarhy ajā
yā yogamāyājani nanda-jāyayā

tataḥ—thereafter; *ca*—indeed; *śauriḥ*—Vasudeva; *bhagavat-praco-ditaḥ*—being instructed by the Supreme Personality of Godhead; *sutam*—his son; *samādāya*—carrying very carefully; *saḥ*—he; *sūtikā-gṛhāt*—from the maternity room; *yadā*—when; *bahiḥ gantum*—to go outside; *iyeṣa*—desired; *tarhi*—exactly at that time; *ajā*—the transcendental energy, who also never takes birth; *yā*—who; *yogamāyā*—is known as Yogamāyā; *ajani*—took birth; *nanda-jāyayā*—from the wife of Nanda Mahārāja.

TRANSLATION

Thereafter, exactly when Vasudeva, being inspired by the Supreme Personality of Godhead, was about to take the newborn child from the delivery room, Yogamāyā, the Lord's spiritual energy, took birth as the daughter of the wife of Mahārāja Nanda.

PURPORT

Śrīla Viśvanātha Cakravartī Ṭhākura discusses that Kṛṣṇa appeared simultaneously as the son of Devakī and as the son of Yaśodā, along with the spiritual energy Yogamāyā. As the son of Devakī, He first appeared as Viṣṇu, and because Vasudeva was not in the position of pure affection for Kṛṣṇa, Vasudeva worshiped his son as Lord Viṣṇu. Yaśodā, however, pleased her son Kṛṣṇa without understanding His Godhood. This is the difference between Kṛṣṇa as the son of Yaśodā and as the son of Devakī. This is explained by Viśvanātha Cakravartī on the authority of *Hari-vaṁśa.*

TEXTS 48–49

तया हृतप्रत्ययसर्ववृत्तिषु
द्वाःस्थेषु पौरेष्वपि शायितेष्वथ ।
द्वारश्च सर्वाः पिहिता दुरत्यया
बृहत्कपाटायसकीलशृङ्खलैः ॥४८॥
ताः कृष्णवाहे वसुदेव आगते
स्वयं व्यवर्यन्त यथा तमो रवेः ।
ववर्ष पर्जन्य उपांशुगर्जितः
शेषोऽन्वगाद् वारि निवारयन् फणैः ॥४९॥

tayā hṛta-pratyaya-sarva-vṛttiṣu
dvāḥ-stheṣu paureṣv api śāyiteṣv atha
dvāraś ca sarvāḥ pihitā duratyayā
bṛhat-kapāṭāyasa-kīla-śṛṅkhalaiḥ

tāḥ kṛṣṇa-vāhe vasudeva āgate
svayaṁ vyavaryanta yathā tamo raveḥ

vavarṣa parjanya upāṁśu-garjitaḥ
śeṣo 'nvagād vāri nivārayan phaṇaiḥ

tayā—by the influence of Yogamāyā; *hṛta-pratyaya*—deprived of all sensation; *sarva-vṛttiṣu*—having all their senses; *dvāḥ-stheṣu*—all the doormen; *paureṣu api*—as well as other members of the house; *śāyiteṣu*—sleeping very deeply; *atha*—when Vasudeva tried to take his transcendental son out of the confinement; *dvāraḥ ca*—as well as the doors; *sarvāḥ*—all; *pihitāḥ*—constructed; *duratyayā*—very hard and firm; *bṛhat-kapāṭa*—and on great doors; *āyasa-kīla-śṛṅkhalaiḥ*—strongly constructed with iron pins and closed with iron chains; *tāḥ*—all of them; *kṛṣṇa-vāhe*—bearing Kṛṣṇa; *vasudeve*—when Vasudeva; *āgate*—appeared; *svayam*—automatically; *vyavaryanta*—opened wide; *yathā*—as; *tamaḥ*—darkness; *raveḥ*—on the appearance of the sun; *vavarṣa*—showered rain; *parjanyaḥ*—the clouds in the sky; *upāṁśu-garjitaḥ*—very mildly resounding and raining very slightly; *śeṣaḥ*—Ananta-nāga; *anvagāt*—followed; *vāri*—showers of rain; *nivārayan*—stopping; *phaṇaiḥ*—by spreading His hoods.

TRANSLATION

By the influence of Yogamāyā, all the doorkeepers fell fast asleep, their senses unable to work, and the other inhabitants of the house also fell deeply asleep. When the sun rises, the darkness automatically disappears; similarly, when Vasudeva appeared, the closed doors, which were strongly pinned with iron and locked with iron chains, opened automatically. Since the clouds in the sky were mildly thundering and showering, Ananta-nāga, an expansion of the Supreme Personality of Godhead, followed Vasudeva, beginning from the door, with hoods expanded to protect Vasudeva and the transcendental child.

PURPORT

Śeṣa-nāga is an expansion of the Supreme Personality of Godhead whose business is to serve the Lord with all necessary paraphernalia. When Vasudeva was carrying the child, Śeṣa-nāga came to serve the Lord and protect Him from the mild showers of rain.

TEXT 50

मघोनि वर्षत्यसकृद् यमानुजा
गम्भीरतोयौघजवोर्मिफेनिला ।
भयानकावर्तशताकुला नदी
मार्गं ददौ सिन्धुरिव श्रियः पतेः ॥५०॥

maghoni varṣaty asakṛd yamānujā
gambhīra-toyaugha-javormi-phenilā
bhayānakāvarta-śatākulā nadī
mārgaṁ dadau sindhur iva śriyaḥ pateḥ

maghoni varṣati—because of Lord Indra's showering rain; *asakṛt*—constantly; *yama-anujā*—the River Yamunā, who is considered the younger sister of Yamarāja; *gambhīra-toya-ogha*—of the very deep water; *java*—by the force; *ūrmi*—by the waves; *phenilā*—full of foam; *bhayānaka*—fierce; *āvarta-śata*—by the whirling waves; *ākulā*—agitated; *nadī*—the river; *mārgam*—way; *dadau*—gave; *sindhuḥ iva*—like the ocean; *śriyaḥ pateḥ*—unto Lord Rāmacandra, the husband of the goddess Sītā.

TRANSLATION

Because of constant rain sent by the demigod Indra, the River Yamunā was filled with deep water, foaming about with fiercely whirling waves. But as the great Indian Ocean had formerly given way to Lord Rāmacandra by allowing Him to construct a bridge, the River Yamunā gave way to Vasudeva and allowed him to cross.

TEXT 51

नन्दव्रजं शौरिरुपेत्य तत्र तान्
गोपान् प्रसुप्तानुपलभ्य निद्रया ।
सुतं यशोदाशयने निधाय त-
त्सुतामुपादाय पुनर्गृहानगात् ॥५१॥

nanda-vrajaṁ śaurir upetya tatra tān
gopān prasuptān upalabhya nidrayā

sutaṁ yaśodā-śayane nidhāya tat-
sutām upādāya punar gṛhān agāt

nanda-vrajam—the village or the house of Nanda Mahārāja; *śauriḥ*—Vasudeva; *upetya*—reaching; *tatra*—there; *tān*—all the members; *gopān*—the cowherd men; *prasuptān*—were fast asleep; *upalabhya*—understanding that; *nidrayā*—in deep sleep; *sutam*—the son (Vasudeva's son); *yaśodā-śayane*—on the bed where mother Yaśodā was sleeping; *nidhāya*—placing; *tat-sutām*—her daughter; *upādāya*—picking up; *punaḥ*—again; *gṛhān*—to his own house; *agāt*—returned.

TRANSLATION

When Vasudeva reached the house of Nanda Mahārāja, he saw that all the cowherd men were fast asleep. Thus he placed his own son on the bed of Yaśodā, picked up her daughter, an expansion of Yogamāyā, and then returned to his residence, the prison house of Kaṁsa.

PURPORT

Vasudeva knew very well that as soon as the daughter was in the prison house of Kaṁsa, Kaṁsa would immediately kill her; but to protect his own child, he had to kill the child of his friend. Nanda Mahārāja was his friend, but out of deep affection and attachment for his own son, he knowingly did this. Śrīla Viśvanātha Cakravartī Ṭhākura says that one cannot be blamed for protecting one's own child at the sacrifice of another's. Furthermore, Vasudeva cannot be accused of callousness, since his actions were impelled by the force of Yogamāyā.

TEXT 52

देवक्याः शयने न्यस्य वसुदेवोऽथ दारिकाम् ।
प्रतिमुच्य पदोर्लोहमास्ते पूर्ववदावृतः ॥५२॥

devakyāḥ śayane nyasya
vasudevo 'tha dārikām
pratimucya pador loham
āste pūrvavad āvṛtaḥ

devakyāḥ—of Devakī; *śayane*—on the bed; *nyasya*—placing; *vasudevaḥ*—Vasudeva; *atha*—thus; *dārikām*—the female child; *pratimucya*—binding himself again; *padoḥ loham*—iron shackles on the two legs; *āste*—remained; *pūrva-vat*—like before; *āvṛtaḥ*—bound.

TRANSLATION

Vasudeva placed the female child on the bed of Devakī, bound his legs with the iron shackles, and thus remained there as before.

TEXT 53

यशोदा नन्दपत्नी च जातं परमबुध्यत ।
न तल्लिङ्गं परिश्रान्ता निद्रयापगतस्मृतिः ॥५३॥

yaśodā nanda-patnī ca
jātaṁ param abudhyata
na tal-liṅgaṁ pariśrāntā
nidrayāpagata-smṛtiḥ

yaśodā—Yaśodā, Kṛṣṇa's mother in Gokula; *nanda-patnī*—the wife of Nanda Mahārāja; *ca*—also; *jātam*—a child was born; *param*—the Supreme Person; *abudhyata*—could understand; *na*—not; *tat-liṅgam*—whether the child was male or female; *pariśrāntā*—because of too much labor; *nidrayā*—when overwhelmed with sleep; *apagata-smṛtiḥ*—having lost consciousness.

TRANSLATION

Exhausted by the labor of childbirth, Yaśodā was overwhelmed with sleep and unable to understand what kind of child had been born to her.

PURPORT

Nanda Mahārāja and Vasudeva were intimate friends, and so were their wives, Yaśodā and Devakī. Although their names were different, they were practically nondifferent personalities. The only difference is that Devakī was able to understand that the Supreme Personality of Godhead had been born to her and had now changed into Kṛṣṇa, whereas Yaśodā was not able to understand what kind of child had been born to her. Yaśodā was such an advanced devotee that she never regarded Kṛṣṇa as the Supreme Personality of Godhead, but simply loved Him as her own child. Devakī, however, knew from the very beginning that although Kṛṣṇa was her son, He was the Supreme Personality of Godhead. In Vṛndāvana, no one regarded Kṛṣṇa as the Supreme Personality of Godhead. When something very wonderful happened because of Kṛṣṇa's activities, the inhabitants of Vṛndāvana—the cowherd men, the cowherd boys, Nanda Mahārāja, Yaśodā and the others—were surprised, but they never considered their son Kṛṣṇa the Supreme Personality of Godhead. Sometimes they suggested that some great demigod had appeared there as Kṛṣṇa. In such an exalted status of devotional service, a devotee forgets the position of Kṛṣṇa and intensely loves the Supreme Personality of Godhead without understanding His position. This is called *kevala-bhakti* and is distinct from the stages of *jñāna* and *jñānamayī bhakti.*

Thus end the Bhaktivedanta purports of the Tenth Canto, Third Chapter, of the Śrīmad-Bhāgavatam, *entitled "The Birth of Lord Kṛṣṇa."*

CHAPTER FOUR

The Atrocities of King Kaṁsa

This chapter describes how Kaṁsa, following the advice of his demoniac friends, considered the persecution of small children to be very diplomatic.

After Vasudeva bound himself with iron shackles as before, all the doors of the prison house closed by the influence of Yogamāyā, who then began crying as a newborn child. This crying awakened the doorkeepers, who immediately informed Kaṁsa that a child had been born to Devakī. Upon hearing this news, Kaṁsa appeared with great force in the maternity room, and in spite of Devakī's pleas that the child be saved, the demon forcibly snatched the child from Devakī's hands and dashed the child against a rock. Unfortunately for Kaṁsa, however, the newborn child slipped away from his hands, rose above his head and appeared as the eight-armed form of Durgā. Durgā then told Kaṁsa, "The enemy you contemplate has taken birth somewhere else. Therefore your plan to persecute all the children will prove futile."

According to the prophecy, the eighth child of Devakī would kill Kaṁsa, and therefore when Kaṁsa saw that the eighth child was a female and heard that his so-called enemy had taken birth elsewhere, he was struck with wonder. He decided to release Devakī and Vasudeva, and he admitted before them the wrongness of his atrocities. Falling at the feet of Devakī and Vasudeva, he begged their pardon and tried to convince them that because the events that had taken place were destined to happen, they should not be unhappy for his having killed so many of their children. Devakī and Vasudeva, being naturally very pious, immediately excused Kaṁsa for his atrocities, and Kaṁsa, after seeing that his sister and brother-in-law were happy, returned to his home.

After the night passed, however, Kaṁsa called for his ministers and informed them of all that had happened. The ministers, who were all demons, advised Kaṁsa that because his enemy had already taken birth somewhere else, all the children born within the past ten days in the villages within Kaṁsa's kingdom should be killed. Although the demigods always feared Kaṁsa, they should not be treated leniently; since they were enemies, Kaṁsa should try his best to uproot their existence. The demoniac ministers further advised that Kaṁsa and the demons continue their enmity toward Viṣṇu because Viṣṇu is the original person among all the demigods. The *brāhmaṇas*, the cows, the *Vedas*, austerity, truthfulness, control of the senses and mind, faithfulness and mercy are among the different parts of the body of Viṣṇu, who is the origin of all the demigods, including Lord Brahmā and Lord Śiva. Therefore, the ministers advised, the demigods, the saintly persons, the cows and the *brāhmaṇas* should be systematically persecuted. Strongly advised in this way by his friends, the demoniac ministers, Kaṁsa approved of their instructions and considered it beneficial to be envious of the *brāhmaṇas*. Following Kaṁsa's orders, therefore, the demons began committing their atrocities all over Vrajabhūmi.

TEXT 1

श्रीशुक उवाच

बहिरन्तःपुरद्वारः सर्वाः पूर्ववदावृताः ।
ततो बालध्वनिं श्रुत्वा गृहपालाः समुत्थिताः ॥ १ ॥

śrī-śuka uvāca
bahir-antaḥ-pura-dvāraḥ
sarvāḥ pūrvavad āvṛtāḥ
tato bāla-dhvaniṁ śrutvā
gṛha-pālāḥ samutthitāḥ

śrī-śukaḥ uvāca—Śrī Śukadeva Gosvāmī said; *bahiḥ-antaḥ-pura-dvāraḥ*—the doors inside and outside the house; *sarvāḥ*—all; *pūrva-vat*—like before; *āvṛtāḥ*—closed; *tataḥ*—thereafter; *bāla-dhvanim*—the crying of the newborn child; *śrutvā*—hearing; *gṛha-pālāḥ*—all the inhabitants of the house, especially the doormen; *samutthitāḥ*—awakened.

TRANSLATION

Śukadeva Gosvāmī continued: My dear King Parīkṣit, the doors inside and outside the house closed as before. Thereafter, the in-

habitants of the house, especially the watchmen, heard the crying of the newborn child and thus awakened from their beds.

PURPORT

The activities of Yogamāyā are distinctly visible in this chapter, in which Devakī and Vasudeva excuse Kaṁsa for his many devious, atrocious activities and Kaṁsa becomes repentant and falls at their feet. Before the awakening of the watchmen and the others in the prison house, many other things happened. Kṛṣṇa was born and transferred to the home of Yaśodā in Gokula, the strong doors opened and again closed, and Vasudeva resumed his former condition of being shackled. The watchmen, however, could not understand all this. They awakened only when they heard the crying of the newborn child, Yogamāyā.

Śrīla Viśvanātha Cakravartī Ṭhākura has remarked that the watchmen were just like dogs. At night the dogs in the street act like watchmen. If one dog barks, many other dogs immediately follow it by barking. Although the street dogs are not appointed by anyone to act as watchmen, they think they are responsible for protecting the neighborhood, and as soon as someone unknown enters it, they all begin to bark. Both Yogamāyā and Mahāmāyā act in all material activities (*prakṛteḥ kriyamāṇāni guṇaiḥ karmāṇi sarvaśaḥ*), but although the energy of the Supreme Personality of Godhead acts under the Supreme Lord's direction (*mayādhyakṣeṇa prakṛtiḥ sūyate sa-carācaram*), doglike watchmen such as politicians and diplomats think that they are protecting their neighborhoods from the dangers of the outside world. These are the actions of *māyā*. But one who surrenders to Kṛṣṇa is relieved of the protection afforded by the dogs and doglike guardians of this material world.

TEXT 2

ते तु तूर्णमुपव्रज्य देवक्या गर्भजन्म तत् ।
आचख्युर्भोजराजाय यदुद्विग्नः प्रतीक्षते ॥ २ ॥

te tu tūrṇam upavrajya
devakyā garbha-janma tat
ācakhyur bhoja-rājāya
yad udvignaḥ pratīkṣate

te—all the watchmen; *tu*—indeed; *tūrṇam*—very quickly; *upavrajya*—going before (the King); *devakyāḥ*—of Devakī; *garbha-janma*—the deliverance from the womb; *tat*—that (child); *ācakhyuḥ*—submitted; *bhoja-rājāya*—unto the King of the Bhojas, Kaṁsa; *yat*—of whom; *udvignaḥ*—with great anxiety; *pratīkṣate*—was waiting (for the child's birth).

TRANSLATION

Thereafter, all the watchmen very quickly approached King Kaṁsa, the ruler of the Bhoja dynasty, and submitted the news of the birth of Devakī's child. Kaṁsa, who had awaited this news very anxiously, immediately took action.

PURPORT

Kaṁsa was very anxiously waiting because of the prophecy that the eighth child of Devakī would kill him. This time, naturally, he was awake and waiting, and when the watchmen approached him, he immediately took action to kill the child.

TEXT 3

स तल्पात् तूर्णमुत्थाय कालोऽयमिति विह्वलः ।
सूतीगृहमगात् तूर्णं प्रस्खलन् मुक्तमूर्धजः ॥ ३ ॥

sa talpāt tūrṇam utthāya
kālo 'yam iti vihvalaḥ
sūtī-gṛham agāt tūrṇaṁ
praskhalan mukta-mūrdhajaḥ

saḥ—he (King Kaṁsa); *talpāt*—from the bed; *tūrṇam*—very quickly; *utthāya*—getting up; *kālaḥ ayam*—here is my death, the supreme time; *iti*—in this way; *vihvalaḥ*—overwhelmed; *sūtī-gṛham*—to the maternity home; *agāt*—went; *tūrṇam*—without delay; *praskhalan*—scattering; *mukta*—had become opened; *mūrdha-jaḥ*—the hair on the head.

TRANSLATION

Kaṁsa immediately got up from bed, thinking, "Here is Kāla, the supreme time factor, which has taken birth to kill me!" Thus

overwhelmed, Kaṁsa, his hair scattered on his head, at once approached the place where the child had been born.

PURPORT

The word *kālaḥ* is significant. Although the child was born to kill Kaṁsa, Kaṁsa thought that this was the proper time to kill the child so that he himself would be saved. *Kāla* is actually another name of the Supreme Personality of Godhead when He appears only for the purpose of killing. When Arjuna inquired from Kṛṣṇa in His universal form, "Who are You?" the Lord presented Himself as *kāla,* death personified to kill. By nature's law, when there is an unwanted increase in population, *kāla* appears, and by some arrangement of the Supreme Personality of Godhead, people are killed wholesale in different ways, by war, pestilence, famine and so on. At that time, even atheistic political leaders go to a church, mosque or temple for protection by God or gods and submissively say, "God willing." Before that, they pay no attention to God, not caring to know God or His will, but when *kāla* appears, they say, "God willing." Death is but another feature of the supreme *kāla,* the Supreme Personality of Godhead. At the time of death, the atheist must submit to this supreme *kāla,* and then the Supreme Personality of Godhead takes away all his possessions (*mṛtyuḥ sarva-haraś cāham*) and forces him to accept another body (*tathā dehāntara-prāptiḥ*). This the atheists do not know, and if they do know, they neglect it so that they may go on with their normal life. The Kṛṣṇa consciousness movement is trying to teach them that although for a few years one may act as a great protector or great watchman, with the appearance of *kāla,* death, one must take another body by the laws of nature. Not knowing this, they unnecessarily waste their time in their occupation as watchdogs and do not try to get the mercy of the Supreme Personality of Godhead. As it is clearly said, *aprāpya māṁ nivartante mṛtyu-saṁsāra-vartmani:* without Kṛṣṇa consciousness, one is condemned to continue wandering in birth and death, not knowing what will happen in one's next birth.

TEXT 4

तमाह भ्रातरं देवी कृपणा करुणं सती ।
स्नुषेयं तव कल्याण स्त्रियं मा हन्तुमर्हसि ॥ ४ ॥

tam āha bhrātaraṁ devī
kṛpaṇā karuṇaṁ satī
snuṣeyaṁ tava kalyāṇa
striyaṁ mā hantum arhasi

tam—unto Kaṁsa; *āha*—said; *bhrātaram*—her brother; *devī*—mother Devakī; *kṛpaṇā*—helplessly; *karuṇam*—piteously; *satī*—the chaste lady; *snuṣā iyam tava*—this child will be your daughter-in-law, the wife of your future son; *kalyāṇa*—O all-auspicious one; *striyam*—a woman; *mā*—not; *hantum*—to kill; *arhasi*—you deserve.

TRANSLATION

Devakī helplessly, piteously appealed to Kaṁsa: My dear brother, all good fortune unto you. Don't kill this girl. She will be your daughter-in-law. Indeed, it is unworthy of you to kill a woman.

PURPORT

Kaṁsa had previously excused Devakī because he thought that a woman should not be killed, especially when pregnant. But now, by the influence of *māyā*, he was prepared to kill a woman—not only a woman, but a small, helpless newborn child. Devakī wanted to save her brother from this terrible, sinful act. Therefore she told him, "Don't be so atrocious as to kill a female child. Let there be all good fortune for you." Demons can do anything for their personal benefit, not considering what is pious or vicious. But Devakī, on the contrary, although safe because she had already given birth to her own son, Kṛṣṇa, was anxious to save the daughter of someone else. This was natural for her.

TEXT 5

बहवो हिंसिता भ्रातः शिशवः पावकोपमाः ।
त्वया दैवनिसृष्टेन पुत्रिकैका प्रदीयताम् ॥ ५ ॥

bahavo hiṁsitā bhrātaḥ
śiśavaḥ pāvakopamāḥ
tvayā daiva-nisṛṣṭena
putrikaikā pradīyatām

bahavaḥ—many; *hiṁsitāḥ*—killed out of envy; *bhrātaḥ*—my dear brother; *śiśavaḥ*—small children; *pāvaka-upamāḥ*—all of them equal to fire in brightness and beauty; *tvayā*—by you; *daiva-nisṛṣṭena*—as spoken by destiny; *putrikā*—daughter; *ekā*—one; *pradīyatām*—give me as your gift.

TRANSLATION

My dear brother, by the influence of destiny you have already killed many babies, each of them as bright and beautiful as fire. But kindly spare this daughter. Give her to me as your gift.

PURPORT

Here we see that Devakī first focused Kaṁsa's attention on his atrocious activities, his killing of her many sons. Then she wanted to compromise with him by saying that whatever he had done was not his fault, but was ordained by destiny. Then she appealed to him to give her the daughter as a gift. Devakī was the daughter of a *kṣatriya* and knew how to play the political game. In politics there are different methods of achieving success: first repression (*dama*), then compromise (*sāma*), and then asking for a gift (*dāna*). Devakī first adopted the policy of repression by directly attacking Kaṁsa for having cruelly, atrociously killed her babies. Then she compromised by saying that this was not his fault, and then she begged for a gift. As we learn from the history of the *Mahābhārata*, or "Greater India," the wives and daughters of the ruling class, the *kṣatriyas*, knew the political game, but we never find that a woman was given the post of chief executive. This is in accordance with the injunctions of *Manu-saṁhitā*, but unfortunately *Manu-saṁhitā* is now being insulted, and the Āryans, the members of Vedic society, cannot do anything. Such is the nature of Kali-yuga.

Nothing happens unless ordained by destiny.

tasyaiva hetoḥ prayateta kovido
na labhyate yad bhramatām upary adhaḥ
tal labhyate duḥkhavad anyataḥ sukhaṁ
kālena sarvatra gabhīra-raṁhasā
(*Bhāg.* 1.5.18)

Devakī knew very well that because the killing of her many children had been ordained by destiny, Kaṁsa was not to be blamed. There was no need to give good instructions to Kaṁsa. *Upadeśo hi murkhāṇāṁ prakopāya na śāntaye* (Cāṇakya Paṇḍita). If a foolish person is given good instructions, he becomes more and more angry. Moreover, a cruel person is more dangerous than a snake. A snake and a cruel person are both cruel, but a cruel person is more dangerous because although a snake can be charmed by *mantras* or subdued by herbs, a cruel person cannot be subdued by any means. Such was the nature of Kaṁsa.

TEXT 6

नन्वहं ते ह्यवरजा दीना हतसुता प्रभो ।
दातुमर्हसि मन्दाया अङ्गेमां चरमां प्रजाम् ॥ ६ ॥

nanv ahaṁ te hy avarajā
dīnā hata-sutā prabho
dātum arhasi mandāyā
aṅgemāṁ caramāṁ prajām

nanu—however; *aham*—I am; *te*—your; *hi*—indeed; *avarajā*—younger sister; *dīnā*—very poor; *hata-sutā*—deprived of all children; *prabho*—O my lord; *dātum arhasi*—you deserve to give (some gift); *mandāyāḥ*—to me, who am so poor; *aṅga*—my dear brother; *imām*—this; *caramām*—last; *prajām*—child.

TRANSLATION

My lord, my brother, I am very poor, being bereft of all my children, but still I am your younger sister, and therefore it would be worthy of you to give me this last child as a gift.

TEXT 7

श्रीशुक उवाच

उपगुह्यात्मजामेवं रुदत्या दीनदीनवत् ।
याचितस्तां विनिर्भर्त्स्य हस्तादाचिच्छिदे खलः॥७॥

śrī-śuka uvāca
upaguhyātmajām evaṁ
rudatyā dīna-dīnavat
yācitas tāṁ vinirbhartsya
hastād ācicchide khalaḥ

śrī-śukaḥ uvāca—Śrī Śukadeva Gosvāmī said; *upaguhya*—embracing; *ātmajām*—her daughter; *evam*—in this way; *rudatyā*—by Devakī, who was crying; *dīna-dīna-vat*—very piteously, like a poor woman; *yācitaḥ*—being begged; *tām*—her (Devakī); *vinirbhartsya*—chastising; *hastāt*—from her hands; *ācicchide*—separated the child by force; *khalaḥ*—Kaṁsa, the most cruel.

TRANSLATION

Śukadeva Gosvāmī continued: Piteously embracing her daughter and crying, Devakī begged Kaṁsa for the child, but he was so cruel that he chastised her and forcibly snatched the child from her hands.

PURPORT

Although Devakī was crying like a very poor woman, actually she was not poor, and therefore the word used here is *dīnavat.* She had already given birth to Kṛṣṇa. Therefore, who could have been richer than she? Even the demigods had come to offer prayers to Devakī, but she played the part of a poor, piteously afflicted woman because she wanted to save the daughter of Yaśodā.

TEXT 8

तां गृहीत्वा चरणयोर्जातमात्रां स्वसुः सुताम् ।
अपोथयच्छिलापृष्ठे स्वार्थोन्मूलितसौहृदः ॥ ८ ॥

tāṁ gṛhītvā caraṇayor
jāta-mātrāṁ svasuḥ sutām
apothayac chilā-pṛṣṭhe
svārthonmūlita-sauhṛdaḥ

tām—the child; *gṛhītvā*—taking by force; *caraṇayoḥ*—by the two legs; *jāta-mātrām*—the newborn child; *svasuḥ*—of his sister; *sutām*—the daughter; *apothayat*—smashed; *śilā-pṛṣṭhe*—on the surface of a stone; *sva-artha-unmūlita*—uprooted because of intense selfishness; *sauhṛdaḥ*—all friendship or family relationships.

TRANSLATION

Having uprooted all relationships with his sister because of intense selfishness, Kaṁsa, who was sitting on his knees, grasped the newborn child by the legs and tried to dash her against the surface of a stone.

TEXT 9

सा तद्धस्तात् समुत्पत्य सद्यो देव्यम्बरं गता ।
अदृश्यतानुजा विष्णोः सायुधाष्टमहाभुजा ॥ ९ ॥

sā tad-dhastāt samutpatya
sadyo devy ambaraṁ gatā
adṛśyatānujā viṣṇoḥ
sāyudhāṣṭa-mahābhujā

sā—that female child; *tat-hastāt*—from the hand of Kaṁsa; *samutpatya*—slipped upward; *sadyaḥ*—immediately; *devī*—the form of a demigoddess; *ambaram*—into the sky; *gatā*—went; *adṛśyata*—was seen; *anujā*—the younger sister; *viṣṇoḥ*—of the Supreme Personality of Godhead; *sa-āyudhā*—with weapons; *aṣṭa*—eight; *mahā-bhujā*—with mighty arms.

TRANSLATION

The child, Yogamāyā-devī, the younger sister of Lord Viṣṇu, slipped upward from Kaṁsa's hands and appeared in the sky as Devī, the goddess Durgā, with eight arms, completely equipped with weapons.

PURPORT

Kaṁsa tried to dash the child downward against a piece of stone, but since she was Yogamāyā, the younger sister of Lord Viṣṇu, she slipped upward and assumed the form of the goddess Durgā. The word *anujā*, meaning "the younger sister," is significant. When Viṣṇu, or Kṛṣṇa, took birth from Devakī, He must have simultaneously taken birth from Yaśodā also. Otherwise how could Yogamāyā have been *anujā*, the Lord's younger sister?

TEXTS 10–11

दिव्यस्रगम्बरालेपरत्नाभरणभूषिता ।
धनुःशूलेषुचर्मासिशङ्खचक्रगदाधरा ॥१०॥
सिद्धचारणगन्धर्वैरप्सरःकिन्नरोरगैः ।
उपाहृतोरुबलिभिः स्तूयमानेदमब्रवीत् ॥११॥

divya-srag-ambarālepa-
ratnābharaṇa-bhūṣitā
dhanuḥ-śūleṣu-carmāsi-
śaṅkha-cakra-gadā-dharā

siddha-cāraṇa-gandharvair
apsaraḥ-kinnaroragaiḥ
upāhṛtoru-balibhiḥ
stūyamānedam abravīt

divya-srak-ambara-ālepa—she then assumed the form of a demigoddess, completely decorated with sandalwood pulp, flower garlands and a nice dress; *ratna-ābharaṇa-bhūṣitā*—decorated with ornaments of valuable jewels; *dhanuḥ-śūla-iṣu-carma-asi*—with bow, trident, arrows, shield and sword; *śaṅkha-cakra-gadā-dharā*—and holding the weapons of Viṣṇu (conchshell, disc and club); *siddha-cāraṇa-gandharvaiḥ*—by the Siddhas, Cāraṇas and Gandharvas; *apsaraḥ-kinnara-uragaiḥ*—and by the Apsarās, Kinnaras and Uragas; *upāhṛta-uru-balibhiḥ*—who brought all kinds of presentations to her; *stūyamānā*—being praised; *idam*—these words; *abravīt*—she said.

TRANSLATION

The goddess Durgā was decorated with flower garlands, smeared with sandalwood pulp and dressed with excellent garments and ornaments made of valuable jewels. Holding in her hands a bow, a

trident, arrows, a shield, a sword, a conchshell, a disc and a club, and being praised by celestial beings like Apsarās, Kinnaras, Uragas, Siddhas, Cāraṇas and Gandharvas, who worshiped her with all kinds of presentations, she spoke as follows.

TEXT 12

किं मया हतया मन्द जातः खलु तवान्तकृत् ।
यत्र क्व वा पूर्वशत्रुर्मा हिंसीः कृपणान् वृथा ॥१२॥

kiṁ mayā hatayā manda
jātaḥ khalu tavānta-kṛt
yatra kva vā pūrva-śatrur
mā hiṁsīḥ kṛpaṇān vṛthā

kim—what is the use; *mayā*—me; *hatayā*—in killing; *manda*—O you fool; *jātaḥ*—has already been born; *khalu*—indeed; *tava anta-kṛt*—who will kill you; *yatra kva vā*—somewhere else; *pūrva-śatruḥ*—your former enemy; *mā*—do not; *hiṁsīḥ*—kill; *kṛpaṇān*—other poor children; *vṛthā*—unnecessarily.

TRANSLATION

O Kaṁsa, you fool, what will be the use of killing me? The Supreme Personality of Godhead, who has been your enemy from the very beginning and who will certainly kill you, has already taken His birth somewhere else. Therefore, do not unnecessarily kill other children.

TEXT 13

इति प्रभाष्य तं देवी माया भगवती भुवि ।
बहुनामनिकेतेषु बहुनामा बभूव ह ॥१३॥

iti prabhāṣya taṁ devī
māyā bhagavatī bhuvi
bahu-nāma-niketeṣu
bahu-nāmā babhūva ha

iti—in this way; *prabhāṣya*—addressing; *tam*—Kaṁsa; *devī*—the goddess Durgā; *māyā*—Yogamāyā; *bhagavatī*—possessing immense power, like that of the Supreme Personality of Godhead; *bhuvi*—on the surface of the earth; *bahu-nāma*—of different names; *niketeṣu*—in different places; *bahu-nāmā*—different names; *babhūva*—became; *ha*—indeed.

TRANSLATION

After speaking to Kaṁsa in this way, the goddess Durgā, Yogamāyā, appeared in different places, such as Vārāṇasī, and became celebrated by different names, such as Annapūrṇā, Durgā, Kālī and Bhadrā.

PURPORT

The goddess Durgā is celebrated in Calcutta as Kālī, in Bombay as Mumbādevī, in Vārāṇasī as Annapūrṇā, in Cuttack as Bhadrakālī and in Ahmedabad as Bhadrā. Thus in different places she is known by different names. Her devotees are known as *śāktas*, or worshipers of the energy of the Supreme Personality of Godhead, whereas worshipers of the Supreme Personality of Godhead Himself are called Vaiṣṇavas. Vaiṣṇavas are destined to return home, back to Godhead, in the spiritual world, whereas the *śāktas* are destined to live within this material world to enjoy different types of material happiness. In the material world, the living entity must accept different types of bodies. *Bhrāmayan sarva-bhūtāni yantrārūḍhāni māyayā* (Bg. 18.61). According to the living entity's desire, Yogamāyā, or Māyā, the goddess Durgā, gives him a particular type of body, which is mentioned as *yantra*, a machine. But the living entities who are promoted to the spiritual world do not return to the prison house of a material body (*tyaktvā dehaṁ punar janma naiti mām eti so 'rjuna*). The words *janma na eti* indicate that these living entities remain in their original, spiritual bodies to enjoy the company of the Supreme Personality of Godhead in the transcendental abodes Vaikuṇṭha and Vṛndāvana.

TEXT 14

तयाभिहितमाकर्ण्य कंसः परमविस्मितः ।
देवकीं वसुदेवं च विमुच्य प्रश्रितोऽब्रवीत् ॥१४॥

tayābhihitam ākarṇya
kaṁsaḥ parama-vismitaḥ
devakīṁ vasudevaṁ ca
vimucya praśrito 'bravīt

tayā—by the goddess Durgā; *abhihitam*—the words spoken; *ākarṇya*—by hearing; *kaṁsaḥ*—Kaṁsa; *parama-vismitaḥ*—was struck with wonder; *devakīm*—unto Devakī; *vasudevam ca*—and Vasudeva; *vimucya*—releasing immediately; *praśritaḥ*—with great humility; *abravīt*—spoke as follows.

TRANSLATION

After hearing the words of the goddess Durgā, Kaṁsa was struck with wonder. Thus he approached his sister Devakī and brother-in-law Vasudeva, released them immediately from their shackles, and very humbly spoke as follows.

PURPORT

Kaṁsa was astonished because the goddess Durgā had become the daughter of Devakī. Since Devakī was a human being, how could the goddess Durgā become her daughter? This was one cause of his astonishment. Also, how is it that the eighth child of Devakī was a female? This also astonished him. *Asuras* are generally devotees of mother Durgā, Śakti, or of demigods, especially Lord Śiva. The appearance of Durgā in her original eight-armed feature, holding various weapons, immediately changed Kaṁsa's mind about Devakī's being an ordinary human. Devakī must have had some transcendental qualities; otherwise why would the goddess Durgā have taken birth from her womb? Under the circumstances, Kaṁsa, struck with wonder, wanted to compensate for his atrocities against his sister Devakī.

TEXT 15

अहो भगिन्यहो भाम मया वां बत पाप्मना ।
पुरुषाद इवापत्यं बहवो हिंसिताः सुताः ॥१५॥

aho bhaginy aho bhāma
mayā vāṁ bata pāpmanā
puruṣāda ivāpatyaṁ
bahavo hiṁsitāḥ sutāḥ

aho—alas; *bhagini*—my dear sister; *aho*—alas; *bhāma*—my dear brother-in-law; *mayā*—by me; *vām*—of you; *bata*—indeed; *pāpmanā*—because of sinful activities; *puruṣa-adaḥ*—a Rākṣasa, man-eater; *iva*—like; *apatyam*—child; *bahavaḥ*—many; *hiṁsitāḥ*—have been killed; *sutāḥ*—sons.

TRANSLATION

Alas, my sister! Alas, my brother-in-law! I am indeed so sinful that exactly like a man-eater [Rākṣasa] who eats his own child, I have killed so many sons born of you.

PURPORT

Rākṣasas are understood to be accustomed to eating their own sons, as snakes and many other animals sometimes do. At the present moment in Kali-yuga, Rākṣasa fathers and mothers are killing their own children in the womb, and some are even eating the fetus with great relish. Thus the so-called civilization is gradually advancing by producing Rākṣasas.

TEXT 16

स त्वहं त्यक्तकारुण्यस्त्यक्तज्ञातिसुहृत् खलः ।
कान्ल्लोकान् वै गमिष्यामि ब्रह्महेव मृतः श्वसन् ॥१६॥

sa tv ahaṁ tyakta-kāruṇyas
tyakta-jñāti-suhṛt khalaḥ
kān lokān vai gamiṣyāmi
brahma-heva mṛtaḥ śvasan

saḥ—that person (Kaṁsa); *tu*—indeed; *aham*—I; *tyakta-kāruṇyaḥ*—devoid of all mercy; *tyakta-jñāti-suhṛt*—my relatives and friends have been rejected by me; *khalaḥ*—cruel; *kān lokān*—which planets;

vai—indeed; *gamiṣyāmi*—shall go; *brahma-hā iva*—like the killer of a *brāhmaṇa; mṛtaḥ śvasan*—either after death or while breathing.

TRANSLATION

Being merciless and cruel, I have forsaken all my relatives and friends. Therefore, like a person who has killed a brāhmaṇa, I do not know to which planet I shall go, either after death or while breathing.

TEXT 17

दैवमप्यनृतं वक्ति न मर्त्या एव केवलम् ।
यद्विश्रम्भादहं पापः स्वसुर्निहतवाञ्छिशून् ॥१७॥

daivam apy anṛtaṁ vakti
na martyā eva kevalam
yad-viśrambhād ahaṁ pāpaḥ
svasur nihatavāñ chiśūn

daivam—providence; *api*—also; *anṛtam*—lies; *vakti*—say; *na*—not; *martyāḥ*—human beings; *eva*—certainly; *kevalam*—only; *yat-viśrambhāt*—because of believing that prophecy; *aham*—I; *pāpaḥ*—the most sinful; *svasuḥ*—of my sister; *nihatavān*—killed; *śiśūn*—so many children.

TRANSLATION

Alas, not only human beings but sometimes even providence lies. And I am so sinful that I believed the omen of providence and killed so many of my sister's children.

TEXT 18

मा शोचतं महाभागावात्मजान् स्वकृतंभुजः ।
जान्तवो न सदैकत्र दैवाधीनास्तदासते ॥१८॥

mā śocataṁ mahā-bhāgāv
ātmajān sva-kṛtaṁ bhujaḥ

jāntavo na sadaikatra
daivādhīnās tadāsate

mā śocatam—kindly do not be aggrieved (for what happened in the past); *mahā-bhāgau*—O you who are learned and fortunate in spiritual knowledge; *ātmajān*—for your sons; *sva-kṛtam*—only because of their own acts; *bhujaḥ*—who are suffering; *jāntavaḥ*—all living entities; *na*—not; *sadā*—always; *ekatra*—in one place; *daiva-adhīnāḥ*—who are under the control of providence; *tadā*—hence; *āsate*—live.

TRANSLATION

O great souls, your children have suffered their own misfortune. Therefore, please do not lament for them. All living entities are under the control of the Supreme, and they cannot always live together.

PURPORT

Kaṁsa addressed his sister and brother-in-law as *mahā-bhāgau* because although he killed their ordinary children, the goddess Durgā took birth from them. Because Devakī bore Durgādevī in her womb, Kaṁsa praised both Devakī and her husband. *Asuras* are very devoted to the goddess Durgā, Kālī and so forth. Kaṁsa, therefore, truly astonished, appreciated the exalted position of his sister and brother-in-law. Durgā is certainly not under the laws of nature, because she herself is the controller of the laws of nature. Ordinary living beings, however, are controlled by these laws (*prakṛteḥ kriyamāṇāni guṇaiḥ karmāṇi sarvaśaḥ*). Consequently, none of us are allowed to live together for any long period. By speaking in this way, Kaṁsa tried to pacify his sister and brother-in-law.

TEXT 19

भुवि भौमानि भूतानि यथा यान्त्यपयान्ति च ।
नायमात्मा तथैतेषु विपर्येति यथैव भूः ॥१९॥

bhuvi bhaumāni bhūtāni
yathā yānty apayānti ca

nāyam ātmā tathaiteṣu
viparyeti yathaiva bhūḥ

bhuvi—on the surface of the world; *bhaumāni*—all material products from earth, such as pots; *bhūtāni*—which are produced; *yathā*—as; *yānti*—appear (in form); *apayānti*—disappear (broken or mixed with the earth); *ca*—and; *na*—not; *ayam ātmā*—the soul or spiritual identity; *tathā*—similarly; *eteṣu*—among all these (products of material elements); *viparyeti*—is changed or broken; *yathā*—as; *eva*—certainly; *bhūḥ*—the earth.

TRANSLATION

In this world, we can see that pots, dolls and other products of the earth appear, break and then disappear, mixing with the earth. Similarly, the bodies of all conditioned living entities are annihilated, but the living entities, like the earth itself, are unchanging and never annihilated [na hanyate hanyamāne śarīre].

PURPORT

Although Kaṁsa is described as a demon, he had good knowledge of the affairs of *ātma-tattva*, the truth of the self. Five thousand years ago, there were kings like Kaṁsa, who is described as an *asura*, but he was better than modern politicians and diplomats, who have no knowledge about *ātma-tattva*. As stated in the *Vedas*, *asaṅgo hy ayaṁ puruṣaḥ:* the spirit soul has no connection with the changes of the material body. The body undergoes six changes—birth, growth, sustenance, by-products, dwindling and then annihilation—but the soul undergoes no such changes. Even after the annihilation of a particular bodily form, the original source of the bodily elements does not change. The living entity enjoys the material body, which appears and disappears, but the five elements earth, water, fire, air and ether remain the same. The example given here is that pots and dolls are produced from the earth, and when broken or destroyed they mingle with their original ingredients. In any case, the source of supply remains the same.

As already discussed, the body is made according to the desires of the soul. The soul desires, and thus the body is formed. Kṛṣṇa therefore says in *Bhagavad-gītā* (18.61):

īśvaraḥ sarva-bhūtānāṁ
hṛd-deśe 'rjuna tiṣṭhati
bhrāmayan sarva-bhūtāni
yantrārūḍhāni māyayā

"The Supreme Lord is situated in everyone's heart, O Arjuna, and is directing the wanderings of all living entities, who are seated as on a machine, made of the material energy." Neither the Supersoul, Paramātmā, nor the individual soul changes its original, spiritual identity. The *ātmā* does not undergo birth, death or changes like the body. Therefore a Vedic aphorism says, *asaṅgo hy ayaṁ puruṣaḥ:* although the soul is conditioned within this material world, he has no connections with the changes of the material body.

TEXT 20

यथानेवंविदो भेदो यत आत्मविपर्ययः ।
देहयोगवियोगौ च संसृतिर्न निवर्तते ॥२०॥

yathānevaṁ-vido bhedo
yata ātma-viparyayaḥ
deha-yoga-viyogau ca
saṁsṛtir na nivartate

yathā—as; *an-evam-vidaḥ*—of a person who has no knowledge (about *ātma-tattva* and the steadiness of the *ātmā* in his own identity, despite the changes of the body); *bhedaḥ*—the idea of difference between body and self; *yataḥ*—because of which; *ātma-viparyayaḥ*—the foolish understanding that one is the body; *deha-yoga-viyogau ca*—and this causes connections and separations among different bodies; *saṁsṛtiḥ*—the continuation of conditioned life; *na*—not; *nivartate*—does stop.

TRANSLATION

One who does not understand the constitutional position of the body and the soul [ātmā] becomes too attached to the bodily concept of life. Consequently, because of attachment to the body and its by-products, he feels affected by union with and separation

from his family, society and nation. As long as this continues, one continues his material life. [Otherwise, one is liberated.]

PURPORT

As confirmed in *Śrīmad-Bhāgavatam* (1.2.6):

sa vai puṁsāṁ paro dharmo
yato bhaktir adhokṣaje
ahaituky apratihatā
yayātmā suprasīdati

The word *dharma* means "engagement." One who is engaged in the service of the Lord (*yato bhaktir adhokṣaje*), without impediment and without cessation, is understood to be situated in his original, spiritual status. When one is promoted to this status, one is always happy in transcendental bliss. Otherwise, as long as one is in the bodily concept of life, one must suffer material conditions. *Janma-mṛtyu-jarā-vyādhi-duḥkha-doṣānudarśanam.* The body is subject to its own principles of birth, death, old age and disease, but one who is situated in spiritual life (*yato bhaktir adhokṣaje*) has no birth, no death, no old age and no disease. One may argue that we may see a person who is spiritually engaged twenty-four hours a day but is still suffering from disease. In fact, however, he is neither suffering nor diseased; otherwise he could not be engaged twenty-four hours a day in spiritual activities. The example may be given in this connection that sometimes dirty foam or garbage is seen floating on the water of the Ganges. This is called *nīra-dharma*, a function of the water. But one who goes to the Ganges does not mind the foam and dirty things floating in the water. With his hand, he pushes away such nasty things, bathes in the Ganges and gains the beneficial results. Therefore, one who is situated in the spiritual status of life is unaffected by foam and garbage—or any superficial dirty things. This is confirmed by Śrīla Rūpa Gosvāmī:

īhā yasya harer dāsye
karmaṇā manasā girā
nikhilāsv apy avasthāsu
jīvan-muktaḥ sa ucyate

"A person acting in the service of Kṛṣṇa with his body, mind and words is a liberated person, even within the material world." (*Bhakti-rasāmṛta-sindhu* 1.2.187) Therefore, one is forbidden to regard the *guru* as an ordinary human being (*guruṣu nara-matir* . . . *nārakī saḥ*). The spiritual master, or *ācārya*, is always situated in the spiritual status of life. Birth, death, old age and disease do not affect him. According to the *Hari-bhakti-vilāsa*, therefore, after the disappearance of an *ācārya*, his body is never burnt to ashes, for it is a spiritual body. The spiritual body is always unaffected by material conditions.

TEXT 21

तस्माद् भद्रे स्वतनयान् मया व्यापादितानपि ।
मानुशोच यतः सर्वः स्वकृतं विन्दतेऽवशः ॥२१॥

tasmād bhadre sva-tanayān
mayā vyāpāditān api
mānuśoca yataḥ sarvaḥ
sva-kṛtaṁ vindate 'vaśaḥ

tasmāt—therefore; *bhadre*—my dear sister (all auspiciousness unto you); *sva-tanayān*—for your own sons; *mayā*—by me; *vyāpāditān*—unfortunately killed; *api*—although; *mā anuśoca*—do not be aggrieved; *yataḥ*—because; *sarvaḥ*—everyone; *sva-kṛtam*—the fruitive results of one's own deeds; *vindate*—suffers or enjoys; *avaśaḥ*—under the control of providence.

TRANSLATION

My dear sister Devakī, all good fortune unto you. Everyone suffers and enjoys the results of his own work under the control of providence. Therefore, although your sons have unfortunately been killed by me, please do not lament for them.

PURPORT

As stated in the *Brahma-saṁhitā* (5.54):

yas tv indra-gopam athavendram aho sva-karma-
bandhānurūpa-phala-bhājanam ātanoti

karmāṇi nirdahati kintu ca bhakti-bhājāṁ
govindam ādi-puruṣaṁ tam ahaṁ bhajāmi

Everyone, beginning from the small insect known as *indra-gopa* up to Indra, the King of the heavenly planets, is obliged to undergo the results of his fruitive activities. We may superficially see that one is suffering or enjoying because of some external causes, but the real cause is one's own fruitive activities. Even when someone kills someone else, it is to be understood that the person who was killed met the fruitive results of his own work and that the man who killed him acted as the agent of material nature. Thus Kaṁsa begged Devakī's pardon by analyzing the matter deeply. He was not the cause of the death of Devakī's sons. Rather, this was their own destiny. Under the circumstances, Devakī should excuse Kaṁsa and forget his past deeds without lamentation. Kaṁsa admitted his own fault, but whatever he had done was under the control of providence. Kaṁsa might have been the immediate cause for the death of Devakī's sons, but the remote cause was their past deeds. This was an actual fact.

TEXT 22

यावद्धतोऽस्मि हन्तास्मीत्यात्मानं मन्यतेऽस्वदृक् ।
तावत्तदभिमान्यज्ञो बाध्यबाधकतामियात् ॥२२॥

yāvad dhato 'smi hantāsmī-
ty ātmānaṁ manyate 'sva-dṛk
tāvat tad-abhimāny ajño
bādhya-bādhakatām iyāt

yāvat—as long as; *hataḥ asmi*—I am now being killed (by others); *hantā asmi*—I am the killer (of others); *iti*—thus; *ātmānam*—own self; *manyate*—he considers; *a-sva-dṛk*—one who has not seen himself (because of the darkness of the bodily conception of life); *tāvat*—for that long; *tat-abhimānī*—regarding himself as the killed or the killer; *ajñaḥ*—a foolish person; *bādhya-bādhakatām*—the worldly transaction of being obliged to execute some responsibility; *iyāt*—continues.

TRANSLATION

In the bodily conception of life, one remains in darkness, without self-realization, thinking, "I am being killed" or "I have killed my enemies." As long as a foolish person thus considers the self to be the killer or the killed, he continues to be responsible for material obligations, and consequently he suffers the reactions of happiness and distress.

PURPORT

By the grace of the Lord, Kaṁsa felt sincere regret for having unnecessarily persecuted such Vaiṣṇavas as Devakī and Vasudeva, and thus he came to the transcendental stage of knowledge. "Because I am situated on the platform of knowledge," Kaṁsa said, "understanding that I am not at all the killer of your sons, I have no responsibility for their death. As long as I thought that I would be killed by your son, I was in ignorance, but now I am free from this ignorance, which was due to a bodily conception of life." As stated in *Bhagavad-gītā* (18.17):

yasya nāhaṅkṛto bhāvo
buddhir yasya na lipyate
hatvāpi sa imāl̐ lokān
na hanti na nibadhyate

"One who is not motivated by false ego, whose intelligence is not entangled, though he kills men in this world, is not the slayer. Nor is he bound by his actions." According to this axiomatic truth, Kaṁsa pleaded that he was not responsible for having killed the sons of Devakī and Vasudeva. "Please try to excuse me for such false, external activities," he said, "and be pacified with this same knowledge."

TEXT 23

क्षमध्वं मम दौरात्म्यं साधवो दीनवत्सलाः ।
इत्युक्त्वाश्रुमुखः पादौ श्यालः स्वस्रोरथाग्रहीत् ॥२३॥

kṣamadhvaṁ mama daurātmyaṁ
sādhavo dīna-vatsalāḥ

ity uktvāśru-mukhaḥ pādau
śyālaḥ svasror athāgrahīt

kṣamadhvam—kindly excuse; *mama*—my; *daurātmyam*—atrocious activities; *sādhavaḥ*—both of you are great saintly persons; *dīna-vatsalāḥ*—and are very kind to poor, cripple-minded persons; *iti uktvā*—saying this; *aśru-mukhaḥ*—his face full of tears; *pādau*—the feet; *śyālaḥ*—his brother-in-law Kaṁsa; *svasroḥ*—of his sister and brother-in-law; *atha*—thus; *agrahīt*—captured.

TRANSLATION

Kaṁsa begged, "My dear sister and brother-in-law, please be merciful to such a poor-hearted person as me, since both of you are saintly persons. Please excuse my atrocities." Having said this, Kaṁsa fell at the feet of Vasudeva and Devakī, his eyes full of tears of regret.

PURPORT

Although Kaṁsa had spoken very nicely on the subject of real knowledge, his past deeds were abominable and atrocious, and therefore he further begged forgiveness from his sister and brother-in-law by falling at their feet and admitting that he was a most sinful person.

TEXT 24

मोचयामास निगडाद् विश्रब्धः कन्यकागिरा ।
देवकीं वसुदेवं च दर्शयन्नात्मसौहृदम् ॥२४॥

mocayām āsa nigaḍād
viśrabdhaḥ kanyakā-girā
devakīṁ vasudevaṁ ca
darśayann ātma-sauhṛdam

mocayām āsa—Kaṁsa released them; *nigaḍāt*—from their iron shackles; *viśrabdhaḥ*—with full confidence; *kanyakā-girā*—in the words of the goddess Durgā; *devakīm*—toward his sister Devakī;

vasudevam ca—and his brother-in-law Vasudeva; *darśayan*—fully exhibiting; *ātma-sauhṛdam*—his family relationship.

TRANSLATION

Fully believing in the words of the goddess Durgā, Kaṁsa exhibited his familial affection for Devakī and Vasudeva by immediately releasing them from their iron shackles.

TEXT 25

भ्रातुः समनुतप्तस्य क्षान्तरोषा च देवकी ।
व्यसृजद् वसुदेवश्च प्रहस्य तमुवाच ह ॥२५॥

bhrātuḥ samanutaptasya
kṣānta-roṣā ca devakī
vyasṛjad vasudevaś ca
prahasya tam uvāca ha

bhrātuḥ—toward her brother Kaṁsa; *samanutaptasya*—because of his being regretful; *kṣānta-roṣā*—was relieved of anger; *ca*—also; *devakī*—Kṛṣṇa's mother, Devakī; *vyasṛjat*—gave up; *vasudevaḥ ca*—Vasudeva also; *prahasya*—smiling; *tam*—unto Kaṁsa; *uvāca*—said; *ha*—in the past.

TRANSLATION

When Devakī saw her brother actually repentant while explaining ordained events, she was relieved of all anger. Similarly, Vasudeva was also free from anger. Smiling, he spoke to Kaṁsa as follows.

PURPORT

Devakī and Vasudeva, both highly elevated personalities, accepted the truth presented by Kaṁsa that everything is ordained by providence. According to the prophecy, Kaṁsa would be killed by the eighth child of Devakī. Therefore, Vasudeva and Devakī saw that behind all these incidents was a great plan devised by the Supreme Personality of Godhead.

Because the Lord had already taken birth, just like a human child, and was in the safe custody of Yaśodā, everything was happening according to plan, and there was no need to continue their ill feeling toward Kaṁsa. Thus they accepted Kaṁsa's words.

TEXT 26

एवमेतन्महाभाग यथा वदसि देहिनाम् ।
अज्ञानप्रभवाहंधीः स्वपरेति भिदा यतः ॥२६॥

evam etan mahā-bhāga
yathā vadasi dehinām
ajñāna-prabhavāhaṁ-dhīḥ
sva-pareti bhidā yataḥ

evam—yes, this is right; *etat*—what you have said; *mahā-bhāga*—O great personality; *yathā*—as; *vadasi*—you are speaking; *dehinām*—about living entities (accepting material bodies); *ajñāna-prabhavā*—by the influence of ignorance; *aham-dhīḥ*—this is my interest (false ego); *sva-parā iti*—this is another's interest; *bhidā*—differentiation; *yataḥ*—because of such a conception of life.

TRANSLATION

O great personality Kaṁsa, only by the influence of ignorance does one accept the material body and bodily ego. What you have said about this philosophy is correct. Persons in the bodily concept of life, lacking self-realization, differentiate in terms of "This is mine" and "This belongs to another."

PURPORT

Everything is done automatically by the laws of nature, which work under the direction of the Supreme Personality of Godhead. There is no question of doing anything independently, for one who has put himself in this material atmosphere is fully under the control of nature's laws. Our main business, therefore, should be to get out of this conditioned life and again become situated in spiritual existence. Only due to ignorance does a person think, "I am a demigod," "I am a human being," "I am a dog," "I am a cat," or, when the ignorance is still further advanced, "I am God." Unless one is fully self-realized, one's life of ignorance will continue.

TEXT 27

शोकहर्षभयद्वेषलोभमोहमदान्विताः ।
मिथो घ्नन्तं न पश्यन्ति भावैर्भावं पृथग्दृशः ॥२७॥

śoka-harṣa-bhaya-dveṣa-
lobha-moha-madānvitāḥ
mitho ghnantaṁ na paśyanti
bhāvair bhāvaṁ pṛthag-dṛśaḥ

śoka—lamentation; *harṣa*—jubilation; *bhaya*—fear; *dveṣa*—envy; *lobha*—greed; *moha*—illusion; *mada*—madness; *anvitāḥ*—endowed with; *mithaḥ*—one another; *ghnantam*—engaged in killing; *na paśyanti*—do not see; *bhāvaiḥ*—because of such differentiation; *bhāvam*—the situation in relation to the Supreme Lord; *pṛthak-dṛśaḥ*—persons who see everything as separate from the control of the Lord.

TRANSLATION

Persons with the vision of differentiation are imbued with the material qualities lamentation, jubilation, fear, envy, greed, illusion and madness. They are influenced by the immediate cause, which they are busy counteracting, because they have no knowledge of the remote, supreme cause, the Personality of Godhead.

PURPORT

Kṛṣṇa is the cause of all causes (*sarva-kāraṇa-kāraṇam*), but one who has no connection with Kṛṣṇa is disturbed by immediate causes and cannot restrain his vision of separation or differences. When an expert physician treats a patient, he tries to find the original cause of the disease and is not diverted by the symptoms of that original cause. Similarly, a devotee is never disturbed by reverses in life. *Tat te 'nukampāṁ susamīkṣamāṇaḥ* (*Bhāg.* 10.14.8). A devotee understands that when he is in distress, this is due to his own past misdeeds, which are now accruing reactions, although by the grace of the Supreme Personality of Godhead these are only very slight. *Karmāṇi nirdahati kintu ca bhakti-bhājām* (*Brahma-saṁhitā* 5.54). When a devotee under the protection of the Supreme Personality of Godhead is to suffer because of faults in his past deeds, he passes through only a little misery by the grace of the Lord. Although the disease of a devotee is due to mistakes committed sometime in the past, he agrees to suffer and tolerate such miseries, and he depends fully on the Supreme Personality of Godhead. Thus he is never affected by material conditions of lamentation, jubilation, fear and so on. A devotee never sees anything to be unconnected with the Supreme Personality of Godhead. Śrīla Madhvācārya, quoting from the *Bhaviṣya Purāṇa*, says:

bhagavad-darśanād yasya
virodhād darśanaṁ pṛthak
pṛthag-dṛṣṭiḥ sa vijñeyo
na tu sad-bheda-darśanaḥ

TEXT 28

श्रीशुक उवाच
कंस एवं प्रसन्नाभ्यां विशुद्धं प्रतिभाषितः ।
देवकीवसुदेवाभ्यामनुज्ञातोऽविशद् गृहम् ।।२८।।

śrī-śuka uvāca
kaṁsa evaṁ prasannābhyāṁ
viśuddhaṁ pratibhāṣitaḥ
devakī-vasudevābhyām
anujñāto 'viśad gṛham

śrī-śukaḥ uvāca—Śrī Śukadeva Gosvāmī said; *kaṁsaḥ*—King Kaṁsa; *evam*—thus; *prasannābhyām*—who were very much appeased; *viśud-dham*—in purity; *pratibhāṣitaḥ*—being answered; *devakī-vasudevā-bhyām*—by Devakī and Vasudeva; *anujñātaḥ*—taking permission; *aviśat*—entered; *gṛham*—his own palace.

TRANSLATION

Śukadeva Gosvāmī continued: Thus having been addressed in purity by Devakī and Vasudeva, who were very much appeased, Kaṁsa felt pleased, and with their permission he entered his home.

TEXT 29

तस्यां रात्र्यां व्यतीतायां कंस आहूय मन्त्रिणः ।
तेभ्य आचष्ट तत् सर्वं यदुक्तं योगनिद्रया ॥२९॥

tasyāṁ rātryāṁ vyatītāyāṁ
kaṁsa āhūya mantriṇaḥ
tebhya ācaṣṭa tat sarvaṁ
yad uktaṁ yoga-nidrayā

tasyām—that; *rātryām*—night; *vyatītāyām*—having passed; *kaṁsaḥ*—King Kaṁsa; *āhūya*—calling for; *mantriṇaḥ*—all the ministers; *tebhyaḥ*—them; *ācaṣṭa*—informed; *tat*—that; *sarvam*—all; *yat uktam*—which was spoken (that Kaṁsa's murderer was already somewhere else); *yoga-nidrayā*—by Yogamāyā, the goddess Durgā.

TRANSLATION

After that night passed, Kaṁsa summoned his ministers and informed them of all that had been spoken by Yogamāyā [who had revealed that He who was to slay Kaṁsa had already been born somewhere else].

PURPORT

The Vedic scripture *Caṇḍī* describes *māyā,* the energy of the Supreme Lord, as *nidrā: durgā devī sarva-bhūteṣu nidrā-rūpeṇa samāsthitaḥ.* The energy of Yogamāyā and Mahāmāyā keeps the living entities sleeping in this material world in the great darkness of ignorance. Yogamāyā, the goddess Durgā, kept Kaṁsa in darkness about Kṛṣṇa's birth and misled him to believe that his enemy Kṛṣṇa had been born elsewhere. Kṛṣṇa was born the son of Devakī, but according to the Lord's original plan, as prophesied to Brahmā, He went to Vṛndāvana to give pleasure to mother Yaśodā and Nanda Mahārāja and other intimate friends and devotees for eleven years. Then He would return to kill Kaṁsa. Because Kaṁsa did not know this, he believed Yogamāyā's statement that Kṛṣṇa was born elsewhere, not of Devakī.

TEXT 30

आकर्ण्य भर्तुर्गदितं तमूचुर्देवशत्रवः ।
देवान् प्रति कृतामर्षा दैतेया नातिकोविदाः ॥३०॥

ākarṇya bhartur gaditaṁ
tam ūcur deva-śatravaḥ
devān prati kṛtāmarṣā
daiteyā nāti-kovidāḥ

ākarṇya—after hearing; *bhartuḥ*—of their master; *gaditam*—the words or statement; *tam ūcuḥ*—replied to him; *deva-śatravaḥ*—all the *asuras*, who were enemies of the demigods; *devān*—the demigods; *prati*—toward; *kṛta-amarṣāḥ*—who were envious; *daiteyāḥ*—the *asuras; na*—not; *ati-kovidāḥ*—who were very expert in executing transactions.

TRANSLATION

After hearing their master's statement, the envious asuras, who were enemies of the demigods and were not very expert in their dealings, advised Kaṁsa as follows.

PURPORT

There are two different types of men—the *asuras* and the *suras.*

dvau bhūta-sargau loke 'smin
daiva āsura eva ca
viṣṇu-bhakta smṛto daiva
āsuras tad-viparyayaḥ
(*Padma Purāṇa*)

Those who are devotees of Lord Viṣṇu, Kṛṣṇa, are *suras*, or *devas*, whereas those who are opposed to the devotees are called *asuras*. Devotees are expert in all transactions (*yasyāsti bhaktir bhagavaty akiñcanā sarvair guṇais tatra samāsate surāḥ*). Therefore they are called *kovida*, which means "expert." *Asuras*, however, although superficially showing expertise in passionate activities, are actually all fools. They are neither sober nor expert. Whatever they do is imperfect. *Moghāśā mogha-karmāṇaḥ*. According to this description of the *asuras* given in *Bhagavad-gītā* (9.12), whatever they do will ultimately be baffled. It was such persons who advised Kaṁsa because they were his chief friends and ministers.

TEXT 31

एवं चेत्तर्हि भोजेन्द्र पुरग्रामव्रजादिषु ।
अनिर्दशान् निर्दशांश्च हनिष्यामोऽद्य वै शिशून् ॥३१॥

evaṁ cet tarhi bhojendra
pura-grāma-vrajādiṣu
anirdaśān nirdaśāṁś ca
haniṣyāmo 'dya vai śiśūn

evam—thus; *cet*—if it is so; *tarhi*—then; *bhoja-indra*—O King of Bhoja; *pura-grāma-vraja-ādiṣu*—in all the towns, villages and pasturing grounds; *anirdaśān*—those who are less than ten days old; *nirdaśān ca*—and those who are just over ten days old; *haniṣyāmaḥ*—we shall kill; *adya*—beginning from today; *vai*—indeed; *śiśūn*—all such children.

TRANSLATION

If this is so, O King of the Bhoja dynasty, beginning today we shall kill all the children born in all the villages, towns and pasturing grounds within the past ten days or slightly more.

TEXT 32

किमुद्यमैः करिष्यन्ति देवाः समरभीरवः ।
नित्यमुद्विग्नमनसो ज्याघोषैर्धनुषस्तव ॥३२॥

kim udyamaiḥ kariṣyanti
devāḥ samara-bhīravaḥ
nityam udvigna-manaso
jyā-ghoṣair dhanuṣas tava

kim—what; *udyamaiḥ*—by their endeavors; *kariṣyanti*—will do; *devāḥ*—all the demigods; *samara-bhīravaḥ*—who are afraid of fighting; *nityam*—always; *udvigna-manasaḥ*—with agitated minds; *jyā-ghoṣaiḥ*—by the sound of the string; *dhanuṣaḥ*—of the bow; *tava*—your.

TRANSLATION

The demigods always fear the sound of your bowstring. They are constantly in anxiety, afraid of fighting. Therefore, what can they do by their endeavors to harm you?

TEXT 33

अस्यतस्ते शरव्रातैर्हन्यमानाः समन्ततः ।
जिजीविषव उत्सृज्य पलायनपरा ययुः ॥३३॥

asyatas te śara-vrātair
hanyamānāḥ samantataḥ
jijīviṣava utsṛjya
palāyana-parā yayuḥ

asyataḥ—pierced by your discharged arrows; *te*—your; *śara-vrātaiḥ*—by the multitude of arrows; *hanyamānāḥ*—being killed; *samantataḥ*—here and there; *jijīviṣavaḥ*—aspiring to live; *utsṛjya*—giving up the battlefield; *palāyana-parāḥ*—intent on escaping; *yayuḥ*—they fled (the fighting).

TRANSLATION

While being pierced by your arrows, which you discharged on all sides, some of them, who were injured by the multitude of arrows but who desired to live, fled the battlefield, intent on escaping.

TEXT 34

केचित् प्राञ्जलयो दीना न्यस्तशस्त्रा दिवौकसः ।
मुक्तकच्छशिखाः केचिद् भीताः स्म इति वादिनः ॥३४॥

kecit prāñjalayo dīnā
nyasta-śastrā divaukasaḥ
mukta-kaccha-śikhāḥ kecid
bhītāḥ sma iti vādinaḥ

kecit—some of them; *prāñjalayaḥ*—folded their hands just to please you; *dīnāḥ*—very poor; *nyasta-śastrāḥ*—being bereft of all weapons; *divaukasaḥ*—the demigods; *mukta-kaccha-śikhāḥ*—their garments and hair loosened and scattered; *kecit*—some of them; *bhītāḥ*—we are very much afraid; *sma*—so became; *iti vādinaḥ*—they spoke thus.

TRANSLATION

Defeated and bereft of all weapons, some of the demigods gave up fighting and praised you with folded hands, and some of them, appearing before you with loosened garments and hair, said, "O lord, we are very much afraid of you."

TEXT 35

न त्वं विस्मृतशस्त्रास्त्रान् विरथान् भयसंवृतान् ।
हंस्यन्यासक्तविमुखान् भग्नचापानयुध्यतः ॥३५॥

na tvaṁ vismṛta-śastrāstrān
virathān bhaya-saṁvṛtān
haṁsy anyāsakta-vimukhān
bhagna-cāpān ayudhyataḥ

na—not; *tvam*—Your Majesty; *vismṛta-śastra-astrān*—those who have forgotten how to use weapons; *virathān*—without chariots; *bhaya-saṁvṛtān*—bewildered by fear; *haṁsi*—does kill; *anya-āsakta-vimukhān*—persons attached not to fighting but to some other subject matter;

bhagna-cāpān—their bows broken; *ayudhyataḥ*—and thus not fighting.

TRANSLATION

When the demigods are bereft of their chariots, when they forget how to use weapons, when they are fearful or attached to something other than fighting, or when their bows are broken and they have thus lost the ability to fight, Your Majesty does not kill them.

PURPORT

There are principles that govern even fighting. If an enemy has no chariot, is unmindful of the fighting art because of fear, or is unwilling to fight, he is not to be killed. Kaṁsa's ministers reminded Kaṁsa that despite his power, he was cognizant of the principles of fighting, and therefore he had excused the demigods because of their incapability. "But the present emergency," the ministers said, "is not intended for such mercy or military etiquette. Now you should prepare to fight under any circumstances." Thus they advised Kaṁsa to give up the traditional etiquette in fighting and chastise the enemy at any cost.

TEXT 36

किं क्षेमशूरैर्विबुधैरसंयुगविकत्थनैः ।
रहोजुषा किं हरिणा शम्भुना वा वनौकसा ।
किमिन्द्रेणाल्पवीर्येण ब्रह्मणा वा तपस्यता ॥३६॥

kiṁ kṣema-śūrair vibudhair
asaṁyuga-vikatthanaiḥ
raho-juṣā kiṁ hariṇā
śambhunā vā vanaukasā
kim indreṇālpa-vīryeṇa
brahmaṇā vā tapasyatā

kim—what is there to fear; *kṣema*—in a place where there is a scarcity of the ability to fight; *śūraiḥ*—by the demigods; *vibudhaiḥ*—by such powerful persons; *asaṁyuga-vikatthanaiḥ*—by boasting and talking uselessly, away from the fighting; *rahaḥ-juṣā*—who is living in a solitary place within the core of the heart; *kim hariṇā*—what is the fear from Lord Viṣṇu; *śambhunā*—(and what is the fear) from Lord Śiva; *vā*—either; *vana-okasā*—who is living in the forest; *kim indreṇa*—what is the fear from Indra; *alpa-vīryeṇa*—he is not at all powerful (having no power to fight with you); *brahmaṇā*—and what is the fear from Brahmā; *vā*—either; *tapasyatā*—who is always engaged in meditation.

TRANSLATION

The demigods boast uselessly while away from the battlefield. Only where there is no fighting can they show their prowess. Therefore, from such demigods we have nothing to fear. As for Lord Viṣṇu, He is in seclusion in the core of the hearts of the yogīs. As for Lord Śiva, he has gone to the forest. And as for Lord Brahmā, he is always engaged in austerities and meditation. The other demigods, headed by Indra, are devoid of prowess. Therefore you have nothing to fear.

PURPORT

Kaṁsa's ministers told Kaṁsa that all the exalted demigods had fled in fear of him. One had gone to the forest, one to the core of the heart, and one to engage in *tapasya.* "Thus you can be free from all fear of the demigods," they said. "Just prepare to fight."

TEXT 37

तथापि देवाः सापत्न्यान्नोपेक्ष्या इति मन्महे ।
ततस्तन्मूलखनने नियुङ्क्ष्वास्माननुव्रतान् ॥३७॥

tathāpi devāḥ sāpatnyān
nopekṣyā iti manmahe
tatas tan-mūla-khanane
niyuṅkṣvāsmān anuvratān

tathā api—still; *devāḥ*—the demigods; *sāpatnyāt*—due to enmity; *na upekṣyāḥ*—should not be neglected; *iti manmahe*—this is our opinion; *tataḥ*—therefore; *tat-mūla-khanane*—to uproot them completely;

niyuṅksva—engage; *asmān*—us; *anuvratān*—who are ready to follow you.

TRANSLATION

Nonetheless, because of their enmity, our opinion is that the demigods should not be neglected. Therefore, to uproot them completely, engage us in fighting with them, for we are ready to follow you.

PURPORT

According to moral instructions, one should not neglect to extinguish fire completely, treat diseases completely, and clear debts completely. Otherwise they will increase and later be difficult to stop. Therefore the minsters advised Kaṁsa to uproot his enemies completely.

TEXT 38

यथामयोऽङ्गे समुपेक्षितो नृभि-
र्न शक्यते रूढपदश्चिकित्सितुम् ।
यथेन्द्रियग्राम उपेक्षितस्तथा
रिपुर्महान् बद्धबलो न चाल्यते ॥३८॥

yathāmayo 'ṅge samupekṣito nṛbhir
na śakyate rūḍha-padaś cikitsitum
yathendriya-grāma upekṣitas tathā
ripur mahān baddha-balo na cālyate

yathā—as; *āmayaḥ*—a disease; *aṅge*—in the body; *samupekṣitaḥ*—being neglected; *nṛbhiḥ*—by men; *na*—not; *śakyate*—is able; *rūḍha-padaḥ*—when it is acute; *cikitsitum*—to be treated; *yathā*—and as; *indriya-grāmaḥ*—the senses; *upekṣitaḥ*—not controlled in the beginning; *tathā*—similarly; *ripuḥ mahān*—a great enemy; *baddha-balaḥ*—if he becomes strong; *na*—not; *cālyate*—can be controlled.

TRANSLATION

As a disease, if initially neglected, becomes acute and impossible to cure, or as the senses, if not controlled at first, are impossible to

control later, an enemy, if neglected in the beginning, later becomes insurmountable.

TEXT 39

मूलं हि विष्णुर्देवानां यत्र धर्मः सनातनः ।
तस्य च ब्रह्म गोविप्रास्तपो यज्ञाः सदक्षिणाः ॥३९॥

mūlaṁ hi viṣṇur devānāṁ
yatra dharmaḥ sanātanaḥ
tasya ca brahma-go-viprās
tapo yajñāḥ sa-dakṣiṇāḥ

mūlam—the foundation; *hi*—indeed; *viṣṇuḥ*—is Lord Viṣṇu; *devānām*—of the demigods; *yatra*—wherein; *dharmaḥ*—religious principles; *sanātanaḥ*—traditional or eternal; *tasya*—of this (foundation); *ca*—also; *brahma*—brahminical civilization; *go*—cow protection; *viprāḥ*—*brāhmaṇas; tapaḥ*—austerity; *yajñāḥ*—performing sacrifices; *sa-dakṣiṇāḥ*—with proper remuneration.

TRANSLATION

The foundation of all the demigods is Lord Viṣṇu, who lives and is worshiped wherever there are religious principles, traditional culture, the Vedas, cows, brāhmaṇas, austerities, and sacrifices with proper remuneration.

PURPORT

Here is a description of *sanātana-dharma*, eternal religious principles, which must include brahminical culture, *brāhmaṇas*, sacrifices and religion. These principles establish the kingdom of Viṣṇu. Without the kingdom of Viṣṇu, the kingdom of God, no one can be happy. *Na te viduḥ svārtha-gatiṁ hi viṣṇum:* in this demoniac civilization, people unfortunately do not understand that the self-interest of human society lies in Viṣṇu. *Durāśayā ye bahir-artha-māninaḥ:* thus they are involved in a hopeless hope. People want to be happy without God consciousness, or Kṛṣṇa consciousness, because they are led by blind leaders who lead human society to chaos. The asuric adherents of Kaṁsa wanted to disrupt the traditional condition of human happiness and thus defeat the *devatās*, the devotees and demigods. Unless the devotees and demigods predominate, the *asuras* will increase, and human society will be in a chaotic condition.

TEXT 40

तस्मात् सर्वात्मना राजन् ब्राह्मणान् ब्रह्मवादिनः।
तपस्विनो यज्ञशीलान् गाश्च हन्मो हविर्दुघाः ॥४०॥

tasmāt sarvātmanā rājan
brāhmaṇān brahma-vādinaḥ
tapasvino yajña-śīlān
gāś ca hanmo havir-dughāḥ

tasmāt—therefore; *sarva-ātmanā*—in every respect; *rājan*—O King; *brāhmaṇān*—the *brāhmaṇas; brahma-vādinaḥ*—who maintain the brahminical culture, centered around Viṣṇu; *tapasvinaḥ*—persons who are engaged in austerities; *yajña-śīlān*—persons engaged in offering sacrifices; *gāḥ ca*—cows and persons engaged in protecting cows; *hanmaḥ*—we shall kill; *haviḥ-dughāḥ*—because they supply milk, from which clarified butter is obtained for the offering of sacrifice.

TRANSLATION

O King, we, who are your adherents in all respects, shall therefore kill the Vedic brāhmaṇas, the persons engaged in offering sacrifices and austerities, and the cows that supply milk, from which clarified butter is obtained for the ingredients of sacrifice.

TEXT 41

विप्रा गावश्च वेदाश्च तपः सत्यं दमः शमः ।
श्रद्धा दया तितिक्षा च क्रतवश्च हरेस्तनूः ॥४१॥

viprā gāvaś ca vedāś ca
tapaḥ satyaṁ damaḥ śamaḥ

śraddhā dayā titikṣā ca
kratavaś ca hares tanūḥ

viprāḥ—the *brāhmaṇas; gāvaḥ ca*—and the cows; *vedāḥ ca*—and the Vedic knowledge; *tapaḥ*—austerity; *satyam*—truthfulness; *damaḥ*—control of the senses; *śamaḥ*—control of the mind; *śraddhā*—faith; *dayā*—mercy; *titikṣā*—tolerance; *ca*—also; *kratavaḥ ca*—as well as sacrifices; *hareḥ tanūḥ*—are the different parts of the body of Lord Viṣṇu.

TRANSLATION

The brāhmaṇas, the cows, Vedic knowledge, austerity, truthfulness, control of the mind and senses, faith, mercy, tolerance and sacrifice are the different parts of the body of Lord Viṣṇu, and they are the paraphernalia for a godly civilization.

PURPORT

When we offer our obeisances to the Personality of Godhead, we say:

namo brahmaṇya-devāya
go-brāhmaṇa-hitāya ca
jagad-dhitāya kṛṣṇāya
govindāya namo namaḥ

When Kṛṣṇa comes to establish real perfection in the social order, He personally gives protection to the cows and the *brāhmaṇas* (*go-brāhmaṇa-hitāya ca*). This is His first interest because without protection of the *brāhmaṇas* and the cows, there can be no human civilization and no question of happy, peaceful life. *Asuras*, therefore, are always interested in killing the *brāhmaṇas* and cows. Especially in this age, Kali-yuga, cows are being killed all over the world, and as soon as there is a movement to establish brahminical civilization, people in general rebel. Thus they regard the Kṛṣṇa consciousness movement as a form of "brainwashing." How can such envious persons be happy in their godless civilization? The Supreme Personality of Godhead punishes them by keeping them in darkness, birth after birth, and pushing them lower and lower into wretched conditions of hellish life. The Kṛṣṇa consciousness movement has started a brahminical civilization, but especially when it is introduced in the Western countries, the *asuras* try to impede it in many ways. Nonetheless, we must push forward this movement tolerantly for the benefit of human society.

TEXT 42

स हि सर्वसुराध्यक्षो ह्यसुरद्विड् गुहाशयः ।
तन्मूला देवताः सर्वाः सेश्वराः सचतुर्मुखाः ।
अयं वै तद्वधोपायो यदृषीणां विहिंसनम् ॥४२॥

sa hi sarva-surādhyakṣo
hy asura-dviḍ guhā-śayaḥ
tan-mūlā devatāḥ sarvāḥ
seśvarāḥ sa-catur-mukhāḥ
ayaṁ vai tad-vadhopāyo
yad ṛṣīṇāṁ vihiṁsanam

saḥ—He (Lord Viṣṇu); *hi*—indeed; *sarva-sura-adhyakṣaḥ*—the leader of all the demigods; *hi*—indeed; *asura-dviṭ*—the enemy of the *asuras; guhā-śayaḥ*—He is the Supersoul within the core of everyone's heart; *tat-mūlāḥ*—taking shelter at His lotus feet; *devatāḥ*—the demigods exist; *sarvāḥ*—all of them; *sa-īśvarāḥ*—including Lord Śiva; *sa-catuḥ-mukhāḥ*—as well as Lord Brahmā, who has four faces; *ayam*—this is; *vai*—indeed; *tat-vadha-upāyaḥ*—the only means of killing Him (Viṣṇu); *yat*—which; *ṛṣīṇām*—of great sages, saintly persons, or Vaiṣṇavas; *vihiṁsanam*—suppression with all kinds of persecution.

TRANSLATION

Lord Viṣṇu, the Supersoul within the core of everyone's heart, is the ultimate enemy of the asuras and is therefore known as asura-dviṭ. He is the leader of all the demigods because all the demigods, including Lord Śiva and Lord Brahmā, exist under His protection. The great saintly persons, sages and Vaiṣṇavas also depend upon Him. To persecute the Vaiṣṇavas, therefore, is the only way to kill Viṣṇu.

PURPORT

The demigods and the Vaiṣṇavas especially are part and parcel of the Supreme Lord, Viṣṇu, because they are always obedient to His orders (*oṁ tad viṣṇoḥ paramaṁ padaṁ sadā paśyanti sūrayaḥ*). The demoniac followers of Kaṁsa thought that if the Vaiṣṇavas, saintly persons and sages were persecuted, the original body of Viṣṇu would naturally be destroyed. Thus they decided to suppress Vaiṣṇavism. The *asuras* perpetually struggle to persecute the Vaiṣṇavas because they do not want Vaiṣṇavism to spread. Vaiṣṇavas preach only devotional service, not encouraging *karmīs, jñānīs* and *yogīs*, because if one must liberate oneself from material, conditional life, one must ultimately become a Vaiṣṇava. Our Kṛṣṇa consciousness movement is directed with this understanding, and therefore the *asuras* always try to suppress it.

TEXT 43

श्रीशुक उवाच

एवं दुर्मन्त्रिभिः कंसः सह सम्मन्त्र्य दुर्मतिः ।
ब्रह्महिंसां हितं मेने कालपाशावृतोऽसुरः ॥४३॥

śrī-śuka uvāca
evaṁ durmantribhiḥ kaṁsaḥ
saha sammantrya durmatiḥ
brahma-hiṁsāṁ hitaṁ mene
kāla-pāśāvṛto 'suraḥ

śrī-śukaḥ uvāca—Śrī Śukadeva Gosvāmī said; *evam*—in this way; *durmantribhiḥ*—his bad ministers; *kaṁsaḥ*—King Kaṁsa; *saha*—along with; *sammantrya*—after considering very elaborately; *durmatiḥ*—without good intelligence; *brahma-hiṁsām*—persecution of the *brāhmaṇas; hitam*—as the best way; *mene*—accepted; *kāla-pāśa-āvṛtaḥ*—being bound by the rules and regulations of Yamarāja; *asuraḥ*—because he was a demon.

TRANSLATION

Śukadeva Gosvāmī continued: Thus, having considered the instructions of his bad ministers, Kaṁsa, who was bound by the laws

of Yamarāja and devoid of good intelligence because he was a demon, decided to persecute the saintly persons, the brāhmaṇas, as the only way to achieve his own good fortune.

PURPORT

Śrīla Locana dāsa Ṭhākura has sung, *āpana karama, bhuñjāye śamana, kahaye locana dāsa.* Instead of taking good instructions from the sages and the *śāstras*, godless nondevotees act whimsically, according to their own plans. Actually, however, no one has his own plans because everyone is bound by the laws of nature and must act according to his tendency in material, conditional life. Therefore one must change one's own decision and follow the decision of Kṛṣṇa and Kṛṣṇa's devotees. Then one is rescued from punishment by Yamarāja. Kaṁsa was not uneducated. It appears from his talks with Vasudeva and Devakī that he knew all about the laws of nature. But because of his association with bad ministers, he could not make a clear decision about his welfare. Therefore the *Caitanya-caritāmṛta* (*Madhya* 22.54) says:

'sādhu-saṅga,' 'sādhu-saṅga'——sarva-śāstre kaya
lava-mātra sādhu-saṅge sarva-siddhi haya

If one desires his real welfare, he must associate with devotees and saintly persons and in this way rectify the material condition of his life.

TEXT 44

सन्दिश्य साधुलोकस्य कदने कदनप्रियान् ।
कामरूपधरान् दिक्षु दानवान् गृहमाविशत् ॥४४॥

sandiśya sādhu-lokasya
kadane kadana-priyān
kāma-rūpa-dharān dikṣu
dānavān gṛham āviśat

sandiśya—after giving permission; *sādhu-lokasya*—of the saintly persons; *kadane*—in persecution; *kadana-priyān*—to the demons, who were very expert at persecuting others; *kāma-rūpa-dharān*—who could assume any form, according to their own desire; *dikṣu*—in all directions; *dānavān*—to the demons; *gṛham āviśat*—Kaṁsa entered his own palace.

TRANSLATION

These demons, the followers of Kaṁsa, were expert at persecuting others, especially the Vaiṣṇavas, and could assume any form they desired. After giving these demons permission to go everywhere and persecute the saintly persons, Kaṁsa entered his palace.

TEXT 45

ते वै रजःप्रकृतयस्तमसा मूढचेतसः ।
सतां विद्वेषमाचेरुरारादागतमृत्यवः ॥४५॥

te vai rajaḥ-prakṛtayas
tamasā mūḍha-cetasaḥ
satāṁ vidveṣam ācerur
ārād āgata-mṛtyavaḥ

te—all the asuric ministers; *vai*—indeed; *rajaḥ-prakṛtayaḥ*—surcharged with the mode of passion; *tamasā*—overwhelmed by the mode of ignorance; *mūḍha-cetasaḥ*—foolish persons; *satām*—of saintly persons; *vidveṣam*—persecution; *āceruḥ*—executed; *ārāt āgata-mṛtyavaḥ*—impending death having already overtaken them.

TRANSLATION

Surcharged with passion and ignorance and not knowing what was good or bad for them, the asuras, for whom impending death was waiting, began the persecution of the saintly persons.

PURPORT

As stated in *Bhagavad-gītā* (2.13):

dehino 'smin yathā dehe
kaumāraṁ yauvanaṁ jarā

tathā dehāntara-prāptir
dhīras tatra na muhyati

"As the embodied soul continually passes, in this body, from boyhood to youth to old age, the soul similarly passes into another body at death. The self-realized soul is not bewildered by such a change." Irresponsible persons, surcharged with passion and ignorance, foolishly do things that are not to be done (*nūnaṁ pramattaḥ kurute vikarma*). But one should know the results of irresponsible actions, as explained in the next verse.

TEXT 46

आयुः श्रियं यशो धर्मं लोकानाशिष एव च ।
हन्ति श्रेयांसि सर्वाणि पुंसो महदतिक्रमः ॥४६॥

āyuḥ śriyaṁ yaśo dharmaṁ
lokān āśiṣa eva ca
hanti śreyāṁsi sarvāṇi
puṁso mahad-atikramaḥ

āyuḥ—the duration of life; *śriyam*—beauty; *yaśaḥ*—fame; *dharmam*—religion; *lokān*—elevation to higher planets; *āśiṣaḥ*—blessings; *eva*—indeed; *ca*—also; *hanti*—destroys; *śreyāṁsi*—benedictions; *sarvāṇi*—all; *puṁsaḥ*—of a person; *mahat-atikramaḥ*—trespassing against great personalities.

TRANSLATION

My dear King, when a man persecutes great souls, all his benedictions of longevity, beauty, fame, religion, blessings and promotion to higher planets will be destroyed.

Thus end the Bhaktivedanta purports of the Tenth Canto, Fourth Chapter, of the Śrīmad-Bhāgavatam, *entitled "The Atrocities of King Kaṁsa."*

CHAPTER FIVE

The Meeting of Nanda Mahārāja and Vasudeva

As described in this chapter, Nanda Mahārāja very gorgeously performed the birth ceremony for his newborn child. Then he went to Kaṁsa to pay taxes due and met his intimate friend Vasudeva.

There was great jubilation all over Vṛndāvana due to Kṛṣṇa's birth. Everyone was overwhelmed with joy. Therefore the King of Vraja, Mahārāja Nanda, wanted to perform the birth ceremony for his child, and this he did. During this great festival, Nanda Mahārāja gave in charity to all present whatever they desired. After the festival, Nanda Mahārāja put the cowherd men in charge of protecting Gokula, and then he went to Mathurā to pay official taxes to Kaṁsa. In Mathurā, Nanda Mahārāja met Vasudeva. Nanda Mahārāja and Vasudeva were brothers, and Vasudeva praised Nanda Mahārāja's good fortune because he knew that Kṛṣṇa had accepted Nanda Mahārāja as His father. When Vasudeva inquired from Nanda Mahārāja about the welfare of the child, Nanda Mahārāja informed him all about Vṛndāvana, and Vasudeva was very much satisfied by this, although he expressed his grief because Devakī's many children had been killed by Kaṁsa. Nanda Mahārāja consoled Vasudeva by saying that everything happens according to destiny and that one who knows this is not aggrieved. Expecting many disturbances in Gokula, Vasudeva then advised Nanda Mahārāja not to wait in Mathurā, but to return to Vṛndāvana as soon as possible. Thus Nanda Mahārāja took leave of Vasudeva and returned to Vṛndāvana with the other cowherd men on their bullock carts.

TEXTS 1–2

श्रीशुक उवाच

नन्दस्त्वात्मज उत्पन्ने जाताह्लादो महामनाः ।
आहूय विप्रान् वेदज्ञान् स्नातः शुचिरलङ्कृतः ॥ १ ॥

वाचयित्वा स्वस्त्ययनं जातकर्मात्मजस्य वै ।
कारयामास विधिवत् पितृदेवार्चनं तथा ॥ २ ॥

śrī-śuka uvāca
nandas tv ātmaja utpanne
jātāhlādo mahā-manāḥ
āhūya viprān veda-jñān
snātaḥ śucir alaṅkṛtaḥ

vācayitvā svastyayanaṁ
jāta-karmātmajasya vai
kārayām āsa vidhivat
pitṛ-devārcanaṁ tathā

śrī-śukaḥ uvāca—Śrī Śukadeva Gosvāmī said; *nandaḥ*—Mahārāja Nanda; *tu*—indeed; *ātmaje*—his son; *utpanne*—having been born; *jāta*—overwhelmed; *āhlādaḥ*—in great jubilation; *mahā-manāḥ*—who was great minded; *āhūya*—invited; *viprān*—the *brāhmaṇas; veda-jñān*—who were fully conversant in Vedic knowledge; *snātaḥ*—taking a full bath; *śuciḥ*—purifying himself; *alaṅkṛtaḥ*—being dressed very nicely with ornaments and fresh garments; *vācayitvā*—after causing to be recited; *svasti-ayanam*—Vedic *mantras* (by the *brāhmaṇas*); *jāta-karma*—the festival for the birth of the child; *ātmajasya*—of his own son; *vai*—indeed; *kārayām āsa*—caused to be performed; *vidhi-vat*—according to the Vedic regulations; *pitṛ-deva-arcanam*—the worship of the forefathers and the demigods; *tathā*—as well as.

TRANSLATION

Śukadeva Gosvāmī said: Nanda Mahārāja was naturally very magnanimous, and when Lord Śrī Kṛṣṇa appeared as his son, he was overwhelmed by jubilation. Therefore, after bathing and purifying himself and dressing himself properly, he invited brāhmaṇas who knew how to recite Vedic mantras. After having these qualified brāhmaṇas recite auspicious Vedic hymns, he arranged to have the Vedic birth ceremony celebrated for his newborn child according to the rules and regulations, and he also arranged for worship of the demigods and forefathers.

PURPORT

Śrīla Viśvanātha Cakravartī Ṭhākura has discussed the significance of the words *nandas tu.* The word *tu,* he says, is not used to fulfill the sentence, because without *tu* the sentence is complete. Therefore the word *tu* is used for a different purpose. Although Kṛṣṇa appeared as the son of Devakī, Devakī and Vasudeva did not enjoy the *jāta-karma,* the festival of the birth ceremony. Instead, this ceremony was enjoyed by Nanda Mahārāja, as stated here (*nandas tv ātmaja utpanne jātāhlādo mahā-manāḥ*). When Nanda Mahārāja met Vasudeva, Vasudeva could not disclose, "Your son Kṛṣṇa is actually my son. You are His father in a different way, spiritually." Because of fear of Kaṁsa, Vasudeva could not observe the festival for Kṛṣṇa's birth. Nanda Mahārāja, however, took full advantage of this opportunity.

The *jāta-karma* ceremony can take place when the umbilical cord, connecting the child and the placenta, is cut. However, since Kṛṣṇa was brought by Vasudeva to the house of Nanda Mahārāja, where was the chance for this to happen? In this regard, Viśvanātha Cakravartī Ṭhākura desires to prove with evidence from many *śāstras* that Kṛṣṇa actually took birth as the son of Yaśodā before the birth of Yogamāyā, who is therefore described as the Lord's younger sister. Even though there may be doubts about the cutting of the umbilical cord, and even though it is possible that this was not done, when the Supreme Personality of Godhead appears, such events are regarded as factual. Kṛṣṇa appeared as Varāhadeva from the nostril of Brahmā, and therefore Brahmā is described as the father of Varāhadeva. Also significant are the words *kārayām āsa vidhivat.* Being overwhelmed with jubilation over the birth of his son, Nanda Mahārāja did not see whether the cord was cut or not. Thus he performed the ceremony very gorgeously. According to the opinion of some authorities, Kṛṣṇa was actually born as the son of Yaśodā. In any case, without regard for material understandings, we can accept that Nanda Mahārāja's celebration for the ceremony of Kṛṣṇa's birth was proper. This ceremony is therefore well known everywhere as Nandotsava.

TEXT 3

धेनूनां नियुते प्रादाद् विप्रेभ्यः समलङ्कृते ।
तिलाद्रीन् सप्त रत्नौघशातकौम्भाम्बरावृतान् ॥ ३ ॥

dhenūnāṁ niyute prādād
viprebhyaḥ samalaṅkṛte
tilādrīn sapta ratnaugha-
śātakaumbhāmbarāvṛtān

dhenūnām—of milk-giving cows; *niyute*—two million; *prādāt*—gave in charity; *viprebhyaḥ*—unto the *brāhmaṇas; samalaṅkṛte*—completely decorated; *tila-adrīn*—hills of grain; *sapta*—seven; *ratna-ogha-śāta-kaumbha-ambara-āvṛtān*—covered with jewels and cloth embroidered with gold.

TRANSLATION

Nanda Mahārāja gave two million cows, completely decorated with cloth and jewels, in charity to the brāhmaṇas. He also gave them seven hills of grain, covered with jewels and with cloth decorated with golden embroidery.

TEXT 4

कालेन स्नानशौचाभ्यां संस्कारैस्तपसेज्यया ।
शुध्यन्ति दानैःसन्तुष्टया द्रव्याण्यात्मात्मविद्यया ॥ ४ ॥

kālena snāna-śaucābhyāṁ
saṁskārais tapasejyayā
śudhyanti dānaiḥ santuṣṭyā
dravyāṇy ātmātma-vidyayā

kālena—by due course of time (the land and other material things become purified); *snāna-śaucābhyām*—by bathing (the body becomes purified) and by cleansing (unclean things become purified); *saṁskāraiḥ*—by purificatory processes (birth becomes purified); *tapasā*—by austerity (the senses become purified); *ijyayā*—by worship (the *brāhmaṇas* become purified); *śudhyanti*—become purified; *dānaiḥ*—by charity (wealth becomes purified); *santuṣṭyā*—by satisfaction (the mind becomes purified); *dravyāṇi*—all material possessions, such as cows, land and gold; *ātmā*—the soul (becomes purified); *ātma-vidyayā*—by self-realization.

TRANSLATION

O King, by the passing of time, land and other material possessions are purified; by bathing, the body is purified; and by being cleansed, unclean things are purified. By purificatory ceremonies, birth is purified; by austerity, the senses are purified; and by worship and charity offered to the brāhmaṇas, material possessions are purified. By satisfaction, the mind is purified; and by self-realization, or Kṛṣṇa consciousness, the soul is purified.

PURPORT

These are śāstric injunctions concerning how one can purify everything according to Vedic civilization. Unless purified, anything we use will infect us with contamination. In India five thousand years ago, even in the villages such as that of Nanda Mahārāja, people knew how to purify things, and thus they enjoyed even material life without contamination.

TEXT 5

सौमङ्गल्यगिरो विप्राः सूतमागधवन्दिनः ।
गायकाश्च जगुर्नेदुर्भेर्यो दुन्दुभयो मुहुः ॥ ५ ॥

saumaṅgalya-giro viprāḥ
sūta-māgadha-vandinaḥ
gāyakāś ca jagur nedur
bheryo dundubhayo muhuḥ

saumaṅgalya-giraḥ—whose chanting of *mantras* and hymns purified the environment by their vibration; *viprāḥ*—the *brāhmaṇas; sūta*—experts in reciting all the histories; *māgadha*—experts in reciting the histories of special royal families; *vandinaḥ*—general professional reciters; *gāyakāḥ*—singers; *ca*—as well as; *jaguḥ*—chanted; *neduḥ*—vibrated; *bheryaḥ*—a kind of musical instrument; *dundubhayaḥ*—a kind of musical instrument; *muhuḥ*—constantly.

TRANSLATION

The brāhmaṇas recited auspicious Vedic hymns, which purified the environment by their vibration. The experts in reciting old

histories like the Purāṇas, the experts in reciting the histories of royal families, and general reciters all chanted, while singers sang and many kinds of musical instruments, like bherīs and dundubhis, played in accompaniment.

TEXT 6

व्रजः सम्मृष्टसंसिक्तद्वाराजिरगृहान्तरः ।
चित्रध्वजपताकास्रक्चैलपल्लवतोरणैः ॥ ६ ॥

vrajaḥ sammṛṣṭa-saṁsikta-
dvārājira-gṛhāntaraḥ
citra-dhvaja-patākā-srak-
caila-pallava-toraṇaiḥ

vrajaḥ—the land occupied by Nanda Mahārāja; *sammṛṣṭa*—very nicely cleaned; *saṁsikta*—very nicely washed; *dvāra*—all the doors or entrances; *ajira*—courtyards; *gṛha-antaraḥ*—everything within the house; *citra*—variegated; *dhvaja*—of festoons; *patākā*—of flags; *srak*—of flower garlands; *caila*—of pieces of cloth; *pallava*—of the leaves of mango trees; *toraṇaiḥ*—(decorated) by gates in different places.

TRANSLATION

Vrajapura, the residence of Nanda Mahārāja, was fully decorated with varieties of festoons and flags, and in different places, gates were made with varieties of flower garlands, pieces of cloth, and mango leaves. The courtyards, the gates near the roads, and everything within the rooms of the houses were perfectly swept and washed with water.

TEXT 7

गावो वृषा वत्सतरा हरिद्रातैलरूषिताः ।
विचित्रधातुबर्हस्रग्वस्त्रकाञ्चनमालिनः ॥ ७ ॥

gāvo vṛṣā vatsatarā
haridrā-taila-rūṣitāḥ

vicitra-dhātu-barhasrag-
vastra-kāñcana-mālinaḥ

gāvaḥ—the cows; *vṛṣāḥ*—the bulls; *vatsatarāḥ*—the calves; *hari-drā*—with a mixture of turmeric; *taila*—and oil; *rūṣitāḥ*—their entire bodies smeared; *vicitra*—decorated varieties of; *dhātu*—colored minerals; *barha-srak*—peacock-feather garlands; *vastra*—cloths; *kāñ-cana*—golden ornaments; *mālinaḥ*—being decorated with garlands.

TRANSLATION

The cows, the bulls and the calves were thoroughly smeared with a mixture of turmeric and oil, mixed with varieties of minerals. Their heads were bedecked with peacock feathers, and they were garlanded and covered with cloth and golden ornaments.

PURPORT

The Supreme Personality of Godhead has instructed in *Bhagavad-gītā* (18.44), *kṛṣi-go-rakṣya-vāṇijyaṁ vaiśya-karma-svabhāvajam:* "Farming, cow protection and trade are the qualities of work for the *vaiśyas.*" Nanda Mahārāja belonged to the *vaiśya* community, the agriculturalist community. How to protect the cows and how rich this community was are explained in these verses. We can hardly imagine that cows, bulls and calves could be cared for so nicely and decorated so well with cloths and valuable golden ornaments. How happy they were. As described elsewhere in the *Bhāgavatam*, during Mahārāja Yudhiṣṭhira's time the cows were so happy that they used to muddy the pasturing ground with milk. This is Indian civilization. Yet in the same place, India, Bhāratavarṣa, how much people are suffering by giving up the Vedic way of life and not understanding the teachings of *Bhagavad-gītā.*

TEXT 8

महार्हवस्त्राभरणकञ्चुकोष्णीषभूषिताः ।
गोपाः समाययू राजन् नानोपायनपाणयः ॥ ८ ॥

mahārha-vastrābharaṇa-
kañcukoṣṇīṣa-bhūṣitāḥ
gopāḥ samāyayū rājan
nānopāyana-pāṇayaḥ

mahā-arha—extremely valuable; *vastra-ābharaṇa*—with garments and ornaments; *kañcuka*—by a particular type of garment used in Vṛndāvana; *uṣṇīṣa*—with turbans; *bhūṣitāḥ*—being nicely dressed; *gopāḥ*—all the cowherd men; *samāyayuḥ*—came there; *rājan*—O King (Mahārāja Parīkṣit); *nānā*—various; *upāyana*—presentations; *pāṇayaḥ*—holding in their hands.

TRANSLATION

O King Parīkṣit, the cowherd men dressed very opulently with valuable ornaments and garments such as coats and turbans. Decorated in this way and carrying various presentations in their hands, they approached the house of Nanda Mahārāja.

PURPORT

When we consider the past condition of the agriculturalist in the village, we can see how opulent he was, simply because of agricultural produce and protection of cows. At the present, however, agriculture having been neglected and cow protection given up, the agriculturalist is suffering pitiably and is dressed in a niggardly torn cloth. This is the distinction between the India of history and the India of the present day. By the atrocious activities of *ugra-karma*, how we are killing the opportunity of human civilization!

TEXT 9

गोप्यश्चाकर्ण्य मुदिता यशोदायाः सुतोद्भवम् ।
आत्मानं भूषयाञ्चक्रुर्वस्त्राकल्पाञ्जनादिभिः ॥ ९ ॥

gopyaś cākarṇya muditā
yaśodāyāḥ sutodbhavam
ātmānaṁ bhūṣayāṁ cakrur
vastrākalpāñjanādibhiḥ

gopyaḥ—the feminine community, the wives of the cowherd men; *ca*—also; *ākarṇya*—after hearing; *muditāḥ*—became very glad; *yaśodāyāḥ*—of mother Yaśodā; *suta-udbhavam*—the birth of a male child; *ātmānam*—personally; *bhūṣayām cakruḥ*—dressed very nicely to attend the festival; *vastra-ākalpa-añjana-ādibhiḥ*—with proper dress, ornaments, black ointment, and so on.

TRANSLATION

The gopī wives of the cowherd men were very pleased to hear that mother Yaśodā had given birth to a son, and they began to decorate themselves very nicely with proper dresses, ornaments, black ointment for the eyes, and so on.

TEXT 10

नवकुङ्कुमकिञ्जल्कमुखपङ्कजभूतयः ।
बलिभिस्त्वरितं जग्मुः पृथुश्रोण्यश्चलत्कुचाः ॥१०॥

nava-kuṅkuma-kiñjalka-
mukha-paṅkaja-bhūtayaḥ
balibhis tvaritaṁ jagmuḥ
pṛthu-śroṇyaś calat-kucāḥ

nava-kuṅkuma-kiñjalka—with saffron and newly grown *kuṅkuma* flower; *mukha-paṅkaja-bhūtayaḥ*—exhibiting an extraordinary beauty in their lotuslike faces; *balibhiḥ*—with presentations in their hands; *tvaritam*—very quickly; *jagmuḥ*—went (to the house of mother Yaśodā); *pṛthu-śroṇyaḥ*—bearing full hips, fulfilling womanly beauty; *calat-kucāḥ*—their developed breasts were moving.

TRANSLATION

Their lotuslike faces extraordinarily beautiful, being decorated with saffron and newly grown kuṅkuma, the wives of the cowherd men hurried to the house of mother Yaśodā with presentations in their hands. Because of natural beauty, the wives had full hips and full breasts, which moved as they hurried along.

PURPORT

The cowherd men and women in the villages lived a very natural life, and the women developed a natural feminine beauty, with full hips and breasts. Because women in modern civilization do not live naturally, their hips and breasts do not develop this natural fullness. Because of artificial living, women have lost their natural beauty, although they claim to be independent and advanced in material civilization. This description of the village women gives a clear example of the contrast between natural life and the artificial life of a condemned society, such as that of the Western countries, where topless, bottomless beauty may be easily purchased in clubs and shops and for public advertisements. The word *balibhiḥ* indicates that the women were carrying gold coins, jeweled necklaces, nice cloths, newly grown grass, sandalwood pulp, flower garlands and similar offerings on plates made of gold. Such offerings are called *bali.* The words *tvaritaṁ jagmuḥ* indicate how happy the village women were to understand that mother Yaśodā had given birth to a wonderful child known as Kṛṣṇa.

TEXT 11

गोप्यः सुमृष्टमणिकुण्डलनिष्ककण्ठ्य-
श्चित्राम्बराः पथि शिखाच्युतमाल्यवर्षाः ।
नन्दालयं सवलया व्रजतीर्विरेजु-
र्व्यालोलकुण्डलपयोधरहारशोभाः ॥११॥

gopyaḥ sumṛṣṭa-maṇi-kuṇḍala-niṣka-kaṇṭhyaś
citrāmbarāḥ pathi śikhā-cyuta-mālya-varṣāḥ
nandālayaṁ sa-valayā vrajatīr virejur
vyālola-kuṇḍala-payodhara-hāra-śobhāḥ

gopyaḥ—the *gopīs; su-mṛṣṭa*—very dazzling; *maṇi*—made of jewels; *kuṇḍala*—wearing earrings; *niṣka-kaṇṭhyaḥ*—and having little keys and lockets hanging from their necks; *citra-ambarāḥ*—dressed with varieties of colored embroidery; *pathi*—on their way to Yaśodāmayī's house; *śikhā-cyuta*—fell from their hair; *mālya-varṣāḥ*—a shower of flower garlands; *nanda-ālayam*—to the house of Mahārāja Nanda; *sa-valayāḥ*—with bangles on their hands; *vrajatīḥ*—while going (in that costume); *virejuḥ*—they looked very, very beautiful; *vyālola*—moving; *kuṇḍala*—with earrings; *payodhara*—with breasts; *hāra*—with flower garlands; *śobhāḥ*—who appeared so beautiful.

TRANSLATION

In the ears of the gopīs were brilliantly polished jeweled earrings, and from their necks hung metal lockets. Their hands were decorated with bangles, their dresses were of varied colors, and from their hair, flowers fell onto the street like showers. Thus while going to the house of Mahārāja Nanda, the gopīs, their earrings, breasts and garlands moving, were brilliantly beautiful.

PURPORT

The description of the *gopīs*, who were going to the house of Mahārāja Nanda to welcome Kṛṣṇa, is especially significant. The *gopīs* were not ordinary women, but expansions of Kṛṣṇa's pleasure potency, as described in the *Brahma-saṁhitā:*

ānanda-cinmaya-rasa-pratibhāvitābhis
tābhir ya eva nija-rūpatayā kalābhiḥ
goloka eva nivasaty akhilātma-bhūto
govindam ādi-puruṣaṁ tam ahaṁ bhajāmi
(5.37)

cintāmaṇi-prakara-sadmasu kalpa-vṛkṣa-
lakṣāvṛteṣu surabhīr abhipālayantam
lakṣmī-sahasra-śata-sambhrama-sevyamānaṁ
govindam ādi-puruṣaṁ tam ahaṁ bhajāmi
(5.29)

Kṛṣṇa is always worshiped by the *gopīs* wherever He goes. Therefore Kṛṣṇa is so vividly described in *Śrīmad-Bhāgavatam*. Śrī Caitanya Mahāprabhu has also described Kṛṣṇa in this way: *ramyā kācid upāsanā vrajavadhū-vargeṇa yā kalpitā.* All these *gopīs* were going to offer Kṛṣṇa their presentations because the *gopīs* are eternal associates of the Lord. Now the *gopīs* were more jubilant because of the news of Kṛṣṇa's appearance in Vṛndāvana.

TEXT 12

ता आशिषः प्रयुञ्जानाश्चिरं पाहीति बालके ।
हरिद्राचूर्णतैलाद्भिः सिञ्चन्त्योऽजनमुज्जगुः ॥१२॥

tā āśiṣaḥ prayuñjānāś
ciraṁ pāhīti bālake
haridrā-cūrṇa-tailādbhiḥ
siñcantyo 'janam ujjaguḥ

tāḥ—all the women, the wives and daughters of the cowherd men; *āśiṣaḥ*—blessings; *prayuñjānāḥ*—offering; *ciram*—for a long time; *pāhi*—may You become the King of Vraja and maintain all its inhabitants; *iti*—thus; *bālake*—unto the newborn child; *haridrā-cūrṇa*—powder of turmeric; *taila-adbhiḥ*—mixed with oil; *siñcantyaḥ*—sprinkling; *ajanam*—the Supreme Personality of Godhead, who is unborn; *ujjaguḥ*—offered prayers.

TRANSLATION

Offering blessings to the newborn child, Kṛṣṇa, the wives and daughters of the cowherd men said, "May You become the King of Vraja and long maintain all its inhabitants." They sprinkled a mixture of turmeric powder, oil and water upon the birthless Supreme Lord and offered their prayers.

TEXT 13

अवाद्यन्त विचित्राणि वादित्राणि महोत्सवे ।
कृष्णे विश्वेश्वरेऽनन्ते नन्दस्य व्रजमागते ॥१३॥

avādyanta vicitrāṇi
vāditrāṇi mahotsave

kṛṣṇe viśveśvare 'nante
nandasya vrajam āgate

avādyanta—vibrated in celebration of Vasudeva's son; *vicitrāṇi*—various; *vāditrāṇi*—musical instruments; *mahā-utsave*—in the great festival; *kṛṣṇe*—when Lord Kṛṣṇa; *viśva-īśvare*—the master of the entire cosmic manifestation; *anante*—unlimitedly; *nandasya*—of Mahārāja Nanda; *vrajam*—at the pasturing place; *āgate*—had so arrived.

TRANSLATION

Now that the all-pervading, unlimited Lord Kṛṣṇa, the master of the cosmic manifestation, had arrived within the estate of Mahārāja Nanda, various types of musical instruments resounded to celebrate the great festival.

PURPORT

The Lord says in *Bhagavad-gītā* (4.7):

yadā yadā hi dharmasya
glānir bhavati bhārata
abhyutthānam adharmasya
tadātmānaṁ sṛjāmy aham

"Whenever and wherever there is a decline in religious practice, O descendant of Bharata, and a predominant rise of irreligion—at that time I descend Myself." Whenever Kṛṣṇa comes, once in a day of Brahmā, He comes to the house of Nanda Mahārāja in Vṛndāvana. Kṛṣṇa is the master of all creation (*sarva-loka-maheśvaram*). Therefore, not only in the neighborhood of Nanda Mahārāja's estate, but all over the universe—and in all the other universes—musical sounds celebrated the auspicious arrival of the Lord.

TEXT 14

गोपाः परस्परं हृष्टा दधिक्षीरघृताम्बुभिः ।
आसिञ्चन्तो विलिम्पन्तो नवनीतैश्च चिक्षिपुः ॥१४॥

gopāḥ parasparaṁ hṛṣṭā
dadhi-kṣīra-ghṛtāmbubhiḥ
āsiñcanto vilimpanto
navanītaiś ca cikṣipuḥ

gopāḥ—the cowherd men; *parasparam*—on one another; *hṛṣṭāḥ*—being so pleased; *dadhi*—with curd; *kṣīra*—with condensed milk; *ghṛta-ambubhiḥ*—with water mixed with butter; *āsiñcantaḥ*—sprinkling; *vilimpantaḥ*—smearing; *navanītaiḥ ca*—and with butter; *cikṣipuḥ*—they threw on one another.

TRANSLATION

In gladness, the cowherd men enjoyed the great festival by splashing one another's bodies with a mixture of curd, condensed milk, butter and water. They threw butter on one another and smeared it on one another's bodies.

PURPORT

From this statement we can understand that five thousand years ago not only was there enough milk, butter and curd to eat, drink and cook with, but when there was a festival it would be thrown about without restriction. There was no limit to how extensively milk, butter, curd and other such products were used in human society. Everyone had an ample stock of milk, and by using it in many varied milk preparations, people would keep good health in natural ways and thus enjoy life in Kṛṣṇa consciousness.

TEXTS 15–16

नन्दो महामनास्तेभ्यो वासोऽलङ्कारगोधनम् ।
सूतमागधवन्दिभ्यो येऽन्ये विद्योपजीविनः ॥१५॥
तैस्तैः कामैरदीनात्मा यथोचितमपूजयत् ।
विष्णोराराधनार्थाय स्वपुत्रस्योदयाय च ॥१६॥

nando mahā-manās tebhyo
vāso 'laṅkāra-go-dhanam

sūta-māgadha-vandibhyo
ye 'nye vidyopajīvinaḥ

tais taiḥ kāmair adīnātmā
yathocitam apūjayat
viṣṇor ārādhanārthāya
sva-putrasyodayāya ca

nandaḥ—Mahārāja Nanda; *mahā-manāḥ*—who among the cowherd men was the greatest of all upright persons; *tebhyaḥ*—unto the cowherd men; *vāsaḥ*—clothing; *alaṅkāra*—ornaments; *go-dhanam*—and cows; *sūta-māgadha-vandibhyaḥ*—unto the *sūtas* (the professional reciters of the old histories), the *māgadhas* (the professional reciters of the histories of royal dynasties) and the *vandīs* (general singers of prayers); *ye anye*—as well as others; *vidyā-upajīvinaḥ*—who were continuing their livelihood on the basis of educational qualifications; *taiḥ taiḥ*—with whatever; *kāmaiḥ*—improvements of desire; *adīna-ātmā*—Mahārāja Nanda, who was so magnanimous; *yathā-ucitam*—as was suitable; *apūjayat*—worshiped them or satisfied them; *viṣṇoḥ ārādhana-arthāya*—for the purpose of satisfying Lord Viṣṇu; *sva-putrasya*—of his own child; *udayāya*—for the improvement in all respects; *ca*—and.

TRANSLATION

The great-minded Mahārāja Nanda gave clothing, ornaments and cows in charity to the cowherd men in order to please Lord Viṣṇu, and thus he improved the condition of his own son in all respects. He distributed charity to the sūtas, the māgadhas, the vandīs, and men of all other professions, according to their educational qualifications, and satisfied everyone's desires.

PURPORT

Although it has become fashionable to speak of *daridra-nārāyaṇa*, the words *viṣṇor ārādhanārthāya* do not mean that all the people satisfied by Nanda Mahārāja in this great ceremony were Viṣṇus. They were not *daridra*, nor were they Nārāyaṇa. Rather, they were devotees of Nārāyaṇa, and by their educational qualifications they would satisfy

Nārāyaṇa. Therefore, satisfying them was an indirect way of satisfying Lord Viṣṇu. *Mad-bhakta-pūjābhyadhikā* (*Bhāg.* 11.19.21). The Lord says, "Worshiping My devotees is better than worshiping Me directly." The *varṇāśrama* system is entirely meant for *viṣṇu-ārādhana*, worship of Lord Viṣṇu. *Varṇāśramācāravatā puruṣeṇa paraḥ pumān/ viṣṇur ārādhyate* (*Viṣṇu Purāṇa* 3.8.9). The ultimate goal of life is to please Lord Viṣṇu, the Supreme Lord. The uncivilized man or materialistic person, however, does not know this aim of life. *Na te viduḥ svārtha-gatiṁ hi viṣṇum* (*Bhāg.* 7.5.31). One's real self-interest lies in satisfying Lord Viṣṇu. Not satisfying Lord Viṣṇu but instead attempting to become happy through material adjustments (*bahir-artha-māninaḥ*) is the wrong way for happiness. Because Viṣṇu is the root of everything, if Viṣṇu is pleased, everyone is pleased; in particular, one's children and family members become happy in all respects. Nanda Mahārāja wanted to see his newborn child happy. That was his purpose. Therefore he wanted to satisfy Lord Viṣṇu, and to satisfy Lord Viṣṇu it was necessary to satisfy His devotees, such as the learned *brāhmaṇas*, *māgadhas* and *sūtas*. Thus, in a roundabout way, ultimately it was Lord Viṣṇu who was to be satisfied.

TEXT 17

रोहिणी च महाभागा नन्दगोपाभिनन्दिता ।
व्यचरद् दिव्यवासस्रक्कण्ठाभरणभूषिता ॥१७॥

rohiṇī ca mahā-bhāgā
nanda-gopābhinanditā
vyacarad divya-vāsa-srak-
kaṇṭhābharaṇa-bhūṣitā

rohiṇī—Rohiṇī, the mother of Baladeva; *ca*—also; *mahā-bhāgā*—the most fortunate mother of Baladeva (greatly fortunate because of having the opportunity to raise Kṛṣṇa and Balarāma together); *nanda-gopā-abhinanditā*—being honored by Mahārāja Nanda and mother Yaśodā; *vyacarat*—was busy wandering here and there; *divya*—beautiful; *vāsa*—with a dress; *srak*—with a garland; *kaṇṭha-ābharaṇa*—and with an ornament covering the neck; *bhūṣitā*—decorated.

TRANSLATION

The most fortunate Rohiṇī, the mother of Baladeva, was honored by Nanda Mahārāja and Yaśodā, and thus she also dressed gorgeously and decorated herself with a necklace, a garland and other ornaments. She was busy wandering here and there to receive the women who were guests at the festival.

PURPORT

Rohiṇī, another wife of Vasudeva's, was also kept under the care of Nanda Mahārāja with her son Baladeva. Because her husband was imprisoned by Kaṁsa, she was not very happy, but on the occasion of Kṛṣṇa-janmāṣṭamī, Nandotsava, when Nanda Mahārāja gave dresses and ornaments to others, he also gave gorgeous garments and ornaments to Rohiṇī so that she could take part in the festival. Thus she also was busy receiving the women who were guests. Because of her good fortune in being able to raise Kṛṣṇa and Balarāma together, she is described as *mahā-bhāgā*, greatly fortunate.

TEXT 18

तत आरभ्य नन्दस्य व्रजः सर्वसमृद्धिमान् ।
हरेर्निवासात्मगुणै रमाक्रीडमभून्नृप ॥१८॥

tata ārabhya nandasya
vrajaḥ sarva-samṛddhimān
harer nivāsātma-guṇai
ramākrīḍam abhūn nṛpa

tataḥ ārabhya—beginning from that time; *nandasya*—of Mahārāja Nanda; *vrajaḥ*—Vrajabhūmi, the land for protecting and breeding cows; *sarva-samṛddhimān*—became opulent with all kinds of riches; *hareḥ nivāsa*—of the residence of the Supreme Personality of Godhead; *ātma-guṇaiḥ*—by the transcendental qualities; *ramā-ākrīḍam*—the place of pastimes for the goddess of fortune; *abhūt*—became; *nṛpa*—O King (Mahārāja Parīkṣit).

TRANSLATION

O Mahārāja Parīkṣit, the home of Nanda Mahārāja is eternally the abode of the Supreme Personality of Godhead and His transcendental qualities and is therefore always naturally endowed with the opulence of all wealth. Yet beginning from Lord Kṛṣṇa's appearance there, it became the place for the pastimes of the goddess of fortune.

PURPORT

As stated in the *Brahma-saṁhitā* (5.29), *lakṣmī-sahasra-śata-sambhrama-sevyamānaṁ govindam ādi-puruṣaṁ tam ahaṁ bhajāmi.* The abode of Kṛṣṇa is always served by hundreds and thousands of goddesses of fortune. Wherever Kṛṣṇa goes, the goddess of fortune naturally resides with Him. The chief of the goddesses of fortune is Śrīmatī Rādhārāṇī. Therefore, Kṛṣṇa's appearance in the land of Vraja indicated that the chief goddess of fortune, Rādhārāṇī, would also appear there very soon. Nanda Mahārāja's abode was already opulent, and since Kṛṣṇa had appeared, it would be opulent in all respects.

TEXT 19

गोपान् गोकुलरक्षायां निरूप्य मथुरां गतः ।
नन्दः कंसस्य वार्षिक्यं करं दातुं कुरूद्वह ॥१९॥

gopān gokula-rakṣāyāṁ
nirūpya mathurāṁ gataḥ
nandaḥ kaṁsasya vārṣikyaṁ
karaṁ dātuṁ kurūdvaha

gopān—the cowherd men; *gokula-rakṣāyām*—in giving protection to the state of Gokula; *nirūpya*—after appointing; *mathurām*—to Mathurā; *gataḥ*—went; *nandaḥ*—Nanda Mahārāja; *kaṁsasya*—of Kaṁsa; *vārṣikyam*—yearly taxes; *karam*—the share of profit; *dātum*—to pay; *kuru-udvaha*—O Mahārāja Parīkṣit, best protector of the Kuru dynasty.

TRANSLATION

Śukadeva Gosvāmī continued: Thereafter, my dear King Parīkṣit, O best protector of the Kuru dynasty, Nanda Mahārāja ap-

pointed the local cowherd men to protect Gokula and then went to Mathurā to pay the yearly taxes to King Kaṁsa.

PURPORT

Because the killing of babies was going on and had already become known, Nanda Mahārāja was very much afraid for his newborn child. Thus he appointed the local cowherd men to protect his home and child. He wanted to go immediately to Mathurā to pay the taxes due and also to offer some presentation for the sake of his newborn son. For the protection of the child, he had worshiped various demigods and forefathers and given charity to everyone's satisfaction. Similarly, Nanda Mahārāja wanted not only to pay Kaṁsa the yearly taxes but also to offer some presentation so that Kaṁsa too would be satisfied. His only concern was how to protect his transcendental child, Kṛṣṇa.

TEXT 20

वसुदेव उपश्रुत्य भ्रातरं नन्दमागतम् ।
ज्ञात्वा दत्तकरं राज्ञे ययौ तदवमोचनम् ॥२०॥

vasudeva upaśrutya
bhrātaraṁ nandam āgatam
jñātvā datta-karaṁ rājñe
yayau tad-avamocanam

vasudevaḥ—Vasudeva; *upaśrutya*—when he heard; *bhrātaram*—that his dear friend and brother; *nandam*—Nanda Mahārāja; *āgatam*—had come to Mathurā; *jñātvā*—when he learned; *datta-karam*—and had already paid the taxes; *rājñe*—unto the King; *yayau*—he went; *tat-avamocanam*—to the residential quarters of Nanda Mahārāja.

TRANSLATION

When Vasudeva heard that Nanda Mahārāja, his very dear friend and brother, had come to Mathurā and already paid the taxes to Kaṁsa, he went to Nanda Mahārāja's residence.

PURPORT

Vasudeva and Nanda Mahārāja were so intimately connected that they lived like brothers. Furthermore, it is learned from the notes of Śrīpāda Madhvācārya that Vasudeva and Nanda Mahārāja were stepbrothers. Vasudeva's father, Śūrasena, married a *vaiśya* girl, and from her Nanda Mahārāja was born. Later, Nanda Mahārāja himself married a *vaiśya* girl, Yaśodā. Therefore his family is celebrated as a *vaiśya* family, and Kṛṣṇa, identifying Himself as their son, took charge of *vaiśya* activities (*kṛṣi-go-rakṣya-vāṇijyam*). Balarāma represents plowing the land for agriculture and therefore always carries in His hand a plow, whereas Kṛṣṇa tends cows and therefore carries a flute in His hand. Thus the two brothers represent *kṛṣi-rakṣya* and *go-rakṣya.*

TEXT 21

तं दृष्ट्वा सहसोत्थाय देहः प्राणमिवागतम् ।
प्रीतः प्रियतमं दोर्भ्यां सस्वजे प्रेमविह्वलः ॥२१॥

taṁ dṛṣṭvā sahasotthāya
dehaḥ prāṇam ivāgatam
prītaḥ priyatamaṁ dorbhyāṁ
sasvaje prema-vihvalaḥ

tam—him (Vasudeva); *dṛṣṭvā*—seeing; *sahasā*—suddenly; *utthāya*—getting up; *dehaḥ*—the same body; *prāṇam*—life; *iva*—as if; *āgatam*—had returned; *prītaḥ*—so pleased; *priya-tamam*—his dear friend and brother; *dorbhyām*—by his two arms; *sasvaje*—embraced; *prema-vihvalaḥ*—overwhelmed with love and affection.

TRANSLATION

When Nanda Mahārāja heard that Vasudeva had come, he was overwhelmed with love and affection, being as pleased as if his body had regained its life. Seeing Vasudeva suddenly present, he got up and embraced him with both arms.

PURPORT

Nanda Mahārāja was older than Vasudeva. Therefore Nanda Mahārāja embraced him, and Vasudeva offered him *namaskāra.*

TEXT 22

पूजितः सुखमासीनः पृष्ट्वानामयमादृतः ।
प्रसक्तधीः स्वात्मजयोरिदमाह विशाम्पते ॥२२॥

pūjitaḥ sukham āsīnaḥ
pṛṣṭvānāmayam ādṛtaḥ
prasakta-dhīḥ svātmajayor
idam āha viśāmpate

pūjitaḥ—Vasudeva having been so dearly welcomed; *sukham āsīnaḥ*—having been given a place to sit comfortably; *pṛṣṭvā*—asking; *anāmayam*—all-auspicious inquiries; *ādṛtaḥ*—being honored and respectfully received; *prasakta-dhīḥ*—because of his being very much attached; *sva-ātmajayoḥ*—to his own two sons, Kṛṣṇa and Balarāma; *idam*—the following; *āha*—inquired; *viśām-pate*—O Mahārāja Parīkṣit.

TRANSLATION

O Mahārāja Parīkṣit, having thus been received and welcomed by Nanda Mahārāja with honor, Vasudeva sat down very peacefully and inquired about his own two sons because of intense love for them.

TEXT 23

दिष्ट्या भ्रातः प्रवयस इदानीमप्रजस्य ते ।
प्रजाशाया निवृत्तस्य प्रजा यत् समपद्यत ॥२३॥

diṣṭyā bhrātaḥ pravayasa
idānīm aprajasya te
prajāśāyā nivṛttasya
prajā yat samapadyata

diṣṭyā—it is by great fortune; *bhrātaḥ*—O my dear brother; *pravayasaḥ*—of you whose age is now quite advanced; *idānīm*—at the present moment; *aprajasya*—of one who did not have a son before; *te*—of you; *prajā-āśāyāḥ nivṛttasya*—of one who was almost hopeless of getting a son at this age; *prajā*—a son; *yat*—whatever; *samapadyata*—has been gotten by chance.

TRANSLATION

My dear brother Nanda Mahārāja, at an advanced age you had no son at all and were hopeless of having one. Therefore, that you now have a son is a sign of great fortune.

PURPORT

At an advanced age one generally cannot beget a male child. If by chance one does beget a child at this age, the child is generally female. Thus Vasudeva indirectly asked Nanda Mahārāja whether he had actually begotten a male child or a female child. Vasudeva knew that Yaśodā had given birth to a female child, whom he had stolen and replaced with a male child. This was a great mystery, and Vasudeva wanted to determine whether this mystery was already known to Nanda Mahārāja. On inquiring, however, he was confident that the mystery of Kṛṣṇa's birth and His being placed in the care of Yaśodā was still hidden. There was no danger, since Kaṁsa at least could not learn what had already happened.

TEXT 24

दिष्ट्या संसारचक्रेऽस्मिन् वर्तमानः पुनर्भवः ।
उपलब्धो भवानद्य दुर्लभं प्रियदर्शनम् ॥२४॥

diṣṭyā saṁsāra-cakre 'smin
vartamānaḥ punar-bhavaḥ
upalabdho bhavān adya
durlabhaṁ priya-darśanam

diṣṭyā—it is also by great fortune; *saṁsāra-cakre asmin*—in this world of birth and death; *vartamānaḥ*—although I was existing; *punaḥ-bhavaḥ*—my meeting with you is just like another birth; *upalabdhaḥ*—being obtained by me; *bhavān*—you; *adya*—today; *durlabham*—although it was never to happen; *priya-darśanam*—to see you again, my very dear friend and brother.

TRANSLATION

It is also by good fortune that I am seeing you. Having obtained this opportunity, I feel as if I have taken birth again. Even though

one is present in this world, to meet with intimate friends and dear relatives in this material world is extremely difficult.

PURPORT

Vasudeva had been imprisoned by Kaṁsa, and therefore, although present in Mathurā, he was unable to see Nanda Mahārāja for many years. Therefore when they met again, Vasudeva considered this meeting to be another birth.

TEXT 25

नैकत्र प्रियसंवासः सुहृदां चित्रकर्मणाम् ।
ओघेन व्यूह्यमानानां प्लवानां स्रोतसो यथा ॥२५॥

naikatra priya-saṁvāsaḥ
suhṛdāṁ citra-karmaṇām
oghena vyūhyamānānāṁ
plavānāṁ srotaso yathā

na—not; *ekatra*—in one place; *priya-saṁvāsaḥ*—living together with dear friends and relatives; *suhṛdām*—of friends; *citra-karmaṇām*—of all of us who have had varieties of reactions to our past *karma; oghena*—by the force; *vyūhyamānānām*—carried away; *plavānām*—of sticks and other objects floating in the water; *srotasaḥ*—of the waves; *yathā*—as.

TRANSLATION

Many planks and sticks, unable to stay together, are carried away by the force of a river's waves. Similarly, although we are intimately related with friends and family members, we are unable to stay together because of our varied past deeds and the waves of time.

PURPORT

Vasudeva was lamenting because he and Nanda Mahārāja could not live together. Yet how could they live together? Vasudeva warns that all of us, even if intimately related, are carried away by the waves of time according to the results of past *karma.*

TEXT 26

कच्चित् पशव्यं निरुजं भूर्यम्बुतृणवीरुधम् ।
बृहद्वनं तदधुना यत्रास्से त्वं सुहृद्वृतः ॥२६॥

kaccit paśavyaṁ nirujaṁ
bhūry-ambu-tṛṇa-vīrudham
bṛhad vanaṁ tad adhunā
yatrāsse tvaṁ suhṛd-vṛtaḥ

kaccit—whether; *paśavyam*—protection of the cows; *nirujam*—without difficulties or disease; *bhūri*—sufficient; *ambu*—water; *tṛṇa*—grass; *vīrudham*—plants; *bṛhat vanam*—the great forest; *tat*—all these arrangements are there; *adhunā*—now; *yatra*—where; *āsse*—are living; *tvam*—you; *suhṛt-vṛtaḥ*—surrounded by friends.

TRANSLATION

My dear friend Nanda Mahārāja, in the place where you are living with your friends, is the forest favorable for the animals, the cows? I hope there is no disease or inconvenience. The place must be full of water, grass and other plants.

PURPORT

For human happiness, one must care for the animals, especially the cows. Vasudeva therefore inquired whether there was a good arrangement for the animals where Nanda Mahārāja lived. For the proper pursuit of human happiness, there must be arrangements for the protection of cows. This means that there must be forests and adequate pasturing grounds full of grass and water. If the animals are happy, there will be an ample supply of milk, from which human beings will benefit by deriving many milk products with which to live happily. As enjoined in *Bhagavad-gītā* (18.44), *kṛṣi-go-rakṣya-vāṇijyaṁ vaiśya-karma-svabhāvajam.* Without giving proper facilities to the animals, how can human society be happy? That people are raising cattle to send to the slaughterhouse is a great sin. By this demoniac enterprise, people are ruining their chance for a truly human life. Because they are not giving any importance to the instructions of Kṛṣṇa, the advancement of their so-called civilization resembles the crazy efforts of men in a lunatic asylum.

TEXT 27

भ्रातर्मम सुतः कच्चिन्मात्रा सह भवद्व्रजे ।
तातं भवन्तं मन्वानो भवद्भ्यामुपलालितः ॥२७॥

bhrātar mama sutaḥ kaccin
mātrā saha bhavad-vraje
tātaṁ bhavantaṁ manvāno
bhavadbhyām upalālitaḥ

bhrātaḥ—my dear brother; *mama*—my; *sutaḥ*—son (Baladeva, born of Rohiṇī); *kaccit*—whether; *mātrā saha*—with His mother, Rohiṇī; *bhavat-vraje*—in your house; *tātam*—as father; *bhavantam*—unto you; *manvānaḥ*—thinking; *bhavadbhyām*—by you and your wife, Yaśodā; *upalālitaḥ*—properly being raised.

TRANSLATION

My son Baladeva, being raised by you and your wife, Yaśodādevī, considers you His father and mother. Is he living very peacefully in your home with His real mother, Rohiṇī?

TEXT 28

पुंसस्त्रिवर्गो विहितः सुहृदो ह्यनुभावितः ।
न तेषु क्लिश्यमानेषु त्रिवर्गोऽर्थाय कल्पते ॥२८॥

puṁsas tri-vargo vihitaḥ
suhṛdo hy anubhāvitaḥ
na teṣu kliśyamāneṣu
tri-vargo 'rthāya kalpate

puṁsaḥ—of a person; *tri-vargaḥ*—the three aims of life (religion, economic development and sense gratification); *vihitaḥ*—enjoined according to Vedic ritualistic ceremonies; *suhṛdaḥ*—toward relatives and friends; *hi*—indeed; *anubhāvitaḥ*—when they are properly in line; *na*—not; *teṣu*—in them; *kliśyamāneṣu*—if they are actually in any difficulty; *tri-vargaḥ*—these three aims of life; *arthāya*—for any purpose; *kalpate*—does become so.

TRANSLATION

When one's friends and relatives are properly situated, one's religion, economic development and sense gratification, as described in the Vedic literatures, are beneficial. Otherwise, if one's friends and relatives are in distress, these three cannot offer any happiness.

PURPORT

Vasudeva regretfully informed Nanda Mahārāja that although he had his wife and children, he could not properly discharge his duty of maintaining them and was therefore unhappy.

TEXT 29

श्रीनन्द उवाच

अहो ते देवकीपुत्राः कंसेन बहवो हताः ।
एकावशिष्टावरजा कन्या सापि दिवं गता ॥२९॥

śrī-nanda uvāca
aho te devakī-putrāḥ
kaṁsena bahavo hatāḥ
ekāvaśiṣṭāvarajā
kanyā sāpi divaṁ gatā

śrī-nandaḥ uvāca—Nanda Mahārāja said; *aho*—alas; *te*—your; *devakī-putrāḥ*—all the sons of your wife Devakī; *kaṁsena*—by King Kaṁsa; *bahavaḥ*—many; *hatāḥ*—have been killed; *ekā*—one; *avaśiṣṭā*—remaining child; *avarajā*—the youngest of all; *kanyā*—a daughter also; *sā api*—she also; *divam gatā*—gone to the heavenly planets.

TRANSLATION

Nanda Mahārāja said: Alas, King Kaṁsa killed so many of your children, born of Devakī. And your one daughter, the youngest child of all, entered the heavenly planets.

PURPORT

When Vasudeva understood from Nanda Mahārāja that the mystery of Kṛṣṇa's birth and His having been exchanged with Yaśodā's daughter was yet undisclosed, he was happy that things were going on nicely. By saying that Vasudeva's daughter, his youngest child, had gone to the heavenly planets, Nanda Mahārāja indicated that he did not know that this daughter was born of Yaśodā and that Vasudeva had exchanged her with Kṛṣṇa. Thus the doubts of Vasudeva were dispelled.

TEXT 30

नूनं ह्यदृष्टनिष्ठोऽयमदृष्टपरमो जनः ।
अदृष्टमात्मनस्तत्त्वं यो वेद न स मुह्यति ॥३०॥

nūnaṁ hy adṛṣṭa-niṣṭho 'yam
adṛṣṭa-paramo janaḥ
adṛṣṭam ātmanas tattvaṁ
yo veda na sa muhyati

nūnam—certainly; *hi*—indeed; *adṛṣṭa*—unseen; *niṣṭhaḥ ayam*—something ends there; *adṛṣṭa*—the unseen destiny; *paramaḥ*—ultimate; *janaḥ*—every living entity within this material world; *adṛṣṭam*—that destiny; *ātmanaḥ*—of oneself; *tattvam*—ultimate truth; *yaḥ*—anyone who; *veda*—knows; *na*—not; *saḥ*—he; *muhyati*—becomes bewildered.

TRANSLATION

Every man is certainly controlled by destiny, which determines the results of one's fruitive activities. In other words, one has a son or daughter because of unseen destiny, and when the son or

daughter is no longer present, this also is due to unseen destiny. Destiny is the ultimate controller of everyone. One who knows this is never bewildered.

PURPORT

Nanda Mahārāja consoled his younger brother Vasudeva by saying that destiny is ultimately responsible for everything. Vasudeva should not be unhappy that his many children had been killed by Kaṁsa or that the last child, the daughter, had gone to the heavenly planets.

TEXT 31

श्रीवसुदेव उवाच
करो वै वार्षिको दत्तो राज्ञे दृष्टा वयं च वः ।
नेह स्थेयं बहुतिथं सन्त्युत्पाताश्च गोकुले ॥३१॥

śrī-vasudeva uvāca
karo vai vārṣiko datto
rājñe dṛṣṭā vayaṁ ca vaḥ
neha stheyaṁ bahu-tithaṁ
santy utpātāś ca gokule

śrī-vasudevaḥ uvāca—Śrī Vasudeva replied; *karaḥ*—the taxes; *vai*—indeed; *vārṣikaḥ*—yearly; *dattaḥ*—have already been paid by you; *rājñe*—to the King; *dṛṣṭāḥ*—have been seen; *vayam ca*—both of us; *vaḥ*—of you; *na*—not; *iha*—in this place; *stheyam*—should be staying; *bahu-titham*—for many days; *santi*—may be; *utpātāḥ ca*—many disturbances; *gokule*—in your home, Gokula.

TRANSLATION

Vasudeva said to Nanda Mahārāja: Now, my dear brother, since you have paid the annual taxes to Kaṁsa and have also seen me, do not stay in this place for many days. It is better to return to Gokula, since I know that there may be some disturbances there.

TEXT 32

श्रीशुक उवाच
इति नन्दादयो गोपाः प्रोक्तास्ते शौरिणा ययुः ।
अनोभिरनडुद्युक्तैस्तमनुज्ञाप्य गोकुलम् ॥३२॥

śrī-śuka uvāca
iti nandādayo gopāḥ
proktās te śauriṇā yayuḥ
anobhir anaḍud-yuktais
tam anujñāpya gokulam

śrī-śukaḥ uvāca—Śrī Śukadeva Gosvāmī said; *iti*—thus; *nanda-ādayaḥ*—Nanda Mahārāja and his companions; *gopāḥ*—the cowherd men; *proktāḥ*—being advised; *te*—they; *śauriṇā*—by Vasudeva; *yayuḥ*—started from that place; *anobhiḥ*—by the bullock carts; *anaḍut-yuktaiḥ*—yoked with oxen; *tam anujñāpya*—taking permission from Vasudeva; *gokulam*—for Gokula.

TRANSLATION

Śukadeva Gosvāmī said: After Vasudeva advised Nanda Mahārāja in this way, Nanda Mahārāja and his associates, the cowherd men, took permission from Vasudeva, yoked their bulls to the bullock carts, and started riding for Gokula.

Thus end the Bhaktivedanta purports to the Tenth Canto, Fifth Chapter, of the Śrīmad-Bhāgavatam, *entitled "The Meeting of Nanda Mahārāja and Vasudeva."*

Appendixes

The Author

His Divine Grace A. C. Bhaktivedanta Swami Prabhupāda appeared in this world in 1896 in Calcutta, India. He first met his spiritual master, Śrīla Bhaktisiddhānta Sarasvatī Gosvāmī, in Calcutta in 1922. Bhaktisiddhānta Sarasvatī, a prominent devotional scholar and the founder of sixty-four Gauḍīya Maṭhas (Vedic institutes), liked this educated young man and convinced him to dedicate his life to teaching Vedic knowledge. Śrīla Prabhupāda became his student, and eleven years later (1933) at Allahabad he became his formally initiated disciple.

At their first meeting, in 1922, Śrīla Bhaktisiddhānta Sarasvatī Ṭhākura requested Śrīla Prabhupāda to broadcast Vedic knowledge through the English language. In the years that followed, Śrīla Prabhupāda wrote a commentary on the *Bhagavad-gītā*, assisted the Gauḍīya Maṭha in its work and, in 1944, without assistance, started an English fortnightly magazine, edited it, typed the manuscripts and checked the galley proofs. He even distributed the individual copies freely and struggled to maintain the publication. Once begun, the magazine never stopped; it is now being continued by his disciples in the West.

Recognizing Śrīla Prabhupāda's philosophical learning and devotion, the Gauḍīya Vaiṣṇava Society honored him in 1947 with the title "Bhaktivedanta." In 1950, at the age of fifty-four, Śrīla Prabhupāda retired from married life, and four years later he adopted the *vānaprastha* (retired) order to devote more time to his studies and writing. Śrīla Prabhupāda traveled to the holy city of Vṛndāvana, where he lived in very humble circumstances in the historic medieval temple of Rādhā-Dāmodara. There he engaged for several years in deep study and writing. He accepted the renounced order of life (*sannyāsa*) in 1959. At Rādhā-Dāmodara, Śrīla Prabhupāda began work on his life's masterpiece: a multivolume translation and commentary on the eighteen thousand verse *Śrīmad-Bhāgavatam* (*Bhāgavata Purāṇa*). He also wrote *Easy Journey to Other Planets.*

After publishing three volumes of *Bhāgavatam,* Śrīla Prabhupāda came to the United States, in 1965, to fulfill the mission of his spiritual master. Since that time, His Divine Grace has written over forty volumes of authoritative translations, commentaries and summary studies of the philosophical and religious classics of India.

In 1965, when he first arrived by freighter in New York City, Śrīla Prabhupāda was practically penniless. It was after almost a year of great difficulty that he established the International Society for Krishna Consciousness in July of 1966. Under his careful guidance, the Society has grown within a decade to a worldwide confederation of almost one hundred *āśramas*, schools, temples, institutes and farm communities.

In 1968, Śrīla Prabhupāda created New Vṛndāvana, an experimental Vedic community in the hills of West Virginia. Inspired by the success of New Vṛndāvana, now a thriving farm community of more than one thousand acres, his students have since founded several similar communities in the United States and abroad.

In 1972, His Divine Grace introduced the Vedic system of primary and secondary education in the West by founding the Gurukula school in Dallas, Texas. The school began with 3 children in 1972, and by the beginning of 1975 the enrollment had grown to 150.

Śrīla Prabhupāda has also inspired the construction of a large international center at Śrīdhāma Māyāpur in West Bengal, India, which is also the site for a planned Institute of Vedic Studies. A similar project is the magnificent Kṛṣṇa-Balarāma Temple and International Guest House in Vṛndāvana, India. These are centers where Westerners can live to gain firsthand experience of Vedic culture.

Śrīla Prabhupāda's most significant contribution, however, is his books. Highly respected by the academic community for their authoritativeness, depth and clarity, they are used as standard textbooks in numerous college courses. His writings have been translated into eleven languages. The Bhaktivedanta Book Trust, established in 1972 exclusively to publish the works of His Divine Grace, has thus become the world's largest publisher of books in the field of Indian religion and philosophy. Its latest project is the publishing of Śrīla Prabhupāda's most recent work: a seventeen-volume translation and commentary—completed by Śrīla Prabhupāda in only eighteen months—on the Bengali religious classic *Śrī Caitanya-caritāmṛta.*

In the past ten years, in spite of his advanced age, Śrīla Prabhupāda has circled the globe twelve times on lecture tours that have taken him to six continents. In spite of such a vigorous schedule, Śrīla Prabhupāda continues to write prolifically. His writings constitute a veritable library of Vedic philosophy, religion, literature and culture.

References

The purports of *Śrīmad-Bhāgavatam* are all confirmed by standard Vedic authorities. The following authentic scriptures are specifically cited in this volume:

Bhagavad-gītā, 17, 22, 24, 25, 28, 38, 40, 41, 42, 44, 48, 51–52, 63, 64, 65, 68, 69, 70, 71, 72, 75, 76, 87, 90, 91, 93, 94, 95, 98, 101, 107, 118, 119–120, 124, 125, 127–128, 129–130, 131, 136, 137–138, 145–146, 150, 153, 156, 159–160, 162–163, 165–166, 173, 174, 175–176, 177–178, 179, 182, 184, 186, 189, 195, 197, 210, 216, 218, 220, 224, 225, 226, 228, 232, 235, 239, 241, 247–248, 250, 251, 256, 265, 267, 287, 292–293, 297, 305, 317–318, 325, 331, 342

Bhakti-rasāmṛta-sindhu, 168, 294–295

Brahma-saṁhitā, 17, 18–19, 44, 46–47, 87, 110, 141, 155n, 160, 165, 187–188, 200, 208, 210, 212, 217, 220, 239, 295–296, 302, 329, 336

Caitanya-bhāgavata, 199

Caitanya-candrāmṛta, 153

Caitanya-caritāmṛta, 20, 68, 101, 144, 146, 171, 192, 241, 258, 316

Caṇḍī, 110, 303

Chāndogya Upaniṣad, 87

Gītā-Govinda, 23

Hari-bhakti-sudhodaya, 103, 175

Glossary

A

Ācārya—a spiritual master who teaches by example.

Ārati—a ceremony for greeting the Lord with offerings of food, lamps, fans, flowers and incense.

Arcanā—the devotional process of Deity worship.

Artha—economic development.

Āśrama—the four spiritual orders of life: celibate student, householder, retired life and renounced life.

Asuras—atheistic demons.

Avatāra—a descent of the Supreme Lord.

B

Bhagavad-gītā—the basic directions for spiritual life spoken by the Lord Himself.

Bhagavān—one who unlimitedly possesses all opulences; a term of address for the Supreme Personality of Godhead.

Bhāgavata-saptāha—a seven-day discourse on *Śrīmad-Bhāgavatam.*

Bhagavat-svarūpa—the personal form of the Lord.

Bhakta—a devotee.

Bhakti-yoga—linking with the Supreme Lord by devotional service.

Brahmacarya—celibate student life; the first order of Vedic spiritual life.

Brahman—the Absolute Truth; especially the impersonal aspect of the Absolute.

Brāhmaṇa—one wise in the *Vedas* who can guide society; the first Vedic social order.

Brahmāṇḍas—the universes.

Brahmāstra—a nuclear weapon produced by chanting *mantras.*

C

Catur-vyūha—the Lord's plenary expansions Vāsudeva, Saṅkarṣaṇa, Pradyumna and Aniruddha

D

Daivas—the demigods or godly persons.

Daridra-nārāyaṇa—"poor Nārāyaṇa," an offensive term used by Māyāvādīs to equate poor men with the Supreme Personality of Godhead.

Dāsya-rasa—the servitorship relationship with the Lord.

Dharma—eternal occupational duty; religious principles.

E

Ekādaśī—a special fast day for increased remembrance of Kṛṣṇa, which comes on the eleventh day of both the waxing and waning moon.

G

Garbhādhāna-saṁskāra—Vedic purificatory ritual for obtaining good progeny; performed by husband and wife before child's conception.

Goloka (Kṛṣṇaloka)—the highest spiritual planet, containing Kṛṣṇa's personal abodes, Dvārakā, Mathurā and Vṛndāvana.

Gopīs—Kṛṣṇa's cowherd girl friends, His most confidential servitors.

Gṛhastha—regulated householder life; the second order of Vedic spiritual life.

Guṇī-bhūta—the first stage of *bhakti.*

Guru—a spiritual master.

H

Hare Kṛṣṇa mantra—*See: Mahā-mantra*

Hlādinī-śakti—the Lord's pleasure potency.

J

Jīva-tattva—the living entities, atomic parts of the Lord.

Jñānī—one who cultivates knowledge by empirical speculation.

K

Kāla-cakra—the wheel of time.

Kali-yuga (Age of Kali)—the present age, characterized by quarrel; it is last in the cycle of four and began five thousand years ago.

Kāma—lust.
Karatālas—hand cymbals used in *kīrtana*.
Karma—fruitive action, for which there is always reaction, good or bad.
Karma-kāṇḍa-vicāra—the rituals for material prosperity prescribed in the *Vedas*.
Karmī—a person satisfied with working hard for flickering sense gratification.
Kevala—the third and highest stage of *bhakti*.
Kīrtana—chanting the glories of the Supreme Lord.
Kṛṣṇaloka—*See:* Goloka
Kṣatriyas—a warrior or administrator; the second Vedic social order.

L

Loka—a planet.

M

Mādhurya-rasa—conjugal love relationship with the Lord.
Mahā-mantra—the great chanting for deliverance:
Hare Kṛṣṇa, Hare Kṛṣṇa, Kṛṣṇa Kṛṣṇa, Hare Hare
Hare Rāma, Hare Rāma, Rāma Rāma, Hare Hare.
Mahā-roga—a severe illness.
Mahat-tattva—the total material energy, from which the material world is manifested.
Mantra—a sound vibration that can deliver the mind from illusion.
Mathurā—Lord Kṛṣṇa's abode, surrounding Vṛndāvana, where He took birth and later returned to after performing His Vṛndāvana pastimes.
Māyā—illusion; forgetfulness of one's relationship with Kṛṣṇa.
Māyāvādīs—impersonal philosophers who say that the Lord cannot have a transcendental body.
Mṛdaṅga—a clay drum used for congregational chanting.
Mūḍha—a fool.
Muni—a sage.

N

Namaskāra—a polite greeting or address.

P

Paraṁ brahma—the Supreme Absolute Truth, Personality of Godhead.
Paramparā—the chain of spiritual masters in disciplic succession.
Pradhāna—the total material energy in its unmanifest state.
Pradhānī-bhūta—the second and intermediate stage of *bhakti.*
Prajāpatis—the populators of the universe.
Prāṇāyāma—control of the breathing process; performed in *aṣṭāṅga-yoga.*
Prasāda—food spiritualized by being offered to the Lord.

R

Rākṣasas—man-eating demons.

S

Sac-cid-ānanda-vigraha—the Lord's transcendental form, which is eternal, full of knowledge and bliss.
Sādhu—a saintly person.
Sakhya-rasa—friend relationship with the Lord.
Śaktyāveśa-avatāra—an empowered incarnation of the Supreme Lord.
Saṅkīrtana—public chanting of the names of God, the approved *yoga* process for this age.
Sannyāsa—renounced life; the fourth order of Vedic spiritual life.
Śānta-rasa—neutral relationship with the Supreme Lord.
Śāstras—revealed scriptures.
Śravaṇaṁ kīrtanaṁ viṣṇoḥ—the devotional processes of hearing and chanting about Lord Viṣṇu.
Sudarśana-cakra—the disc weapon of the Supreme Lord.
Śuddha-sattva—the state of pure, transcendental goodness (not to be confused with material goodness).
Śūdra—a laborer; the fourth of the Vedic social orders.
Svāmī—one who controls his mind and senses; title of one in the renounced order of life.
Svarūpa-siddhi—the perfection of attaining one's original, spiritual form.

T

Tapasya—austerity; accepting some voluntary inconvenience for a higher purpose.

Tilaka—auspicious clay marks that sanctify a devotee's body as a temple of the Lord.

U

Ugra-karma—evil activities.

V

Vaikuṇṭha—the spiritual world.

Vaiṣṇava—a devotee of Lord Viṣṇu, Kṛṣṇa.

Vaiśyas—farmers and merchants; the third Vedic social order.

Vānaprastha—one who has retired from family life; the third order of Vedic spiritual life.

Varṇa—the four occupational divisions of society: the intellectual class, the administrative class, the mercantile class, and the laborer class.

Varṇāśrama—the Vedic social system of four social and four spiritual orders.

Vātsalya-rasa—parental relationship with the Lord.

Vedas—the original revealed scriptures, first spoken by the Lord Himself.

Vimuktas—persons liberated from the material world.

Viṣṇu, Lord—Kṛṣṇa's expansion for the creation and maintenance of the material universes.

Viṣṇu-mūrtis—the various forms of the Lord.

Viṣṇu-tattva—the original Personality of Godhead's primary expansions, each of whom is equally God.

Vṛndāvana—Kṛṣṇa's personal abode, where He fully manifests His quality of sweetness.

Vyāsadeva—Kṛṣṇa's incarnation, at the end of Dvāpara-yuga, for compiling the *Vedas*.

Y

Yajña—an activity performed to satisfy either Lord Viṣṇu or the demigods.

Yogī—a transcendentalist who, in one way or another, is striving for union with the Supreme.

Yugas—ages in the life of a universe, occurring in a repeated cycle of four.

Sanskrit Pronunciation Guide

Vowels

अ a आ ā इ i ई ī उ u ऊ ū ऋ ṛ ॠ ṝ

ऌ ḷ ए e ऐ ai ओ o औ au

ं ṁ *(anusvāra)* ः ḥ *(visarga)*

Consonants

Gutturals:	क ka	ख kha	ग ga	घ gha	ङ ṅa
Palatals:	च ca	छ cha	ज ja	झ jha	ञ ña
Cerebrals:	ट ṭa	ठ ṭha	ड ḍa	ढ ḍha	ण ṇa
Dentals:	त ta	थ tha	द da	ध dha	न na
Labials:	प pa	फ pha	ब ba	भ bha	म ma
Semivowels:	य ya	र ra	ल la	व va	
Sibilants:	श śa	ष ṣa	स sa		
Aspirate:	ह ha	ऽ ' *(avagraha)* – the apostrophe			

The numerals are: ० -0 १ -1 २ -2 ३ -3 ४ -4 ५ -5 ६ -6 ७ -7 ८ -8 ९ -9

The vowels above should be pronounced as follows:

a – like the *a* in org*a*n or the *u* in b*u*t.
ā – like the *a* in f*a*r but held twice as long as short *a*.
i – like the *i* in p*i*n.
ī – like the *i* in p*i*que but held twice as long as short *i*.

u – like the *u* in p*u*sh.
ū – like the *u* in r*u*le but held twice as long as short *u*.
ṛ – like the *ri* in *ri*m.
ṝ – like *ree* in *ree*d.
ḷ – like *l* followed by *ṛ* (*lṛ*).
e – like the *e* in th*ey*.
ai – like the *ai* in *ai*sle.
o – like the *o* in g*o*.
au – like the *ow* in h*ow*.
ṁ (*anusvāra*) – a resonant nasal like the *n* in the French word *bon*.
ḥ (*visarga*) – a final *h*-sound: *aḥ* is pronounced like *aha*; *iḥ* like *ihi*.

The vowels are written as follows after a consonant:

ा ā ि i ी ī ु u ू ū ृ ṛ ॄ ṝ े e ै ai ो o ौ au

For example: क ka का kā कि ki की kī कु ku कू kū
कृ kṛ कॄ kṝ के ke कै kai को ko कौ kau

The vowel "a" is implied after a consonant with no vowel symbol.

The symbol virāma (्) indicates that there is no final vowel: क्

The consonants are pronounced as follows:

k – as in *k*ite
kh – as in Ec*kh*art
g – as in *g*ive
gh – as in di*g-h*ard
ṅ – as in si*ng*
c – as in *ch*air
ch – as in staun*ch-h*eart
j – as in *j*oy
jh – as in he*dgeh*og
ñ – as in ca*ny*on
ṭ – as in *t*ub
ṭh – as in ligh*t-h*eart
ḍ – as in *d*ove
ḍha- as in re*d-h*ot
ṇ – as r*na* (prepare to say the *r* and say *na*).

Cerebrals are pronounced with tongue to roof of mouth, but the following dentals are pronounced with tongue against teeth:

t – as in *t*ub but with tongue against teeth.
th – as in ligh*t-h*eart but with tongue against teeth.

d – as in *d*ove but with tongue against teeth.
dh – as in re*d-h*ot but with tongue against teeth.
n – as in *n*ut but with tongue between teeth.
p – as in *p*ine
ph – as in u*ph*ill (not *f*)
b – as in *b*ird
bh – as in ru*b-h*ard
m – as in *m*other
y – as in *y*es
r – as in *r*un
l – as in *l*ight
v – as in *v*ine
ś (palatal) – as in the *s* in the German word *sprechen*
ṣ (cerebral) – as the *sh* in *sh*ine
s – as in *s*un
h – as in *h*ome

Generally two or more consonants in conjunction are written together in a special form, as for example: क्ष kṣa त्र tra

There is no strong accentuation of syllables in Sanskrit, or pausing between words in a line, only a flowing of short and long (twice as long as the short) syllables. A long syllable is one whose vowel is long (ā, ī, ū, e, ai, o, au), or whose short vowel is followed by more than one consonant (including anusvāra and visarga). Aspirated consonants (such as kha and gha) count as only single consonants.

Index of Sanskrit Verses

This index constitutes a complete listing of the first and third lines of each of the Sanskrit poetry verses of this volume of *Śrīmad-Bhāgavatam*, arranged in English alphabetical order. The first column gives the Sanskrit transliteration, and the second and third columns, respectively, list the chapter-verse reference and page number for each verse.

General Index

Numerals in boldface type indicate references to translations of the verses of *Śrīmad-Bhāgavatam.*

A

Abhaya defined, 196
Abhayaṁ sarvadā tasmai
  verse quoted, 157
Abhyāsa-yoga-yuktena
  quoted, 71
Abhyutthānam adharmasya
  verse quoted, 40, 118, 120, 145–146, 155n, 195, 331
Ābrahma-bhuvanāl lokāḥ
  quoted, 241
Absolute Truth
  devotional service reveals, 156
  Lord Kṛṣṇa as, 34, **156**, 158, 160
  personal & impersonal realization of, 75
  See also: Kṛṣṇa, Lord; Supreme Lord
Abudhaḥ defined, 223
Ācāryas (saintly authorities)
  duty of, 171
  Lord as reached via, **170–171**, 172
  scholars ignore, 184
  See also: Spiritual master; *names of specific ācāryas*
Acintya-bhedābheda (oneness-and-difference) philosophy, 128, 236
Activities
  of God. *See:* Kṛṣṇa, Lord, pastimes of; Supreme Lord, activities of
  of irresponsible persons, 318
  in Kṛṣṇa consciousness movement, 192
  See also: Endeavor; Fruitive activities; *Karma;* Sinful activities
Adānta-gobhir viśatāṁ tamisraṁ
  quoted, 149
  verse quoted, 34–35
Aditi, Devakī was, **261**
Administrators. *See:* Kings; *Kṣatriyas;* Leaders, government; Politicians
Advaitam acyutam anādim ananta-rūpam
  quoted, 87
Adyāpiha caitanya e saba līla kare
  verse quoted, 199
Āgamāpāyino 'nityās
  verse quoted, 91
Age of Kali. *See:* Kali-yuga
Aghāsura, **119**
Agriculturalists. *See: Vaiśyas*
Ahaituky apratihatā
  verse quoted, 294
Aham ādir hi devānām
  quoted, 87, 235
Ahaṁ sarvasya prabhavo
  quoted, 235
Ahaṁ tvāṁ sarva-pāpebhyo
  quoted, 28
Ahaṅkāra (false ego). *See:* Bodily concept
Ahaṅkāra itīyaṁ me
  verse quoted, 216, 224
Ahaṅkāra vimūḍhātmā
  quoted, 52
  verse quoted, 51–52
Aitadātmyam idaṁ sarvam
  quoted, 224
Ajo 'pi sann avyayātmā
  quoted, 210
Akrūra, 122, 193
Āmāra ājñāya guru hañā tāra' ei deśa
  verse quoted, 144
Amara-kośa, cited on sex life, 259
Ambarīṣa Mahārāja, 69
Ambuja defined, 34
Amitān yodhayed yas tu
  verse quoted, 106
Aṁśena defined, 102

B

C

M

O

Ocean *(continued)*
Causal, Mahā-Viṣṇu lies on, 217, 221
Indian, gave way to Lord Rāma, **270**
of milk, demigods prayed to Viṣṇu at, **43**, 108
Ocean and material world, analogy of, **168**, 169, **170–171**, 172
Old age, female children begotten in, 340
Oṁ as Vedic confirmation, 136
Omen of Kaṁsa's doom, **59**, 60
Oṁ namo bhagavate vāsudevāya
quoted, 156
Oṁ tad viṣṇoḥ paramaṁ padam
quoted, 234, 315
Oneness & difference of Lord & creation (*acintya-bhedābheda* philosophy), 128, 236
Opulence(s)
of agriculturalist in past, 326
of devotee, 178
of Lord, 141, 177–178
love for Lord in, 247
of Nanda's residence, **336**
Orders, social. *See: Brāhmaṇas; Kṣatriyas;* Society, human, occupational divisions in; *Vaiśyas*
Oversoul. *See:* Supersoul

P

Pada-ratnāvalī-ṭīkā, cited on Māyādevī's names, 134
Padma Purāṇa, quotations from
on *ācārya-sampradāya*, 172
on hearing from nondevotees as forbidden, 22, 191
on Kṛṣṇa and His name, 47
on Lord known by devotional service, 185–186
on *suras* & *asuras*, 304
Pain. *See:* Suffering
Pañcālas, **121**
Pāṇḍavas, Kṛṣṇa saved, **27–28**, 29
Parama-puruṣa defined, 43
Paramātmā. *See:* Supersoul
Paraṁ bhāvam ajānanto
verse quoted, 250
Paraṁ brahma paraṁ dhāma
quoted, 236
verse quoted, 44
Parameśvara defined, 43
Paraṁ padam defined, 28
Paramparā defined, **21**
Parāsya śaktir vividhaiva śrūyate
quoted, 51, 234, 266, 267
verse quoted, 159, 226
Parāvareśo mahad-aṁśa-yukto
quoted, 138
Parents, child not ultimately protected by, 157
See also: Father; Marriage
Parīkṣit Mahārāja
fasted before death, **34**
greatness of, 36–38
Kṛṣṇa saved, **28**, 29
liberation of, 105, 107, 168
quoted on disappearance of Kṛṣṇa & Yadu dynasty, 266
Paritrāṇāya sādhūnāṁ
quoted, 42, 93, **147**, 167, 230
verse quoted, 95, 120
Passion, mode of (*rajo-guṇa*)
for creation of cosmos, **227**–228
destiny in, 72
irresponsible persons in, 318
Pastimes of Kṛṣṇa. *See:* Kṛṣṇa, Lord, pastimes of
Paśu-ghna defined, 23, 24, 103, 105–106
Patita-pāvana-hetu tava avatāra
quoted, 257
Pauruṣaṁ dhāma defined, 140
Payo-dāna-mukhenāpi
verse quoted, 109
Perfection
by chanting Hare Kṛṣṇa, 257
by devotional service, 29, 174
by Kṛṣṇa consciousness, 68, 138
See also: Success
Persons. *See:* Animals; Human beings; Living entities; Soul, conditioned; Supreme Lord

Q

R

S

U

V